Kubernetes for vSphere Administrators

Kubernetes for vSphere Administrators
Copyright © 2022 by Cormac Hogan.

International Standard Book Number: **9798837800467**

Version: 1.0

About the author

Cormac Hogan is a Chief Technologist in the Office of the CTO in the Cloud Infrastructure Business Group at VMware, focusing predominantly on Kubernetes platforms running on vSphere. Cormac has previously held roles in VMware's Engineering, Technical Marketing and Support organizations. Cormac is the owner of CormacHogan.com, a blog site dedicated to storage, virtualization, and container orchestration. He is also the author of the "vSAN Deep Dive" series of books. He can be followed on Twitter @CormacJHogan.

Index

Preface

I had the idea to write this book for some time. The initial trigger was hearing statements similar to "vSphere administrators would not transition to a Platform Operator role". By Platform Operator, I mean someone who would manage developer environments, environments which typically utilized Kubernetes. This role is also referred to as DevOps. I knew this statement to be untrue. vSphere administrators are more than capable of transitioning to this role. Many of them had already stepped up from their roles as Windows and Linux administrators to become vSphere administrators. They learnt virtualisation; they learnt storage management through VMFS and vSAN, along with protocols such as iSCSI and Fibre Channel. They learnt network administration through virtual networks and NSX-T, getting to grips with features like distributed switches and concepts such as NIC teaming and VLAN Tagging. They know how to automate the deployment of infrastructure and workloads through many different tools, ranging from vRealize Automation to PowerCLI, from Ansible to Terraform. They used a plethora of management and monitoring tools to keep an eye on the capacity requirements and performance of both the infrastructure and the applications that run on it. They can figure out if an application is bound by CPU, memory, network, or storage, and forecast when additional resources are required. I honestly couldn't understand why would anyone think vSphere administrators could not step into the role of creating, managing, and monitoring Kubernetes clusters and the development infrastructure that sits on top of it? It's just another platform after all, with the Kubernetes clusters running on a vSphere platform as a set of virtual machines in many cases.

Who better than a vSphere administrator to appreciate the full stack, from physical hosts up through the virtualization layer to the virtual machines that run Kubernetes and the container workloads? Sure, there is a lot to learn. An awful lot! There are a whole range of new concepts to get our heads around, such as containers, twelve-factored applications, eventual consistency, YAML manifests, and kubectl. Not to mention that by stepping into a DevOps role, you may now need to look at more than Kubernetes. You might get asked to assist in the building, running and troubleshooting of pipelines, an orchestration mechanism that converts developer code into a container image and puts it into production on a Kubernetes cluster. But keep in mind that these pipelines are just another automation mechanism, with their own nuances and requirements. And although continuous integration (CI) and continuous deployment (CD) pipelines are not the focus of this book, readers should be aware that this is just another type of automation, all of which can be learnt. I make some cursory introduction to this topic in chapter 8.

This book, by itself, will not convert a vSphere administrator into a DevOps. Instead, it is intended to provide vSphere administrators with a reference guide as they take their first steps with Kubernetes. It will try to demystify some of the terminologies around the Kubernetes platform and provide some very clear and concise examples to help. It will also try to map Kubernetes constructs to vSphere constructs, and the link between the two platforms when Kubernetes is running on vSphere. We look at various Kubernetes distributions from VMware, notably Tanzu Kubernetes Grid (TKG) and vSphere with Tanzu. The latter product has been created specifically with vSphere administrators in mind. Don't worry about that for the moment – the book will devote some time to explaining the different parts of the Tanzu portfolio related to Kubernetes. With that said, the Tanzu Kubernetes distributions are built on upstream Kubernetes, so much of the guidance provided throughout the book will also be relevant to other Kubernetes distributions. I hope you enjoy it, and more importantly, you find it helpful.

Cormac Hogan (May 2022)

You, the reader

This book targets IT professionals who are involved in the day-to-day running of VMware vSphere environments where Kubernetes clusters are deployed, or perhaps, will soon be deployed. It should prove helpful to vSphere administrators who may be looking at stepping into the world of containers, Kubernetes, and DevOps. This book assumes a familiarity with the vSphere platform and other VMware products found in the Software-Defined Data Centre (SDDC). It assumes little or no familiarity with Kubernetes, so will cover the basics of the Kubernetes platform before getting into the details of running Kubernetes on vSphere.

Note that after most of the introductory topics, I begin making specific callouts to the role of the vSphere administrator and the role of the Platform Operator. The Platform Operator is the person who consumes vSphere resources to build out developer platforms for their end-users, typically developers. Developers normally don't care about infrastructure, they just want to test, run and debug their code as quickly as possible, through some sort of pipeline or supply chain mechanism. Thus, this relationship between the vSphere administrator and Platform Operator is the focus of this book. I would also encourage readers to learn as much as possible about the role of the Platform Operator in your organization as this may be a role you might consider for your career progression. Again, I feel that vSphere administrators, with their existing knowledge of infrastructure, would make excellent Platform Operators.

All of the examples used in this book can be found in the following Git repository - https://github.com/cormachogan/vsphere-book-examples. Feel free to download and use as required.

Please note that, on occasion, I have taken the liberty of abbreviating the outputs from some of the CLI commands. This applies to docker, kubectl and tanzu CLIs. The reason for this is that many of the outputs are extremely verbose and are very difficult to read once printed. I've also taken the liberty of obfuscating some IP addresses from the figures, just as a security precaution. Lastly, to make a distinction between the command and output, I placed all of the commands in **bold**. I hope this does not detract from the usefulness of this book, or the learning experience that this book will convey to vSphere administrators wishing to take their first steps into the world of Kubernetes.

Kudos

A word of thanks to my book reviewers, Duncan Epping, Paudie O'Riordan and Myles Gray. These are the people that I continuously learn from and rely on. They did an awesome job giving me many tips, pointers, and corrections through multiple drafts of this book. However, any errors or mistakes that remain in the book are entirely my responsibility. You can read lots of good information about VMware on Duncan's blog at https://yellow-bricks.com and Myles has a great DevSecOps blog at https://blah.cloud.

Dedication

"The Only Constant in Life Is Change."
- Heraclitus

"Everything, everything'll be just fine
Everything, everything'll be alright, alright"
- The Middle, Jimmy Eat World

01

Introduction to Containers

One of the main purposes of Kubernetes is to manage or orchestrate container-based workloads. Therefore, it is not possible to talk about Kubernetes without first describing what a container is. We are going to look at features of containers outside of Kubernetes in this chapter, mostly to give you an appreciation of why developers like to use them for building applications. We will finish off this chapter with some considerations around how to automatically build code into containers, and what the Platform Operator role needs to consider when it comes to containers.

What is a container?

In its simplest form, a container can be considered a very special operating system process, representing an application that runs in an operating system. I say they are special, only because they leverage features for limiting and isolating host resources. In the early days of containers, they were often compared to virtual machines, and some very simplistic viewpoints compared them to virtual machines "without the need for an operating system". In some respects, I suppose this is correct. But since a container is a process running in an operating system, they still require an operating system to run. Admittedly, many containers may run in the same operating system, since again the container is just a process. But the neat thing about containers is portability. Developers can create their container-based app on their laptop, and then deploy it to an on-premises based Kubernetes distribution such as Tanzu Kubernetes, or to a cloud-based Kubernetes distribution, such as Google Kubernetes Engine

OK, so what is in a container? A container contains an image which is the application. But it also contains all of the binaries and libraries that you need to run the application. When the container is run, two operating system features are used to provide an allocation of resources to the application and isolate it from other containers running on the same underlying operating system. These features are known respectively as control groups (or *cgroups* for short) and *namespaces*. The very special process that represents the container is run in its own namespace and is given its own CPU and Memory resources, its own copy of the host network stack and its own file system on which to run. As a vSphere administrator, this is enough of a high-level overview without getting into the nuts and bolts of container technology. The following diagram will hopefully show the relationship between the container processes, their respective namespaces and related cgroups.

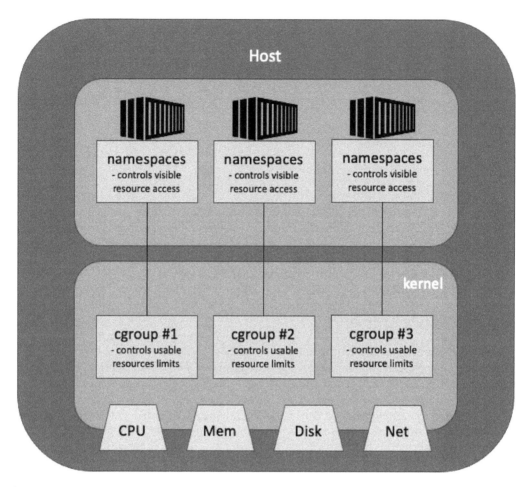

Figure 1: Namespaces and cgroups

Why containers?

While container technology had existed for many years, it was not until Docker (the company) came along and made it very easy for developers to package their containers using Docker (the product) and make them portable, that containers began to gain popularity.

Think back just 5 years, when containers first started to become popular. Before containers, developers typically created a large monolithic executable of the application. vSphere administrators took care of the virtual machine (VM) creation, the installation of the guest operating system, and the customization of the operating system through VMware tools and other mechanisms. Finally, the application could be installed in the VM. There are many ways that a vSphere administrator can automate this whole process and use features of the vSphere stack to provide availability, load-balancing and performance using vSphere High Availability (HA), vSphere Distributed Resource Scheduler (DRS), and Fault Tolerance. However, providing updates to a large monolithic application was a challenge for developers. Even for minor updates to a small section of the application, different development teams would have to work together, merge their work, and test all of the interoperability between the various components that made up the application before it could be released.

What containers did was allow for these large monolithic applications to be broken up into their constituent parts, referred to as refactoring, which could then be worked on independently. For example, the application might have comprised of some front-end web server, some middleware and finally a back-end database. By containerizing the application, and splitting each of these services into its own containerized workload, development teams could work on them at a more granular level. This makes the release cycle easier, as it does not require testing and verifying the whole of the application each time. Also, and probably more critically, by adhering to the Twelve-Factor App – https://12factor.net - paradigm, containerized applications can now be inherently portable, have built-in resiliency, and be scaled in and scaled out as necessary based on the load experienced by different parts of the application. These factors have all contributed to the rise in containerized applications and the term Microservices. Microservices are when an application is distributed across many containers, and each container provides unique functionality for the application.

In effect, developers can now package up their applications in containers that they build on their laptops or desktops and know that the application will run consistently in a variety of different environments, whether they be on-premises in a data center or a cloud environment.

I will add one comment and say that refactoring a large, monolithic application into a containerized application is a significant undertaking, taking many months or even years. Some bespoke monolithic applications may never be refactored. Thus, I believe we are going to see both large monolithic apps running in VMs, as well as new containerized twelve-factor applications running side by side for many years.

A simple container demonstration

This example will show some simple container operations. To do this, a container runtime, sometimes referred to as the container engine, needs to be installed. The container runtime understands how to run containers on the host operating system. In other words, they know how to create the cgroups and namespaces required to run containers. Examples of container runtimes are dockerd (moby), containerd, CRI-O and runC.

There are various ways of getting container runtimes. These can be installed on your desktop in several different ways. Docker provides Docker Desktop for free - https://www.docker.com/products/docker-desktop/ - as long as you are a small business. Otherwise, you have to pay a subscription. An alternate way is via Rancher Desktop - https://rancherdesktop.io/ - which is an open-source application which will run both Kubernetes and a container runtime on your desktop. It also allows you to disable Kubernetes and allow the container runtime to continue running, which is useful. I am using dockerd (moby) container runtime for the following examples, allowing me to use the docker client command-line utility. There are many other ways of getting container runtimes. Feel free to choose your preferred method.

Checking Docker version

The *docker version* command will show which version of the client and server are installed. This example is using docker community edition version 20.10.12 for the client and 20.10.11 for the docker engine. Yours may be different, and that is also fine.

```
chogan@chogan-a01 ~ % docker version
Client: Docker Engine - Community
 Version:           20.10.12
 API version:       1.41
 Go version:        go1.17.5
 Git commit:        e91ed5707e
 Built:             Sun Dec 12 06:28:24 2021
 OS/Arch:           darwin/amd64
 Context:           default
 Experimental:      true

Server:
 Engine:
  Version:          20.10.11
  API version:      1.41 (minimum version 1.12)
  Go version:       go1.16.10
  Git commit:       847da184ad5048b27f5bdf9d53d070f731b43180
  Built:            Fri Nov 19 03:41:34 2021
  OS/Arch:          linux/amd64
  Experimental:     false
 containerd:
  Version:          v1.5.8
  GitCommit:        1e5ef943eb76627a6d3b6de8cd1ef6537f393a71
 runc:
  Version:          1.0.0-rc95
  GitCommit:        b9ee9c6314599f1b4a7f497e1f1f856fe433d3b7
 docker-init:
  Version:          0.19.0
  GitCommit:
```

To look at the running containers on a host system, use the command *docker ps*. If you haven't got a running container on your system, this command won't return anything.

```
% docker ps
```

We can now run our very first container. There is a very simple hello-world container that we can use. To run it, simply type *docker run hello-world*.

```
% docker run hello-world
Unable to find image 'hello-world:latest' locally
latest: Pulling from library/hello-world
2db29710123e: Pull complete
Digest: sha256:80f31da1ac7b312ba29d65080fddf797dd76acfb870e677f390d5acba9741b17
Status: Downloaded newer image for hello-world:latest

Hello from Docker!
This message shows that your installation appears to be working correctly.

To generate this message, Docker took the following steps:
 1. The Docker client contacted the Docker daemon.
 2. The Docker daemon pulled the "hello-world" image from the Docker Hub.
    (amd64)
 3. The Docker daemon created a new container from that image which runs the
```

```
       executable that produces the output you are currently reading.
   4.  The Docker daemon streamed that output to the Docker client, which sent it
       to your terminal.

To try something more ambitious, you can run an Ubuntu container with:
 $ docker run -it ubuntu bash

Share images, automate workflows, and more with a free Docker ID:
 https://hub.docker.com/

For more examples and ideas, visit:
 https://docs.docker.com/get-started/
```

Several things happened here. First, the docker client asks the docker daemon to run the container. The docker daemon checks the list of images on the host operating system to see if the *hello-world* image is already available locally. It did not find it locally, so instead it must *pull* it from an external image registry, which is `hub.docker.com`. This is where the container image is stored. After pulling it down, the container image is then executed. The application or executable in the container displays the welcome message from Docker. The text explains exactly what happened. It's a good first example, and also shows you what you can try next. Regarding the reference to the `:latest` appended to the container name, this is called the tag, and is a directive to pull the "latest" version of the image. The tag can be changed to pull other versions of the container image if necessary.

Now, let's run *docker ps* once again. What do you think it should show?

```
% docker ps
```

Why do we not see the hello-world container? The reason is that the container has run, done its required task and exited. It is no longer running so *docker ps* won't display it. However, if there was a container process running previously, and it has since exited, using *docker ps -a* will show containers that were running but are no longer running.

```
% docker ps -a
CONTAINER ID  IMAGE         COMMAND    CREATED        STATUS                  PORTS
NAMES
bf0220cd4c60  hello-world   "/hello"  5 minutes ago  Exited (0) 5 minutes ago
bold_chandrasekhar
```

The output has wrapped across 2 lines, making it a little difficult to read. But it is possible to see that the image name is hello-world, the command which was run within the container image is "/hello", which when run, displayed the text in the previous output. It is no longer running, as it exited 5 minutes ago. Finally, the runtime name assigned to the container is `bold_chandrasekhar`. These are randomized names used by the container runtime to assign to containers. A name of your own choice could be specified on the docker command line. We will see an example of this later.

The image for hello-world has now been pulled down to the host operating system, in this case, my Apple MacBook. I can use another docker command, *docker image,* to check the images that have been downloaded to my host. To list images that have been pulled to my host, use the command *docker image ls.*

```
% docker image ls
REPOSITORY          TAG         IMAGE ID        CREATED        SIZE
hello-world         latest      feb5d9fea6a5    8 months ago   13.3kB
```

Since the container image is now stored locally on my host, future requests to run the container image do not need to download the image from the docker hub registry. They can and will use the downloaded image. Let's now run the hello-world container again.

% **docker run hello-world**

```
Hello from Docker!
This message shows that your installation appears to be working correctly.

To generate this message, Docker took the following steps:
 1. The Docker client contacted the Docker daemon.
 2. The Docker daemon pulled the "hello-world" image from the Docker Hub.
    (amd64)
 3. The Docker daemon created a new container from that image which runs the
    executable that produces the output you are currently reading.
 4. The Docker daemon streamed that output to the Docker client, which sent it
    to your terminal.

To try something more ambitious, you can run an Ubuntu container with:
 $ docker run -it ubuntu bash

Share images, automate workflows, and more with a free Docker ID:
 https://hub.docker.com/

For more examples and ideas, visit:
 https://docs.docker.com/get-started/
```

Why don't we take the advice displayed in the hello-world output and try something more ambitious? Note the *docker run -it ubuntu bash* command. This is again a request to run a container image called ubuntu, which as you might suspect, runs an Ubuntu distribution in a container. The option *-i* is a request to run the container in interactive mode, keeping standard input (stdin) open on the container so that we can interact with it. The *-t* short for tty, which is basically how terminal access is provided. A combination of the -i and -t provide keyboard and terminal access to the container. The final argument, *bash*, is the command to run on the container. This command is available on the ubuntu container image, among others. In effect, we should end up with an interaction bash shell on the Ubuntu container once the command is run.

```
% docker run -it ubuntu bash
Unable to find image 'ubuntu:latest' locally
latest: Pulling from library/ubuntu
125a6e411906: Pull complete
Digest: sha256:26c68657ccce2cb0a31b330cb0be2b5e108d467f641c62e13ab40cbec258c68d
Status: Downloaded newer image for ubuntu:latest
root@e4562f27ed65:/#
```

Looks like this is successful. We have been presented with what appears to be a bash shell on the container image. Let's check if it is Ubuntu.

```
root@e4562f27ed65:/# cat /etc/os-release
PRETTY_NAME="Ubuntu 22.04 LTS"
NAME="Ubuntu"
VERSION_ID="22.04"
VERSION="22.04 LTS (Jammy Jellyfish)"
VERSION_CODENAME=jammy
ID=ubuntu
ID_LIKE=debian
HOME_URL="https://www.ubuntu.com/"
```

```
SUPPORT_URL="https://help.ubuntu.com/"
BUG_REPORT_URL="https://bugs.launchpad.net/ubuntu/"
PRIVACY_POLICY_URL="https://www.ubuntu.com/legal/terms-and-policies/privacy-policy"
UBUNTU_CODENAME=jammy
root@e4562f27ed65:/#
```

Yep! This is Ubuntu. Looks like it is working. Type *exit* to leave the container bash shell.

I would like to add one more container example to our list. In the previous examples, we were looking at containers which were in attached mode; in other words, running in the foreground. What if we wanted to launch a container image and have it run in the background, dropping us back to our host prompt so that we could get on with other work? This is achieved by running the container with the *-d* for detached option. This time a new container image called nginx is used. Nginx provides a sample web server deployment. The command will also include the option -p to map container port 80 to host port 8080. By connecting to host port 8080 (in my case, on my Apple Mac), the request is routed to container port 80.

```
% docker run -d nginx -p 8080:80
Unable to find image 'nginx:latest' locally
latest: Pulling from library/nginx
42c077c10790: Pull complete
62c70f376f6a: Pull complete
915cc9bd79c2: Pull complete
75a963e94de0: Pull complete
7b1fab684d70: Pull complete
db24d06d5af4: Pull complete
Digest: sha256:2bcabc23b45489fb0885d69a06ba1d648aeda973fae7bb981bafbb884165e514
Status: Downloaded newer image for nginx:latest
d5809f3fb0c0973be132717923c1e8e936033fcbdb48dea445f9940d036c662b
```

The container ID is displayed at the end of the output. It is very long. You do not need to type all of this in every time you want to reference the container. You can use a shortened version. The first part of the container ID is displayed in the *docker ps* command. Using this command, we can also check if the container is running. This short version can be used to interact with the container.

```
% docker ps
CONTAINER ID   IMAGE    COMMAND           CREATED         STATUS          PORTS
NAMES
d5809f3fb0c0   nginx    "/docker-entrypoint...."  40 seconds ago  Up 37 seconds
0.0.0.0:8080->80/tcp, :::8080->80/tcp    nostalgic_varahamihira
```

It would appear that the nginx container is running successfully. Note that this container includes some port entries, highlighting the fact that container port 80 is being mapped to host port 8080. This is how the Nginx web server can be accessed from your laptop or desktop. Point your browser to http://localhost:8080 to see the Nginx splash screen. For even greater detail about the container, use the command *docker inspect <container-id>*. This will provide detail about the container, its image, its networking settings, and a whole slew of other settings, most of which are not necessary to understand for our purposes. It can still be a useful command, however.

You may wonder why there are so many pulls being done in the last command. It is because this nginx container is made up of multiple layers, each layer building on top of the previous one. One layer might be the OS running on the container, and another might be the Nginx web server application. Shortly, we will build our own container and you will how these layers work in more detail. Let's now clean up what was previously created. There should be three images on the host at this point.

```
% docker images
REPOSITORY          TAG           IMAGE ID        CREATED        SIZE
nginx               latest        0e901e68141f    2 days ago     142MB
ubuntu              latest        d2e4e1f51132    4 weeks ago    77.8MB
hello-world         latest        feb5d9fea6a5    8 months ago   13.3kB
```

Let's begin by trying to delete the nginx image.

```
% docker image rm nginx:latest
Error response from daemon: conflict: unable to remove repository reference "nginx:latest"
(must force) - container eeeb2c5def69 is using its referenced image 0e901e68141f
```

The image is still in use. Let's stop the nginx container and try again.

```
% docker ps | grep nginx
7fe9d87b5bb5    nginx       "/docker-entrypoint.…"    15 minutes ago   Up 15 minutes
0.0.0.0:8080->80/tcp, :::8080->80/tcp    infallible_vaughan
```

```
% docker stop 7fe9d87b5bb5
7fe9d87b5bb5
```

```
% docker ps | grep nginx
```

```
% docker ps -a | grep nginx
7fe9d87b5bb5    nginx       "/docker-entrypoint.…"    15 minutes ago   Exited (0) 8 seconds ago
infallible_vaughan
```

At this point, the container has been stopped. Let's try to delete it once more.

```
% docker image rm nginx:latest
Error response from daemon: conflict: unable to remove repository reference "nginx:latest"
(must force) - container 7fe9d87b5bb5 is using its referenced image 0e901e68141f
```

Stopping the container is not enough since the container can be started again (as shown below). The image needs to be available to start the container. Therefore the image cannot be removed. The container must be deleted to remove any reference to the image. Only then can the image be removed. Note that if any container continues to reference the image, it cannot be removed unless the *force* option is applied.

```
% docker start 7fe9d87b5bb5
7fe9d87b5bb5
```

```
% docker ps | grep nginx
7fe9d87b5bb5    nginx                     "/docker-entrypoint.…"    17 minutes ago    Up 5
seconds    0.0.0.0:8080->80/tcp, :::8080->80/tcp    infallible_vaughan
```

```
% docker stop 7fe9d87b5bb5
7fe9d87b5bb5
```

```
% docker rm 7fe9d87b5bb5
7fe9d87b5bb5
```

```
% docker image rm nginx:latest
Untagged: nginx:latest
Untagged: nginx@sha256:2bcabc23b45489fb0885d69a06ba1d648aeda973fae7bb981bafbb884165e514
Deleted: sha256:0e901e68141fd02f237cf63eb842529f8a9500636a9419e3cf4fb986b8fe3d5d
Deleted: sha256:1e877fb1acf761377390ab38bbad050a1d5296f1b4f51878c2695d4ecdb98c62
Deleted: sha256:834e54d50f731515065370d1c15f0ed47d2f7b6a7b0452646db80f14ace9b8de
Deleted: sha256:d28ca7ee17ff94497071d5c075b4099a4f2c950a3471fc49bdf9876227970b24
Deleted: sha256:096f97ba95539883af393732efac02acdd0e2ae587a5479d97065b64b4eded8c
Deleted: sha256:de7e3b2a7430261fde88313fbf784a63c2229ce369b9116053786845c39058d5
```

```
Deleted: sha256:ad6562704f3759fb50f0d3de5f80a38f65a85e709b77fd24491253990f30b6be
```

Container images consume space on your local host. It is wise to do some regular housekeeping and clean out the ones that you are no longer using.

In the previous examples, we have seen what might be called stateless containers. In other words, containers that do not need to persist any data to disk. Any writes to disk from within these containers are made to the local filesystem within the container. This data is lost when the container is deleted. Let's look at how containers can make data persistent, even if the container itself comes and goes. These types of containers are often referred to as stateful containers.

Container Storage

Persistent storage can be provided to containers by adding specific parameters at container creation time. The volumes can be created in advance of the container or can be created when the container is run. In the following example, a very simple volume is first created. The volume is added to the *docker run* command line, requesting that the volume be mounted to a specific mount point, /demo, in the container. The *df* command is then used to verify that the mount request has succeeded.

```
% docker volume create corvol1
corvol1

% docker volume ls
DRIVER      VOLUME NAME
local       corvol1

% docker run -it -v corvol1:/demo ubuntu bash
root@1e48dcf177ea:/#

root@1e48dcf177ea:/# df -h
Filesystem                      Size  Used Avail Use% Mounted on
overlay                          98G  2.1G   91G   3% /
tmpfs                            64M     0   64M   0% /dev
tmpfs                           2.0G     0  2.0G   0% /sys/fs/cgroup
shm                              64M     0   64M   0% /dev/shm
/dev/disk/by-label/data-volume   98G  2.1G   91G   3% /demo
tmpfs                           2.0G     0  2.0G   0% /proc/acpi
tmpfs                           2.0G     0  2.0G   0% /proc/scsi
tmpfs                           2.0G     0  2.0G   0% /sys/firmware
```

The request appears to have been successful. I created a volume called corvol1 using the *docker volume create* command. I requested that the volume be mounted to /demo when the ubuntu container is created. And when it is queried using the *df* command from within the container, we can see it has been successfully mounted.

This docker volume can exist outside the lifecycle of the container. Deleting the container does not delete the volume. This is an important feature of container volumes – they are not tied to the container lifecycle. The volume is stored on the host. In this case, it is on part of the local disk that is 'managed' by docker (usually /var/lib/docker/volumes). If using a MacBook, docker is likely launched in a virtual machine (VM), and this path won't exist on the host, but on the VM. This can be a bit confusing. For example, Rancher Desktop v1.4.1 launches an Alpine Linux v3.5 VM. This is where the container runtime and K3s (a lightweight Kubernetes distribution - https://k3s.io/) are run. It is also where the volume path mentioned above resides. It is in the VM, not on the Mac. If you wish to examine the Rancher Desktop VM running on MacOS, the command *rdctl shell* can be used. The capacities and sizes displayed in the output above also come from this VM, not the host.

Later, when we get into containers being orchestrated by Kubernetes, we will see examples of how containers (inside of Pods) can consume storage from vSphere datastores when they need to persist data.

Container Networking

Several networks may be visible after your container runtime has been installed. By running *docker network ls*, you may observe a bridge network, a host network and possibly others. A bridge network is the default network used by containers and uses a CIDR (shorthand for Classless Inter-Domain Routing) of 172.17.0.0/16. Any containers attached to the same bridge network should be able to communicate with one another over this range of IP addresses. Containers on different bridge networks should not be able to communicate with one another. A host network, as its name suggests, allows a container to use the network of the host. A network of type "None" means that all networking is disabled for any containers using this network. Here is a sample from my Docker environment. Yours may differ depending on the container engine.

```
% docker network ls
NETWORK ID      NAME      DRIVER    SCOPE
3aea554e789b    bridge    bridge    local
345fbdfda66f    host      host      local
eca9e6155f02    none      null      local
```

The interesting thing about docker networks is that it is possible to ping containers that reside on the default bridge network by IP address but not by hostname. To allow containers to communicate via both IP address and hostname, a new user-defined bridge network must be created. This allows the resolution of container names to IP addresses through a capability called automatic service discovery. Let's create a new network to demonstrate. The commands to create a bridge are shown below. The network type defaults to bridge in a *create* command, so it does not need to be specified.

```
% docker network create cormac-network
f613a979f8b774d30b4086c43a7889111402e05bd19ccea46f096d513e4f168a

% docker network inspect cormac-network | more
[
    {
        "Name": "cormac-network",
        "Id": "f613a979f8b774d30b4086c43a7889111402e05bd19ccea46f096d513e4f168a",
        "Created": "2022-05-31T09:42:27.3404948122Z",
        "Scope": "local",
        "Driver": "bridge",
        "EnableIPv6": false,
        "IPAM": {
            "Driver": "default",
            "Options": {},
            "Config": [
                {
                    "Subnet": "172.22.0.0/16",
                    "Gateway": "172.22.0.1"
                }
            ]
        },
```

Note that this new bridge network has been assigned a CIDR of 172.22.0.0/16. Let's now create 2 new containers based on our previously used ubuntu image. These containers do not have any network tooling installed by default, so we will add those, and then try the test. Note that when these containers are run, the network is now specified, and they use the newly created user-defined bridge network. The '-h' option is used to specify the hostname of the container.

```
% docker run -it -h ubuntu1 --network cormac-network ubuntu bash
root@ubuntu1:/# apt-get update
root@ubuntu1:/# apt-get install iputils-ping -y
root@ubuntu1:/# apt-get install iproute2 -y
```

In another window/shell, run the following:

```
% docker run -it -h ubuntu2 --network cormac-network ubuntu bash
root@ubuntu2:/# apt-get update
root@ubuntu2:/# apt-get install iputils-ping -y
root@ubuntu2:/# apt-get install iproute2 -y
```

With the appropriate tooling installed, we can now query the IP address of the containers and try our ping tests. Start with the first container. The loopback interface is deliberately not displayed.

```
root@ubuntu1:/# ip a
.
.
.
61: eth0@if62: <BROADCAST,MULTICAST,UP,LOWER_UP> mtu 1500 qdisc noqueue state UP group
default
    link/ether 02:42:ac:16:00:03 brd ff:ff:ff:ff:ff:ff link-netnsid 0
    inet 172.22.0.3/16 brd 172.22.255.255 scope global eth0
       valid_lft forever preferred_lft forever
```

Then run the same command on the other container:

```
root@ubuntu2:/# ip a
.
.
.
59: eth0@if60: <BROADCAST,MULTICAST,UP,LOWER_UP> mtu 1500 qdisc noqueue state UP group
default
    link/ether 02:42:ac:16:00:02 brd ff:ff:ff:ff:ff:ff link-netnsid 0
    inet 172.22.0.2/16 brd 172.22.255.255 scope global eth0
       valid_lft forever preferred_lft forever
```

We can see that both containers are on the new user-defined bridge network since they have been allocated IP addresses from the 172.22.0.0/16 range and not from the 172.17.0.0/16 range associated with the default bridge network. Let's now try the *ping* test, first using the IP address of the remote container and then using the hostname.

```
root@ubuntu1:/# ping -c 3 172.22.0.2
PING 172.22.0.2 (172.22.0.2) 56(84) bytes of data.
64 bytes from 172.22.0.2: icmp_seq=1 ttl=64 time=0.070 ms
64 bytes from 172.22.0.2: icmp_seq=2 ttl=64 time=0.324 ms
64 bytes from 172.22.0.2: icmp_seq=3 ttl=64 time=0.139 ms

--- 172.22.0.2 ping statistics ---
3 packets transmitted, 3 received, 0% packet loss, time 2091ms
rtt min/avg/max/mdev = 0.070/0.177/0.324/0.107 ms
```

```
root@ubuntu1:/# ping -c 3 ubuntu2
PING ubuntu2 (172.22.0.2) 56(84) bytes of data.
64 bytes from af1286f2d882.cormac-network (172.22.0.2): icmp_seq=1 ttl=64 time=0.188 ms
64 bytes from af1286f2d882.cormac-network (172.22.0.2): icmp_seq=2 ttl=64 time=0.266 ms
64 bytes from af1286f2d882.cormac-network (172.22.0.2): icmp_seq=3 ttl=64 time=0.231 ms

--- ubuntu2 ping statistics ---
3 packets transmitted, 3 received, 0% packet loss, time 2004ms
rtt min/avg/max/mdev = 0.188/0.228/0.266/0.031 ms
```

Success! Containers that have been deployed on the same bridge network can communicate with one another, and if it is a user-defined bridge network, they can reach each other via hostnames. Let's do one final test with networking. Let's prove that it is not possible to reach containers across different bridge networks. I will deploy one more ubuntu container but leave it to deploy to the default bridge network. I will then see if it can reach the other containers that I have already deployed on their own bridge network.

Here is the result when I try to ping one of the existing containers from my new container on the default bridge:

```
root@dd58d6006ec6:/# ip a
.
.
.
63: eth0@if64: <BROADCAST,MULTICAST,UP,LOWER_UP> mtu 1500 qdisc noqueue state UP group
default
    link/ether 02:42:ac:11:00:03 brd ff:ff:ff:ff:ff:ff link-netnsid 0
    inet 172.17.0.3/16 brd 172.17.255.255 scope global eth0
       valid_lft forever preferred_lft forever

root@dd58d6006ec6:/# ping 172.22.0.2
PING 172.22.0.2 (172.22.0.2) 56(84) bytes of data.
```

No response, as expected, proving that containers can't reach other containers on different bridge networks. Again, this is just a flavour of container networking. Kubernetes distributions utilize what is known as a Container Network Interface (CNI), to configure networking for containers. Much greater detail around container networking and CNI will be provided when we get to examine container deployments within Kubernetes clusters that are deployed on vSphere, and consuming vSphere networking or indeed, NSX-T.

Create your container with docker build

As mentioned, the nice thing about containers is their portability. It means that developers can build something that should be able to run anywhere, assuming that the location in which the container is running has a suitable container runtime, e.g., containerd. In this section, I want to demonstrate a small example of creating some "code" and then building a customized container image which will allow that code to be run. This section will introduce the concept of a Dockerfile and the *docker build* command. As you will see, the Dockerfile is nothing more than a list of instructions or commands to *docker build*. A Dockerfile consists of a standard set of instructions such as `FROM`, `CMD`, `COPY`, `RUN` to name just a few. In this example, a very simple container image will be built using the Ubuntu image seen earlier.

We mentioned container layering earlier when we pulled the nginx image. Building our own container, we will see the concept of layers within an image in more detail. Essentially, when we build our own container image, we are placing a new layer (which we can read and write to) on top of some read-only layers. One layer will be the ubuntu OS, followed by another layer of Apache2 web server. We are then going to make some configuration changes to the Apache2 setup, introducing yet another layer. The commands within the Dockerfile trigger the generation of new layers, each layer containing the file generated by the command in the Dockerfile.

As mentioned, the container will be modified from the original image as the Apache2 web server will be installed. A new `index.html` file, which is created locally, will be copied from the desktop to the container. This will replace the default Apache2 `index.html` landing page in `/var/www/html`. To access the web server, port 80 will be opened on the container image. The web server will also be run in the foreground to keep the container running.

First, make a new directory on your desktop. Change to this new directory, and then create a file called Dockerfile and another called `index.html`. Simply run a *touch* command to do this.

```
% mkdir apache2
% cd apache2
% touch Dockerfile
% touch index.html
```

Using an editor of your choice (e.g., vi, nano), edit `index.html` and populate the contents with the following.

```
<html>
<head>
  <title> My first containerized app! </title>
</head>
<body>
  <p> This website is running in a container! </p>
</body>
</html>
```

Next, edit Dockerfile and populate the contents with the following.

```
FROM ubuntu:latest
RUN apt-get update; \
apt-get install apache2 -y; \
mv /var/www/html/index.html /var/www/html/index.html.orig
COPY index.html /var/www/html
EXPOSE 80
ENTRYPOINT ["/usr/sbin/apache2ctl", "-D", "FOREGROUND"]
```

Let's highlight these directives for the build process in more detail. The first is that we are building this container image using an existing Ubuntu image, as specified in the FROM line. Several commands will be RUN in the image, namely an *apt-get update* and an *apt-get install apache -y*. Another command moves the current `index.html` to `index.html.orig` in `/var/www/html`. In the COPY line, the `index.html` file which resides in the same folder as our Dockerfile is copied to `/var/www/html` on the container image. The Dockerfile also includes a directive to EXPOSE port 80, since we wish to be able to reach the web server on port 80. Lastly, we are going to use ENTRYPOINT to run the Apache web server in the foreground. ENTRYPOINT and CMD do very similar things on containers, but there is a subtle difference. CMD allows you to override the executable parameters that you pass to a container whereas ENTRYPOINT does not. So this container will only run the apache2ctl command in the foreground, and nothing else. This turns the container into an executable.

We can now proceed to build the container image. To do that, run the *docker build* command in the directory where the Dockerfile was created. I have included an optional (-t) tag command to make the container image easier to recognize. This could also be done later on if required. I also removed a lot of the additional output from the *apt-get* commands so that we can see the various steps of the build process, and I have also placed a gap between each of the steps, something which would not observe in a normal build process. This should make it easier to identify where each of the Dockerfile directives is occurring.

```
% docker build -t cormac/apache2 .
Sending build context to Docker daemon  4.096kB

Step 1/5 : FROM ubuntu:latest
latest: Pulling from library/ubuntu
125a6e411906: Pull complete
Digest: sha256:26c68657ccce2cb0a31b330cb0be2b5e108d467f641c62e13ab40cbec258c68d
Status: Downloaded newer image for ubuntu:latest
 ---> d2e4e1f51132

Step 2/5 : RUN apt-get update; apt-get install apache2 -y; mv /var/www/html/index.html
/var/www/html/index.html.orig
 ---> Running in ca6c0b746218
Removing intermediate container ca6c0b746218
 ---> 093111417835

Step 3/5 : COPY index.html /var/www/html
 ---> 9dc44ad2f566

Step 4/5 : EXPOSE 80
 ---> Running in b6bd1c5a1ac1
Removing intermediate container b6bd1c5a1ac1
 ---> ea3fb4f03145

Step 5/5 : ENTRYPOINT ["/usr/sbin/apache2ctl", "-D", "FOREGROUND"]
 ---> Running in 5ec1ae951b78
Removing intermediate container 5ec1ae951b78
 ---> 22d2b0d59805
Successfully built 22d2b0d59805
Successfully tagged cormac/apache2:latest
```

The new image should now be available.

```
% docker images
REPOSITORY          TAG           IMAGE ID        CREATED            SIZE
cormac/apache2      latest        22d2b0d59805    About a minute ago 226MB
```

To see the different layers that make up the container image, you can use the *docker history* command. This will display the various commands, and thus the different layers, that were used to create the container.

```
% docker history cormac/apache2
IMAGE            CREATED              BY                                              SIZE
COMMENT
22d2b0d59805     About a minute ago   /bin/sh -c #(nop)  ENTRYPOINT ["/usr/sbin/ap…   0B
ea3fb4f03145     About a minute ago   /bin/sh -c #(nop)  EXPOSE 80                    0B
9dc44ad2f566     About a minute ago   /bin/sh -c #(nop) COPY file:cf34c0d953fea9c5…   143B
093111417835     About a minute ago   /bin/sh -c apt-get update; apt-get install a…   148MB
d2e4e1f51132     4 weeks ago          /bin/sh -c #(nop)  CMD ["bash"]                 0B
<missing>        4 weeks ago          /bin/sh -c #(nop) ADD file:37744639836b248c8…   77.8MB
```

And finally, we can run the container image. I am providing a hostname for the container using -h, as the Apache2 web server application will complain if one is not provided. I am using -d to run it in detached mode, and -p to set the port mappings, with port 80 in the container mapped to 8080 on the local host/laptop/desktop.

```
% docker run -h web-server.mydomain.com -d -p 8080:80 cormac/apache2
63880d6c04b3a95aab56390f29da559cea9730fc1fb0e4448897811248a151bc
```

Let's check that the image is running using the *docker ps* command.

```
% docker ps
CONTAINER ID   IMAGE           COMMAND              CREATED         STATUS
PORTS                          NAMES
63880d6c04b3   cormac/apache2  "/usr/sbin/apache2ct…"  12 seconds ago  Up 10 seconds
0.0.0.0:8080->80/tcp, :::8080->80/tcp   dreamy_franklin
```

Success! The container is up and running. Note the port mappings (which have wrapped to the second line of output). Port 80 on the container is mapped to port 8080 on the host. To verify that the web server is up and running in the container, it should be possible to see the modified web server landing page by pointing a browser to `http://localhost:8080` on the host.

You might wonder if it is still possible to get shell access to this running container. The answer is yes. A *docker exec* command can be used to run commands on the container, including the ability to check the hostname of the running container.

```
% docker exec -ti 63880d6c04b3 hostname
web-server.mydomain.com
```

We can check if the directives that were put in the build file have been followed by opening a bash session to the container:

```
% docker exec -it 63880d6c04b3 bash
root@web-server:/# cd /var/www/html

root@web-server:/var/www/html# ls
index.html  index.html.orig

root@web-server:/var/www/html# cat index.html
<html>
<head>
  <title> My first containerized app! </title>
</head>
<body>
  <p> This website is running in a container! </p>
</body>
</html>
```

Everything looks good. The original `index.html` has been moved to `index.html.orig` and the new `index.html` has been copied in place as requested.

Congratulations! You've just built your first container. And while you may not need to do anything like this with containers as a vSphere administrator, or even as a Kubernetes Operator in a DevOps role, this exercise should at the very least give you an idea about how containers are put together. This will also help you to understand some of the upcoming concepts around Kubernetes, especially Pods. A Pod, as you will soon see, is the Kubernetes compute construct that manages containers.

It is also useful to note that this is a significant part of the DevOps role, albeit we are looking at a very simplified approach. A major part of many DevOps pipelines is getting developer code containerized. Not only that, but you also have to maintain the image on which the code is built, e.g., the Ubuntu image we used at the beginning of the Dockerfile. You may also be tasked with ensuring that this image is secure and be responsible for ensuring that the image is sufficiently patched and up to date. All of these things tend to be the responsibility of whoever is in the DevOps role. Another consideration is where to store the new image once it is created. You'll probably need to look at some form of secure image registry, whether that is an on-premises registry such as Harbor from VMware, or some external registry like Docker Hub. Again, the responsibility of managing and maintaining the image registry, from both an availability and recovery perspective, may well fall under the responsibility of whoever takes on the DevOps role. We will look at the Harbor image registry later in the book, but as you can see, there are lots of things to think about.

Create your own application with docker-compose

We've just seen how to build a single container with *docker build* and the Dockerfile. However, applications will most likely be made up of multiple containers, some of which might be stateless and others which might be stateful (requiring persistent storage). The application may require multiple different services (web server, middleware, back-end database). To enable developers to describe an application and not just individual containers, Docker created a feature called Compose. This allows developers to describe the application as a set of services via a YAML manifest file. Compose has commands which let you stop, start, and rebuild services. It also allows you to check the status of the running services and monitor the logs.

To show how it works, we will use a very simple example once more. We will continue the previous example of our Apache2 web server built on the Ubuntu image, but rather than specifying the hostname and port mappings on the command line, we will describe them in a service which added to the `docker-compose.yaml` file in the same directory as Dockerfile.

Note: Some Docker distributions may include the *docker-compose* binary. Others may not, so you may need to download and install *docker-compose* to complete this exercise.

To begin, remove the previous container and image.

```
% docker ps
CONTAINER ID   IMAGE            COMMAND                 CREATED         STATUS
PORTS                                    NAMES
63880d6c04b3   cormac/apache2  "/usr/sbin/apache2ct…"  5 seconds ago  Up 2 seconds
0.0.0.0:8080->80/tcp, :::8080->80/tcp    optimistic_neumann

% docker stop 63880d6c04b3

% docker rm 63880d6c04b3

% docker images
REPOSITORY          TAG          IMAGE ID        CREATED         SIZE
cormac/apache2      latest       e562324e1d3a    33 minutes ago  226MB
```

```
% docker image rm cormac/apache2

% touch docker-compose.yaml
```

Using an editor of your choice (e.g., vi, nano), edit the newly created `docker-compose.yaml` file and populate the contents with the following.

```
version: "2.0"
services:
  webserver:
    build: .
    hostname: web-server
    domainname: mydomain.com
    ports:
      - "8080:80"
```

This compose file is building one service, called web-server. The web-server service will build the image per the Dockerfile that is still present in the current directory, represented by "." in the build line. This is the same container that was built with the *docker build* in the previous exercise. A `hostname` and `domainname` entries are added to the file to avoid the Apache2 web server complaining about not having a hostname. The container exposes the default port for the Apache2 web server, port 80, which is then mapped to port 8080 on the host.

To build and run the application, type *docker-compose up*. You should now be able to point your browser to http://localhost:8080 and once again see the modified landing page.

```
% docker-compose up
Sending build context to Docker daemon      485B
Step 1/5 : FROM ubuntu:latest
 ---> d2e4e1f51132
Step 2/5 : RUN apt-get update; apt-get install apache2 -y; mv /var/www/html/index.html
/var/www/html/index.html.orig
 ---> Using cache
 ---> 6e5b2ecd1725
Step 3/5 : COPY index.html /var/www/html
 ---> Using cache
 ---> a66071b900cc
Step 4/5 : EXPOSE 80
 ---> Using cache
 ---> 647d8c13b5ef
Step 5/5 : ENTRYPOINT ["/usr/sbin/apache2ctl", "-D", "FOREGROUND"]
 ---> Using cache
 ---> a88a3dbfb027
Successfully built a88a3dbfb027
Successfully tagged apache2_web:latest
[+] Running 2/2
 ⠿ Network apache2_default  Created
0.1s
 ⠿ Container apache2-web-1  Created
0.1s
Attaching to apache2-web-1
```

Note that the *docker-compose* command does not exit. However, the web server should still be accessible at http://localhost:8080. Hit Control-C and it will cancel the service. To run the service in "detached" mode and return to your shell prompt, add a "-d" option to the command. The status of the compose services can be queried using the *docker-compose ps* command.

```
% docker-compose up -d
[+] Running 1/1
 ⠿ Container apache2-web-1  Started                        0.5s
```

This creates the image and starts the container. Note that the name of the image now reflects the service name.

```
% docker-compose ps
NAME            COMMAND                SERVICE STATUS  PORTS
apache2-web-1 "/usr/sbin/apache2ct…" web     running 0.0.0.0:8080->80/tcp, :::8080->80/tcp

% docker images
REPOSITORY                TAG             IMAGE ID        CREATED         SIZE
apache2_web               latest          5cbd5273d9fa    7 seconds ago   226MB

% docker ps
CONTAINER ID   IMAGE         COMMAND            CREATED          STATUS
fd98e17d3c9d   apache2_web   "/usr/sbin/apache2ct…"  29 seconds ago   Up 28 seconds
```

The application services can be stopped and started with *docker-compose stop* and *docker-compose start* respectively.

```
% docker-compose stop
[+] Running 1/1
 ⠿ Container apache2-web-1  Stopped                        10.3s

% docker-compose start
[+] Running 1/1
 ⠿ Container apache2-web-1  Started                        0.5s
```

If you wish to remove the whole application and services, along with the containers, you can use *docker-compose down*.

```
% docker-compose down
[+] Running 2/2
 ⠿ Container apache2-web-1  Removed                        10.3s
 ⠿ Network apache2_default  Removed
```

As I said, this is a very simple example. Docker Compose can be used to create much more complex, multi-container applications with a variety of different services. However, this is hopefully providing you with some appreciation of the flexibility of containers, what can be achieved with them, and why developers like them so much.

Summary

Let's remind ourselves why we are looking at containers. Containers are the building blocks of the new modern applications. Traditionally applications were large, monolithic executables. New paradigms, such as the Twelve-Factor App approach is seeing applications distributed into multiple parts, where each part can be separately containerized. We've seen how to deploy containers, as well as build our own simple container. But when a container is part of a distributed, modern application, made up of many other containers, how do you go about managing it? In chapter 2, the concept of Container Orchestration is introduced. Container Orchestrators allow for containerized apps to be created, deleted, scaled in, scaled out, and facilitates many of the other features discussed in the Twelve-Factor App designs. Today, the Container Orchestrator of choice is, of course, Kubernetes.

02

Introduction to Kubernetes

There are many books on the market that discuss Kubernetes and Kubernetes constructs in detail. Indeed, a quick internet search will lead you to websites which provide detailed explanations much of the topics in this chapter. The goal here is not to provide a deep dive into these constructs. Instead, this chapter is designed to provide you, the vSphere administrator with enough information to understand the basics of Kubernetes. It will not focus on a particular brand of VMware Kubernetes, i.e., one of the Tanzu brands. VMware Kubernetes distributions will be looked at in detail in later chapters. This chapters take a more generic view of Kubernetes

No introduction to Kubernetes would be complete without a reference to the shorthand K8s nomenclature, although I don't use it in this book. It simply means Kubernetes with the opening letter 'K' followed by 8 more letters and closing with an 's'. Now you know.

Why Kubernetes?

After reading chapter 1, you might be wondering why we need Kubernetes if containers are so flexible. In a nutshell, Kubernetes allows us to manage containers at scale, or indeed, manage the applications running in containers at scale. The term container "orchestration" is used a lot, but in essence, Kubernetes is a platform that allows us to provision, scale in and out, update and upgrade, and generally, life cycle manages container-based applications. Of course, there is much more to Kubernetes than just containers. In chapter 1 we mentioned Microservices. These are distributed applications leveraging containers. This introduces the concept of Service Mesh. Service Mesh deals with the partitioning or segmentation of applications at a network and security level, allowing all the constituent parts of a distributed microservices application to securely communicate with each other. However, Microservices and Service Mesh are beyond the scope of what we wish to discuss in this chapter. Instead, our focus will be on the basics of Kubernetes.

The Kubernetes Cluster

A Kubernetes cluster is made up of two distinct components: one or more control plane nodes and one or more worker nodes. When deployed on vSphere, Kubernetes nodes are virtual machines. However, Kubernetes can also be deployed onto bare-metal servers as well as be deployed as a set of containers. On the topic of worker nodes, a new concept called NodePools has recently started to emerge. This allows for the creation of pools of worker nodes with different characteristics, such as different CPU, Memory, and Storage configurations. For this chapter, we will stick with the worker node terminology, but later, we will look at the NodePool concept in more detail.

Note: KinD, short for Kubernetes in Docker, is a very popular Kubernetes distribution for laptops and desktops, where the major Kubernetes components are run in containers. However, KinD does require a docker client and container runtime to be usable. Other popular Kubernetes distributions that can be deployed on your laptop and desktop include Rancher Desktop mentioned in chapter 1 and TCE - Tanzu Community Edition (https://tanzucommunityedition.io/), amongst others. Some distributions such as TCE do not provide a container runtime, so will require the user to install one on their desktop. Other distributions such as Rancher Desktop come with container runtimes such as containerd and dockerd (moby) included. Rancher Desktop deploys with a single control plane node using a lightweight Kubernetes distribution called K3s (https://k3s.io/).

Let's look at some of the components that make up a Kubernetes cluster in more detail. Note that this is not an architectural deep dive into Kubernetes. We just want to have enough information so that we know what we are looking at when we are navigating in a Kubernetes cluster as a vSphere administrator who is interested in the Kubernetes platform.

As mentioned, a Kubernetes cluster is typically made up of two types of nodes, control plane nodes and worker nodes. When Kubernetes is deployed on vSphere, a Kubernetes node is a virtual machine (VM). In the next section, we will look at the role of each type of node.

Control Plane

The control plane, as its name suggests is where the smarts of the Kubernetes cluster reside. In a Kubernetes control plane, a key-value store called **etcd** manages the configuration data as well as the state of the cluster. Basically, it holds the cluster configuration. The **API server** takes care of all of the interactions that take place between core components and etcd. Core components are constantly watching the API server for any changes related to the state of the system. If there is a change to an application definition, for example, everyone watching gets a notification of the change. Another important component is the **scheduler**, which figures out where to provision new Pods (the Kubernetes objects which encapsulate applications) by considering such things as Pod and node affinity and anti-affinity rules. The scheduler is responsible for finding the best node on which to run a newly created Pod.

Another core component is the **kube-controller.** It is responsible for running what are known as control loops, which are also commonly called reconcilers. Since Kubernetes is a declarative system, the purpose of these control loops is to watch the actual state of the system. If it is different from the desired/declared state, they initiate operations to make the actual state the same as the desired state. An example of this could be something as simple as attaching a Persistent Volume to a Pod. When an application is deployed in Kubernetes, the application definition is persisted on the control plane. The API server maintains both an in-memory cache of the desired state (what the system desired state is) and another in-memory cache of the actual state (real-world observed state). When these caches differ, the controller is responsible for initiating tasks to rectify the difference.

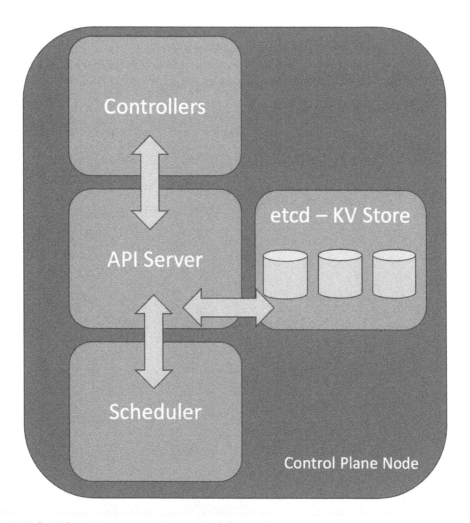

Figure 2: Major Kubernetes components - control plane node

Worker Nodes

Let's now talk about the worker nodes in a Kubernetes cluster. **Kube-proxy** is the component that configures node networking to route network requests from virtual IP addresses of a Kubernetes service to the endpoint implementing the service, anywhere in the cluster. This simply means that it doesn't matter which worker node a Pod is deployed onto, it will be accessible. There is a Kube-proxy implemented on every node. Kube-proxy works with a Container Network Interface, or CNI for short, to implement Kubernetes networking. Popular CNIs include Flannel, Calico and Antrea.

The main component on the worker nodes is the **kubelet**. In some respects, you can think of this as the Kubernetes agent running on the worker nodes. The kubelet provides several functions. Some of its primary functions are to check with the API server to find which Pods should be running on the node where the kubelet is running, as well as report the state of its running Pods back to the API server. It also works with the Container Storage Interface, or CSI for short to handle the formatting and mounting of persistent volumes to Pods.

The final major component is the **container runtime**. We've spoken quite a lot about this in chapter 1 when we discussed containers. The container runtime understands how to create the `cgroups` and `namespaces` required to run containers. And as mentioned, there are many container runtimes available. Therefore, the container runtime may vary from Kubernetes distribution to Kubernetes distribution.

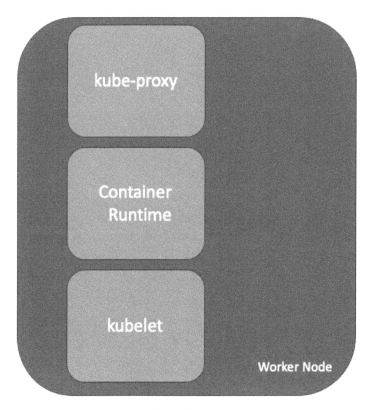

Figure 3: Major Kubernetes components - worker node

One other component found on the cluster is **DNS**. Whilst not a core component (it is called an add-on), it is required. As its name might imply, this is the DNS service for creating DNS records and assigning fully qualified domain names to virtual IP addresses assigned to Kubernetes services. You may see this implemented as CoreDNS or KubeDNS, depending on the distribution of Kubernetes. It is important to note that containers deployed in the Kubernetes cluster automatically include this DNS server in their searches. Many other add-ons and services have a dependency on DNS.

So how does it all tie together? Let's say we deploy a new application onto a Kubernetes cluster. The scheduler will notice the new Pod has not yet been scheduled (for the purposes of this discussion, we can think of a Pod as being the Kubernetes management construct wrapped around a container). The scheduler now runs its algorithm to find out the best Kubernetes node on which to run the Pod. The scheduler then updates the API server for the Pod to indicate where it should be scheduled. The kubelet on the chosen node is monitoring the API server. It observes that a new Pod has been scheduled on it by the scheduler. But this Pod is not running. The kubelet on the chosen node will now start the Pod. The kubelet continuously monitors the Pod to make sure it is running and will restart it if it crashes. It also runs any reconciliation control loops to bring Pods to the declared state if its actual state does not match. This is how it will remain until it is deleted.

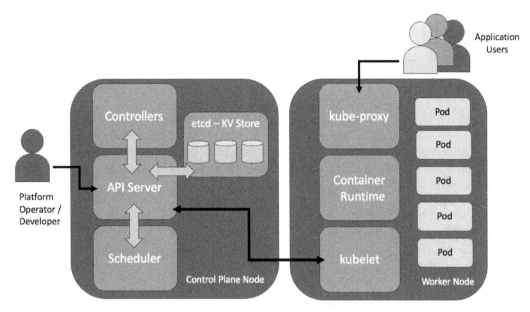

Figure 4: Major Kubernetes components - cluster

When you delete the application, all of the components watching it will receive the deletion event. The kubelet will notice that Pod no longer exists on the API server, so it will then go ahead and delete it from its node.

In the next section, we look at some of the basic building blocks of Kubernetes. We will start with some of the most common objects and then delve into some of the more complex ones.

The basics - KUBECONFIG

First, however, it is important to understand how communication between a user (Kubernetes Platform Operator, developer, SRE, etc.) and the Kubernetes cluster takes place. Access to a cluster is provided via a configuration that is defined in the KUBECONFIG, a file that is typically found in $HOME/.kube/config on the user desktop. This file may contain multiple contexts if the user is working on multiple Kubernetes clusters. The context for a particular cluster is a copy of a file that is typically located in /etc/kubernetes/admin.conf on the Kubernetes cluster's control plane nodes. A sample KUBECONFIG looks something like the following:

```
- cluster:
    certificate-authority-data:xxx
    server: https://192.168.0.1:6443
  name: workload1
contexts:
- context:
    cluster: workload1
    user: workload1-admin
  name: workload1-admin@workload1
current-context: workload1
- name: workload1-admin
```

```
user:
  client-certificate-data: xxx
  client-key-data: xxx
```

I've simplified this config file by removing the contents of certain fields, such as certificate-authority-data, client-certificate-data and client-key-data. From the command line of the local desktop or laptop, a user can use *kubectl* to select a context and assuming the server details and privileges are all correct, communicates with that Kubernetes cluster via additional *kubectl* commands.

In the example below, there are two contexts in my KUBECONFIG file. The current context is denoted by the * in the CURRENT column. Initially, it is set to the context called `rancher-desktop`. After changing to the `workload1-admin` context, you can see the * in the CURRENT column now associated with this cluster. Any commands that I now run via *kubectl* are against the `workload1` Kubernetes cluster.

```
% kubectl config get-contexts
CURRENT   NAME                        CLUSTER           AUTHINFO           NAMESPACE
*         rancher-desktop             rancher-desktop   rancher-desktop
          workload1-admin@workload1   workload1         workload1-admin


% kubectl config use-context workload1-admin@workload1
Switched to context "workload1-admin@workload1".


% kubectl config get-contexts
CURRENT   NAME                        CLUSTER           AUTHINFO           NAMESPACE
          rancher-desktop             rancher-desktop   rancher-desktop
*         workload1-admin@workload1   workload1         workload1-admin
```

In chapter 7, a closer look at the workings of kubeconfig will be examined. In particular, there will be examples of how to create a kubeconfig for a single user or developer who has specific privileges on the Kubernetes cluster. This allows a Platform Operator to control who has access to the cluster, rather than giving out admin privileges to every user. There will also be an example which shows how to merge a newly created kubeconfig with the general ~/.kube/config file, so you don't have to manually edit/merge the files. This will be particularly useful for a Platform Operator responsible for managing many different Kubernetes clusters.

To follow along with the upcoming exercises, you don't need to have access to a Kubernetes cluster. I am using *kubectl* commands to explain certain concepts, but it is not necessary to try them out in practice. However, if you do wish to follow along, you can use any Kubernetes cluster of your choosing. You will also need to install the *kubectl* binary, which is available from several sources and supports most operating system distributions. Note that you may also need to install the docker client and a container runtime to allow some of the laptop/desktop distributions to work. Once you have a Kubernetes cluster up and running (even the simplest kind – Kubernetes in Docker – cluster would suffice), and have successfully set the context, you can try out some of the following exercises. VMware even began shipping 'kind' with Fusion and Workstation products back in 2020. There is a blog post detailing how to get started with it on Fusion here - https://cormachogan.com/2020/09/17/vmware-fusion-v12-kubernetes-kind-integration/. Note that some of the exercises will be demonstrating interoperability between Kubernetes and vSphere, so some of the examples will not be valid for the desktop distributions of Kubernetes since they don't have a vSphere platform underneath. In future chapters, we will be going through the process of deploying Kubernetes clusters on vSphere, and at that point, all the examples in this chapter will be valid.

The basics - YAML (Yet Another Markup Language)

This is probably the most painful part of Kubernetes, especially for those of us who have spent a long time using a user interface to manage and monitor vSphere infrastructure. All communication to the Kubernetes API server is using the *kubectl* command. However, to ask Kubernetes to create something for you, whether it is a Pod, a service, or a volume, you typically pass a manifest file that contains some YAML text with details about the object. Not only that, but the YAML content needs exact formatting with specific space indentation. This is a challenge for those of us who are used to clicking around a UI to get most things done. However, don't let it put you off. Most YAML files that you will create will be copied and pasted from somewhere else, with just some minor tweaking to make them suit your needs. There is going to be ample opportunity to familiarise ourselves with YAML over the remainder of this book. We will return to it time and again. The book is littered with examples of YAML manifests, and by the end of the book, these will be second nature to you, whether you like it or not. Once the YAML manifest is created, we use *kubectl* to send the contents to the Kubernetes API server for implementation.

Namespaces

Namespaces provide a sort of multi-tenancy for a Kubernetes cluster. In effect, they can be used to enable different projects for different teams of developers to share a cluster, with each team working within their own namespace. There are several pre-defined namespaces in a Kubernetes cluster. Some namespaces are used by Kubernetes itself, i.e., the namespace `kube-system`. Others are created and used by add-ons to the cluster. Lastly, there is always a `default` namespace. When no namespace is specified as part of a YAML manifest, objects such as Pods, volumes, etc will be created in this namespace. Similarly, when kubectl commands are run to query objects such as Pods and volumes and no namespace is specified on the commands line, it is the objects from the default namespace that are displayed.

Note: The concept of namespaces can be a bit confusing. Already in this book, we have come across namespaces which control container access to host resources. vSphere with Tanzu also has the concept of namespaces, often referred to as vSphere Namespaces. Do not confuse either of these with the Kubernetes namespaces that are being discussed here. vSphere Namespaces shall be explained when vSphere with Tanzu is covered in chapter 6.

To query the namespaces that are on a Kubernetes cluster, the command *kubectl get ns* (ns short for namespace) can be used. This is an upstream Kubernetes cluster, deployed as a set of VMs on a vSphere platform, where the vSphere CSI driver add-on has also been installed.

```
% kubectl get ns
NAME                STATUS    AGE
default             Active    110d
kube-node-lease     Active    110d
kube-public         Active    110d
kube-system         Active    110d
vmware-system-csi   Active    110d
```

Here is the output from the Kubernetes deployed by Rancher Desktop on my laptop.

```
% kubectl get ns
NAME              STATUS    AGE
default           Active    18h
kube-system       Active    18h
kube-public       Active    18h
kube-node-lease   Active    18h
```

As you can see, these are pretty much the same set of namespaces. The upstream cluster has the vSphere CSI driver installed which will allow it to consume vSphere storage for persistent volumes – more on this shortly. To get details about a particular namespace, including information around resource quota and limits, a *kubectl describe ns <ns name>* can be used.

```
% kubectl describe ns default
Name:          default
Labels:        kubernetes.io/metadata.name=default
Annotations:   <none>
Status:        Active

No resource quota.

No LimitRange resource.
```

To query the objects within a namespace, the command *kubectl get <object> -n <namespace>* can be used, where the object is the type of Kubernetes object you are interested in, e.g., Pod, volume, etc. To look at the Pods in the `vmware-system-csi` namespace, for example, you can run the following:

```
% kubectl get pod -n vmware-system-csi
NAME                                      READY   STATUS    RESTARTS       AGE
vsphere-csi-controller-7b87c8b9bc-fg8c4   7/7     Running   9 (27d ago)    89d
vsphere-csi-node-ggkng                    3/3     Running   0              110d
vsphere-csi-node-r6pfh                    3/3     Running   5 (102d ago)   110d
vsphere-csi-node-tsd4r                    3/3     Running   3 (102d ago)   110d
```

The Ready field reports how many containers are in the Pod and if they are online and available. Restarts report the number of times containers in the Pod have been restarted by the **kubelet**.

If you wanted to query the Kubernetes cluster for a particular object across all namespaces, you can use the *-A* option to specify all namespaces. In the next example, I am going to query for services using svc for short. Services will be covered in a lot of detail shortly, but for the moment a service can be considered an abstraction for a set of Pods, where network access to the group of Pods is presented as a unique IP address (a ClusterIP) and name. Services are a mechanism to provide continuous access to the application, even as individual Pods in the group of Pods come and go.

In the first output, I am only showing the services in the `default` namespace since I did not specify any namespace on the command line. So only those services in the default namespace are returned. In the second command, I included the *-A* so that all services across all namespaces are displayed. The services output will vary from Kubernetes distribution to distribution, so you may be different to what is shown here. At the very least, you will probably see a `Kubernetes` service and a `kube-dns` service.

```
% kubectl get service
NAME         TYPE        CLUSTER-IP    EXTERNAL-IP   PORT(S)    AGE
kubernetes   ClusterIP   10.96.0.1     <none>        443/TCP    110d
```

```
% kubectl get service -A
NAMESPACE           NAME             TYPE       CLUSTER-IP        PORT(S)
default             kubernetes       ClusterIP  10.96.0.1         443/TCP
kube-system         kube-dns         ClusterIP  10.96.0.10        53/UDP,53/TCP,9153/TCP
kube-system         kubelet          ClusterIP  None              10250/TCP,10255/TCP,4194/TCP
vmware-system-csi   vsphere-csi-ctlr ClusterIP  10.107.176.153    2112/TCP,2113/TCP
```

Note the difference in the outputs. The -A option places the namespace name as the first column. Something else which might be confusing at first is that some objects are cluster scoped, not namespace scoped. Therefore you do not need to include the -A option to query them. Examples of globally scoped objects are StorageClass and Persistent Volumes. When these entities are queried, all instances in the cluster are returned.

We mentioned a few different types of Kubernetes objects in the last few examples. Let's look at the most common objects next.

Pods

In chapter 1 we spent a lot of time looking at all aspects of a container. In Kubernetes, a Pod is a construct which contains one or more containers. The term derives from a Pod of whales, which relates to the Docker logo of a whale. Pods are units of computes which can be created, deleted, or queried. All containers within a Pod are scheduled together; they also share storage and network resources.

Note that standalone Pods by themselves are considered ephemeral. If anything happens to the Kubernetes node on which the Pod is scheduled, for example, a drain operation as part of an upgrade, or an eviction due to resource constraints, the Pod is deleted. A Pod cannot self-heal. Thus, there are other constructs within Kubernetes to provide high availability to Pods. These constructs are used depending on whether the Pod is stateless (does not persist data) or is stateful (has a requirement to persist data). Thus, we will talk about Pod storage requirements next, before talking about other highly available Kubernetes constructs.

For quite a long time in the very early days of this technology, containers were considered to be useful only for stateless workloads. In other words, developers spun up one or more containers, did some units of work within the containers, and extracted the result. Any write operations by the application that took place during those units of work were sent to ephemeral on-disk files. Afterwards, the developers simply deleted the containers – along with any stored data. However, it quickly became clear that there could be considerable value in being able to persist the resulting data within the volume, and re-use it for future units of work. Not only that but a way to persist data when a container failed or crashed was also desirable. Thus, a mechanism to provide persistent storage for containers was needed. This gave rise to Persistent Volumes (PV) and Persistent Volume Claims (PVC) in Kubernetes. But before delving into the details of PVs and PVCs, we should first discuss another Kubernetes construct, StorageClass, which selects the correct storage driver and class of storage for provisioning persistent storage for Pods. In vSphere environments, this can be thought of as selecting the correct vSphere datastore to persist any data created within a Pod.

Let's proceed and create our very first Pod. This is a very simple Pod manifest which uses a container image called busybox. This container provides a number of Unix utilities in a single executable and is very useful for testing purposes. Create a file called busybox-simple.yaml using your choice of editor and add the following contents to it.

Important: As mentioned, the indentations are extremely important in YAML manifests. Certain fields are expected to be located at certain indentation points. Make note of the exact indentations when making copies of any of the YAML manifests shown in this book. Indentations are spaces. Tabs are not used. Rather than copying and pasting from the book, retrieve the sample manifests shown here from the Git repository highlighted at the beginning and end of the book.

```
kind: Pod
apiVersion: v1
metadata:
  name: busybox-simple
spec:
  containers:
  - name: busybox
    image: busybox
    command: [ "sleep", "1000000" ]
```

The kind is of type Pod, a compute object in Kubernetes. The API version is v1. We can also tell that it is a stable API version. Sometimes you may see references to alpha and beta in the API version when newer features are being tested. The metadata section contains the name of the Pod. One would also commonly specify a namespace in the metadata section. This tells Kubernetes where to place the Pod. Since no namespace is specified, the Pod is going to be placed in the `default` namespace. In the spec section, there is a single container definition. It has been named busybox and uses an image called busybox. If this image does not already exist on the node on which the Pod is scheduled, it will need to be pulled from an external registry (e.g. Docker Hub). We also need to launch a task on the Pod to prevent it from automatically exiting, simply because we have not given it any work to do. In this case, a simple *sleep* command is run. The sleep units are in seconds, so this will keep the Pod running long enough for us to query it. To create the Pod, we use *kubectl apply -f* and provide the manifest as the argument.

```
% kubectl apply -f busybox-simple.yaml
pod/busybox-simple created
```

```
% kubectl get pod
NAME             READY   STATUS    RESTARTS   AGE
busybox-simple   1/1     Running   0          4s
```

The Ready field refers to the number of containers within the Pod that are running and healthy. In this case, there is only a single container in the Pod. Later, we shall see Pods that have multiple containers. It looks like the Pod is up and running. Other useful commands to try at this point are the *kubectl describe pod busybox-simple*, which will display information such as which Kubernetes worker node the Pod has been scheduled onto, as well as IP address and image information. It will also display events related to the Pod, as shown here:

```
Events:
  Type     Reason      Age    From                Message
  ----     ------      ----   ----                -------
  Normal   Scheduled   18m    default-scheduler   Successfully assigned default/busybox-simple
to worker0
  Normal   Pulling     17m    kubelet             Pulling image "busybox"
  Normal   Pulled      17m    kubelet             Successfully pulled image "busybox" in
1.367615319s
  Normal   Created     17m    kubelet             Created container busybox
  Normal   Started     17m    kubelet             Started container busybox
```

Now that we have created a Pod, let's look how at we can remove it. There are a couple of ways that you can delete this Pod. You could run a *kubectl delete pod busybox-simple* . Or, similar to how we created the Pod, you could point to the file used to create the Pod as follows:

```
% kubectl delete -f busybox-simple.yaml
pod "busybox-simple" deleted
```

The Pod is now deleted.

At this point, you are probably thinking that this is very similar to the Docker Compose mechanism seen in chapter 1. You would be correct in thinking that. However, shortly we will see some of the benefits of Kubernetes over standalone containers when it comes to making an application highly available, as well as how to scale applications in and out quite seamlessly.

Pod Resources

Pods can be deployed with resource requests and limits. These resource requests and limits pertain specifically to CPU and Memory requirements. The Kubernetes worker nodes are then examined to determine which is a suitable candidate on which to schedule the Pod. The kubelet on the node then passes these resource requirements to the container runtime, which in turn sets up the kernel cgroup on the host operating system to enforce the resource requirements. Here is an example Pod with some resource requirements included in the manifest.

```
kind: Pod
apiVersion: v1
metadata:
  name: busybox-simple-with-res
spec:
  containers:
  - name: busybox
    image: busybox
    command: [ "sleep", "1000000" ]
    resources:
      requests:
        memory: "64Mi"
        cpu: "250m"
      limits:
        memory: "128Mi"
        cpu: "500m"
```

Coming from vSphere, some of the terminology here is a bit strange, especially for CPU. CPU resources are specified as a portion of a whole CPU. I've seen the term millicpu or millicore used to describe it. In this example, the Pod has requested 250 millicpu, or 0.25 CPU. The CPU limit is set to 500 millicpu or 0.5 CPU. Memory is a little easier to understand, though it can be specified with several different units. In this example, the Pod has a request of 128 MiB of memory, and a limit of 256MiB of memory. Keep in mind that each container within the Pod can have its own set of resources, so the resource requirements of a Pod can quickly add up. Limits and requests can be observed by doing a *kubectl describe* on the Pod.

Also, consider that the resources available to a Pod are limited to the resources available to the Kubernetes worker node on which it is deployed. If resources on the worker node become scarce, it is possible that the Pod could be *evicted* if its resource limits are reached. At that point, the vSphere administrator may be called upon to use vSphere tools to examine resource usage at the Kubernetes node / VM level.

StorageClass

When Kubernetes is running on a vSphere environment, it is possible to take a static approach to storage allocation. By this, I mean that a vSphere administrator can manually create virtual disks (VMDKs) on a vSphere datastore. Then a Platform Operator could create YAML manifest files to reference the newly created VMDKs and use them as Kubernetes persistent volumes. Once the manifest is applied, it would request the kubelet on the worker node to attach the static pre-existing VMDK, then format it, and finally take care of mounting the volume to the Pod, making it available to the containers running in the Pod.

But this would be a tedious process. vSphere administrators do not want to be in the business of creating individual VMDKs in vSphere. Platform Operators do not want to be creating multiple PV YAML manifest files to map each VMDK as a PV to the Pods/containers. What is much more desirable is a dynamic process to achieve this. In other words, tell Kubernetes that the Pod requires a volume of a specific size and a specific access mode from a particular vSphere datastore, and have the volume dynamically provisioned. StorageClasses, alongside the Persistent Volumes Claims, or PVCs for short, enable this functionality.

The importance of StorageClass is that it allows the selection of a particular type of storage, a class of storage if you will. Some distributions of Kubernetes, such as Rancher Desktop, will provide a StorageClass for you to use automatically, as your typical desktop will not have access to a range of different storage platforms or devices. You can check if there are some StorageClass available on your distribution by running *kubectl get sc* (sc short for StorageClass).

```
% kubectl get sc
NAME                PROVISIONER          RECLAIM  VOLUMEBINDINGMODE   ALLVOLEX  AGE
local-path (default) rancher.io/local-path Delete   WaitForFirstConsumer false    18h
```

Let's discuss one of the fields in the above output. The `Provisioner` is essentially the driver in Kubernetes that will provide the storage. As you can imagine, there could be several different storage drivers/provisioners installed on a Kubernetes cluster, each driver responsible for provisioning volumes on different back-end storage types. The StorageClass construct allows us to select these different provisioners to provision volumes on different physical storages. The other details, such as reclaim and volume binding mode, as well as allow volume expansion, will be discussed shortly, and again in more detail when we talk about persistent volumes and persistent volume claims.

In upstream Kubernetes, there is no pre-defined StorageClass. These have to be created by the platform operator or developer. For Kubernetes deployments on vSphere, a StorageClass allows for the selection of an appropriate vSphere datastore on which to provision a persistent volume. This is achieved by specifying both a provisioner and a parameter called storagePolicyName in the StorageClass manifest file. Here is an example of a StorageClass YAML manifest which is used to select a datastore on vSphere for the creation of block volumes. It is in fact a vSAN datastore that is being selected, vSAN being VMware's hyper-converged infrastructure (HCI) solution.

```
kind: StorageClass
apiVersion: storage.k8s.io/v1
metadata:
  name: my-first-sc
  annotations:
    storageclass.kubernetes.io/is-default-class: "true"
provisioner: csi.vsphere.vmware.com
```

```
allowVolumeExpansion: true
parameters:
  storagepolicyname: "vSAN Default Storage Policy"
  csi.storage.k8s.io/fstype: "ext4"
```

Let's take a look at the contents. First, it is of the kind StorageClass. The API version is currently v1, and it is stable. The metadata section contains the name of the storage class and an annotation. This annotation sets this as the default storage class. This means that if a persistent volume is requested and the storage class is not specified, this default storage class will be used.

The `provisioner`, in this case, is the vSphere CSI driver, short for Container Storage Interface. This is the storage driver developed by VMware to enable Kubernetes to consume vSphere storage. More on this driver later, but suffice to say that when it gets a request to create a volume, it knows to reach out to the vCenter Server and ask it to build a volume on behalf of Kubernetes, and of course return information about the volume to Kubernetes.

Note: You should be cognizant of the fact that there are many, many CSI drivers available for Kubernetes. Most storage vendors now provide their CSI drivers for their proprietary storage. The vSphere CSI driver will work on any storage that has been formatted for vSphere, implying support for VMFS, NFS, vVols (short for Virtual Volumes) and vSAN. However, it is not uncommon to find Kubernetes distributions with more than one CSI driver, and thus multiple storage classes with different provisioner entries referencing different back-end storage types.

Continuing with the contents of the StorageClass manifest above, the `allowVolumeExpansion` parameter is probably self-explanatory in that this StorageClass will allow volumes to be grown in size, should this prove to be a requirement later on. Some provisioners may not support online volume expansion, and for those that do, it is important to specify that it is allowed in the StorageClass manifest or else it won't be available as a feature.

We then come to the `parameters` section of the StorageClass. This first parameter relates to a storage policy, something specific to a vSphere environment. This allows persistent volumes to be backed by different classes of vSphere storage. For example consider vSAN, VMware's hyper-converged infrastructure (HCI) storage offering. It offers a range of different volume configurations (e.g. RAID-1, RAID-5, RAID-6, Stripe Width, etc). A bunch of different storage classes representing each of the different capabilities could be created. As volumes are provisioned with different storage classes, they get instantiated as virtual disks (VMDKs) with different capabilities on the underlying vSAN datastore. In this case, the `storagePolicyName` is set to "vSAN Default Storage Policy" which offers RAID-1 protection. Thus, any persistent volumes that are created with this StorageClass will be instantiated as a RAID-1 volume on the vSAN datastore, which one assumes is a valid datastore to choose in this environment.

Last but not least, there is one additional parameter, fstype. This defines the formatting for the volume that is to be attached to the Pod, then formatted and mounted to the containers in the Pod. Here, the request is to format the volume as "ext4", a common Linux filesystem format. Other parameters could be specified, but these are more advanced and we will return to those shortly. Now that the StorageClass manifest is created, let's look at the Persistent Volume (PV).

Let's now look at a StorageClass which can be used to select vSAN File Service file volumes.

```
kind: StorageClass
apiVersion: storage.k8s.io/v1
metadata:
```

```
  name: my-second-sc
provisioner: csi.vsphere.vmware.com
parameters:
  storagepolicyname: "vSAN Default Storage Policy"
  csi.storage.k8s.io/fstype: "nfs4"
```

There are several differences when compared to the previous StorageClass. The annotation to set the default StorageClass is removed. Thus, this is not considered the default storage class. The attribute to allow volume expansion has also been removed since this is not possible on volumes created by vSAN File Service. Lastly, the fstype parameter has been changed from "ext4" to "nfs4". This distinction is enough to tell the vSphere CSI driver (the provisioner) that this is a request for a file volume from vSAN File Service rather than for a block volume created on the vSAN datastore. But as you can see, the same policy is referenced in both StorageClass. This means that it does not matter if the volume requested is block or file, either will be protected by vSAN using the default policy settings. More details around volume management will be discussed in chapter 5 when a closer look at the vSphere CSI driver takes place. There is a significant role for the vSphere administrator here, identifying different classes of vSphere storage, working with the Platform Operator to identify application needs, and allocating storage appropriately.

Persistent Volumes

A Persistent Volume, or PV for short, is an allocation of storage resources that can be used by a containerized application to store data. In the case of Kubernetes running on vSphere and using vSphere datastores, persistent volumes map to VMDKs on the datastore. Note however that these are a special type of virtual disk. The VMDK that are instantiated on the datastore to back a PV are a special virtual disk known as a First Class Disk (FCD) or Improved Virtual Disks (IVD) and enable disk-centric operations outside of the lifecycle of the virtual machine, e.g., snapshot, restore, clone, etc. These IVDs are known to the vCenter Server and are uniquely identifiable, unlike traditional VMDKs. Since we would like to do certain operations to persistent volumes which are not related to the Kubernetes worker node, IVDs are used to back Kubernetes volumes on vSphere.

Persistent Volumes are not tied to the lifecycle of a Pod. They can exist independent of any Pod that uses them. Indeed, a Pod can be deleted and can be recreated to use the same PV without any loss of data from the PV.

As discussed, Persistent Volumes can be provisioned statically, i.e., created manually outside of Kubernetes, and then mapped to a Persistent Volume construct. However, they can also be provisioned dynamically through a Persistent Volume Claim (PVC), which is far more useful. Let's talk about that next.

Persistent Volume Claims

There is no need to create individual static persistent volumes in Kubernetes. Instead, all that is required is to create a manifest for a PVC, persistent volume claim. This should dynamically instantiate a persistent volume. In this next example, we will look once again at Rancher Desktop. Previously we saw that Rancher Desktop comes with a pre-defined StorageClass called local-path, so there is no need for a StorageClass to be manually created in this case. Instead, what we will do is create a PVC manifest, to request the creation of a persistent volume. Here is an example of such a manifest. Create this manifest on your laptop/desktop, add the contents and save it. I have called the file `local-path-pvc.yaml`.

```
apiVersion: v1
kind: PersistentVolumeClaim
metadata:
  name: my-first-local-path-pvc
  namespace: default
spec:
  storageClassName: local-path
  accessModes:
    - ReadWriteOnce
  resources:
    requests:
      storage: 1Gi
```

This manifest is for an object of kind Persistent Volume Claim, and the API version is v1. Again, this is a stable kind, with no references to alpha or beta. The metadata contains the name and the namespace where the PVC should be created. Note that objects will automatically be created in the default namespace if no namespace is provided. We now come to the interesting part which is the spec. The first spec entry is a reference to the StorageClassName, in this case `local-path`. This means that the PVC request should use the provisioner and storage referenced by the storage class. In this case, it is a request to create a volume on our laptop/desktop using the `local-path` provisioner from Rancher.

Now we come to the attribute `spec.accessModes`. As the name implies, this is controlling access to the volume. The two most common access modes for Kubernetes PVs are read-write-once (RWO) and read-write-many (RWX). RWO access mode implies that a persistent volume can only be accessed from a single Pod. RWX access mode implies that a persistent volume can be accessed from multiple Pods. Thus RWOs are typically block volumes, whereas RWXs are typically file shares. This manifest contains a request for a read-write-once volume that will be dedicated to a single Pod (although it can be shared by all containers in the same Pod).

Another attribute of a Persistent Volume Claim manifest is `resources.requests.storage` which is also part of the `spec` and is where the size of the Persistent Volume is specified. In this case, it is a request to create a 1GB volume.

Let's create the PVC using *kubectl apply -f <pvc manifest>* and see if the resulting PV is dynamically created.

```
% kubectl apply -f local-path-pvc.yaml
persistentvolumeclaim/my-first-local-path-pvc created

% kubectl get pvc
NAME                        STATUS   VOLUME   CAPACITY   ACCESS MODES   STORAGECLASS   AGE
my-first-local-path-pvc     Pending                                     local-path     13s
```

Interestingly, the PV has not been created. The PVC is in a state of pending. Let's see if we can understand why it is pending. Let's run a *kubectl describe* on the PVC and see if there are any relevant events.

```
% kubectl describe pvc
Name:          my-first-local-path-pvc
Namespace:     default
StorageClass:  local-path
Status:        Pending
Volume:
Labels:        <none>
Annotations:   <none>
Finalizers:    [kubernetes.io/pvc-protection]
Capacity:
Access Modes:
VolumeMode:    Filesystem
Used By:       <none>
Events:
  Type    Reason              Age            From                        Message
  ----    ------              ----           ----                        -------
  Normal  WaitForFirstConsumer 4s (x3 over 21s) persistentvolume-controller  waiting for
first consumer to be created before binding
```

As we can see, the PVC is waiting for the first consumer to be created before binding. This is because the `VolumeBindingMode` in the StorageClass is set to `WaitforFirstConsumer`. A consumer in this case is a Pod, i.e. something that will use the PVC and PV. This brings us back to some of the StorageClass attributes seen earlier. One of those was `VolumeBindingMode`. When this is set to `WaitForFirstConsumer`, it means that the Pod must be scheduled first, and then the PV is attached to the same worker node which is running the Pod. The creation of the PVC will enter a pending state until a consumer (Pod) is created. This mode is also used in multiple availability zones (multi-AZ for short) environments where the Kubernetes cluster is spread across several different vSphere Clusters, and where there may be no shared storage across the environments. More on this later when we get into more detailed topology discussions. Other volume binding modes include `Immediate`, which simply means that the PV is created immediately and without any thought given to the Pods scheduling requirements. If the Pod cannot be scheduled on the node where the PV is attached, then the Pod may not come online and will remain Pending.

Let's proceed with creating a Pod that will consume the volume and allow the PVC and PV to be created. The following Pod manifest, `busybox-local-path.yaml`, should achieve that.

```
kind: Pod
apiVersion: v1
metadata:
  name: busybox-local-path-pod
spec:
  containers:
  - name: busybox
    image: busybox
    volumeMounts:
    - name: demo-vol
      mountPath: "/demo"
    command: [ "sleep", "1000000" ]
  volumes:
    - name: demo-vol
      persistentVolumeClaim:
        claimName: my-first-local-path-pvc
```

This Pod YAML manifest is configured to consume a persistent volume. Note that in the `spec.volumes` section we define the name of the volume as well as a reference to the PVC we just created, `my-first-local-path-pvc`. Then in the `spec.containers` section, there is also a volumeMounts section which references the name of the volume placed in the `spec.volumes` section. There is also a `mountPath` which describes where the volume should be mounted in the Pod (or, to be specific, where the volume should be mounted in the container busybox in the Pod busybox-local-path-pod). But since there is only a single container in this Pod, we can talk generally about the Pod and container as being the same. Since the container is not running anything or providing any sort of service, a *sleep* command is issued to it to keep it running. One final thing to mention about this manifest. The Pod does not have a namespace specified in the metadata section. Therefore, it will get created in the `default` namespace. This is fine since the PVC was also created in the `default` namespace. Note that the Pod and the PVC need to be in the same namespace for this to succeed, so it is important to ensure that the namespace metadata is set correctly for Pods and PVCs that are using non-default namespaces.

Let's now create the Pod and see if we see also see the creation of the PVC and PV succeed.

```
% kubectl apply -f busybox-local-path.yaml
pod/busybox-local-path-pod created

% kubectl get pod
NAME                    READY   STATUS    RESTARTS   AGE
busybox-local-path-pod  1/1     Running   0          12s

% kubectl get pvc
NAME                     STATUS   VOLUME                                         CAPACITY
ACCESS MODES   STORAGECLASS   AGE
my-first-local-path-pvc  Bound    pvc-4ac06416-49ad-4a5f-bd15-0658aee13d98       1Gi
RWO            local-path     27s

% kubectl get pv
NAME                                                         CAPACITY   ACCESS MODES
RECLAIM POLICY   STATUS   CLAIM                              STORAGECLASS   REASON   AGE
persistentvolume/pvc-4ac06416-49ad-4a5f-bd15-0658aee13d98   1Gi        RWO
Delete           Bound    default/my-first-local-path-pvc    local-path              18s
```

Success! The Pod has been created and so has the Persistent Volume. We should do an additional test, and just make sure the volume is available to the container inside of Pod. It is possible to use *kubectl exec* to start a shell and verify that there is indeed persistent storage available. The command below is opening a `sh` shell session to the container busybox in the Pod busybox-local-path-pod. The *-it* is reminiscent of similar options to the *docker exec* command in that it opens an interactive tty session to the container. The *-c* specifies the container, but since there is only a single container in this Pod, this could be omitted from the command.

```
% kubectl exec -it busybox-local-path-pod -c busybox -- sh
/ # df -Th /demo
Filesystem               Type        Size    Used Available Use% Mounted on
/dev/disk/by-label/data-volume
                         ext4        97.9G   889.9M   92.0G   1% /demo
/ # cd /demo
/demo # mkdir test
/demo # cd test
/demo/test # echo "Hello World" > testfile
/demo/test # cat testfile
Hello World
```

This looks good. The persistent volume has been mounted onto /demo and has been formatted as an ext4 filesystem. It is approximately 1G in size, give or take some capacity for the formatting of the filesystem as ext4. I can write to the volume, suggesting everything is working as expected.

The interesting thing about persistent volumes is that they can exist outside the context of a Pod. Let's now delete the Pod and re-examine the PVC and PV. Then let's create the Pod once again, referencing the same PVC. This should remount the same formatted PV to the Pod and allow our previously written data to once again be accessible. Note once again that there is no need to specify a namespace since the Pod and PVC are created in the *default* namespace. PVs are global and are not scoped to any namespace. Thus, all PVs are listed when queried.

```
% kubectl get pod
NAME                         READY   STATUS    RESTARTS   AGE
busybox-local-path-pod       1/1     Running   0          61m

% kubectl delete pod busybox-local-path-pod
pod "busybox-local-path-pod" deleted
```

The Pod is deleted. Let's check on the PVC and PV. As expected, these are still present.

```
% kubectl get pvc,pv
NAME                                                    STATUS    VOLUME
CAPACITY   ACCESS MODES    STORAGECLASS    AGE
persistentvolumeclaim/my-first-local-path-pvc    Bound     pvc-4ac06416-49ad-4a5f-bd15-
0658aee13d98    1Gi          RWO              local-path      62m

NAME                                                              CAPACITY   ACCESS MODES
RECLAIM POLICY   STATUS   CLAIM                                   STORAGECLASS   REASON   AGE
persistentvolume/pvc-4ac06416-49ad-4a5f-bd15-0658aee13d98    1Gi          RWO
Delete           Bound    default/my-first-local-path-pvc    local-path               61m
```

Let's create the Pod once more. The Pod manifest continues to reference the same PVC.

```
% kubectl apply -f busybox-local-path.yaml
pod/busybox-local-path-pod created

% kubectl get pod
NAME                         READY   STATUS    RESTARTS   AGE
busybox-local-path-pod       1/1     Running   0          6s
```

The Pod is up and running once again. Let's see if the volume has been mounted and if the data is persisted from the last iteration. Note that this time the *exec* command is not specifying the container since there is only a single container in the Pod.

```
% kubectl exec -it busybox-local-path-pod -- sh
/ # cd /demo
/demo # ls
test
/demo # cd test
/demo/test # ls
testfile
/demo/test # cat testfile
Hello World
```

As we can see, the data is still available. The PV continued to be available even when the Pod that was using it was deleted and restarted. Standalone Pod and PV lifecycles are not connected.

The `ReclaimPolicy` in the StorageClass gets associated with the PVC. Setting this to `Delete` means that when the PVC is deleted, the PV is also deleted. Other ReclaimPolicy settings such as `Retain` are also available. Retain means that the PV persists even when the PVC is deleted.

You can clean up these objects using the *kubectl delete* command seen earlier. Since the PV has been built with a ReclaimPolicy of Delete, deleting the PVC should automatically remove the PV as well. Objects can be deleted by referencing them directly, e.g., *kubectl delete pvc my-first-local-path-pvc* or by referencing the YAML manifest used to create the PVC using the *-f* option in the delete command.

```
% kubectl delete pod busybox-local-path-pod
pod "busybox-local-path-pod" deleted

% kubectl get pvc
NAME                     STATUS   VOLUME                                        CAPACITY
ACCESS MODES   STORAGECLASS   AGE
my-first-local-path-pvc  Bound    pvc-4ac06416-49ad-4a5f-bd15-0658aee13d98   1Gi
RWO            local-path     116m

% kubectl get pv
NAME                                        CAPACITY   ACCESS MODES   RECLAIM POLICY
STATUS   CLAIM                              STORAGECLASS   REASON   AGE
pvc-4ac06416-49ad-4a5f-bd15-0658aee13d98   1Gi        RWO            Delete
Bound    default/my-first-local-path-pvc    local-path              115m

% kubectl delete pvc my-first-local-path-pvc
persistentvolumeclaim "my-first-local-path-pvc" deleted

% kubectl get pvc
No resources found in default namespace.

% kubectl get pv
No resources found
```

Persistent Volume Claims on vSphere

Since this is a book that is aimed at the vSphere administrator, let's look at a Kubernetes distribution that is deployed as a set of VMs on a vSphere platform. As we stated in the previous section on persistent volumes, there is no need to create individual static persistent volumes in Kubernetes. This can be handled dynamically through a PVC, a persistent volume claim. This method dynamically instantiates persistent volumes. In the case of vSphere, PVCs dynamically create VMDKs on the vSphere storage. The resulting PV gets assigned the attributes defined in the storage policy parameter found in the StorageClass. Let's take a look at a simple PVC YAML next, where the Kubernetes cluster has been deployed onto vSphere, and the underlying datastore is provided by vSAN.

```
kind: PersistentVolumeClaim
apiVersion: v1
metadata:
  name: my-first-pv-claim
spec:
  storageClassName: my-first-sc
  accessModes:
    - ReadWriteOnce
  resources:
    requests:
      storage: 2Gi
```

Comparing this to the previous PVC manifest, the metadata in this manifest only contains the name. The namespace is omitted so the PVC will therefore be created in the `default` namespace. The first entry in the `spec` is a reference to the StorageClass that we created earlier, `my-first-sc`. This means that the PVC request should use the provisioner and storage referenced by that StorageClass. In this case, it is a request to create the volume on the vSAN datastore using the default vSAN policy.

Now we come to the attributes `spec.accessModes`. As discussed previously, this is controlling access to the volume. As a reminder, the read-write-once (RWO) access mode implies that persistent volumes created from this claim can only be accessed by a single Pod. Finally, as per `resources.requests.storage` in the `spec`, this is a request to create a 2GB volume.

For completeness' sake, here is an example of a PVC for an RWX file volume. Notice that the only difference between the read-write-once and read-write-many PVC is the different `spec.storageClassName` and of course the `spec.accessModes` setting of ReadWriteMany instead of ReadWriteOnce. The differences between the different access modes will be covered in detail in chapter 5, but for now, you can understand read-write-once (RWO) volumes to be those volumes that can only be mounted by a single Pod, and a read-write-many (RWX) volume to be one that can be mounted by multiple Pods. The reason for the different StorageClass references is for choosing a different filesystem format. The read-write-once block volumes provisioned on vSAN in this example are of type ext4, whereas read-write-many file volumes are of type nfs4. The latter tells the provisioner (the vSphere CSI driver) to create a vSAN File Service file volume rather than a block volume directly on the vSAN datastore.

```
apiVersion: v1
kind: PersistentVolumeClaim
metadata:
  name: vsan-file-claim
spec:
  storageClassName: my-second-sc
  accessModes:
    - ReadWriteMany
  resources:
    requests:
      storage: 2Gi
```

Note that, at the time of writing, RWX volumes can only be dynamically created when used in conjunction with vSAN File Service. vSAN File Service has been available since the vSphere 7.0 release. The vSphere CSI driver does not currently support multi-attach RWX block volumes. We will revisit this functionality later on in the book. For now, let's proceed with the creation of the StorageClass and read-write-once block PVC, and examine the resulting block PV.

I have merged both the StorageClass and Persistent Volume Claim manifest together, which can be done by separating the individual manifests with a --- divider. This is a useful way of keeping all manifests related to the same application in one file. To reiterate, this example can only be run on a Kubernetes cluster that has been deployed on a vSphere environment which has a vSAN HCI storage system. The Kubernetes cluster will also require the vSphere CSI driver installed, which is a manual task for upstream Kubernetes distributions, although it is automatically installed as part of the Tanzu Kubernetes clusters. This procedure will also be covered later in the book.

If you do have a Kubernetes cluster on vSphere with vSAN to test with, you can run this example by creating a YAML manifest called `vsphere-sc-pvc.yaml` and populating it with the following:

```
kind: StorageClass
apiVersion: storage.k8s.io/v1
metadata:
  name: my-first-sc
provisioner: csi.vsphere.vmware.com
allowVolumeExpansion: true
parameters:
  storagepolicyname: "vSAN Default Storage Policy"
  csi.storage.k8s.io/fstype: "ext4"
---
apiVersion: v1
kind: PersistentVolumeClaim
metadata:
  name: my-first-pvc
spec:
  storageClassName: my-first-sc
  accessModes:
    - ReadWriteOnce
  resources:
    requests:
      storage: 2Gi
```

We can now proceed with the creation of the StorageClass and PVC. This is done by applying the manifest using *kubectl apply*. Once applied, we can check to see if the resulting PV gets dynamically created as well. Note that all of the objects can be queried via *kubectl get* commands, using shortened object names such as 'sc' for storage class, 'pvc' for persistent volume claim and 'pv' for persistent volume.

```
% kubectl apply -f vsphere-sc-pvc.yaml
storageclass.storage.k8s.io/my-first-sc created
persistentvolumeclaim/my-first-pvc created

% kubectl get sc
NAME         PROVISIONER            RECLAIMPOLICY  VOLBINDODE  ALLOWVOLEXPANSION  AGE
my-first-sc  csi.vsphere.vmware.com Delete         Immediate   true               2m27s

% kubectl get pvc
NAME          STATUS VOLUME      CAPACITY  ACCESS MODE  STORAGECLASS  AGE
my-first-pvc  Bound  pvc-e27414.. 2Gi      RWO          my-first-sc   2m30s

% kubectl get pv
NAME         CAP  ACC  RECLAIM  STATUS  CLAIM                 STORAGECLASS  AGE
pvc-e27414.. 2Gi  RWO  Delete   Bound   default/my-first-pvc  my-first-sc   2m31s
```

Success! The StorageClass, PVC and PV were all created successfully. In both the PVC and PV output, the StorageClass reference is visible. The Access Mode for the PVC and PV report RWO (Read Write Once), meaning that they are only available to a single Pod, although all containers within the Pod can share access. On this occasion, the PVC and PV could be successfully created without the need for a Pod. This is because the VolumeBindingMode is set to Immediate in the StorageClass and not WaitForFirstConsumer which we saw in the earlier example with Rancher Desktop.

We now have a PV to write data to. Let's create a Pod to consume the PV. Here is another Pod YAML manifest, like what we saw previously. To recap, the spec.volumes section contains the name of a volume as well as a reference to the PVC we just created. Then in the spec.containers section, the volumeMounts section references the name of the volume from the spec.volumes section. The mountPath describes where the volume should be mounted in the Pod (or to be specific, where the volume should be mounted in the container busybox in the Pod busybox-persistent-pod). But once again, there is only a single container in this Pod.

```
kind: Pod
apiVersion: v1
metadata:
  name: busybox-persistent-pod
spec:
  containers:
  - name: busybox
    image: busybox
    volumeMounts:
    - name: demo-vol
      mountPath: "/demo"
    command: [ "sleep", "1000000" ]
  volumes:
    - name: demo-vol
      persistentVolumeClaim:
        claimName: my-first-pvc
```

Let's build this Pod, and then check to see if we have been able to mount the volume successfully onto /demo.

```
 % kubectl apply -f busybox-persistent.yaml
pod/busybox-persistent-pod created
```

```
% kubectl get pods
NAME                        READY    STATUS             RESTARTS    AGE
busybox-persistent-pod      0/1      ContainerCreating  0           5s
```

```
% kubectl get pods
NAME                        READY    STATUS     RESTARTS    AGE
busybox-persistent-pod      1/1      Running    0           14s
```

```
% kubectl exec -it busybox-persistent-pod -- df -Th /demo
Filesystem          Type          Size      Used    Available    Use%    Mounted on
/dev/sda            ext4          1.9G      6.0M        1.8G      0%      /demo
```

This appears to have been successful. The Pod entered a running state, and when we ran the *df -Th /demo* command on the container, it returns that /demo is mounted. It also appears to be a block device (/dev/sda) which is ~2G in size and is formatted as "ext4" which is what was requested as per the StorageClass.

We're going to leave storage there for now. We will revisit it later when we talk about the vSphere CSI driver and highlight some of the objects that get created on a vSphere datastore when it is being consumed for Kubernetes volumes.

Namespaces, Pods, PVCs, and PVs are some of the fundamental building blocks found in Kubernetes. We will now expand on this and introduce some more complex building blocks, which provide greater resilience and availability for your containerized applications.

Deployments & ReplicaSets

Now that we have seen how to deploy stateful and stateless Pods, the next question is how do we make our applications highly available in Kubernetes? In other words, if a Pod fails, how do we avoid the application being impacted. Does a Platform Operator want to be involved in restarting any Pods that might have failed? The answer here is, of course, no. The desire is to have Kubernetes "supervise" the application in some way, and if a Pod fails, have Kubernetes recreate and restart it. In some cases, there may be no need to replicate the data – perhaps the application just provides some front-end functionality, like a web server, and we just want Kubernetes to maintain a desired number of Pods for this app. This is where the resources/objects called Deployments (with ReplicaSets) come in. These allow for a desired number of Pods to be created, scaled in and out, and recreated/restarted in the event of a failure.

Deployments and ReplicaSets go hand in hand. You can think of Deployments as managing ReplicaSets, and ReplicaSets, in turn, managing Pods. You might ask why there are these levels of abstractions. Well, the ReplicaSet will ensure that the correct number of Pods are created and kept running, as per the `Replica` entry in the Deployment YAML manifest. A Deployment object then manages how ReplicaSets behave. For instance, in the case of an upgrade of the application, a Deployment may create new ReplicaSets to roll out the updated application, and when that has been completed it will take care of terminating and removing the older ReplicaSets which continues to maintain the older Pods running the previous version of the application. As we will see later if the whole ReplicaSet is deleted, it is recreated and it in turn will recreate the required number of replica Pods.

```
apiVersion: apps/v1
kind: Deployment
metadata:
  name: demo-deployment
  labels:
    app: demo
spec:
  replicas: 1
  selector:
    matchLabels:
      app: demo
  template:
    metadata:
      labels:
        app: demo
    spec:
      containers:
      - name: busybox
        image: busybox
        command: [ "sleep", "1000000" ]
```

The main items to highlight here are the `spec.replicas` and the `spec.selector` fields. The `selector` field is how we tell the Deployment which Pods it needs to manage. By setting the `spec.selector.matchLabels.app` to demo, any Pods that have a matching `label` of demo will be managed. This deployment is going to start with a single replica. In our case, it is another busybox container. Once created, check on the Deployment (deploy), ReplicaSets (rs) and Pods.

```
% kubectl apply -f deployment-simple.yaml
deployment.apps/demo-deployment created

% kubectl get deploy
NAME              READY   UP-TO-DATE   AVAILABLE   AGE
demo-deployment   1/1     1            1           7s

% kubectl get rs
NAME                         DESIRED   CURRENT   READY   AGE
demo-deployment-7f94b66bc4   1         1         1       13s
```

```
% kubectl get pods
NAME                                   READY   STATUS    RESTARTS   AGE
demo-deployment-7f94b66bc4-7f7xq       1/1     Running   0          17s
```

Everything looks good. From the above, it should be clear that this Deployment has a single ReplicaSet, and that in turn manages a single Pod running the busybox container image. Note that there are no volumes or mounts. Let's now do a scale-out test, where we will scale the deployment to 3 replicas. This should result in a total of 3 Pods deployed.

```
% kubectl scale deploy demo-deployment --replicas=3
deployment.apps/demo-deployment scaled

% kubectl get deploy
NAME              READY   UP-TO-DATE   AVAILABLE   AGE
demo-deployment   3/3     3            3           13m

% kubectl get rs
NAME                         DESIRED   CURRENT   READY   AGE
demo-deployment-7f94b66bc4   3         3         3       13m

% kubectl get pods
NAME                               READY   STATUS    RESTARTS   AGE
demo-deployment-7f94b66bc4-7f7xq   1/1     Running   0          14m
demo-deployment-7f94b66bc4-fwm52   1/1     Running   0          19s
demo-deployment-7f94b66bc4-6fwxp   1/1     Running   0          19s
```

Now we said that Deployments provide the availability to applications. Let's test that out next by deleting one of the Pods in the Deployment.

```
% kubectl delete pod demo-deployment-7f94b66bc4-6fwxp
pod "demo-deployment-7f94b66bc4-6fwxp" deleted

% kubectl get pods
NAME                               READY   STATUS    RESTARTS   AGE
demo-deployment-7f94b66bc4-7f7xq   1/1     Running   0          18m
demo-deployment-7f94b66bc4-fwm52   1/1     Running   0          5m
demo-deployment-7f94b66bc4-6lvmp   1/1     Running   0          34s
```

It appears to have worked seamlessly. A replacement Pod has been scheduled in place of the Pod that was deleted, maintaining the correct number of "replicas". By using a *kubectl describe* on the ReplicaSet, we can see the events. There is a new "Created pod" event to coincide with the time that the original Pod was deleted, as shown below.

```
Events:
  Type    Reason           Age     From                   Message
  ----    ------           ----    ----                   -------
  Normal  SuccessfulCreate 20m     replicaset-controller  Created pod: demo-deployment-
7f94b66bc4-7f7xq
  Normal  SuccessfulCreate 7m      replicaset-controller  Created pod: demo-deployment-
7f94b66bc4-fwm52
  Normal  SuccessfulCreate 7m      replicaset-controller  Created pod: demo-deployment-
7f94b66bc4-6fwxp
  Normal  SuccessfulCreate 2m34s   replicaset-controller  Created pod: demo-deployment-
7f94b66bc4-6lvmp
```

What about deleting the whole ReplicaSet? Let's try it. We should see the Pods that were associated with the original ReplicaSet get deleted along with the original ReplicaSet, but then we should see a new ReplicaSet get instantiated with the correct number of replicas, i.e. Pods.

```
% kubectl delete rs demo-deployment-7f94b66bc4
replicaset.apps "demo-deployment-7f94b66bc4" deleted

% kubectl get pods
NAME                               READY   STATUS             RESTARTS   AGE
demo-deployment-7f94b66bc4-6lvmp   1/1     Terminating        0          5m11s
demo-deployment-7f94b66bc4-fwm52   1/1     Terminating        0          9m37s
demo-deployment-7f94b66bc4-7f7xq   1/1     Terminating        0          23m
demo-deployment-7f94b66bc4-vt68z   0/1     ContainerCreating  0          4s
demo-deployment-7f94b66bc4-lfn2n   0/1     ContainerCreating  0          4s
demo-deployment-7f94b66bc4-t724n   0/1     ContainerCreating  0          4s
```

And after a short time:

```
% kubectl get pods
NAME                               READY   STATUS    RESTARTS   AGE
demo-deployment-7f94b66bc4-vt68z   1/1     Running   0          88s
demo-deployment-7f94b66bc4-t724n   1/1     Running   0          88s
demo-deployment-7f94b66bc4-lfn2n   1/1     Running   0          88s

% kubectl get rs
NAME                         DESIRED   CURRENT   READY   AGE
demo-deployment-7f94b66bc4   3         3         3       90s
```

Let's finish by scaling down the ReplicaSet to 1. The command to do this is almost identical to the scale-up command we used previously.

```
% kubectl scale deploy demo-deployment --replicas=1
deployment.apps/demo-deployment scaled

% kubectl get pods
NAME                               READY   STATUS    RESTARTS   AGE
demo-deployment-7f94b66bc4-t724n   1/1     Running   0          7m36s

% kubectl get rs
NAME                         DESIRED   CURRENT   READY   AGE
demo-deployment-7f94b66bc4   1         1         1       7m39s

% kubectl get deployment
NAME              READY   UP-TO-DATE   AVAILABLE   AGE
demo-deployment   1/1     1            1           30m
```

Hopefully, this has given you an idea of the usefulness of Deployments and ReplicaSets. If a Pod fails in a Deployment, a new Pod is created to ensure the desired state of the application is met, as described in the Deployment manifest. While Deployments are typically associated with stateless applications, they could also be used with stateful applications. If each Pod shared access to the same volume (from a highly available NFS share on some external storage, for example) then a Deployment might be ideal to make this application highly available in Kubernetes.

One final item to highlight with Deployments & ReplicaSets is the nomenclature. As you may have noticed, the naming convention of the Pods in the ReplicaSet does not make it very clear the order in which Pods were created, nor which Pod would be removed if we were to scale the number of replicas down to a smaller number. This is one of the main disadvantages of Deployments. The nomenclature used by StatefulSets, which is discussed next, makes it easy to understand the order in which Pods are deployed, which Pod is using which PV, and also which order Pods would be removed if the application was scaled down or shutdown.

StatefulSets

We have just looked at Deployments, which is focused on maintaining the availability of Pods. Now we will look at another way of creating highly available applications through the use of StatefulSets. Some of the primary differences between StatefulSets and Deployments have been highlighted already. Deployments start and stop Pods in a very random order which is not ideal for certain distributed applications. Another significant difference is that one could use StatefulSets to "supervise" both Pods <u>and</u> storage. This makes the creation of dynamic PVs on behalf of Pods much easier, as well as facilitates the scale-out of both Pods and PVs. And of course, a StatefulSet will take care of the recreation of either object should they fail.

So while Deployments and ReplicaSets are only used for supervising Pods, StatefulSets can be thought of as supervising both Pods and PVs.

When would you use a Deployment and when would you use a StatefulSet? The answer is, of course, it depends on the application. Assume there is a stateless application where you did not need storage. Then a Deployment is perfect. Another example is when there is an application where all Pods wrote to the same ReadWriteMany shared external storage, such as an NFS file share. In that case, there is only a need to manage the Pods, ensuring that the desired number of Pods are running. Again, a Deployment would be ideal as it ensures that the correct number of Pods desired by the application is available.

A StatefulSet would be used where you need to manage the availability of both the compute (Pods) and the storage (PVs). Now, when we discussed containers in chapter 1, we said that many newer apps are being designed with containerization and distribution in mind, and are adhering to the twelve-factor app paradigm. One of these design features is built-in replication. This allows the application to protect itself, and recover from certain failures. An example of an application which has such features is the Cassandra NoSQL database.

However, for an application like Cassandra to use built-in replication, each Pod would require its own storage. While it is possible to achieve this with a shared storage system such as NFS, which was mentioned previously, in many cases the Kubernetes cluster could be distributed across multiple sites and multiple infrastructures which do not share storage. Thus, you would need to provide the Pods with their own "local" storage and allow the application to replicate the data between sites.

Another consideration with such an application is that as you scaled it in and out, both the Pods and the storage would need to scale uniformly. This means that new persistent volumes are allocated to each new Pod. Should a Pod go down, impacting a part of this application, the remaining Pods continue to run the application. They can do this since they have their unique full copies of the replicated data. Thus the application can remain online and available. A StatefulSet will attempt to maintain the correct number of replicas, in this case, the correct number of Pods & PVs, to ensure that the application remains available.

A StatefulSet can create PVCs (and of course PVs) as necessary. It does it through the use of a `volumeClaimTemplate` in its manifest YAML file. This is where you add the reference to the

StorageClass and the specification of the volume you wish to create. This is then included as a `volumeMount` for a container within the Pod. On applying the manifest YAML for the StatefulSet, you should observe the Pods and PVCs getting created and named with an incremental numeric sequence. This makes it much easier to understand the start-up, scale-in, scale-out and shutdown sequence of Pods. The StorageClass that is referenced by the StatefulSet will need to exist for the PVC creation to work.

Once again, the manifest I am about to show here contains two kinds. The first is for a Service, and the second is for the StatefulSet. We have not discussed Services yet, but they will come up shortly. Let's just say that the Service is necessary to set up consistent communication to the Pods of the Cassandra application running in the StatefulSet. Now, this is a large manifest which contains a lot of application-specific information. I will explain the more pertinent sections but don't worry if you don't grasp fully what it is doing – understanding the behaviour of the NoSQL database is not necessary to understand the behaviour of a StatefulSet. However, I like this as a sample application (although this version is a bit dated) as it has some useful tooling built-in to assist with figuring out what is happening.

This may look complex, but once I describe it in the following section, it will become clear what this manifest is requesting.

```yaml
apiVersion: v1
kind: Service
metadata:
  labels:
    app: cassandra
  name: cassandra
  namespace: cassandra
spec:
  clusterIP: None
  selector:
    app: cassandra
---
apiVersion: apps/v1
kind: StatefulSet
metadata:
  name: cassandra
  namespace: cassandra
  labels:
    app: cassandra
spec:
  serviceName: cassandra
  replicas: 3
  selector:
    matchLabels:
      app: cassandra
  template:
    metadata:
      labels:
        app: cassandra
    spec:
      containers:
      - name: cassandra
        image: gcr.io/google-samples/cassandra:v11
        ports:
        - containerPort: 7000
          name: intra-node
        - containerPort: 7001
          name: tls-intra-node
```

```yaml
        - containerPort: 7199
          name: jmx
        - containerPort: 9042
          name: cql
        resources:
          limits:
            cpu: "500m"
            memory: 1Gi
          requests:
            cpu: "500m"
            memory: 1Gi
        securityContext:
          capabilities:
            add:
              - IPC_LOCK
        lifecycle:
          preStop:
            exec:
              command:
              - /bin/sh
              - -c
              - nodetool drain
        env:
          - name: MAX_HEAP_SIZE
            value: 512M
          - name: HEAP_NEWSIZE
            value: 100M
          - name: CASSANDRA_SEEDS
            value: "cassandra-0.cassandra.cassandra.svc.cluster.local"
          - name: CASSANDRA_CLUSTER_NAME
            value: "K8Demo"
          - name: CASSANDRA_DC
            value: "DC1-K8Demo"
          - name: CASSANDRA_RACK
            value: "Rack1-K8Demo"
          - name: POD_IP
            valueFrom:
              fieldRef:
                fieldPath: status.podIP
        readinessProbe:
          exec:
            command:
            - /bin/bash
            - -c
            - /ready-probe.sh
          initialDelaySeconds: 15
          timeoutSeconds: 5
        volumeMounts:
        - name: cassandra-data
          mountPath: /cassandra_data
  volumeClaimTemplates:
  - metadata:
      name: cassandra-data
    spec:
      accessModes: [ "ReadWriteOnce" ]
      storageClassName: my-first-sc
      resources:
        requests:
          storage: 1Gi
```

Much of the information at the beginning of the StatefulSet manifest is very similar to what we saw in the Deployment section previously. The `spec.replicas` and the `spec.selector` fields tell the StatefulSet which Pods it needs to manage.

```
spec:
..
  replicas: 3
  selector:
    matchLabels:
      app: cassandra
```

By setting the `selector.matchLabels.app` to cassandra under `spec`, any Pods that have a matching `label` of cassandra will be managed. This StatefulSet is going to get created with three replicas. This means three Pods and three PVC/PVs. We will see shortly how the Pods are numbered cassandra-X according to the order that which they are created. The same is true for the PVCs. Again, there is only a single container called cassandra in each Pod. The container image is going to be pulled from `gcr.io/google-samples` (gcr.io is the Google container registry). The version of Cassandra is `v11`, which I mentioned is quite old. Ports and resources are probably self-explanatory, but these are the ports that will be exposed on the containers and the amount of CPU and memory that is being requested but also limited to the Pods.

```
  template:
..
    spec:
      containers:
      - name: cassandra
        image: gcr.io/google-samples/cassandra:v11
        ports:
        - containerPort: 7000
          name: intra-node
        - containerPort: 7001
          name: tls-intra-node
        - containerPort: 7199
          name: jmx
        - containerPort: 9042
          name: cql
        resources:
          limits:
            cpu: "500m"
            memory: 1Gi
          requests:
            cpu: "500m"
            memory: 1Gi
```

In the lifecycle section, there is a directive to execute the command *nodetool drain* on the application in the container/Pod before it is shut down. The *nodetool* command allows interaction with the Cassandra application.

```
        lifecycle:
          preStop:
            exec:
              command:
              - /bin/sh
              - -c
              - nodetool drain
```

The env section defines a bunch of variables that are passed to the nodes when the application is started. One of these variables, `CASSANDRA_SEEDS`, defines which is the primary node. The value here represents the fully qualified name of the primary node, and the rest of the name assumes that the node is created in the namespace called cassandra and that the service used by the StatefulSet is also called cassandra.

```
env:
  - name: MAX_HEAP_SIZE
    value: 512M
  - name: HEAP_NEWSIZE
    value: 100M
  - name: CASSANDRA_SEEDS
    value: "cassandra-0.cassandra.cassandra.svc.cluster.local"
  - name: CASSANDRA_CLUSTER_NAME
    value: "K8Demo"
  - name: CASSANDRA_DC
    value: "DC1-K8Demo"
  - name: CASSANDRA_RACK
    value: "Rack1-K8Demo"
  - name: POD_IP
    valueFrom:
      fieldRef:
        fieldPath: status.podIP
```

There is also a readiness probe which is a common application feature and allows Kubernetes to check if the application is up and running. This is simply running a script on the Pod called `ready-node.sh` which checks to see if the application is up and running on the current Pod. If it is, the script returns a 0 to indicate the Pod is ready. If it is not, it returns a 1 to indicate that the Pod is not ready.

```
readinessProbe:
  exec:
    command:
    - /bin/bash
    - -c
    - /ready-probe.sh
  initialDelaySeconds: 15
  timeoutSeconds: 5
```

The `volumeMount` entry is stating that the volumes created in the `volumeClaimTemplate` are formatted and mounted to `/cassandra_data` on the Pods. Note that the volumes are RWO, and are referencing the StorageClass `my-first-sc`, which we have already created.

```
      volumeMounts:
      - name: cassandra-data
        mountPath: /cassandra_data
volumeClaimTemplates:
- metadata:
    name: cassandra-data
  spec:
    accessModes: [ "ReadWriteOnce" ]
    storageClassName: my-first-sc
    resources:
      requests:
        storage: 1Gi
```

Before deploying this StatefulSet, create a namespace called cassandra using *kubectl create ns cassandra*. Next, deploy the Service and StatefulSet manifest above, and then monitor the creation of the various objects. Note that this deployment does take some time, and you may have to wait several minutes before everything is ready. Note that all the *kubectl get* commands here use a *-n cassandra* since this is the namespace where all the components are created. Service is abbreviated to `svc` and StatefulSet is abbreviated to `sts` in the following section.

```
% kubectl create ns cassandra
namespace/cassandra created
```

```
% kubectl apply -f cassandra-sts.yaml
service/cassandra created
statefulset.apps/cassandra created
```

```
% kubectl get svc -n cassandra
NAME        TYPE        CLUSTER-IP    EXTERNAL-IP    PORT(S)    AGE
cassandra   ClusterIP   None          <none>         <none>     8s
```

```
% kubectl get sts -n cassandra
NAME        READY   AGE
cassandra   0/3     15s
```

```
% kubectl get pods -n cassandra
NAME          READY   STATUS    RESTARTS   AGE
cassandra-0   0/1     Running   0          23s
```

```
% kubectl get pvc -n cassandra
NAME                        STATUS   VOLUME                                        CAPACITY
ACCESS MODES   STORAGECLASS   AGE
cassandra-data-cassandra-0  Bound    pvc-8e1746ca-fcee-4297-8e2b-b7ac264ec421      1Gi
RWO            my-first-sc    35s
```

```
% kubectl get pv -n cassandra
NAME                                      CAPACITY   ACCESS MODES   RECLAIM POLICY
STATUS   CLAIM                            STORAGECLASS   REASON   AGE
pvc-8e1746ca-fcee-4297-8e2b-b7ac264ec421  1Gi            RWO         Delete
Bound    cassandra/cassandra-data-cassandra-0   my-first-sc              40s
pvc-d7df2c83-6f30-4139-a7cd-35c051075207  1Gi            RWO         Delete
Bound    cassandra/cassandra-data-cassandra-1   my-first-sc              5s
```

As we can see, things are beginning to roll out. After a minute or so, repeat the *kubectl get* commands to see if things have progressed.

```
% kubectl get sts -n cassandra
NAME        READY   AGE
cassandra   3/3     5m34s
```

```
% kubectl get pods -n cassandra
NAME          READY   STATUS    RESTARTS   AGE
cassandra-0   1/1     Running   0          5m38s
cassandra-1   1/1     Running   0          5m2s
cassandra-2   1/1     Running   0          3m48s
```

```
% kubectl get pvc -n cassandra
NAME                        STATUS   VOLUME             CAP   ACCESS   STORAGECLASS   AGE
cassandra-data-cassandra-0  Bound    pvc-8e1746ca-..421  1Gi   RWO      my-first-sc    5m42s
cassandra-data-cassandra-1  Bound    pvc-d7df2c83-..07   1Gi   RWO      my-first-sc    5m6s
cassandra-data-cassandra-2  Bound    pvc-ff5c9aee-..82   1Gi   RWO      my-first-sc    3m52s
```

```
% kubectl get pv -n cassandra
NAME                CAP   ACC   RECLAIM  STATUS   CLAIM                                   AGE
pvc-8e1746ca-..421  1Gi   RWO   Delete   Bound    cassandra/cassandra-data-cassandra-0    5m44s
pvc-d7df2c83-..207  1Gi   RWO   Delete   Bound    cassandra/cassandra-data-cassandra-1    5m9s
```

```
pvc-ff5c9aee-..982  1Gi  RWO  Delete  Bound  cassandra/cassandra-data-cassandra-2  3m54s
```

The StatefulSet now appears to have been successfully deployed. We can see 3 Pods, 3 PVCs and 3 PVs. The names of the Pods and PVCs make it easy to understand the relationship between them, i.e., which Pod is using which PVC and PV.

I also mentioned that I like using this Cassandra NoSQL StatefulSet as it has some built-in tooling so we can query the application. Note that many of the characteristics of the Cassandra environment reported in the output of such commands, such as Datacenter and Rack, were passed in through environment variables in the StatefulSet manifest. You can check the environment variables by running the following command.

```
% kubectl exec -it cassandra-0 -n cassandra -- env | grep CASSANDRA_
CASSANDRA_SEEDS=cassandra-0.cassandra.cassandra.svc.cluster.local
CASSANDRA_CLUSTER_NAME=K8Demo
CASSANDRA_DC=DC1-K8Demo
CASSANDRA_RACK=Rack1-K8Demo
```

In this next example, the *nodetool status* command connects to the primary container in the Cassandra application and requests a status report on all the Cassandra nodes in Cassandra. Again, since there is only one container per Pod, there is no need to specify the container at the command line.

```
% kubectl exec -it cassandra-0 -n cassandra -- nodetool status
Datacenter: DC1-K8Demo
======================
Status=Up/Down
|/ State=Normal/Leaving/Joining/Moving
-- Address      Load       Tokens Owns (effective)  Host ID                               Rack
UN 10.244.2.80  75.99 KiB  32     61.0%  0e0e4a2b-be71-4018-8f0b-b086c74a9c07  Rack1-K8Demo
UN 10.244.1.51  100.12 KiB 32     72.8%  aef46ea6-e6ae-42d6-b53b-e5c4fa477f2e  Rack1-K8Demo
UN 10.244.2.79  104.42 KiB 32     66.2%  276caf92-195b-4067-944a-c912c76acf68  Rack1-K8Demo
```

The status and state are reporting UN, telling us that all the Cassandra nodes are Up and Normal. Let's now scale out the StatefulSet to 4 replicas instead of 3, and hopefully, we will observe a new Pod and a new PVC/PC created. Again, this may take a minute or so before the application returns a ready state through its `readynode.sh` script. Feel free to open a bash shell to any of the Cassandra Pods and examine this script – it is located on the root (/) folder of each Pod. You'll see that all it is doing is checking for the UN status of the Cassandra node for the current Pod and returning either a 0 (ready) or 1 (Not Ready). Once we get a 0 returned, i.e., the node has a UN state, the Pod is set to Ready.

```
% kubectl scale sts cassandra --replicas=4 -n cassandra
statefulset.apps/cassandra scaled

% kubectl get sts -n cassandra
NAME        READY  AGE
cassandra   3/4    15m

% kubectl get pods -n cassandra
NAME          READY  STATUS            RESTARTS  AGE
cassandra-0   1/1    Running           0         15m
cassandra-1   1/1    Running           0         14m
cassandra-2   1/1    Running           0         13m
cassandra-3   0/1    ContainerCreating 0         7s
```

```
% kubectl get pvc -n cassandra
NAME                          STATUS   VOLUME                                        CAPACITY
ACCESS MODES   STORAGECLASS   AGE
cassandra-data-cassandra-0    Bound    pvc-8e1746ca-fcee-4297-8e2b-b7ac264ec421      1Gi
RWO            my-first-sc    15m
cassandra-data-cassandra-1    Bound    pvc-d7df2c83-6f30-4139-a7cd-35c051075207      1Gi
RWO            my-first-sc    14m
cassandra-data-cassandra-2    Bound    pvc-ff5c9aee-98d7-4bae-a8bc-13c561887982      1Gi
RWO            my-first-sc    13m
cassandra-data-cassandra-3    Bound    pvc-ae403db9-d0ad-4be4-a9a2-6d14b7c41be5      1Gi
RWO            my-first-sc    11s

% kubectl get pv -n cassandra
NAME                                         CAPACITY   ACCESS MODES   RECLAIM POLICY
STATUS    CLAIM                                         STORAGECLASS   REASON    AGE
pvc-8e1746ca-fcee-4297-8e2b-b7ac264ec421     1Gi           RWO          Delete
Bound     cassandra/cassandra-data-cassandra-0          my-first-sc              15m
pvc-ae403db9-d0ad-4be4-a9a2-6d14b7c41be5     1Gi           RWO          Delete
Bound     cassandra/cassandra-data-cassandra-3          my-first-sc              14s
pvc-d7df2c83-6f30-4139-a7cd-35c051075207     1Gi           RWO          Delete
Bound     cassandra/cassandra-data-cassandra-1          my-first-sc              14m
pvc-ff5c9aee-98d7-4bae-a8bc-13c561887982     1Gi           RWO          Delete
Bound     cassandra/cassandra-data-cassandra-2          my-first-sc              13m
```

The new Pod is on its way up, and before too long we should see an updated StatefulSet with 4 replicas. Again, note the numerations associated with the new Pod and PVC (-3) which allows you to identify the most recent edition.

```
% kubectl get sts -n cassandra
NAME        READY   AGE
cassandra   4/4     17m
```

Let's do one final StatefulSet test, and that is to delete a Pod. Since the role of a StatefulSet is to maintain the availability of Kubernetes components for the application, a new Pod should be instantiated to replace the failed Pod. Let's monitor the Cassandra application as we do it, using the built-in *nodetool* command available in the app.

```
% kubectl delete pod cassandra-1 -n cassandra
pod "cassandra-1" deleted

% kubectl get pods -n cassandra
NAME          READY   STATUS    RESTARTS   AGE
cassandra-0   1/1     Running   0          26m
cassandra-1   0/1     Running   0          3s
cassandra-2   1/1     Running   0          24m
cassandra-3   1/1     Running   0          11m

% kubectl exec -it cassandra-0 -n cassandra -- nodetool status
Datacenter: DC1-K8Demo
======================
Status=Up/Down
|/ State=Normal/Leaving/Joining/Moving
--  Address      Load        Tokens Owns (effective)   Host ID                                 Rack
UN  10.244.1.52  114.18 KiB  32     49.4%              92030cd4-4e60-4425-9d3b-0ce51f2e1975    Rack1-K8Demo
UN  10.244.2.80  75.99 KiB   32     46.0%              0e0e4a2b-be71-4018-8f0b-b086c74a9c07    Rack1-K8Demo
DN  10.244.1.51  100.12 KiB  32     53.4%              aef46ea6-e6ae-42d6-b53b-e5c4fa477f2e    Rack1-K8Demo
UN  10.244.2.79  104.42 KiB  32     51.2%              276caf92-195b-4067-944a-c912c76acf68    Rack1-K8Demo
```

We can see that a new Pod is created almost immediately after the original one is deleted, but that it is currently not ready. By checking the application, we can see that one of the hosts in the

Cassandra setup is in a DN – Down but Normal – state. Presumably, there is some synchronization that might need to take place to bring it online, but I will qualify that statement by saying that I am no expert on the inner workings of the Cassandra NoSQL database. However, after a few moments, the Pod returns to a ready state and all hosts are UN – Up and Normal – one again.

```
% kubectl get pods -n cassandra
NAME         READY   STATUS    RESTARTS   AGE
cassandra-0  1/1     Running   0          26m
cassandra-1  1/1     Running   0          48s
cassandra-2  1/1     Running   0          25m
cassandra-3  1/1     Running   0          11m

% kubectl exec -it cassandra-0 -n cassandra -- nodetool status
Datacenter: DC1-K8Demo
======================
Status=Up/Down
|/ State=Normal/Leaving/Joining/Moving
-- Address      Load       Tokens Owns (effective)      Host ID                              Rack
UN 10.244.1.52 114.18 KiB 32     49.4%    92030cd4-4e60-4425-9d3b-0ce51f2e1975  Rack1-K8Demo
UN 10.244.1.53 123.6  KiB 32     53.4%    aef46ea6-e6ae-42d6-b53b-e5c4fa477f2e  Rack1-K8Demo
UN 10.244.2.80  75.99 KiB 32     46.0%    0e0e4a2b-be71-4018-8f0b-b086c74a9c07  Rack1-K8Demo
UN 10.244.2.79 111.19 KiB 32     51.2%    276caf92-195b-4067-944a-c912c76acf68  Rack1-K8Demo
```

At this point, you should have a good appreciation of what a StatefulSet is and how useful it is to be able to scale in and out applications that require persistent storage. You should also understand now, at this point, the difference between standalone Pods, Deployments and StatefulSets, and the usefulness of each.

DaemonSet

I just wanted to add a small note about DaemonSets as you may come across these from time to time when working with Kubernetes. We briefly mentioned them in the context of the kube-proxy earlier. DaemonSets ensure that a copy of a Pod is run on every node in the Kubernetes cluster. These are often found with system resources and with add-ons such as a Container Network Interface (CNI) where every node requires networking services or a Container Storage Interface (CSI) where every node requires storage services. As a cluster is scaled out with new nodes added, a DaemonSet ensure that the new nodes also get a copy of the Pod. Here is a DaemonSets called `kube-proxy` taken from my upstream Kubernetes cluster. Note the use of *-n kube-system* which runs the query on the `kube-system` namespace only. If I omitted the name of the DaemonSet, all DaemonSets from the namespace would be returned. If I used the *-A* option instead of specifying a namespace, all namespaces would be checked for a match.

```
% kubectl get ds kube-proxy -n kube-system
NAME        DESIRED   CURRENT   READY   UP-TO-DATE   AVAILABLE   NODE SELECTOR          AGE
kube-proxy  3         3         3       3            3           kubernetes.io/os=linux 114d
```

Networking Services

Services are a fundamental building block of Kubernetes applications. Services address an issue where Pods can come and go, such as what we have already observed with Deployments and with StatefulSets. Each time a Pod is restarted, it will most likely get a new IP address. This makes it difficult to maintain connectivity/communication with them, especially for clients. Through

Services, Kubernetes provides a mechanism to assign an internal IP address for the lifespan of an application. Clients can then be configured to talk to the Service, and traffic to the Service will be load balanced across all the Endpoints (i.e., Pods) that are connected to it. Thus, clients don't need to rely on the IP addresses of individual Pods to maintain connectivity. This is the reason why two CIDRs or network ranges are typically provided when setting up Kubernetes. There is a Pod CIDR and a Service CIDR, although in many cases there is a default range for each.

Note: Some of the following content might be a little advanced for a vSphere administrator. We are certainly starting to get into some of the fundamentals of Kubernetes. Again, coming away from this topic with an understanding of Services will be sufficient, and networking will of course be revisited when we look at the integration points with vSphere regularly throughout the book. Don't worry if you don't understand everything initially as these concepts will be explored and reinforced with additional examples later.

When a service is created, it typically gets (1) a virtual IP address, (2) a DNS entry (assuming DNS is configured) and (3) networking rules that 'proxy' or redirect the network traffic to the Endpoint that provides the service. When that virtual IP address receives traffic, **kube-proxy** is responsible for redirecting the traffic to the correct Endpoint. Thus, in an application made up of multiple Pods, Services enable a front-end Pod on one Kubernetes worker node would be able to seamlessly communicate with a back-end Pod on a completely different Kubernetes worker node in the same Kubernetes cluster. There are several different Service types, which are now discussed in further detail.

The default Service type is ClusterIP. By default, **ClusterIP** does not take an argument when declared in the Service manifest. It is set to blank or empty. Earlier, we came across another ClusterIP setting when creating a "**headless**" service for the Cassandra StatefulSet demo. This was where service type **ClusterIP** was set to **None**. There is another option is to set ClusterIP to an actual IP address, but this is not explored in this book.

Another Service type that shall be examined is **NodePort** whereby a service can be exposed directly via a port on the Kubernetes nodes.

A final Service type that we will look at is **LoadBalancer**, which also allows external clients outside of the K8s cluster to access an application running in K8s. In this section, we are going to delve into the most common services in much greater detail and try to explain what is happening when a Service is created.

ClusterIP

The ClusterIP service type is used internally within the Kubernetes cluster. These service types are not accessible from outside the cluster. However, the ClusterIP service type can have several different values when it comes to services. Let's look at the most common ones, and how they differ.

ClusterIP set to "" (blank)

This is the default service type in Kubernetes. With ClusterIP set to "" or blank, the service is accessible within the Kubernetes cluster only – no external access is allowed from outside of the cluster. With this ClusterIP type, an IP address and DNS name are created for the service which represents the group of back-end Pods/Endpoints. The assumption here is that DNS has been implemented on the Kubernetes cluster. If it has been enabled, then the Service types should be resolvable from within the Kubernetes cluster by using the DNS name of the Service. The Service also load-balances requests across all the back-end Pods that are part of the application.

Let's assume that a Cluster of type "" (blank) service has been assigned to a group of Pods running some application such as a web server. Access to the application is available via the virtual IP address of the service (a cluster-internal IP). Assuming DNS is in place, access is also available via the DNS name assigned to the Service. When a client accesses the Service via the virtual IP address or DNS name, the first request proxies (by kube-proxy) to the first Pod, the second request goes to the second Pod, and so on in a round-robin fashion. Requests are load-balanced across all Pods in the group.

Let's look at an actual example. In this demonstration, I am going to create a new Deployment which will create Pods that contain a Nginx web server. This will be deployed to a new namespace called web. I will also create a Service for the Nginx application so the communication to the web server doesn't rely on the Pods' IP addresses, which as we stated, can change as Pods come and go. Here is the manifest that I built for both the Deployment and Service in the web namespace:

```
apiVersion: v1
kind: Service
metadata:
  labels:
    app: nginx
  name: nginx-svc
  namespace: web
spec:
  clusterIP: ""
  ports:
    - name: http
      port: 80
  selector:
    app: nginx
---
apiVersion: apps/v1
kind: Deployment
metadata:
  name: nginx-deployment
  namespace: web
spec:
  selector:
    matchLabels:
      app: nginx
  replicas: 2
  template:
    metadata:
      labels:
        app: nginx
    spec:
      containers:
      - name: nginx
        image: nginx:latest
        ports:
        - containerPort: 80
```

The service manifest has the clusterIP set to "" (blank or empty). Note also the port entry in Service spec is set to 80, and matches the containerPort in the deployment manifest. The relationship between the Deployment and the Service is achieved by setting the spec.selector in the Service to look for the label `app: nginx`. This label has been set in the Deployment `template`, so any Pods created by the Deployment will have this label. This is what creates the association between Service and Pod/Endpoint.

```
% kubectl create ns web
namespace/web created
```

```
% kubectl apply -f clusterip-blank-svc.yaml
service/nginx-svc created
deployment.apps/nginx-deployment created
```

```
% kubectl get deploy -n web
NAME                READY   UP-TO-DATE   AVAILABLE   AGE
nginx-deployment    2/2     2            2           13s
```

The Deployment has been created successfully. Let's query some of the other objects that have been created. However, rather than constantly appending a *-n web* to each *kubectl* command that I type, I am going to modify the context to the web namespace. Then I can simply type the *kubectl* commands without the need to specify the namespace. The IP addresses of the Pods can be seen if the *-o wide* option is used with the command. These IP addresses are derived from the Pod CIDR IP address range which would have been provided at Kubernetes cluster creation time, or defaulted to a specific range if not specified.

```
% kubectl config set-context --current --namespace=web
Context "k8s-admin@k8s" modified.
```

```
% kubectl get deploy
NAME                READY   UP-TO-DATE   AVAILABLE   AGE
nginx-deployment    2/2     2            2           65s
```

```
% kubectl get pods -o wide
NAME                                  READY   STATUS    RESTARTS   AGE   IP             NODE
nginx-deployment-8d545c96d-dbfpg      1/1     Running   0          82s   10.244.2.82    k8s-wk1
nginx-deployment-8d545c96d-t5qkb      1/1     Running   0          82s   10.244.1.55    k8s-wk0
```

The Pods managed by the Deployment/ReplicaSet are up and running. They also have their IP addresses assigned. Let's now look at the Service and the Endpoints.

```
% kubectl get svc nginx-svc
NAME        TYPE        CLUSTER-IP       EXTERNAL-IP   PORT(S)   AGE    SELECTOR
nginx-svc   ClusterIP   10.102.241.233   <none>        80/TCP    104s   app=nginx
```

We can see that an IP address has been assigned to the Service. These IP addresses are derived from the Service CIDR IP address range which would have been provided at Kubernetes cluster creation time, or defaulted to a specific range if not specified. The selector used for the service is also displayed. Again, it is any Pods that have the label `app=nginx` get associated with the service. Let's now check the Endpoints.

```
% kubectl get endpoints
NAME        ENDPOINTS                            AGE
nginx-svc   10.244.1.55:80,10.244.2.82:80        112s
```

```
% kubectl describe endpoints nginx-svc
Name:          nginx-svc
Namespace:     web
Labels:        app=nginx
Annotations:   endpoints.kubernetes.io/last-change-trigger-time: 2022-06-02T08:03:44Z
```

```
Subsets:
  Addresses:          10.244.1.55,10.244.2.82
  NotReadyAddresses:  <none>
  Ports:
    Name  Port  Protocol
    ----  ----  --------
    http  80    TCP

Events:  <none>
```

The Endpoint's addresses matches the addresses of the Pods in the Nginx Deployment. Therefore any requests that arrive into this Service will be proxied or redirected to the Pods. The Endpoint ports are set to port 80, for http. Just to reiterate, it doesn't matter if these Pods come and go, the Service will be updated with any new Endpoint IP addresses and communication to the application (Nginx web service) will not be impacted.

Let's now scale the application from 2 replicas to 3 and see what happens. The ability to scale applications like this is one of the most significant benefits of Kubernetes. Note that applications can be scaled in as well as out. Usually, this is an operation that would be undertaken when the load increases or decreases on an application.

```
% kubectl scale deploy nginx-deployment --replicas=3
deployment.apps/nginx-deployment scaled

% kubectl get deploy
NAME               READY   UP-TO-DATE   AVAILABLE   AGE
nginx-deployment   3/3     3            3           16m

% kubectl get pods -o wide
NAME                                READY   STATUS    RESTARTS   AGE   IP            NODE
nginx-deployment-8d545c96d-dbfpg    1/1     Running   0          16m   10.244.2.82   k8s-wk1
nginx-deployment-8d545c96d-hqkz6    1/1     Running   0          20s   10.244.1.56   k8s-wk0
nginx-deployment-8d545c96d-t5qkb    1/1     Running   0          16m   10.244.1.55   k8s-wk0

% kubectl get endpoints
NAME        ENDPOINTS                                          AGE
nginx-svc   10.244.1.55:80,10.244.1.56:80,10.244.2.82:80      16m
```

We can see that a new Pod has been created and its IP address has been added to the Endpoints that the Service is using. Thus, any requests to the Nginx Service will now be balanced across the three Pods. Let's check on the DNS settings next.

To examine the DNS assignments, I am going to create another Pod in the same namespace. This is because, as mentioned a few times already, ClusterIP does not allow external access to a Service. The Service is only accessible from within the Kubernetes cluster. Here is the manifest for the simple busybox that I am going to create. Note that it is in the same namespace as the Deployment and that there is no label set in its metadata.

```
apiVersion: v1
kind: Pod
metadata:
  name: web-busybox
  namespace: web
spec:
  containers:
  - name: busybox
    image: busybox
    command: [ "sleep", "1000000" ]
```

Let's create it and check its IP address.

```
% kubectl apply -f clusterip-busybox.yaml
pod/web-busybox created
```

```
% kubectl get pods -o wide
NAME                                 READY   STATUS    RESTARTS   AGE     IP            NODE
nginx-deployment-8d545c96d-dbfpg     1/1     Running   0          24m     10.244.2.82   k8s-wk1
nginx-deployment-8d545c96d-hqkz6     1/1     Running   0          8m30s   10.244.1.56   k8s-wk0
nginx-deployment-8d545c96d-t5qkb     1/1     Running   0          24m     10.244.1.55   k8s-wk0
web-busybox                          1/1     Running   0          14s     10.244.1.57   k8s-wk0
```

The new Pod is up and running. However, there is no app=nginx label associated with the new Pod. This means that the Nginx Service should not be associated with the new Pod in any way. Let's check the Endpoints once again to make sure.

```
% kubectl get endpoints
NAME        ENDPOINTS                                             AGE
nginx-svc   10.244.1.55:80,10.244.1.56:80,10.244.2.82:80         31m
```

As expected, there is no change to the Endpoints. The Nginx Service is only redirecting requests to the Nginx Pods, and not to the new Busybox Pod. Let's now *exec* a shell session to the Busybox Pod and examine the Service. Since DNS is configured on this cluster, the first thing we will do is a *nslookup* on the Nginx Service, nginx-svc. Note that we expect the DNS name to be <service>.<namespace>.svc.cluster.local. The IP address that we shall attempt to resolve is 10.102.241.233, which is the IP address associated with the nginx Service, and which we examined in the *kubectl get svc* command earlier.

```
% kubectl exec -it web-busybox -- sh
/ # nslookup 10.102.241.233
Server:        10.96.0.10
Address:10.96.0.10:53

233.241.102.10.in-addr.arpa       name = nginx-svc.web.svc.cluster.local

/ # nslookup nginx-svc
Server:        10.96.0.10
Address:10.96.0.10:53

Name:    nginx-svc.web.svc.cluster.local
Address: 10.102.241.233
```

This all looks good. Let's check the application. I should be able to display the Nginx landing page from the web server if I connect to the Service.

```
/ # wget -O - nginx-svc.web.svc.cluster.local
Connecting to nginx-svc.web.svc.cluster.local (10.102.241.233:80)
writing to stdout
<!DOCTYPE html>
<html>
<head>
<title>Welcome to nginx!</title>
<style>
html { color-scheme: light dark; }
body { width: 35em; margin: 0 auto;
font-family: Tahoma, Verdana, Arial, sans-serif; }
</style>
</head>
```

```
<body>
<h1>Welcome to nginx!</h1>
.
.
written to stdout
/#
```

Success! Using *nslookup* in the Busybox Pod, we were able to resolve the IP address of the Service to a DNS name - `nginx-svc.web.svc.cluster.local`. We were also able to use *wget* to pull the Nginx landing page using the DNS name of the Service. The DNS name was provided by the DNS service in the Kubernetes cluster. Every service on the cluster gets a DNS name. The web reference is taken from the namespace where the nginx service is running. This namespace was specified in the deployment manifest back at the start of the exercise. The *wget* request went to the Service IP address of `10.102.241.233`. This request was then redirected to one of the Pod/Endpoints to get the Welcome page display above. All appears to be working as expected.

Note that it is still possible to use the IP address of the Pod to access the Nginx landing page. But, at the risk of repeating myself, we don't want to communicate to the Pods directly since they are ephemeral and can come and go. The Service construct provides a level of stability to application communications in Kubernetes.

```
/ # wget -O - 10.244.2.82
Connecting to 10.244.2.82 (10.244.2.82:80)
writing to stdout
<!DOCTYPE html>
<html>
<head>
<title>Welcome to nginx!</title>
<style>
html { color-scheme: light dark; }
body { width: 35em; margin: 0 auto;
font-family: Tahoma, Verdana, Arial, sans-serif; }
</style>
</head>
<body>
<h1>Welcome to nginx!</h1>
```

OK – that's all well and good, but you are probably wondering where the IP addresses for the Pods and the Services come from. These are provided as part of the Kubernetes Cluster configuration, where you typically must assign a CIDR range for both Pods and Services. Later in the book, when we look at deploying a Kubernetes cluster in detail, we will look at how you can configure these ranges.

ClusterIP set to None (aka headless)

With ClusterIP explicitly set to **None**, the Service is once again accessible within the cluster only. However, the difference between this setting compared to ClusterIP set to "" (blank) is that there is no IP address associated with the None type ClusterIP service. Instead, any resolution of the Service name returns the IP addresses of the Pod Endpoints that back the Service.

This service is typically used when you want to control which specific Pod or Pods you want to communicate with, rather than simply communicate with them through a single Service IP address. This was the Service type implemented in the previous StatefulSet example with the Casandra NoSQL database.

Let's build out a new deployment, as shown below. I am going to place this into a separate namespace called web2. This time the label will be called `nginx2`, to differentiate it from the previous deployment. As an aside, you are hopefully getting an appreciation of the importance of labels within Kubernetes. Note that the name of the Service and the Deployment are the same as before, but since they are being deployed to a different namespace. This is fine since these objects are namespace scoped. The main difference this time is that the `ClusterIP` is now set to `None` in the Service manifest.

```
apiVersion: v1
kind: Service
metadata:
  labels:
    app: nginx2
  name: nginx-svc
  namespace: web2
spec:
  clusterIP: None
  ports:
    - name: http
      port: 80
  selector:
    app: nginx2
---
apiVersion: apps/v1
kind: Deployment
metadata:
  name: nginx-deployment
  namespace: web2
spec:
  selector:
    matchLabels:
      app: nginx2
  replicas: 2
  template:
    metadata:
      labels:
        app: nginx2
    spec:
      containers:
      - name: nginx
        image: nginx:latest
        ports:
        - containerPort: 80
```

Let's build the application in the new web2 namespace. I am using a new command, *kubectl get all*, to check the objects. This name is a bit misleading, in that it doesn't show all objects as the name suggests. However, it does allow us to query most of the objects that we are interested in with one command. A standout item is that there is now no IP address associated with the Service, even though the ClusterIP is the type of Service. This is where the term "headless" originated. There is no front-end service for the application. Instead, communication resolves directly to the back-end Pods/Endpoints.

```
% kubectl create ns web2
namespace/web2 created

% kubectl apply -f clusterip-headless-svc.yaml
service/nginx-svc created
deployment.apps/nginx-deployment created
```

```
% kubectl get all -n web2
NAME                                   READY   STATUS    RESTARTS   AGE
pod/nginx-deployment-79c8885ff8-kjpqt  1/1     Running   0          9s
pod/nginx-deployment-79c8885ff8-pvl46  1/1     Running   0          9s

NAME                 TYPE        CLUSTER-IP   EXTERNAL-IP   PORT(S)   AGE
service/nginx-svc    ClusterIP   None         <none>        80/TCP    9s

NAME                              READY   UP-TO-DATE   AVAILABLE   AGE
deployment.apps/nginx-deployment  2/2     2            2           9s

NAME                                        DESIRED   CURRENT   READY   AGE
replicaset.apps/nginx-deployment-79c8885ff8  2         2         2       9s
```

Everything looks good. Let's switch to the web2 namespace context and check the Endpoints next.

```
% kubectl config set-context --current --namespace=web2
Context "k8s-admin@k8s" modified.

% kubectl get endpoints
NAME        ENDPOINTS                         AGE
nginx-svc   10.244.1.58:80,10.244.2.83:80     21m

% kubectl get pods -o wide
NAME                                READY   STATUS    RESTARTS   AGE   IP            NODE
nginx-deployment-79c8885ff8-kjpqt   1/1     Running   0          21m   10.244.1.58   k8s-wk0
nginx-deployment-79c8885ff8-pvl46   1/1     Running   0          21m   10.244.2.83   k8s-wk1
```

This all looks to be working as expected. As said, the purpose of setting ClusterIP to None is to allow communication directly to the Pods, not a Service. Once again, we will create a simple Busybox Pod in the same namespace as the Deployment, and as before, use the tools available on the Pod (*nslookup*, *wget*) to check how this Service behaves differently from the default ClusterIP setting. For completeness, here is the manifest for the Busybox Pod, with the namespace entry now set to web2.

```
apiVersion: v1
kind: Pod
metadata:
  name: web-busybox
  namespace: web2
spec:
  containers:
  - name: busybox
    image: busybox
    command: [ "sleep", "1000000" ]
```

Create the busybox Pod and check the IP addresses once more.

```
% kubectl apply -f clusterip-headless-busybox.yaml
pod/web-busybox created

% kubectl get pods -o wide
NAME                                READY   STATUS    RESTARTS   AGE   IP            NODE
nginx-deployment-79c8885ff8-kjpqt   1/1     Running   0          27m   10.244.1.58   k8s-wk0
nginx-deployment-79c8885ff8-pvl46   1/1     Running   0          27m   10.244.2.83   k8s-wk1
web-busybox                         1/1     Running   0          6s    10.244.2.84   k8s-wk1
```

Now when the Service name is resolved from the busybox Pod, the list of IP addresses for the backend Pods is returned rather than a unique IP for the Service itself. You can also see the request going to the different Pods on a round-robin basis.

```
% kubectl exec -it web-busybox -- sh
/ # nslookup nginx-svc
Server:        10.96.0.10
Address:10.96.0.10:53

Name:    nginx-svc.web2.svc.cluster.local
Address: 10.244.2.83
Name:    nginx-svc.web2.svc.cluster.local
Address: 10.244.1.58
```

Let's try to retrieve the landing page.

```
/ # wget -O - nginx-svc
Connecting to nginx-svc (10.244.2.83:80)
writing to stdout
<!DOCTYPE html>
<html>
<head>
<title>Welcome to nginx!</title>
```

If you look at the connecting line, you can see that it is now going directly to a Pod's IP address, the first Pod in the list when we resolved the Service. Let's run it again.

```
/ # wget -O - nginx-svc
Connecting to nginx-svc (10.244.1.58:80)
writing to stdout
<!DOCTYPE html>
<html>
<head>
<title>Welcome to nginx!</title>
```

And now it is going to the second Pod's IP Address. Hopefully, this provides a useful insight into the different behaviours of ClusterIP.

NodePort

So far, we have only discussed ClusterIP, which only allows services to be exposed inside of the Kubernetes cluster. The next service type to discuss is NodePort. NodePort allows for the exposing a service outside of a Kubernetes cluster, but rather than using a dedicated virtual IP address, it exposes the service via a port on the Kubernetes nodes in the cluster. Access to the service is then made via a reference to the node IP address plus the exposed port. Let's look at an example of that next. First, let's display the nodes in my cluster, and then we can look at the manifest file which now sets the type to **NodePort**. I have a single control plane node and two worker nodes. Note the internal IP addresses of the nodes, as it is these that will be used to access the application.

```
% kubectl get nodes -o wide
NAME     STATUS ROLES         AGE  VERSION INTERNAL-IP   EXTERNAL-IP OS-IMAGE
K8s-cp0  Ready  control-plane 111d v1.23.3 192.168.51.40 <none>      Ubuntu 21.10
K8s-wk0  Ready  <none>        111d v1.23.3 192.168.51.47 <none>      Ubuntu 21.10
K8s-wk1  Ready  <none>        111d v1.23.3 192.168.51.42 <none>      Ubuntu 21.10
```

Some of the tailing columns from the -o wide output have been removed for formatting. I'm going to create another deployment with Nginx, but this time the Service `spec.type` will be set to `NodePort`. Once again, I'm deploying to a new namespace, web3, and I have also changed the labels on the Service and Deployment. After the deployment, a new Service of type `NodePort` should be visible.

```
apiVersion: v1
kind: Service
metadata:
  labels:
    app: nginx3
  name: nginx-svc
  namespace: web3
spec:
  type: NodePort
  ports:
    - name: http
      port: 80
  selector:
    app: nginx3
---
apiVersion: apps/v1
kind: Deployment
metadata:
  name: nginx-deployment
  namespace: web3
spec:
  selector:
    matchLabels:
      app: nginx3
  replicas: 2
  template:
    metadata:
      labels:
        app: nginx3
    spec:
      containers:
      - name: nginx
        image: nginx:latest
        ports:
        - containerPort: 80
```

```
% kubectl create ns web3
namespace/web3 created

% kubectl apply -f nodeport-svc.yaml
service/nginx-svc created
deployment.apps/nginx-deployment created

% kubectl get all -n web3
NAME                                          READY    STATUS     RESTARTS    AGE
pod/nginx-deployment-5bf9b56d77-gh65d         1/1      Running    0           9s
pod/nginx-deployment-5bf9b56d77-zvd2f         1/1      Running    0           9s

NAME                 TYPE         CLUSTER-IP      EXTERNAL-IP     PORT(S)         AGE
service/nginx-svc    NodePort     10.96.7.126     <none>          80:30179/TCP    9s

NAME                               READY    UP-TO-DATE    AVAILABLE    AGE
deployment.apps/nginx-deployment   2/2      2             2            9s

NAME                                          DESIRED    CURRENT    READY    AGE
```

```
replicaset.apps/nginx-deployment-5bf9b56d77   2          2          2          9s
```

```
% kubectl get pods -o wide -n web3
NAME                                    READY  STATUS   RESTARTS  AGE  IP            NODE
nginx-deployment-5bf9b56d77-gh65d       1/1    Running  0         16m  10.244.2.85   k8s-wk1
nginx-deployment-5bf9b56d77-zvd2f       1/1    Running  0         16m  10.244.1.59   k8s-wk0
```

```
% kubectl get endpoints -n web3
NAME        ENDPOINTS                       AGE
nginx-svc   10.244.1.59:80,10.244.2.85:80   16s
```

Everything appears to have come online successfully. Note that the service `nginx-svc` is now of type NodePort. The other thing that is interesting to note about the service is the Port. Container Port 80 has now been allocated a Node Port 30179. This port comes from a range of node ports configured when the Kubernetes cluster is created, the default range being 30000 to 32767. Now, if we connect to this port on any of the Kubernetes nodes in the cluster, we should be able to reach our containerized application, the Nginx web server. The actual node port could be specified in the Service manifest, but if none is specified, one is randomly chosen from the available node port range.

Let's try to connect to the application from outside the Kubernetes cluster. We have the IP addresses of the Kubernetes nodes from the previous *kubectl get nodes -o wide* output. Now we simply need to specify the node IP address and node port when making the request. In this example, I am running a *curl* command from my laptop to the combined node IP address and node port.

```
% curl -L http://192.168.51.42:30179
<!DOCTYPE html>
<html>
<head>
<title>Welcome to nginx!</title>
<h1>Welcome to nginx!</h1>
```

Success! We can reach the application from an external client, e.g., a laptop or desktop, to reach the application. Even if we send the request to a node where the Pod isn't running, the request will be proxied appropriately to an endpoint that can respond. Therefore, you can point to any node in the cluster and expect to get a response. This is very different to ClusterIP which does not allow external access from outside the Kubernetes cluster to the Service.

LoadBalancer

As we have seen, ClusterIP services are only accessible from within the cluster. A service of NodePort exposes a service externally. However, a more elegant solution for external connectivity to applications is to use a Service type of LoadBalancer to expose a service externally using its own unique IP address.

When Service type LoadBalancer is used, Kubernetes provides functionality that is like ClusterIP="" (blank), and any incoming requests will be load-balanced across all back-end Pods. However, the external load balancer functionality is not built into Kubernetes. It must be provided by some external provider outside of Kubernetes. On vSphere, especially vSphere with Tanzu, several external Load Balancer providers are supported. For example, there is an HA-Proxy appliance, the NSX Advanced Load Balancer (formerly Avi Vantage) as well as the L4 Load Balancer provided by the Edge device in NSX-T. Assuming NSX-T is used, as soon as `type: LoadBalancer` is specified in the Service manifest file, NSX-T will retrieve an available address from the preconfigured pool of Load Balancer IP addresses and allocate it to the Service. As the Service receives client requests on the external IP address, the LoadBalancer Service (which has been updated with Endpoint entries for the Pods) redirects or proxies these requests to the backend Pods.

We are not yet at the point where we can start to provision the external load balancers mentioned above. Instead, we will create our very own simple Load Balancer in the Kubernetes cluster and use this to demonstrate the functionality mentioned previously. I am going to use a load balancer provider called MetalLB (https://metallb.universe.tf/) which can be deployed directly into the Kubernetes cluster. It comes as two distinct components; the *controller* Deployment is the cluster-wide controller that handles IP address assignments, and the *speaker* DaemonSet is the component that speaks the protocol(s) of your choice to make the Services reachable. Two manifests are available. One sets up the namespace and the other creates all the components. The latter creates the Service accounts for the controller and speaker, along with the Role Based Access Control (RBAC) permissions that the components need to function. This is not an area that we have discussed yet, but it is something we will discuss later in the book. However, it is not necessary to understand these concepts for the purposes of understanding the LoadBalancer Service type. One final item needed is a configuration file, in the form of a ConfigMap. This is another Kubernetes construct. MetalLB uses the ConfigMap construct to define the protocol and range of IP addresses that will be provided when there is a request for a LoadBalancer Service type. Below is a sample ConfigMap. I have selected a /24 range of IP addresses on the 192.168.200.0 network. The protocol is set to `layer2`, meaning we don't need to worry about any protocol-specific configuration like BGP (Border Gateway Protocol). We are only interested in provisioning IP addresses. You can of course change the address range to something that is available and reachable in your environment. This range can also be made much smaller if necessary.

```
apiVersion: v1
kind: ConfigMap
metadata:
  namespace: metallb-system
  name: config
data:
  config: |
    address-pools:
    - name: default
      protocol: layer2
      addresses:
      - 192.168.200.1-192.168.200.254
```

The two manifests for namespace and speaker are available via https://metallb.universe.tf/installation/. Apply them to your Kubernetes cluster.

```
% kubectl apply -f \
https://raw.githubusercontent.com/metallb/metallb/v0.12.1/manifests/namespace.yaml
namespace/metallb-system created

% kubectl apply -f \
https://raw.githubusercontent.com/metallb/metallb/v0.12.1/manifests/metallb.yaml
Warning: policy/v1beta1 PodSecurityPolicy is deprecated in v1.21+, unavailable in v1.25+
podsecuritypolicy.policy/controller created
podsecuritypolicy.policy/speaker created
serviceaccount/controller created
```

```
serviceaccount/speaker created
clusterrole.rbac.authorization.k8s.io/metallb-system:controller created
clusterrole.rbac.authorization.k8s.io/metallb-system:speaker created
role.rbac.authorization.k8s.io/config-watcher created
role.rbac.authorization.k8s.io/pod-lister created
role.rbac.authorization.k8s.io/controller created
clusterrolebinding.rbac.authorization.k8s.io/metallb-system:controller created
clusterrolebinding.rbac.authorization.k8s.io/metallb-system:speaker created
rolebinding.rbac.authorization.k8s.io/config-watcher created
rolebinding.rbac.authorization.k8s.io/pod-lister created
rolebinding.rbac.authorization.k8s.io/controller created
daemonset.apps/speaker created
deployment.apps/controller created
```

There are several objects being deployed here that have not yet been discussed in the book, e.g.,
Role and RoleBinding, ClusterRole and ClusterRoleBinding, but which will be examined later in the
context of Identity Management. However, some objects should be familiar to you by now, such as
the DaemonSet and the Deployment. All objects should appear ready after a short period. Remember
to specify the namespace when querying.

```
% kubectl get all -n metallb-system
NAME                             READY   STATUS    RESTARTS   AGE
pod/controller-57fd9c5bb-rxnbs   1/1     Running   0          49s
pod/speaker-ch2cz                1/1     Running   0          49s
pod/speaker-jz9db                1/1     Running   0          49s
pod/speaker-z8smt                1/1     Running   0          49s

NAME                    DESIRED   CURRENT   READY   UP-TO-DATE   AVAILABLE   NODE
SELECTOR           AGE
daemonset.apps/speaker  3         3         3       3            3
kubernetes.io/os=linux  50s

NAME                         READY   UP-TO-DATE   AVAILABLE   AGE
deployment.apps/controller   1/1     1            1           50s

NAME                                     DESIRED   CURRENT   READY   AGE
replicaset.apps/controller-57fd9c5bb     1         1         1       50s
```

Now create and apply the ConfigMap above. A load balancer provider should now be available to
your Kubernetes cluster.

```
% kubectl apply -f metallb-configmap.yml
configmap/config created
```

If we proceed to build an application which requires a Load Balancer service, we should see it get
allocated an IP address from the range of IP addresses defined in the ConfigMap. This is the same
Service and Deployment that we have used on several occasions at this point. As with the previous
examples, I have placed this Service and Deployment in its own namespace called web4. I've also
adjusted the labels so that they are unique for this application. Lastly, the only major change from
the last example is that the Service type has been set to LoadBalancer.

```
apiVersion: v1
kind: Service
metadata:
  labels:
    app: nginx4
  name: nginx-svc
  namespace: web4
spec:
```

```
    type: LoadBalancer
    ports:
      - name: http
        port: 80
    selector:
      app: nginx4
---
apiVersion: apps/v1
kind: Deployment
metadata:
  name: nginx-deployment
  namespace: web4
spec:
  selector:
    matchLabels:
      app: nginx4
  replicas: 2
  template:
    metadata:
      labels:
        app: nginx4
    spec:
      containers:
      - name: nginx
        image: nginx:latest
        ports:
        - containerPort: 80
```

Let's deploy it and check to see if it has picked up an external IP address from the load balancer.

```
% kubectl create ns web4
namespace/web4 created
```

```
% kubectl apply -f loadbalancer-svc.yaml
service/nginx-svc created
deployment.apps/nginx-deployment created
```

```
% kubectl get all -n web4
NAME                                         READY   STATUS    RESTARTS   AGE
pod/nginx-deployment-6b89486868-6fhrr        1/1     Running   0          7s
pod/nginx-deployment-6b89486868-fqlkt        1/1     Running   0          7s

NAME                TYPE           CLUSTER-IP      EXTERNAL-IP     PORT(S)        AGE
service/nginx-svc   LoadBalancer   10.104.28.217   192.168.200.1   80:30762/TCP   8s

NAME                               READY   UP-TO-DATE   AVAILABLE   AGE
deployment.apps/nginx-deployment   2/2     2            2           7s

NAME                                          DESIRED   CURRENT   READY   AGE
replicaset.apps/nginx-deployment-6b89486868   2         2         2       7s
```

Success! There is an external IP address associated with the Service. It is the first IP address in the range that was placed in the load balancer configuration file. Assuming this is a valid IP address in the environment, it should be possible to run either a *wget* or *curl* against it, or point a browser at this address and view the Nginx landing page. Note that most cloud providers will provide a load balancer service for their Kubernetes distributions. However, for on-premises deployments on vSphere, a load balancer will need to be provided manually. The options for load balancers when running Kubernetes on vSphere will be discussed in detail later in the book. For now, it is enough to understand the concept of a LoadBalancer type service.

Note that the service has both an internal Cluster-IP IP address and an external IP address. Any requests to access the service from inside the cluster would continue to use the internal IP address.

At this point, you should have a reasonable understanding of Services. You should be aware that some Services, such as ClusterIP, provide internal-only communication within the Kubernetes cluster. Some ClusterIP settings provide a front-end IP address for the service and load balance requests across the Pods, whilst other allows access directly to the Pods. Other Services, such as NodePort and LoadBalancer allow external communication to the applications running in the Kubernetes Cluster. And you should also be aware that the LoadBalancer Service requires an external provider since there is none built into the cluster.

Ingress

Ingresses achieve a similar function as a Load Balancer in so far as they provide a means of allowing external traffic into your cluster. But they are significantly different in how they do this. If we take the Load Balancer Service type first, then for every service that is exposed via a Load Balancer, a unique external IP address needs to be assigned to each service. If you have a lot of services, you will require a lot of IP addresses.

Ingress, on the other hand, is not a Service. It behaves as a sort of entry point to your cluster, using a single IP address, and sits in front of multiple services. The request can then be 'routed' to the appropriate Service, based on how the request is made. The most common example of where ingress is used is with web servers. For example, I may run an online store, where different services are offered, e.g. searching for an item, adding an item to the basket, displaying basket contents, etc. Depending on the URL, I can redirect that request to a different service at the back-end, all from the same website/URL. So `my-web.com/add-to-basket` could be directed to the 'add-to-basket' service backed by a set of Pods running a particular service, whilst `my-web.com/search` could be redirected to a different service backed by a different set of Pods.

To summarize, how this differs from a Load Balancer service is that a Load Balancer distributes requests across back-end Pods of the same type offering a service, consuming a unique external IP address per service. Whereas ingress will route requests to a specific back-end service (based on a URL, for example) when there are multiple different services available in the back-end. As mentioned, one typically comes across ingress when you have multiple services exposed via the same IP address, and all these services uses the same layer 7 (L7) protocol, which more often than not is HTTP. Note that there is a dependency on a LoadBalancer service – you will not be able to use the Ingress feature without a load balancer.

Be aware that an Ingress object does nothing by itself; it requires an ingress controller to operate. One popular open source Ingress Controller for Kubernetes is Contour (https://projectcontour.io/). VMware acquired Contour along with the Heptio acquisition. This was a company built by the founders of the Kubernetes project. Contour works by deploying Envoy, an open source edge and service proxy. What is neat about Contour is that supports dynamic configuration updates. Let's begin with deploying the Contour quick start manifest which contain all the necessary components.

```
% kubectl apply -f https://projectcontour.io/quickstart/contour.yaml
namespace/projectcontour created
serviceaccount/contour created
```

```
serviceaccount/envoy created
configmap/contour created
customresourcedefinition.apiextensions.k8s.io/contourconfigurations.projectcontour.io
created
customresourcedefinition.apiextensions.k8s.io/contourdeployments.projectcontour.io created
customresourcedefinition.apiextensions.k8s.io/extensionservices.projectcontour.io created
customresourcedefinition.apiextensions.k8s.io/httpproxies.projectcontour.io created
customresourcedefinition.apiextensions.k8s.io/tlscertificatedelegations.projectcontour.io
created
serviceaccount/contour-certgen created
rolebinding.rbac.authorization.k8s.io/contour created
role.rbac.authorization.k8s.io/contour-certgen created
job.batch/contour-certgen-v1.21.0 created
clusterrolebinding.rbac.authorization.k8s.io/contour created
rolebinding.rbac.authorization.k8s.io/contour-rolebinding created
clusterrole.rbac.authorization.k8s.io/contour created
role.rbac.authorization.k8s.io/contour created
service/contour created
service/envoy created
deployment.apps/contour created
daemonset.apps/envoy created
```

Next, let's verify that the installation has been successful.

```
% kubectl get pods -n projectcontour -o wide
NAME                           READY   STATUS      RESTARTS   AGE    IP             NODE
contour-55544b8fdc-k6l79       1/1     Running     0          72s    10.244.1.67    k8s-wk0
contour-55544b8fdc-smt82       1/1     Running     0          72s    10.244.2.92    k8s-wk1
contour-certgen-v1.21.0-lh75b  0/1     Completed   0          75s    10.244.1.66    k8s-wk0
envoy-d4595                    2/2     Running     0          72s    10.244.2.93    k8s-wk1
envoy-fs52g                    2/2     Running     0          72s    10.244.1.68    k8s-wk0
```

Everything looks good from a Pod perspective. Also, check the Services. Envoy has a requirement on a LoadBalancer type service, so make sure an External IP address has been allocated by the Load Balancer provider.

```
% kubectl get svc -n projectcontour -o wide
NAME      TYPE           CLUSTER-IP      EXTERNAL-IP      PORT(S)                      AGE
contour   ClusterIP      10.104.111.70   <none>           8001/TCP                     22s
envoy     LoadBalancer   10.109.253.77   192.168.51.177   80:31972/TCP,443:31080/TCP   22s
```

Now we need to create an application (or applications) that can demonstrate this Ingress. I am once again going to use a simple Apache2 web server deployments, just like we did in chapter 1. I am going to run two servers behind a single URL / IP address using an ingress service. When my service is in receipt of a request to access /index-a, I am going to redirect the request to the 'a' service and 'a' web server, and hit the index page on Pod 'a', Similarly, on receipt of a request to access /index-b, I am redirect the request to the 'b' service and 'b' web server, and hit the index page on Pod 'b'. For this, I am going to build some new docker images for my Pod containers, so we can easily tell which services/Pods we are landing on, a or b.

After building these containers, I am going to tag and push them up to an image registry. This is an important task for the DevOps role. In this example, I am going to push them up to an account that I have created on docker hub. Other registries are available. Once they are on an external registry, they can be consumed by the Pods that I create on my Kubernetes cluster for the application.

First, let's revisit the docker build process from chapter 1. I have created a new directory on my laptop called ingress. In this directory, I have created a new index.html file, called index-a.html.

```
<html>
<head>
  <title> Welcome to Service A! </title>
</head>
<body>
  <p> Welcome to Service A! </p>
</body>
</html>
```

I have created a new Dockerfile, but this time it is going to create a new file in `/var/www/html` called `index-a.yaml` which is copied from my local desktop. Here is the new Dockerfile.

```
FROM ubuntu:latest
RUN apt-get update; \
apt-get install apache2 -y
COPY index-a.html /var/www/html/index-a.html
EXPOSE 80
ENTRYPOINT ["/usr/sbin/apache2ctl", "-D", "FOREGROUND"]
```

As before, let's build the Dockerfile, and we should observe the layers putting together our new container image. This should all be pretty familiar since it is a repeat of what we did in chapter 1. I am going to tag it as `ingress-demo-a`.

```
% docker build -t cormac/ingress-demo-a .
Sending build context to Docker daemon  4.096kB
Sending build context to Docker daemon  3.072kB
Step 1/5 : FROM ubuntu:latest
 ---> d2e4e1f51132
Step 2/5 : RUN apt-get update; apt-get install apache2 -y
 ---> Running in 0a2cdf65ddda
Removing intermediate container 0a2cdf65ddda
 ---> 80988477b9c7
Step 3/5 : COPY index-a.html /var/www/html/index-a.html
 ---> 455822bc5dab
Step 4/5 : EXPOSE 80
 ---> Running in 13c8c438699c
Removing intermediate container 13c8c438699c
 ---> eaee6b6864d1
Step 5/5 : ENTRYPOINT ["/usr/sbin/apache2ctl", "-D", "FOREGROUND"]
 ---> Running in d25a096dcdb5
Removing intermediate container d25a096dcdb5
 ---> 987848af1a4a
Successfully built 987848af1a4a
Successfully tagged cormac/ingress-demo-a:latest
```

Let's run the container, and check it is working.

```
% docker images
cormac/ingress-demo-a              latest               987848af1a4a  About a minute
ago   226MB

% docker run -d -p 8080:80 -h ingress-demo.mydomain.com cormac/ingress-demo
f2f05141db3a12dd23b4cef4ae9bd866a9408161ce246b702f68c0cbcc1c10f8

% docker ps
CONTAINER ID   IMAGE              COMMAND             CREATED         STATUS
PORTS                             NAMES
048476b1dc13   cormac/ingress-demo-a   "/usr/sbin/apache2ct…"  15 seconds ago  Up 13
seconds   0.0.0.0:8080->80/tcp, :::8080->80/tcp   eager_kowalevski
```

One final check to make sure it is displaying the expected landing page, this time using *curl*.

```
% curl -0 http://localhost:8080/index-a.html
<html>
<head>
  <title> Welcome to Service A! </title>
</head>
<body>
  <p> Welcome to Service A! </p>
</body>
</html>
```

Stop and remove the new container.

```
% docker stop 048476b1dc13
048476b1dc13

% docker rm 048476b1dc13
048476b1dc13
```

Now repeat the whole process for the second web server. Create a new folder, and add a new `index-b.html` and a new `Dockerfile`. Here are the respective files, almost identical to what we did for 'a'. Here is the index html file:

```
<html>
<head>
  <title> Welcome to Service B! </title>
</head>
<body>
  <p> Welcome to Service B! </p>
</body>
</html>
```

And here is the new Dockerfile.

```
FROM ubuntu:latest
RUN apt-get update; \
apt-get install apache2 -y
COPY index-b.html /var/www/html/index-b.html
EXPOSE 80
ENTRYPOINT ["/usr/sbin/apache2ctl", "-D", "FOREGROUND"]
```

Once again, we build the image:

```
% docker build -t cormac/ingress-demo-b .
Sending build context to Docker daemon  3.072kB
Step 1/5 : FROM ubuntu:latest
 ---> d2e4e1f51132
Step 2/5 : RUN apt-get update; apt-get install apache2 -y
 ---> Using cache
 ---> 80988477b9c7
Step 3/5 : COPY index-b.html /var/www/html/index-b.html
 ---> ae5c4ace8bf3
Step 4/5 : EXPOSE 80
 ---> Running in 1a487d5a65fc
Removing intermediate container 1a487d5a65fc
 ---> 6db9edf1c04c
Step 5/5 : ENTRYPOINT ["/usr/sbin/apache2ctl", "-D", "FOREGROUND"]
 ---> Running in 731d34ea838d
```

```
Removing intermediate container 731d34ea838d
 ---> c794e8163ef1
Successfully built c794e8163ef1
Successfully tagged cormac/ingress-demo-b:latest
```

Let's run it, and test it like we did for 'a'.

```
% docker run -d -p 8080:80 -h ingress-demo.mydomain.com cormac/ingress-demo-b
d4f6a92aa23c1b907789e759a16f700ce21bd683cd9679a878869598fa3293e3
```

```
% curl -0 http://localhost:8080/index-b.html
<html>
<head>
  <title> Welcome to Service B! </title>
</head>
<body>
  <p> Welcome to Service B! </p>
</body>
</html>
```

Looks good to me! The web server landing page reports service 'b'. You can now stop and delete this container.

```
% docker stop d4f6a92aa23c
d4f6a92aa23c
```

```
% docker rm d4f6a92aa23c
d4f6a92aa23c
```

Now the images need to be stored somewhere that Kubernetes can reach them. This is typically a Container Image Registry. It allows container images to be pushed (saved) and pulled (retrieved).

Note: Managing container images on behalf of developers is one of the major tasks of a Platform Operator. Throughout this book, different container registries are examined, and how to securely interact with them is also discussed.

The first step is to login to container registry where the container image should be stored. You will need to create an account on the container registry to be able to use it. Next, a `tag` is created on the local image which points to an external registry. Once it is tagged, a push command will `push` the image up to the external registry. Then when the YAML manifest for the web server application is built on Kubernetes, a path to the image location on the registry can be provided. When the Pod is deployed in Kubernetes, the image is *pulled* from the container registry.

Let's see a container registry interaction in action. The *docker login* command logs into the external docker hub registry (hub.docker.com). If you've already logged, credentials will have been saved locally, meaning you do not need to provide them again. When logging in for the first time, the credentials must be provided.

```
% docker login
Login with your Docker ID to push and pull images from Docker Hub. If you don't have a
Docker ID, head over to https://hub.docker.com to create one.
Username: cormachogan
Password: **********
Login Succeeded
```

```
% docker images | grep ingress
cormac/ingress-demo-b          latest       c794e8163ef1   4 minutes ago   226MB
cormac/ingress-demo-a          latest       987848af1a4a   12 minutes ago  226MB
```

```
% docker tag cormac/ingress-demo-a:latest cormachogan/ingress-demo-a:latest
```

```
% docker push cormachogan/ingress-demo-a:latest
The push refers to repository [docker.io/cormachogan/ingress-demo-a]
528c2f733cb3: Pushed
606b22dd796a: Pushed
e59fc9495612: Pushed
latest:   digest:   sha256:24f592dde4c30660fe65c784158c7f88f82ec16bc255e5a05841be154b9a500d
size: 948
```

Success! The image has been successfully tagged and pushed to docker hub. I now have a location where the image can be retrieved from. Repeat the process for the second 'b' image.

```
% docker tag cormac/ingress-demo-b:latest cormachogan/ingress-demo-b:latest
```

```
% docker push cormachogan/ingress-demo-b:latest
The push refers to repository [docker.io/cormachogan/ingress-demo-b]
bd1992406371: Pushed
cab5549bfdfb: Mounted from cormachogan/ingress-demo-a
e59fc9495612: Mounted from cormachogan/ingress-demo-a
latest: digest: sha256:9b161359757a459035610e0b8cde47a56b3baeb3348d7e68deb35a0deb505223
size: 948
```

You may have noticed that the second push was much quicker. This is because a number of layers of the image are already on the registry, since the first image was pushed. Therefore, there is no need to push those layers again. Now that the images are available on the external registry, our attention can turn back to Kubernetes. Five manifests will be created in total. Obviously, there will be an ingress manifest, but we are also going to create 2 deployment manifests and 2 service manifests, one for each component of our web service, 'a' and 'b'.

Here is the combined Deployment and Service manifest for web server 'a'. There is not much to say about this as we have seen similar manifests multiple times already in the book. The only item of significance is the image entry, which is now pointing to my image registry on docker hub.

```
apiVersion: apps/v1
kind: Deployment
metadata:
  name: web-a-deployment
spec:
  selector:
    matchLabels:
      app: web-a
  replicas: 1
  template:
    metadata:
      labels:
        app: web-a
    spec:
      containers:
      - name: web-a
        image: cormachogan/ingress-demo-a:latest
        ports:
        - containerPort: 80
---
apiVersion: v1
kind: Service
```

```
metadata:
  labels:
    app: web-a
  name: web-a
spec:
  ports:
  - port: 80
    protocol: TCP
  selector:
    app: web-a
  sessionAffinity: None
  type: ClusterIP
```

Here is the combined Deployment and Service manifest for web server 'b'. It is almost identical to 'a' except that it is using a different image, the image with the 'b' web server landing page rather than the 'a' web server landing page.

```
apiVersion: apps/v1
kind: Deployment
metadata:
  name: web-b-deployment
spec:
  selector:
    matchLabels:
      app: web-b
  replicas: 1
  template:
    metadata:
      labels:
        app: web-b
    spec:
      containers:
      - name: web-b
        image: cormachogan/ingress-demo-b:latest
        ports:
        - containerPort: 80
---
apiVersion: v1
kind: Service
metadata:
  labels:
    app: web-b
  name: web-b
spec:
  ports:
  - port: 80
    protocol: TCP
  selector:
    app: web-b
  sessionAffinity: None
  type: ClusterIP
```

Here is the ingress manifest.

```
apiVersion: networking.k8s.io/v1
kind: Ingress
metadata:
  name: web
spec:
  rules:
  - host: web.mydomain.com
    http:
```

```
      paths:
      - path: /index-a.html
        pathType: Prefix
        backend:
          service:
            name: web-a
            port:
              number: 80
      - path: /index-b.html
        pathType: Prefix
        backend:
          service:
            name: web-b
            port:
              number: 80
```

The rules section of the manifest is looking at the path, and redirecting the request to the appropriate service. The idea here is that an end-user connects to the host `web.mydomain.com` (a DNS name assigned to the Ingress), and depending on whether the full URL is `web.mydomain.com/index-a.html` or `web.mydomain.com/index-b.html`, the request will be routed to the appropriate service, and the appropriate Pod/Container/application. This should display the correct (a or b) index page that was modified in the image. Note that the URL `web.mydomain.com` is resolving to the IP address assigned to the Envoy service by the Load Balancer provisioner. If you are doing this in an environment where it is not feasible to add this to the DNS, add the name and IP address to your local /etc/hosts file – the name simply needs to resolve to the IP address. Earlier, we checked to make sure that Envoy was assigned an external IP address by the Load Balancer at the beginning on this Ingress section. The Load Balancer provider can be the simple MetalLB that we deployed in an earlier exercise.

Let's deploy the manifests and check to see if the Ingress is working as expected.

```
% kubectl apply -f web-a-deploy.yaml
deployment.apps/web-a-deployment created
service/web-a created

% kubectl apply -f web-b-deploy.yaml
deployment.apps/web-b-deployment created
service/web-b created

% kubectl get svc
NAME          TYPE        CLUSTER-IP       EXTERNAL-IP    PORT(S)    AGE
kubernetes    ClusterIP   10.96.0.1        <none>         443/TCP    113d
web-a         ClusterIP   10.96.193.167    <none>         80/TCP     11s
web-b         ClusterIP   10.106.255.214   <none>         80/TCP     5s

% kubectl get deploy
NAME                READY   UP-TO-DATE   AVAILABLE   AGE
web-a-deployment    1/1     1            1           15s
web-b-deployment    1/1     1            1           9s
```

So far, everything looks good. Let's now create and check on the ingress.

```
% kubectl apply -f web-ingress.yaml
ingress.networking.k8s.io/web created

% kubectl get ingress
NAME   CLASS    HOSTS              ADDRESS          PORTS   AGE
web    <none>   web.mydomain.com   192.168.51.177   80      3m28s
```

The ingress looks good. The correct FQDN appears in the hosts section of the output, and it has been allocated a VIP address. Note that it is using the same IP address that was assigned to Envoy. Let's now try our test by curling to different URLs and hopefully seeing the rules defined in the ingress manifest working as expected.

```
% curl -0 http://web.mydomain.com/index-a.html
<html>
<head>
  <title> Welcome to Service A! </title>
</head>
<body>
  <p> Welcome to Service A! </p>
</body>
</html>

% curl -0 http://web.mydomain.com/index-b.html
<html>
<head>
  <title> Welcome to Service B! </title>
</head>
<body>
  <p> Welcome to Service B! </p>
</body>
</html>
```

Success! Everything is working as expected. Depending on the URL, the request is being directed to the appropriate Service and web server in the backend. The Ingress is doing its job, and all of this has been achieved through a single allocated IP address from the Load Balancer. In this way, access can be provided to multiple services and applications running in Kubernetes without consuming a vast range of Load Balancer IP addresses. We can visualize the ingress working something like what is shown below.

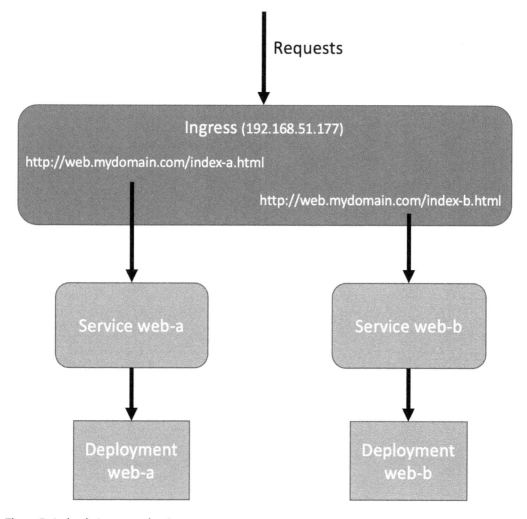

Figure 5: A simple Ingress using Contour

Later, we shall see how vSphere with Tanzu on NSX-T uses and Ingress to control and provide accesses to all the services inside of a vSphere Namespace. Ingress provides a very useful and important mechanism in Kubernetes.

Kubernetes Operators / Custom Resource Definitions

Throughout this book, you will come across references to custom resources and custom resource definitions. These are mechanisms which extend Kubernetes. They allow third parties, including VMware, to add their bespoke Kubernetes objects. They are used extensively. Kubernetes Operators make use of the custom resources to manage applications and resources. Thus, operators and custom resources go together most of the time. By way of example, on a standard TKG cluster deployed via the TKG Service, the Antrea CNI creates several custom resource definitions, which can be listed with the following command:

```
% kubectl get crd
NAME                                                             CREATED AT
antreaagentinfos.clusterinformation.antrea.tanzu.vmware.com      2022-06-16T14:55:33Z
antreacontrollerinfos.clusterinformation.antrea.tanzu.vmware.com 2022-06-16T14:55:33Z
clustergroups.core.antrea.tanzu.vmware.com                       2022-06-20T16:17:03Z
clusternetworkpolicies.security.antrea.tanzu.vmware.com          2022-06-16T14:55:34Z
externalentities.core.antrea.tanzu.vmware.com                    2022-06-16T14:55:34Z
networkpolicies.security.antrea.tanzu.vmware.com                 2022-06-16T14:55:34Z
tierentitlementbindings.crd.antrea.tanzu.vmware.com              2022-06-20T16:17:04Z
tierentitlements.crd.antrea.tanzu.vmware.com                     2022-06-20T16:17:04Z
tiers.security.antrea.tanzu.vmware.com                           2022-06-16T14:55:34Z
traceflows.ops.antrea.tanzu.vmware.com                           2022-06-16T14:55:34Z
```

These custom resource definitions are then used to build customer resources, which are Kubernetes entities. To see if any custom resources have been created using the custom resource definition, the custom resource name can be queried directly. For example, an `antreagentinfos` object is created on every node. As shown below.

```
% kubectl get antreaagentinfos -A
NAME                                              AGE
tkg-cluster-01-control-plane-ls79h                2d17h
tkg-cluster-01-worker-pool-1-6ss8h-c7db67f69-9dx78 2d17h
tkg-cluster-01-worker-pool-1-6ss8h-c7db67f69-lq42q 2d17h
```

It is not necessary to get into the details of operators or customer resource definitions. It is enough for a vSphere administrator to understand that they are simply a way to extend Kubernetes clusters with third party applications.

Editing Kubernetes Objects

While we have seen several kubectl commands in this chapter, there is one command that you will come across regularly that has not yet been discussed. This is the *kubectl edit* command, where the manifests of Kubernetes objects can be modified live, or 'on-the-fly', so to speak. As one might expect, this opens an editor on your desktop/laptop, and often this is not an editor that you might be familiar with, e.g., the vi/vim editor. To specify a preferred editor, e.g., nano, use the environment variable KUBE_EDITOR, e.g., *export KUBE_EDITOR=/usr/bin/nano*. This variable setting could be added into your .profile or .bash_profile (depending on your shell) to have it set every time you login. We will see some examples of editing manifests or existing objects later in the book.

Summary

In this chapter, we have seen quite a number of Kubernetes constructs. We have seen some of the compute constructs such as Pods, and some of the resiliency constructs such as Deployments and StatefulSets. We have seen storage constructs like StorageClass, PVCs and PVs. We looked at a number of different Service types for Pod networking, before finally taking a look at the Ingress construct. There are of course many additional Kubernetes constructs that we have not looked at yet. These include Secrets, ConfigMaps, Roles and RoleBindings, ClusterRoles and ClusterRoleBindings, Service Accounts, to name but a few. These will be examined in closer detail as we come across additional examples later in the book. However, hopefully this chapter has given you a reasonable understanding of some of the most common major constructs that make up Kubernetes. Our next step is to look at the various ways that Kubernetes clusters are created on vSphere.

03

Creating a Kubernetes Cluster on vSphere

In chapter 2, a number of ways to deploy Kubernetes to your local laptop/desktop were discussed. For example, KinD (Kubernetes in Docker) is a common distribution that you can deploy locally to your laptop or your desktop to get familiar with Kubernetes concepts. Tanzu Community Edition and Rancher Desktop are other available options. However, since this book is primarily aimed at vSphere administrators who might be involved in managing vSphere platforms where Kubernetes is deployed, we are going to look at various ways of getting Kubernetes up and running on a vSphere platform. We are going to begin with some of the more manual tools and procedures using kubeadm and clusterctl. We will then move on to looking at the Tanzu Kubernetes Grid and vSphere with Tanzu which make the deployment of Kubernetes cluster on vSphere much easier.

VMs as Kubernetes Nodes - Requirements

If you are manually building a Kubernetes cluster on vSphere, there are a few requirements regarding the virtual machines that you plan to use as Kubernetes nodes. Every virtual machine must run a hardware version that is 15 or higher. If you have a virtual machine with a lower hardware version, it needs to be upgraded. Secondly, every node requires that the `disk.EnableUUID` parameter is set to True in the VM Advanced Configuration. This is required so that attached VMDKs present a consistent UUID to the virtual machine. This allows disks (i.e., persistent volumes) to be mounted properly. The final requirement is to add a new Paravirtual type of SCSI controller to the VM. This will also be used to attach VMDKs when there is a request for a persistent volume in a Pod/container on the Kubernetes worker node. With these settings in place, the VM is now ready to be used as a Kubernetes node. Note that at the time of writing, the vSphere CSI v2.5 has only alpha support for Windows containers. Thus, this chapter will focus on Kubernetes clusters deployed on virtual machines with Linux Guest operating systems installed.

Build a Kubernetes cluster with Kubeadm

Let's look at the first of the older, manual methods used to deploy Kubernetes on vSphere – kubeadm. In the examples that follow, Kubernetes will be deployed as a set of virtual machines to a vSphere 7.0U3 (build 19480866) environment. The Kubernetes distribution that I am using is v1.23.3. I also plan to install vSphere CSI driver version 2.4. I mention this because instructions regarding the installation of the vSphere CSI do change regularly, so the steps followed here should be deemed informational and may be out of date for later releases available at the time of publication. I recommend checking the official documentation, especially for the vSphere CSI driver, to see if any of the install instructions have been updated.

To use kubeadm to build a Kubernetes cluster, you must first prepare the virtual machines that will make up the control plane and worker nodes. You'll have to create one or more user accounts, decide how to enable SSH access, deploy a container runtime such as Docker, and install the relevant tooling such as kubectl, kubeadm and kubelet. There are many guides and tutorials available online on how to do this and are beyond the scope of this book. However, once these requirements are in place, the next step is to initialize the cluster using *kubeadm init*. In this example, I am also providing the *–pod-network-cidr* which defined the network range that should be assigned to Pods. I am not providing a service CIDR, which implies that I am going to use the defaults.

This *kubeadm init* command, run on the virtual machine, will build the first control plane node in the cluster. You can increase the verbosity of the output with a -v option, e.g. -v3. Most of verbose output will display the pre-checks, making sure that the appropriate manifests are present, container runtime is up, and networking is working.

```
$ sudo kubeadm init --pod-network-cidr=10.244.0.0/16
[init] Using Kubernetes version: v1.23.3
[preflight] Running pre-flight checks
[preflight] Pulling images required for setting up a Kubernetes cluster
[preflight] This might take a minute or two, depending on the speed of your internet
connection
[preflight] You can also perform this action in beforehand using 'kubeadm config images
pull'
[certs] Using certificateDir folder "/etc/kubernetes/pki"
[certs] Generating "ca" certificate and key
[certs] Generating "apiserver" certificate and key
[certs] apiserver serving cert is signed for DNS names [k8s-cp0 kubernetes
kubernetes.default kubernetes.default.svc kubernetes.default.svc.cluster.local] and IPs
[10.96.0.1 192.168.51.40]
[certs] Generating "apiserver-kubelet-client" certificate and key
[certs] Generating "front-proxy-ca" certificate and key
[certs] Generating "front-proxy-client" certificate and key
[certs] Generating "etcd/ca" certificate and key
[certs] Generating "etcd/server" certificate and key
[certs] etcd/server serving cert is signed for DNS names [k8s-cp0 localhost] and IPs
[192.168.51.40 127.0.0.1 ::1]
[certs] Generating "etcd/peer" certificate and key
[certs] etcd/peer serving cert is signed for DNS names [k8s-cp0 localhost] and IPs
[192.168.51.40 127.0.0.1 ::1]
[certs] Generating "etcd/healthcheck-client" certificate and key
[certs] Generating "apiserver-etcd-client" certificate and key
[certs] Generating "sa" key and public key
[kubeconfig] Using kubeconfig folder "/etc/kubernetes"
[kubeconfig] Writing "admin.conf" kubeconfig file
[kubeconfig] Writing "kubelet.conf" kubeconfig file
[kubeconfig] Writing "controller-manager.conf" kubeconfig file
[kubeconfig] Writing "scheduler.conf" kubeconfig file
[kubelet-start] Writing kubelet environment file with flags to file
"/var/lib/kubelet/kubeadm-flags.env"
[kubelet-start] Writing kubelet configuration to file "/var/lib/kubelet/config.yaml"
[kubelet-start] Starting the kubelet
[control-plane] Using manifest folder "/etc/kubernetes/manifests"
[control-plane] Creating static Pod manifest for "kube-apiserver"
[control-plane] Creating static Pod manifest for "kube-controller-manager"
[control-plane] Creating static Pod manifest for "kube-scheduler"
[etcd] Creating static Pod manifest for local etcd in "/etc/kubernetes/manifests"
[wait-control-plane] Waiting for the kubelet to boot up the control plane as static Pods
from directory "/etc/kubernetes/manifests". This can take up to 4m0s
[apiclient] All control plane components are healthy after 6.503287 seconds
```

```
[upload-config] Storing the configuration used in ConfigMap "kubeadm-config" in the "kube-system" Namespace
[kubelet] Creating a ConfigMap "kubelet-config-1.23" in namespace kube-system with the configuration for the kubelets in the cluster
NOTE: The "kubelet-config-1.23" naming of the kubelet ConfigMap is deprecated. Once the UnversionedKubeletConfigMap feature gate graduates to Beta the default name will become just "kubelet-config". Kubeadm upgrade will handle this transition transparently.
[upload-certs] Skipping phase. Please see --upload-certs
[mark-control-plane] Marking the node k8s-cp0 as control-plane by adding the labels:
[node-role.kubernetes.io/master(deprecated) node-role.kubernetes.io/control-plane
node.kubernetes.io/exclude-from-external-load-balancers]
[mark-control-plane] Marking the node k8s-cp0 as control-plane by adding the taints [node-role.kubernetes.io/master:NoSchedule]
[bootstrap-token] Using token: d2t54j.gw3jk2d475yw9o5c
[bootstrap-token] Configuring bootstrap tokens, cluster-info ConfigMap, RBAC Roles
[bootstrap-token] configured RBAC rules to allow Node Bootstrap tokens to get nodes
[bootstrap-token] configured RBAC rules to allow Node Bootstrap tokens to post CSRs in order for nodes to get long term certificate credentials
[bootstrap-token] configured RBAC rules to allow the csrapprover controller automatically approve CSRs from a Node Bootstrap Token
[bootstrap-token] configured RBAC rules to allow certificate rotation for all node client certificates in the cluster
[bootstrap-token] Creating the "cluster-info" ConfigMap in the "kube-public" namespace
[kubelet-finalize] Updating "/etc/kubernetes/kubelet.conf" to point to a rotatable kubelet client certificate and key
[addons] Applied essential addon: CoreDNS
[addons] Applied essential addon: kube-proxy

Your Kubernetes control-plane has initialized successfully!

To start using your cluster, you need to run the following as a regular user:

  mkdir -p $HOME/.kube
  sudo cp -i /etc/kubernetes/admin.conf $HOME/.kube/config
  sudo chown $(id -u):$(id -g) $HOME/.kube/config

Alternatively, if you are the root user, you can run:

  export KUBECONFIG=/etc/kubernetes/admin.conf

You should now deploy a pod network to the cluster.
Run "kubectl apply -f [podnetwork].yaml" with one of the options listed at:
  https://kubernetes.io/docs/concepts/cluster-administration/addons/

Then you can join any number of worker nodes by running the following on each as root:

kubeadm join 192.168.51.40:6443 --token d2t54j.gw3jk2d475yw9o5c \
--discovery-token-ca-cert-hash
sha256:3be77679e99574015bb295381809166471b959e4e69e84430ebc9c449e51516a
```

The initialization of the first control plane node in the cluster appears to have been successful. We see references to many of the core components that we discussed at the beginning of chapter 2, such as etcd, API server and kubelet. Much of the initial setup relates to certificates, which are used extensively in Kubernetes to establish trust between many of the components. Various configuration files are created before a number of 'static' Pods are created which will run core services such as the API server and scheduler. We also see some addons around DNS and the kube-proxy. Near the end, after the run has succeeded, the output provides us with a KUBECONFIG file so that we can access the cluster. It even shows us how to make a copy of it so we can access the cluster as a non-root user. Finally, the output even provides us with a *kubeadm* command to join worker nodes to the cluster at the very end of the output. Of course, the worker node will also need to be prepared, same as the control plane nodes.

There are a few things to do before we get to add the workers though. Another piece of guidance in the above output is the requirement to deploy a Pod network to the cluster. In essence, what this is saying is that we need a CNI, a Container Network Interface, deployed to the cluster. Funnily enough, we are not prompted to install a CPI, a Cloud Provider Interface, or a CSI, a Container Storage Interface. Let's address each of those three items next, as these are necessary for Kubernetes clusters deployed on vSphere.

Container Network Interface (CNI)

Like many things in the Kubernetes space, there are a wide variety of CNI's available. Some of the most common ones are Flannel, Calico and even VMware's own Antrea. Setting up the CNI is usually as simply as deploying a YAML manifest. You can do this immediately after the *kubeadm init* command. In the example below, I am applying the Flannel CNI to the cluster.

DNS requires networking connectivity, so until a CNI is installed, the DNS containers will not be available. Note that you only need to do this task once on the control plane "master" node.

```
$ kubectl apply -f \
https://raw.githubusercontent.com/flannel-io/flannel/master/Documentation/kube-flannel.yml
Warning: policy/v1beta1 PodSecurityPolicy is deprecated in v1.21+, unavailable in v1.25+
podsecuritypolicy.policy/psp.flannel.unprivileged created
clusterrole.rbac.authorization.k8s.io/flannel created
clusterrolebinding.rbac.authorization.k8s.io/flannel created
serviceaccount/flannel unchanged
configmap/kube-flannel-cfg configured
daemonset.apps/kube-flannel-ds created
```

Once the CNI components are up and running, the rest of the Kubernetes cluster should become healthy as well, i.e., the DNS pods.

```
$ kubectl get pods -A
NAMESPACE     NAME                                READY  STATUS   RESTARTS  AGE
kube-system   coredns-64897985d-9z5hx             1/1    Running  0         3m28s
kube-system   coredns-64897985d-pjwct             1/1    Running  0         3m28s
kube-system   etcd-k8s-cp0                        1/1    Running  2         3m42s
kube-system   kube-apiserver-k8s-cp0              1/1    Running  2         3m42s
kube-system   kube-controller-manager-k8s-cp0     1/1    Running  0         3m42s
kube-system   kube-flannel-ds-957h1               1/1    Running  0         7s
kube-system   kube-proxy-chw9g                    1/1    Running  0         3m28s
kube-system   kube-scheduler-k8s-cp0              1/1    Running  2         3m42s
```

The next step is to deploy the CPI, the Cloud Provider Interface.

vSphere Cloud Provider Interface (CPI)

Let's look at the configuration for the vSphere Cloud Provider Interface, formerly known as the CCM, the vSphere Cloud Controller Manager. The Cloud Provider Interface (CPI) is responsible for controlling platform-specific operations, often referred to as control loops, within Kubernetes. Some of the roles of CPI are as follows:

- Initialize Kubernetes nodes with specific zone/region labels
- Obtain a node's IP addresses and hostname
- Check to see if the node has been deleted on the underlying vSphere platform. If the node has been deleted, then the CPI should also handle deleting the Kubernetes node object.

Some CPIs include a Load Balancer control loop, a cloud specific ingress controller which will configure a Load Balancer as required. However, there is no native Load Balancer service for vSphere as already mentioned. The Load Balancer can be provided by either the HA-Proxy appliance, the NSX Advanced Load Balancer (ALB) or NSX-T. There used to be a volume controller in early versions of the CPI. This functionality has moved to the CSI, the Container Storage Interface. Therefore, installation of the CSI is another manual step we will have to take as we manually create the Kubernetes cluster with *kubeadm*. We will do this after the CPI is installed.

To begin deploying the vSphere CPI, all nodes in the cluster, including the control plane nodes, must be tainted with the following:

```
node.cloudprovider.kubernetes.io/uninitialized=true:NoSchedule.
```

Taints are a way for a node to stop Pods from being scheduled on it. At present, there is only a single control plane node in our cluster, so that is the only one which needs to be tainted.

```
$ kubectl taint node k8s-cp0 \
node.cloudprovider.kubernetes.io/uninitialized=true:NoSchedule
node/k8s-cp0 tainted
```

You can check the taints with the following command, outputting the node information in JSON format, and then using the command *jq* to transform JSON data into a more readable format. The *jq* utility may not be automatically available on your host, so you may need to download it and install it to run this command.

```
$ kubectl get nodes -o json | jq '.items[].spec.taints'
[
  {
    "effect": "NoSchedule",
    "key": "node.cloudprovider.kubernetes.io/uninitialized",
    "value": "true"
  },
  {
    "effect": "NoSchedule",
    "key": "node-role.kubernetes.io/master"
  }
]
```

As soon as the CPI controller is started, and the node is initialised, the taint will be automatically removed by the kubelet. The next step is to download the manifests for the vSphere CPI. The recommended way is to set the major version of the Kubernetes distribution in an environment variable, and then use the *wget* to retrieve it as shown here.

```
$ VERSION=1.23; export VERSION
```

```
$ sudo wget https://raw.githubusercontent.com/kubernetes/cloud-provider-vsphere/release-
$VERSION/releases/v$VERSION/vsphere-cloud-controller-manager.yaml
--2022-06-04 08:48:28--  https://raw.githubusercontent.com/kubernetes/cloud-provider-
vsphere/release-1.23/releases/v1.23/vsphere-cloud-controller-manager.yaml
Resolving raw.githubusercontent.com (raw.githubusercontent.com)... 185.199.111.133,
185.199.108.133, 185.199.110.133, ...
Connecting to raw.githubusercontent.com
(raw.githubusercontent.com)|185.199.111.133|:443... connected.
HTTP request sent, awaiting response... 200 OK
Length: 5870 (5.7K) [text/plain]
Saving to: 'vsphere-cloud-controller-manager.yaml'

vsphere-cloud-controller-manager.yaml
100%[=====================================================================>]   5.73K  --
.-KB/s    in 0s

2022-06-04 08:48:28 (69.9 MB/s) - 'vsphere-cloud-controller-manager.yaml' saved
[5870/5870]
```

The downloaded manifest contains a **Secret** and a **ConfigMap**. We have only briefly touched on these Kubernetes objects, when a ConfigMap was examined with the MetalLB in the load balancer section of chapter 2. A Secret in this example is used to store user credentials required by Pods to access the vCenter Server. It contains information such as the IP address of the vCenter Server as well as username and password credentials. It will allow the CPI to successfully connect to the vSphere platform to check and retrieve required information. As well as the Secret, there is a ConfigMap. This also stores data, but usually non-confidential information. The ConfigMap has a data field, and using this content, a vSphere.conf file is being created. In this data field, information is added about vCenter port, data centre and whether or not the vCenter is using self-signed certs. Both of these objects together are configured to pass information to the CPI Pod about how to access and navigate the vSphere environment.

This manifest file must be edited and the configuration needs to be populated with valid information about the local vSphere environment. Below is the unmodified Secret and ConfigMap from the downloaded CPI manifest to show what needs to be modified.

```
apiVersion: v1
kind: Secret
metadata:
  name: vsphere-cloud-secret
  labels:
    vsphere-cpi-infra: secret
    component: cloud-controller-manager
  namespace: kube-system
  # NOTE: this is just an example configuration, update with real values based on your
environment
stringData:
  10.0.0.1.username: "<ENTER_YOUR_VCENTER_USERNAME>"
  10.0.0.1.password: "<ENTER_YOUR_VCENTER_PASSWORD>"
  1.2.3.4.username: "<ENTER_YOUR_VCENTER_USERNAME>"
  1.2.3.4.password: "<ENTER_YOUR_VCENTER_PASSWORD>"
---
apiVersion: v1
kind: ConfigMap
metadata:
  name: vsphere-cloud-config
  labels:
    vsphere-cpi-infra: config
    component: cloud-controller-manager
  namespace: kube-system
data:
```

```
  # NOTE: this is just an example configuration, update with real values based on your
environment
  vsphere.conf: |
    # Global properties in this section will be used for all specified vCenters unless
overriden in the VirtualCenter section.
    global:
      port: 443
      # set insecureFlag to true if the vCenter uses a self-signed cert
      insecureFlag: true
      # settings for using k8s secret
      secretName: vsphere-cloud-secret
      secretNamespace: kube-system

    # vcenter section
    vcenter:
      your-vcenter-name-here:
        server: 10.0.0.1
        user: use-your-vcenter-user-here
        password: use-your-vcenter-password-here
        datacenters:
          - hrwest
          - hreast
      could-be-a-tenant-label:
        server: 1.2.3.4
        datacenters:
          - mytenantdc
        secretName: cpi-engineering-secret
        secretNamespace: kube-system

    # labels for regions and zones
    labels:
      region: k8s-region
      zone: k8s-zone
```

Below is a possible example of a completed manifest for the `vsphere-cloud-controller-manager.yaml` file with some sample values.

```
apiVersion: v1
kind: Secret
metadata:
  name: vsphere-cloud-secret
  labels:
    vsphere-cpi-infra: secret
    component: cloud-controller-manager
  namespace: kube-system
stringData:
  192.168.51.1.username: "Administrator@vSphere.local"
  192.168.51.1.password: "VMware123!"
---
apiVersion: v1
kind: ConfigMap
metadata:
  name: vsphere-cloud-config
  labels:
    vsphere-cpi-infra: config
    component: cloud-controller-manager
  namespace: kube-system
data:
  vsphere.conf: |
    # Global properties in this section will be used for all specified vCenters unless
overriden in VirtualCenter section.
    global:
      port: 443
```

```
    # set insecureFlag to true if the vCenter uses a self-signed cert
    insecureFlag: true
    # settings for using k8s secret
    secretName: vsphere-cloud-secret
    secretNamespace: kube-system

  # vcenter section
  vcenter:
    vCenter-01:
      server: 192.168.51.1
      user: Administrator@vsphere.local
      password: VMware123!
      datacenters:
        - MyDatacenter
```

Once the edits and modifications have been made to the manifest for the Secret and the ConfigMap, the manifest can now be applied to the Kubernetes cluster.

```
$ kubectl apply -f vsphere-cloud-controller-manager.yaml
serviceaccount/cloud-controller-manager created
secret/vsphere-cloud-secret created
configmap/vsphere-cloud-config created
rolebinding.rbac.authorization.k8s.io/servicecatalog.k8s.io:apiserver-authentication-
reader created
clusterrolebinding.rbac.authorization.k8s.io/system:cloud-controller-manager created
clusterrole.rbac.authorization.k8s.io/system:cloud-controller-manager created
daemonset.apps/vsphere-cloud-controller-manager created
```

Once the CPI components are created, you can check for a field called `ProviderID` on the nodes. This indicates that the node has been successfully initialized by the CPI.

```
$ kubectl describe nodes | grep "ProviderID"
ProviderID:                    vsphere://422465a5-a287-b488-e3c8-50d2f7fde489
```

This looks good. One final test is to check if the CPI Pod (vsphere-cloud-controller-manager) is running on the cluster. It would seem so from this output. One could always use the *kubectl logs* command to verify that there are no issues reported by the CPI Pod.

```
$ kubectl get pods -A
NAMESPACE     NAME                                          READY   STATUS    RESTARTS   AGE
kube-system   coredns-64897985d-9z5hx                       1/1     Running   0          8m16s
kube-system   coredns-64897985d-pjwct                       1/1     Running   0          8m16s
kube-system   etcd-k8s-cp0                                   1/1     Running   2          8m30s
kube-system   kube-apiserver-k8s-cp0                         1/1     Running   2          8m30s
kube-system   kube-controller-manager-k8s-cp0               1/1     Running   0          8m30s
kube-system   kube-flannel-ds-4bc5n                          1/1     Running   0          3m21s
kube-system   kube-proxy-6xxqp                               1/1     Running   0          3m44s
kube-system   kube-scheduler-k8s-cp0                         1/1     Running   2          8m30s
kube-system   vsphere-cloud-controller-manager-2bwws        1/1     Running   0          6s
```

vSphere Container Storage Interface (CSI)

Similar to the CNI, there are many Container Storage Interfaces available in the market. Almost every storage vendor that I know of provide their own CSI driver. Since this is a deployment to a vSphere platform, and since I am mostly interested in creating persistent volumes on vSphere datastores and not directly on a storage array, I will install the vSphere CSI plugin onto this Kubernetes cluster.

The CSI driver, when used on Kubernetes, also requires the use of the vSphere Cloud Provider Interface, which we have already deployed. There are 5 steps to installing the vSphere CSI driver (v2.4) onto a vanilla, upstream / generic Kubernetes cluster. Later versions of CSI are available, with v2.5.1 being the most recent at the time of writing.

1. Create a `vmware-system-csi` namespace on the Kubernetes cluster
2. Taint the control plane nodes of the cluster. Not all nodes need to be tainted, only control plane nodes. Since we still only have a single control plane node, this is relatively straightforward.
3. Create a configuration file (`csi-vsphere.conf`) in the `/etc/kubernetes` directory on the control plane node. This file, similar to what we saw with the CPI configuration, contains details to allow CSI Pods to connect to vSphere. The configuration file name is important as it is refenced in the CSI deployment manifest.
4. Create a Kubernetes Secret from the configuration file
5. Install the vSphere CSI driver

Let's go through the steps next. Applying this first manifest creates the namespace.

```
$ kubectl apply -f https://raw.githubusercontent.com/kubernetes-sigs/vsphere-csi-
driver/v2.4.0/manifests/vanilla/namespace.yaml

$ cat /etc/kubernetes/csi-vsphere.conf
[Global]
cluster-id = "k8s"
[VirtualCenter "192.168.51.1"]
insecure-flag = "true"
user = "administrator@vsphere.local"
password = "VMware123!"
port = "443"
datacenters = "Datacenter"

$ kubectl create secret generic vsphere-config-secret \
--from-file=csi-vsphere.conf --namespace=vmware-system-csi
secret/vsphere-config-secret created

$ kubectl get secret vsphere-config-secret --namespace=vmware-system-csi
NAME                     TYPE      DATA   AGE
vsphere-config-secret    Opaque    1      7s

$ kubectl apply -f https://raw.githubusercontent.com/kubernetes-sigs/vsphere-csi-
driver/v2.4.0/manifests/vanilla/vsphere-csi-driver.yaml
csidriver.storage.k8s.io/csi.vsphere.vmware.com created
serviceaccount/vsphere-csi-controller created
clusterrole.rbac.authorization.k8s.io/vsphere-csi-controller-role created
clusterrolebinding.rbac.authorization.k8s.io/vsphere-csi-controller-binding created
serviceaccount/vsphere-csi-node created
clusterrole.rbac.authorization.k8s.io/vsphere-csi-node-cluster-role created
clusterrolebinding.rbac.authorization.k8s.io/vsphere-csi-node-cluster-role-binding created
role.rbac.authorization.k8s.io/vsphere-csi-node-role created
rolebinding.rbac.authorization.k8s.io/vsphere-csi-node-binding created
configmap/internal-feature-states.csi.vsphere.vmware.com created
service/vsphere-csi-controller created
deployment.apps/vsphere-csi-controller created
daemonset.apps/vsphere-csi-node created
daemonset.apps/vsphere-csi-node-windows created
```

```
$ kubectl get pods -A
NAMESPACE          NAME                                       READY STATUS    RESTARTS AGE
kube-system        coredns-64897985d-9z5hx                    1/1   Running   0        36m
kube-system        coredns-64897985d-pjwct                    1/1   Running   0        36m
kube-system        etcd-k8s-cp0                          1/1   Running   2        37m
kube-system        kube-apiserver-k8s-cp0                     1/1   Running   2        37m
kube-system        kube-controller-manager-k8s-cp0            1/1   Running   0        37m
kube-system        kube-flannel-ds-4bc5n                      1/1   Running   0        32m
kube-system        kube-proxy-6xxqp                           1/1   Running   0        32m
kube-system        kube-scheduler-k8s-cp0                     1/1   Running   2        37m
kube-system        vsphere-cloud-controller-manager-rjhj2     1/1   Running   0        26m
vmware-system-csi  vsphere-csi-controller-85d4475856-f6wlj    6/6   Running   0        25s
vmware-system-csi  vsphere-csi-node-btmsw                     3/3   Running   0        25s
```

Success! Everything is in place to allow us to proceed with creating the worker nodes. Remember the guidance at the beginning of this chapter, however. The VM that is about to become a worker node needs to have a particular revision of VM Hardware. It also needs the `disk.enableUUID` parameter set to True in the advanced settings. It also needs a paravirtual SCSI adapter created. On top of that, it needs the container runtime installed, and the necessary Kubernetes tools, such as *kubeadm, kubelet* and *kubectl*. Let's assume all that is in place. The following command, as seen at the end of the *kubeadm init* when the control plane node was initialized, will automatically add a new CNI (kube-flannel) daemon set, a new kube-proxy and a new CSI (vsphere-csi-node) to the list of components running on the cluster when the command is run on the worker node.

```
$ sudo kubeadm join 192.168.57.40:6443 --token d2t54j.gw3jk2d475yw9o5c \
--discovery-token-ca-cert-hash
sha256:3be77679e99574015bb295381809166471b959e4e69e84430ebc9c449e51516a
[sudo] password for ubuntu: *******
[preflight] Running pre-flight checks
[preflight] Reading configuration from the cluster...
[preflight] FYI: You can look at this config file with 'kubectl -n kube-system get cm
kubeadm-config -o yaml'
W0210 10:29:56.200337    4830 utils.go:69] The recommended value for "resolvConf" in
"KubeletConfiguration" is: /run/systemd/resolve/resolv.conf; the provided value is:
/run/systemd/resolve/resolv.conf
[kubelet-start] Writing kubelet configuration to file "/var/lib/kubelet/config.yaml"
[kubelet-start] Writing kubelet environment file with flags to file
"/var/lib/kubelet/kubeadm-flags.env"
[kubelet-start] Starting the kubelet
[kubelet-start] Waiting for the kubelet to perform the TLS Bootstrap...
This node has joined the cluster:
* Certificate signing request was sent to apiserver and a response was received.
* The Kubelet was informed of the new secure connection details.
Run 'kubectl get nodes' on the control-plane to see this node join the cluster.
```

Check that the new node is available, as per the recommendation on the last line of the output.

```
$ kubectl get nodes
NAME        STATUS   ROLES                  AGE     VERSION
k8s-cp0     Ready    control-plane,master   18m     v1.23.3
k8s-wk0     Ready    <none>                 4m8s    v1.23.3
```

And let's check the new Pods.

```
$ kubectl get pods -A
NAMESPACE          NAME                             READY STATUS    RESTARTS AGE
kube-system        coredns-64897985d-9z5hx          1/1   Running   0        53m
kube-system        coredns-64897985d-pjwct          1/1   Running   0        53m
kube-system        etcd-k8s-cp0                     1/1   Running   2        53m
kube-system        kube-apiserver-k8s-cp0           1/1   Running   2        54m
```

```
kube-system        kube-controller-manager-k8s-cp0        1/1    Running  0    54m
kube-system        kube-flannel-ds-4bc5n                  1/1    Running  0    49m
kube-system        kube-flannel-ds-957h1                  1/1    Running  0     3m
kube-system        kube-proxy-6xxqp                       1/1    Running  0    49m
kube-system        kube-proxy-chw9g                       1/1    Running  0     3m
kube-system        kube-scheduler-k8s-cp0                 1/1    Running  2    53m
kube-system        vsphere-cloud-controller-manager-rjhj2 1/1    Running  0    10m
vmware-system-csi  vsphere-csi-controller-7b87c8b9bc-fg8c4 6/6   Running  0     8m
vmware-system-csi  vsphere-csi-node-ggkng                 3/3    Running  0     8m
vmware-system-csi  vsphere-csi-node-r6pfh                 3/3    Running  0     3m
```

Everything looks good. Our Kubernetes cluster has been configured, and the CNI, CPI and CSI have all been added successfully. Note that this has only shown the basic configuration of the vSphere CSI plug-in. We haven't looked at the roles provided by the containers within the different CSI Pods either. Later on, we will return to this topic as this is where one can implement controls over vSAN File Service for read-write-many persistent volumes(PVs), and also where one can implement labels and zones to control application and PV deployment in a geographically dispersed vSphere environment. More on this when we discuss multi-AZ deployments, AZ short for availability zones. However, the purpose of this section was to show one of the manual ways in which Kubernetes can be deployed on vSphere using kubeadm. Those advanced topics will be revisited later in the book.

Build a Kubernetes cluster with Cluster API

After reading the last topic on *kubeadm*, it should be obvious that standing up a Kubernetes cluster in this way is quite a bit of work. You might be wondering if there is an easier way. Many others have thought the same. Enter Cluster API. The goal of Cluster API is to enable cluster operations such as create, configure, manage, monitor and delete inside of Kubernetes. In other words, have Kubernetes manage other Kubernetes clusters. This is a sort of chicken and egg situation. First, you need add the Cluster API components to a Kubernetes cluster before you can use them to build new Kubernetes clusters. Thus, Cluster API has the concept of a management cluster. This is basically a Kubernetes cluster which has the Cluster API components installed. It also has one or more infrastructure providers installed. The infrastructure provider will know the nuances of the particular platform onto which you are trying to provision new Kubernetes clusters. For instance, there is an infrastructure provider for vSphere. This management cluster is now responsible for the lifecycle of workload clusters. A workload cluster is simply a Kubernetes cluster which is provisioned and managed by a management cluster. Note that the management cluster does not need to reside on the same infrastructure on which you are provisioning workload clusters. The management cluster could run on your local laptop or desktop, as we will see shortly.

To see Cluster API in operation, we mentioned that you need an existing Kubernetes cluster. For simplicity, I will use a Rancher Desktop. You could use any other Kubernetes type, e.g., KinD or Tanzu Community Edition, both which was mentioned previously. The Rancher Desktop Kubernetes cluster will be initialized with the appropriate Cluster API components so that it can assume the role of a management cluster, and enable us to deploy one or more workload clusters. This is done using the *clusterctl* binary, which will also need to be installed. You will be then able to compare this approach with the kubeadm approach taken previously, and decide if it is an easier and more intuitive way of building Kubernetes cluster. Extensive documentation on Cluster API is available in the Cluster API book (https://cluster-api.sigs.k8s.io/user/quick-start.html).

Rancher Desktop deploys with a single control plane node on my desktop. It uses a lightweight Kubernetes distribution called K3s (https://k3s.io/). This will become our Cluster API management cluster.

```
% kubectl get nodes
NAME                   STATUS   ROLES                  AGE    VERSION
lima-rancher-desktop   Ready    control-plane,master   3d4h   v1.23.6+k3s1
```

The next step is to download the `clusterctl` binary. The `clusterctl` tool is how we enable Cluster API, and specifically how we create the management cluster. It can be downloaded from GitHub. Here is a way to download version v1.1.4, as per the Cluster API quick start guide. After downloading it, I make it executable and move it to my PATH. Afterwards I check the version.

```
% curl -L https://github.com/kubernetes-sigs/cluster-
api/releases/download/v1.1.4/clusterctl-darwin-amd64 -o clusterctl

  % Total    % Received % Xferd  Average Speed   Time    Time     Time  Current
                                 Dload  Upload   Total   Spent    Left  Speed
  0       0    0       0    0       0      0       0 --:--:-- --:--:-- --:--:--      0
100  59.0M  100  59.0M    0       0   1410k       0  0:00:42  0:00:42 --:--:--   869k
```

```
% chmod +x ./clusterctl
```

```
% sudo mv ./clusterctl /usr/local/bin/clusterctl
```

```
% clusterctl version
clusterctl version: &version.Info{Major:"1", Minor:"1", GitVersion:"v1.1.4",
GitCommit:"1c3a1526f101d4b07d2eec757fe75e8701cf6212", GitTreeState:"clean",
BuildDate:"2022-06-03T17:14:56Z", GoVersion:"go1.17.3", Compiler:"gc",
Platform:"darwin/amd64"}
```

Now that we have the *clusterctl* binary downloaded, the Cluster API management cluster can be initialized. Verify that you are using the correct cluster context. Let's also check the Pod listing of the Kubernetes cluster so we can identify any newer Pods that are created by this process.

```
% kubectl config current-context
rancher-desktop
```

```
% kubectl get pods -A
NAMESPACE     NAME                                     READY   STATUS      RESTARTS      AGE
kube-system   helm-install-traefik-crd-24mdg           0/1     Completed   0             3d5h
kube-system   helm-install-traefik-6frgn               0/1     Completed   1             3d5h
default       demo-deployment-7f94b66bc4-t724n         1/1     Running     2 (21h ago)   3d2h
kube-system   svclb-traefik-ft6fs                      2/2     Running     4 (21h ago)   3d5h
kube-system   coredns-d76bd69b-5tnj2                   1/1     Running     2 (21h ago)   3d5h
kube-system   traefik-df4ff85d6-r9v5p                  1/1     Running     2 (21h ago)   3d5h
kube-system   local-path-provisioner-6c79684f77-b6lqh  1/1     Running     4 (10m ago)   3d5h
kube-system   metrics-server-7cd5fcb6b7-mstgb          1/1     Running     4 (10m ago)   3d5
```

The vSphere provider components requires two environment variables to be set, VSPHERE_USERNAME and VSPHERE_PASSWORD.

```
% VSPHERE_USERNAME='administrator@vsphere.local';export VSPHERE_USERNAME
% VSPHERE_PASSWORD='VMware123!';export VSPHERE_PASSWORD
```

The initialization of the cluster API management cluster can now begin, adding the appropriate providers for building Kubernetes workload clusters on vSphere. The following command will install a total of four providers onto the management cluster.

```
% clusterctl init --infrastructure vsphere
Fetching providers
Installing cert-manager Version="v1.7.2"
Waiting for cert-manager to be available...
Installing Provider="cluster-api" Version="v1.1.4" TargetNamespace="capi-system"
Installing Provider="bootstrap-kubeadm" Version="v1.1.4" TargetNamespace="capi-kubeadm-
bootstrap-system"
Installing Provider="control-plane-kubeadm" Version="v1.1.4" TargetNamespace="capi-
kubeadm-control-plane-system"
Installing Provider="infrastructure-vsphere" Version="v1.2.0" TargetNamespace="capv-
system"

Your management cluster has been initialized successfully!

You can now create your first workload cluster by running the following:

  clusterctl generate cluster [name] --kubernetes-version [version] | kubectl apply -f -
```

The management cluster is now initialized. Let's see which new components have been added to the cluster. Please note that some of the columns have been removed and other have been edited to allow for better formatting of the output. However, you may assume that all the new Pods related to Cluster API are up and running.

```
% kubectl get pods -A
NAMESPACE                             NAME                                             READY
kube-system                           helm-install-traefik-crd-24mdg                   0/1
kube-system                           helm-install-traefik-6frgn                       0/1
kube-system                           svclb-traefik-ft6fs                              2/2
kube-system                           coredns-d76bd69b-5tnj2                           1/1
kube-system                           traefik-df4ff85d6-r9v5p                          1/1
kube-system                           local-path-provisioner-b6lqh                     1/1
kube-system                           metrics-server-7cd5fcb6b7-mstgb                  1/1
cert-manager                          cert-manager-cainjector-48897                    1/1
cert-manager                          cert-manager-d5x8w                               1/1
cert-manager                          cert-manager-webhook-5mfkd                       1/1
capi-system                           capi-controller-manager-7nqtn                    1/1
capi-kubeadm-bootstrap-system         capi-kubeadm-bootstrap-controller-manager-64cfz  1/1
capi-kubeadm-control-plane-system     capi-kubeadm-control-plane-controller-manager-glm9p 1/1
capv-system                           capv-controller-manager-qwbgr                    1/1
```

The `capi` Pods are those related to Cluster API. The `capv` Pod is specifically for Cluster API on vSphere. Cluster API uses *kubeadm* to bootstrap the control plane. As we have seen previously, the purpose of kubeadm is to create Kubernetes clusters. The kubeadm bootstrap provider generates cluster certificates, and initializes the control plane. It waits until the control plane initialization is complete before creating other nodes (e.g. worker nodes) and joining them to the cluster. The control plane initialization is machine-based which means that (in the case of vSphere at least), virtual machines are provisioned to build the control plane, and these is turn are used to create the system Pods for Kubernetes services such as `kube-apiserver`, `kube-controller-manager` and `kube-scheduler`.

The next step is to ensure that there is a virtual machine template available on the vSphere infrastructure where you wish to deploy Kubernetes. The name of the VM template must match the VSPHERE_TEMPLATE environment variable. This environment variable refers to a virtual machine template in the vSphere inventory which must be uploaded in advance. This is the template which will be used for creating the VMs that will provide the Kubernetes workload cluster control plane and worker nodes. This template must be a supported CAPV machine images. For more information about the machine images, refer to https://github.com/kubernetes-sigs/cluster-api-provider-vsphere/blob/main/docs/getting_started.md#uploading-the-machine-images.

Once the machine image is uploaded and the template is created, everything is now in place to allow us to build a workload cluster. There are however a significant number of additional environment variables which need to be configured before initiating the build. The vSphere provider will require variables that provide the IP address of the vCenter Server, vCenter Server credentials and a number of inventory items such as data centre and datastore. Once the environment variables have been populated, a new workload cluster can be created. All the requirements are in the Cluster API documentation for the vSphere provider. It may be easier to place these in a shell script, and then run a *source* commands on the script to set all of the environment variables at once. Here is an example of such a script.

```
# The vCenter Server IP or FQDN
export VSPHERE_SERVER="10.0.0.1"
# The vSphere datacenter to deploy the management cluster on
export VSPHERE_DATACENTER="SDDC-Datacenter"
# The vSphere datastore to deploy the management cluster on
export VSPHERE_DATASTORE="vsanDatastore"
# The VM network to deploy the management cluster on
export VSPHERE_NETWORK="VM Network"
# The vSphere resource pool for your VMs
export VSPHERE_RESOURCE_POOL="*/Resources"
# The VM folder for your VMs. Set to "" to use the root vSphere folder
export VSPHERE_FOLDER="vm"
# The VM template to use for your VMs
export VSPHERE_TEMPLATE="ubuntu-1804-kube-v1.17.3"
# The public ssh authorized key on all machines
export VSPHERE_SSH_AUTHORIZED_KEY="ssh-rsa AAAAB3N..."
# The certificate thumbprint for the vCenter Server
export VSPHERE_TLS_THUMBPRINT="97:48:03:8D:78:A9..."
# The storage policy to be used (optional). Set to "" if not required
export VSPHERE_STORAGE_POLICY="policy-one"
# The IP address used for the control plane endpoint
export CONTROL_PLANE_ENDPOINT_IP="1.2.3.4"
```

To a vSphere administrator, most of the environment variables described above should be easy to comprehend. The majority refer to components of the vSphere infrastructure. Some variables may need additional explanation however.

If you are planning to assist with the management and running of the Kubernetes clusters, you will probably want to be able to SSH to the Kubernetes cluster nodes after deployment. At the very least, someone will need to be able to access the nodes for the purposes of troubleshooting. The environment variable VSPHERE_SSH_AUTHORIZED_KEY contains the key of the user who wishes to be able to access the nodes after they have been deployed. This is the public key that is typically found in ~/.ssh/id_rsa.pub on the users laptop or desktop. If it does not exist, it can quickly be created with the *ssh-keygen* command.

The VSPHERE_TLS_THUMBPRINT is used to establish trust with the vCenter Server. This thumbprint can be retrieved by pointing a browser at the vSphere UI where the Kubernetes cluster is to be deployed, selecting the Secure icon on the browser and examining the certificate details.

From there, it is possible to retrieve the SHA1 fingerprint. An alternative way is to SSH as root onto the vCenter Server and runs the following command:

```
# openssl x509 -in /etc/vmware-vpx/ssl/rui.crt -fingerprint -sha1 -noout
```

A VSPHERE_STORAGE_POLICY gives control over the class of storage that you wish to consume for the nodes. This is an optional setting. If set however, the reference storage policy must exist.

Finally, CONTROL_PLANE_ENDPOINT_IP is the virtual IP address assigned to the Kubernetes cluster control plane. This is implemented through `kube-vip`, a mechanism that provides a front-end virtual IP address for the Kubernetes control plane. This provides a level of availability since communication to the Kubernetes cluster control plane is via this VIP and not directly to a single control plane node. Should a control plane node fail, communication with the API server is not impacted. When the cluster is created, a Pod called kube-vip is created for this purpose. This Pod uses the IP address specified in this variable to serve API requests. Kube-vip assigns the control plane endpoint IP address to one control plane node at a time. Thus, while kube-vip provides high availability to the control plane in the workload cluster, it does not behave as a true load balancer for the control plane.

Once the environment variables have been exported, the following command creates a single manifest (YAML) output that contains all of the objects to build a new workload cluster, such as `Cluster`, `vSphereCluster`, `vSphereMachineTemplate`, `MachineDeployment`, `Machine` and `KubeadmControlPlane`. In this example, the cluster is called `vsphere-quickstart` with 1 control plane node and 2 worker nodes. The Kubernetes version in the command line needs to match the CAPV machine image template which was deployed to the vSphere platform. In this example, it is v1.23.5.

```
$ clusterctl generate cluster vsphere-quickstart \
--infrastructure vsphere \
--kubernetes-version v1.23.5 \
--control-plane-machine-count 1 \
--worker-machine-count 2 \
> cluster.yaml

$ kubectl apply -f cluster.yaml
cluster.cluster.x-k8s.io/vsphere-quickstart created
vspherecluster.infrastructure.cluster.x-k8s.io/vsphere-quickstart created
vspheremachinetemplate.infrastructure.cluster.x-k8s.io/vsphere-quickstart created
kubeadmcontrolplane.controlplane.cluster.x-k8s.io/vsphere-quickstart created
kubeadmconfigtemplate.bootstrap.cluster.x-k8s.io/vsphere-quickstart-md-0 created
machinedeployment.cluster.x-k8s.io/vsphere-quickstart-md-0 created
clusterresourceset.addons.cluster.x-k8s.io/vsphere-quickstart-crs-0 created
secret/vsphere-quickstart created
secret/vsphere-csi-controller created
configmap/vsphere-csi-controller-role created
configmap/vsphere-csi-controller-binding created
secret/csi-vsphere-config created
configmap/csi.vsphere.vmware.com created
configmap/vsphere-csi-node created
configmap/vsphere-csi-controller created
secret/cloud-controller-manager created
secret/cloud-provider-vsphere-credentials created
configmap/cpi-manifests created
```

This will begin the process of deploying three new VMs on your vSphere infrastructure, one for the control plane node and two for the worker nodes. The size and resource usage of these VMs is the same as the template VSPHERE_TEMPLATE. These VMs will begin to appear in the vSphere inventory. What is interesting is that the vSphere Cloud Provider (CPI) and vSphere CSI plugin is part of the deployment. Thus, there is no need to concern ourselves with manually installing the CPI or CSI in a Kubernetes cluster that has been deployed with Cluster API. However, there is no CNI installed. This is something that will still be required.

The *clusterctl* command can be used to monitor the state of the newly created cluster, e.g.

```
% clusterctl describe cluster vsphere-quickstart
NAME                                                  READY  SEVERITY  REASON
SINCE   MESSAGE
Cluster/vsphere-quickstart                            False  Info
WaitingForControlPlane          5s
├─ClusterInfrastructure - VSphereCluster/vsphere-quickstart  True
5s
├─ControlPlane - KubeadmControlPlane/vsphere-quickstart
│ └─Machine/vsphere-quickstart-h57pw                  False  Info
WaitingForBootstrapData         2s     1 of 2 completed
└─Workers
  └─MachineDeployment/vsphere-quickstart-md-0         False  Warning
WaitingForAvailableMachines     7s     Minimum availability requires 2 replicas, current
0 available
    └─2 Machines...                                   False  Info
WaitingForControlPlaneAvailable 4s     See vsphere-quickstart-md-0-55b55fd787-k9hx6,
vsphere-quickstart-md-0-55b55fd787-snncw
```

If the configuration file is correct, then soon after applying the cluster manifest, it should be possible to observe cloning operations taking place on the vSphere UI tasks view as the VMs that make up the Kubernetes cluster nodes get created.

We can also use *clusterctl* to download the KUBECONFIG for the new workload cluster. With the workload context, it is now possible to display the list of nodes in the workload cluster. Here the KUBECONFIG has been copied to a local file rather than `~/.kube/config`. We can still use this standalone KUBECONFIG file by using the `--kubeconfig` option to the *kubectl* command.

```
% clusterctl get kubeconfig vsphere-quickstart > quickstart-kubeconfig

% kubectl get nodes --kubeconfig quickstart-kubeconfig
NAME                                     STATUS    ROLES                  AGE   VERSION
vsphere-quickstart-md-0-55b55fd787-dr7p2 NotReady  <none>                 27s   v1.23.5
vsphere-quickstart-md-0-55b55fd787-pmr41 NotReady  <none>                 22s   v1.23.5
vsphere-quickstart-nkv7r                 NotReady  control-plane,master   84s   v1.23.5
```

After a while, the 3 nodes that make up the cluster appear. However, they are currently in a **NotReady** state as highlighted above. This is because the CNI (Container Network Interface) has not yet been deployed, so Pod to Pod communication across nodes is not yet possible. Let's choose Calico, a well-known CNI. It can be deployed as follows, referencing the quickstart-kubeconfig file built previously:

```
$ kubectl apply -f https://docs.projectcalico.org/manifests/calico.yaml \
--kubeconfig quickstart-kubeconfig
configmap/calico-config created
customresourcedefinition.apiextensions.k8s.io/bgpconfigurations.crd.projectcalico.org
created
customresourcedefinition.apiextensions.k8s.io/bgppeers.crd.projectcalico.org created
customresourcedefinition.apiextensions.k8s.io/blockaffinities.crd.projectcalico.org
created
```

```
customresourcedefinition.apiextensions.k8s.io/clusterinformations.crd.projectcalico.org
created
customresourcedefinition.apiextensions.k8s.io/felixconfigurations.crd.projectcalico.org
created
customresourcedefinition.apiextensions.k8s.io/globalnetworkpolicies.crd.projectcalico.org
created
customresourcedefinition.apiextensions.k8s.io/globalnetworksets.crd.projectcalico.org
created
customresourcedefinition.apiextensions.k8s.io/hostendpoints.crd.projectcalico.org created
customresourcedefinition.apiextensions.k8s.io/ipamblocks.crd.projectcalico.org created
customresourcedefinition.apiextensions.k8s.io/ipamconfigs.crd.projectcalico.org created
customresourcedefinition.apiextensions.k8s.io/ipamhandles.crd.projectcalico.org created
customresourcedefinition.apiextensions.k8s.io/ippools.crd.projectcalico.org created
customresourcedefinition.apiextensions.k8s.io/kubecontrollersconfigurations.crd.projectcal
ico.org created
customresourcedefinition.apiextensions.k8s.io/networkpolicies.crd.projectcalico.org
created
customresourcedefinition.apiextensions.k8s.io/networksets.crd.projectcalico.org created
clusterrole.rbac.authorization.k8s.io/calico-kube-controllers created
clusterrolebinding.rbac.authorization.k8s.io/calico-kube-controllers created
clusterrole.rbac.authorization.k8s.io/calico-node created
clusterrolebinding.rbac.authorization.k8s.io/calico-node created
daemonset.apps/calico-node created
serviceaccount/calico-node created
deployment.apps/calico-kube-controllers created
serviceaccount/calico-kube-controllers created
poddisruptionbudget.policy/calico-kube-controllers created
```

In a short space of time, the nodes should enter a **Ready** state.

```
% kubectl get nodes --kubeconfig quickstart-kubeconfig
NAME                                        STATUS   ROLES                   AGE     VERSION
vsphere-quickstart-md-0-55b55fd787-dr7p2    Ready    <none>                  3m6s    v1.23.5
vsphere-quickstart-md-0-55b55fd787-pmr4l    Ready    <none>                  3m1s    v1.23.5
vsphere-quickstart-nkv7r                    Ready    control-plane,master    4m3s    v1.23.5
```

Let's also take a look at what the Cluster API objects, and what state they are in.

```
% clusterctl describe cluster vsphere-quickstart
NAME                                                              READY SEVERITY REASON SINCE
Cluster/vsphere-quickstart                                        True                  8m7s
├─ClusterInfrastructure - VSphereCluster/vsphere-quickstart      True                  9m15s
├─ControlPlane - KubeadmControlPlane/vsphere-quickstart          True                  8m7s
│ └─Machine/vsphere-quickstart-nkv7r                             True                  8m9s
└─Workers
  └─MachineDeployment/vsphere-quickstart-md-0                    True                  4m20s
    └─2 Machines...                                              True                  6m59s
```

Success! Everything looks ready here too. The workload cluster is now up and running, using the local Rancher Desktop (K3s) distribution as the management cluster. We installed the Cluster API components and the provisioner for vSphere onto K3s. This cluster now knows how to deploy Kubernetes clusters onto vSphere environments. We setup all the necessary environment variables, added the node/VM template to the vSphere infrastructure, and rolled out a new Kubernetes cluster. While the initial setup may seem a little complicated, once it is done once, we now have a repeatable mechanism for deploying out Kubernetes clusters onto our vSphere platform. The process also took care of the installation of both the CPI and CSI, but we did have to install our own CNI to complete the setup process to bring everything online.

I mentioned that Cluster API introduces a range of custom resources to the Kubernetes management cluster. These new objects can all be queried with *kubectl get*, and *kubectl describe* if more detail about an object is required. This can be very useful when troubleshooting a Cluster API deployment on vSphere that does not appear to be working as expected. For example, a describe of a machine could reveal a reason why cloning failed. In this case, the environment variable holding the network portgroup was set to a portgroup that did not exist:

```
% kubectl describe machine vsphere-quickstart-qfwlg
.
.
Status:
  Bootstrap Ready:  true
  Conditions:
    Last Transition Time:   2022-06-04T15:10:44Z
    Message:                1 of 2 completed
    Reason:                 CloningFailed
    Severity:               Warning
    Status:                 False
    Type:                   Ready
    Last Transition Time:   2022-06-04T15:09:58Z
    Status:                 True
    Type:                   BootstrapReady
    Last Transition Time:   2022-06-04T15:10:44Z
    Message:                error getting network specs for "infrastructure.cluster.x-
k8s.io/v1beta1, Kind=VSphereVM default/vsphere-quickstart-qfwlg": unable to find network
"VM51-DportGroup": network 'VM51-DportGroup' not found
    Reason:                 CloningFailed
```

Various components can be removed from the management cluster individually. For example, if you wanted to remove one of the infrastructure providers, run a *clusterctl delete --infrastructure <infra>* command.

```
% clusterctl delete
Error: At least one of --core, --bootstrap, --control-plane, --infrastructure should be
specified or the --all flag should be set
```

Finally, if you wish to remove all Cluster API extensions from the management cluster, and return the cluster to its former self as a plain Kubernetes cluster, the command *clusterctl delete --all* will take care it. Note that this does not delete any of the workload clusters that you have deployed. These will have to be deleted separately, using a *kubectl delete -f* against the cluster manifest.

```
% clusterctl delete --all
Deleting Provider="cluster-api" Version="v1.1.4" Namespace="capi-system"
Deleting Provider="bootstrap-kubeadm" Version="v1.1.4" Namespace="capi-kubeadm-bootstrap-
system"
Deleting Provider="control-plane-kubeadm" Version="v1.1.4" Namespace="capi-kubeadm-
control-plane-system"
Deleting Provider="infrastructure-vsphere" Version="v1.2.0" Namespace="capv-system"
```

Overall, Cluster API does look like a more elegant approach to *kubeadm* for deploying Kubernetes clusters is a repeatable manner. Admittedly, you have to prepare the ground work for this approach, getting the correct image installed on the vSphere environment as a template, and then setting all of the environment variables needed by Cluster API for the creation of the management cluster and then the workload clusters. However, once these are in place, it seems to be a much easier approach than setting up new Kubernetes clusters each and every time via *kubeadm*.

The Tanzu team at VMware also believe that ClusterAPI is a better approach. In fact, many of them are contributors to the Cluster API project. In the next section, we are going to look at TKG, the flagship Kubernetes from VMware which is available on multiple cloud environments, not just vSphere. We will go through the process of deploying a dedicated management cluster, and then show how to deploy workload clusters once the management cluster is up and running. However, rather than using Rancher Desktop and K3s, the management cluster and the workload clusters will both run on vSphere.

Build a Tanzu Kubernetes Grid (TKG) with tanzu CLI

Now it is time to look at Tanzu Kubernetes Grid (TKG), VMware's own brand of Kubernetes. The important thing to note is that TKG clusters are upstream compatible clusters. The Tanzu team uses a selection of open-source products to create a Kubernetes distribution that can be tested, signed, and supported by VMware. In this section, the standalone TKG product, sometimes referred to as TKGm or TKG multi-cloud, will be examined in detail. This product can be deployed on several different cloud platforms, but the focus here is on vSphere. We will go through the process of setting up a management cluster, and once that is complete, a workload cluster will be rolled out. This is very similar to the workflow that we saw in the Cluster API section in the previous section, but some of the enhancements made by the VMware engineering teams to make this as seamless as possible will be observed. As you may have guessed, TKG relies heavily on the Cluster API functionality for the creation of workload clusters. Whilst the management cluster is used to create and manage workload clusters on a specific cloud provider (in this case, vSphere), it is also where services for the workload clusters are configured.

TKG version 1.5.4 (the latest version at the time of writing) is supported on vSphere environments that are at vSphere 6.7U3 and later. TKG has built-in support for nodes running Photon OS version 3 and Ubuntu version 20.04 operating systems, although it is possible to build your own images should this be a requirement.

Similar to Cluster API, a base OVA image needs to be imported into the vSphere as a template to build the clusters. At the time of writing, the supported images for the management cluster are Ubuntu v20.04 (Kubernetes v1.22.9) and Photon v3 (Kubernetes v1.22.9). These are available from the Tanzu Kubernetes Grid download page on the VMware Customer Connect site. The workload clusters have a number of different Kubernetes versions available which will be looked at shortly.

TKG offers a few options for the management and workload cluster API Servers VIP addresses. Similar to vanilla Cluster API, kube-vip can be used with TKG to define a virtual IP for the API servers on both the management cluster and any workload clusters. However kube-vip cannot be used for Load Balancer services within the clusters. If this is a requirement, TKG can leverage the NSX Advanced Load Balancer for both the cluster API Servers VIP addresses and for Load Balancer services IP addresses. Integration with the NSX ALB will be shown in detail shortly.

Finally, you will need DHCP to be available on the vSphere network portgroup where the nodes that make up the TKG clusters reside. There is no way to assign static IP addresses to the TKG nodes at the time of writing.

Note: The information presented above is correct at the time of going to press, but I would once again urge all readers to validate this information against the latest documentation before placing a TKG cluster into production.

Tanzu CLI

To deploy TKG, a *tanzu* command line interface (CLI) must be installed. This provides the mechanism to create the management and workload clusters, like the *clusterctl* command seen in the Cluster API section. Versions are available for Linux, Mac, and Windows. These are also available from the Tanzu Kubernetes Grid download page on the VMware Customer Connect site. Note that in order to install the Tanzu CLI, a Docker client must be available. This is because kind (Kubernetes in Docker) is required to bootstrap the management cluster. Refer back to chapter 1 where a number of options for Docker were provided. You will also need to have a *kubectl* binary available in order to successfully deploy a management cluster. This is also available from the VMware Customer Connect site. The following steps detail how to extract and install the Tanzu CLI after it has been download to my Mac desktop. The steps will be similar for other operating systems.

```
% gunzip tanzu-cli-bundle-darwin-amd64.tar.gz

% tar xvf tanzu-cli-bundle-darwin-amd64.tar
x cli/
x cli/core/
x cli/core/plugin.yaml
x cli/core/v0.11.6/
x cli/core/v0.11.6/tanzu-core-darwin_amd64
x cli/tanzu-framework-plugins-standalone-darwin-amd64.tar.gz
x cli/tanzu-framework-plugins-context-darwin-amd64.tar.gz
x cli/ytt-darwin-amd64-v0.37.0+vmware.1.gz
x cli/kapp-darwin-amd64-v0.42.0+vmware.2.gz
x cli/imgpkg-darwin-amd64-v0.22.0+vmware.1.gz
x cli/kbld-darwin-amd64-v0.31.0+vmware.1.gz
x cli/vendir-darwin-amd64-v0.23.1+vmware.1.gz

% cd cli

% sudo install core/v0.11.6/tanzu-core-darwin_amd64 /usr/local/bin/tanzu

% tanzu version
version: v0.11.6
buildDate: 2022-05-20
sha: 90440e2b
```

The version returned above is correct. TKG v1.5.4 uses Tanzu Framework v0.11.6. What is reported is the Tanzu Framework version, not the TKG version.

The first step after installing the CLI is to initialize it with the *tanzu init* command. If this is a new deployment, this step installs the necessary core plugins to allow the creation of management and workload clusters. This creates a configuration file called `config.yaml` is `.config/tanzu`.

```
% tanzu init
Checking for required plugins...
Installing plugin 'login:v0.11.6'
Installing plugin 'management-cluster:v0.11.6'
Installing plugin 'package:v0.11.6'
Installing plugin 'pinniped-auth:v0.11.6'
Installing plugin 'secret:v0.11.6'
Successfully installed all required plugins
✓  successfully initialized CLI
```

The list of installed plugins can be displayed using *tanzu plugin list*. I've added some spaces in the output to make them a little easier to read.

```
% tanzu plugin list
NAME                  DESCRIPTION                    SCOPE       DISCOVERY  VERSION  STATUS

login                 to the platform                Standalone  default    v0.11.6  installed

management-cluster    Kubernetes management-cluster  Standalone  default    v0.11.6  installed
                      operations

package               Tanzu package management       Standalone  default    v0.11.6  installed

pinniped-auth         Pinniped authentication ops    Standalone  default    v0.11.6  installed
                      operations (usually not
                      directly invoked)

secret                Tanzu secret management        Standalone  default    v0.11.6  installed
```

There is one more set of tools required before we can create our first management cluster. These are collectively known as the Carvel tools. A description of these tools is as follows:

- `ytt` - a tool for templating and patching YAML files
- `kapp` – a tool to install, upgrade, and delete multiple Kubernetes resources
- `kbld` – a tool for image-building
- `imgpkg` – a tool to manage container images

These tools are bundled with Tanzu CLI in the cli folder – they simply need to be installed. Below are the details for installing the binaries on a MacOS. The instructions for other distributions can be found in the official VMware Tanzu documentation.

```
% gunzip ytt-darwin-amd64-v0.37.0+vmware.1.gz
% chmod ugo+x ytt-darwin-amd64-v0.37.0+vmware.1
% mv ./ytt-darwin-amd64-v0.37.0+vmware.1 /usr/local/bin/ytt

% gunzip kapp-darwin-amd64-v0.42.0+vmware.2.gz
% chmod ugo+x kapp-darwin-amd64-v0.42.0+vmware.2
% mv ./kapp-darwin-amd64-v0.42.0+vmware.2 /usr/local/bin/kapp

% gunzip kbld-darwin-amd64-v0.31.0+vmware.1.gz
% chmod ugo+x kbld-darwin-amd64-v0.31.0+vmware.1
% mv kbld-darwin-amd64-v0.31.0+vmware.1 /usr/local/bin/kbld

% gunzip imgpkg-darwin-amd64-v0.22.0+vmware.1.gz
% chmod ugo+x imgpkg-darwin-amd64-v0.22.0+vmware.1
% mv imgpkg-darwin-amd64-v0.22.0+vmware.1 /usr/local/bin/imgpkg
```

All the tooling is now in place to enable us to build our first TKG management cluster. To begin with, Tanzu CLI will be used to launch a UI. In that UI, various details about the vSphere infrastructure and other management cluster requirements will be populated. The UI can be used to launch the creation of the management cluster, but it also provides the option of creating a configuration file which can be used for the creation of additional management clusters, but which can also form the basis for the creation and configuration of workload clusters.

TKG Management Cluster Creation

To launch the UI for the installer, the *tanzu mc create --ui* command is used. The *mc* is short for management cluster. This creates a temporary management cluster using a `kind` (Kubernetes in Docker) cluster on the bootstrap machine. This bootstrap cluster is then used to build the Tanzu Kubernetes Grid management cluster on a specific platform, which in our case is vSphere.

Note that docker must be running before you can run this command. This is needed for the initial bootstrap cluster. If it isn't running, the command will fail.

```
% tanzu mc create --ui

Validating the pre-requisites...
Serving kickstart UI at http://127.0.0.1:8080
```

This command will also download any necessary BOMs (Bill of Materials) and providers to `.config/tanzu/tkg`. The BOMs include a list of TKG and TKr (Tanzu Kubernetes releases). When launched on my Mac, a new browser window opens and displays the TKG installer. As you can see, different cloud providers are supported. This is obviously a deployment on vSphere, so that is what should be selected.

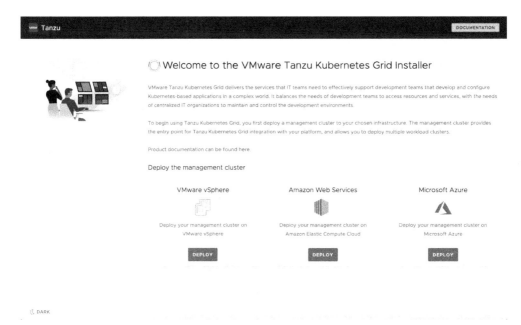

Figure 6: TKG Installer UI

This will drop us into the IaaS Provider section. Here we need to populate information about the vCenter Server, Username and Password fields, and decide if you want thumbprint verification. Then click on Connect.

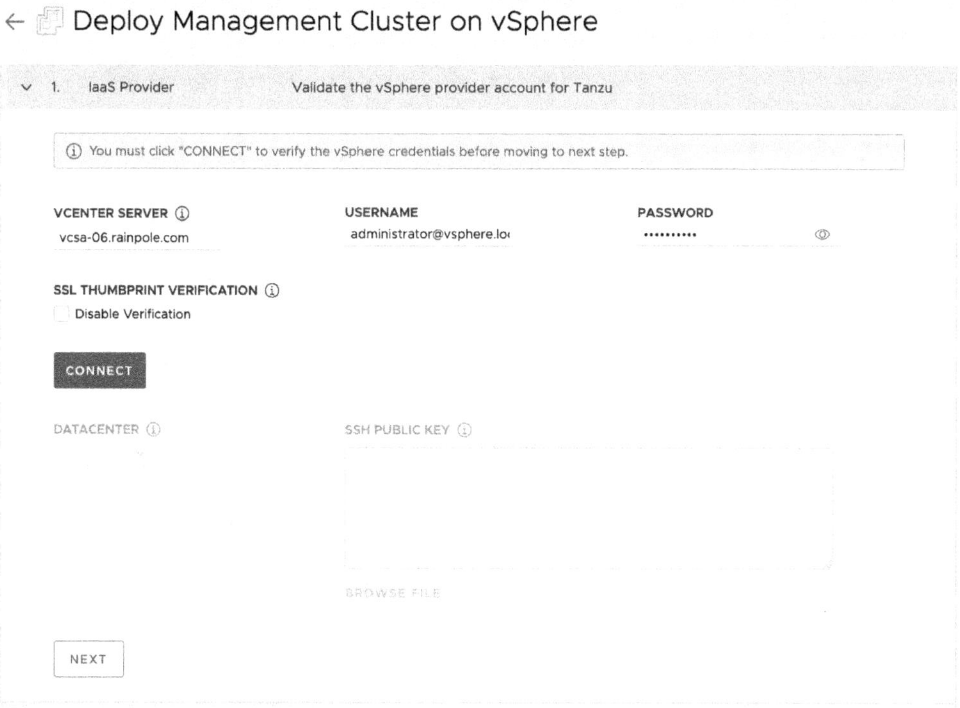

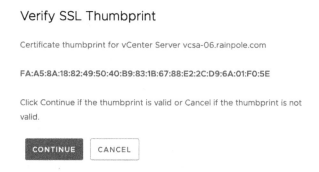

Figure 7: TKG Installer UI - IaaS Provider

Once the "Connect" button has been clicked, you will see several pop-ups. If SSL Thumbprint Verification was not disabled, you will be asked to verify the vCenter SHA1 fingerprint as follows:

Verify SSL Thumbprint

Certificate thumbprint for vCenter Server vcsa-06.rainpole.com

FA:A5:8A:18:82:49:50:40:B9:83:1B:67:88:E2:2C:D9:6A:01:F0:5E

Click Continue if the thumbprint is valid or Cancel if the thumbprint is not valid.

CONTINUE   CANCEL

Figure 8: TKG Installer UI - SSL Thumbprint

Immediately after clicking Continue, you will be prompted with an option to switch to vSphere with Tanzu. Since this is a deployment on vSphere, vSphere with Tanzu is the preferred way to deploy TKG on vSphere. We will look at vSphere with Tanzu in much greater detail in the next section. However, for the purposes of this exercise, click on the 'Deploy TKG Management Cluster' button.

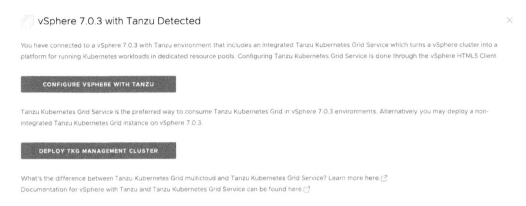

Figure 9: TKG Installer UI – vSphere Deployment Selection

This now allows us to populate the remaining IaaS Provider fields, which includes selection of the data center as well as the SSH Public Key of the user who wishes to SSH onto the TKG nodes after they have been deployed. A list of data center objects from the vCenter Server will be available from the dropdown menu. Select the appropriate one which is where the TKG clusters (both management and workload) will be deployed. We already discussed the SSH Public Key in the Cluster API section previously. Refer back to this section to locate the public key, and how to generate one if it does not exist.

Figure 10: TKG Installer UI – Data Center and SSH Public Key

Once the Data Center and SSH Public Key fields are populated, click next to continue. This will bring us to the management cluster settings. Here, you choose whether the Management Cluster is a development environment or a production environment. This decides the size of the management cluster control plane, either one node for dev or three nodes for prod.

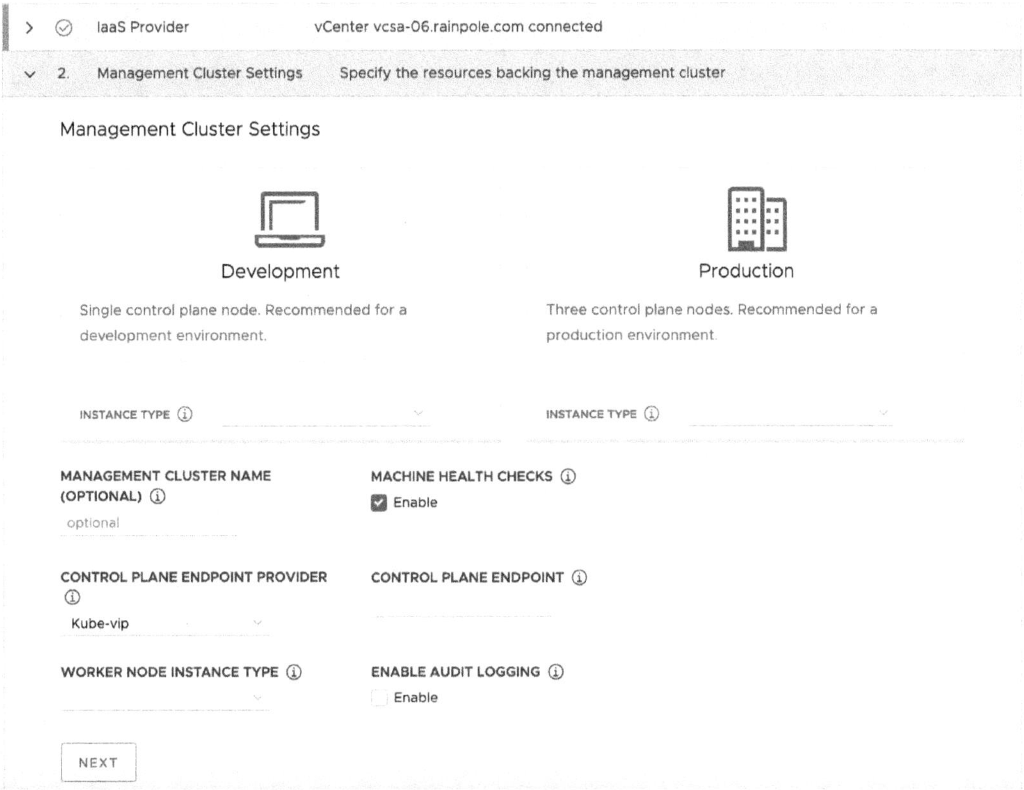

Figure 11: TKG Installer UI – Management Cluster Settings (empty)

The size of the nodes (virtual machines) is also chosen in the management cluster settings, both for the control plane and worker nodes. There are four options available, depending on the size of control plane node that you wish to create.

- **Small**: 2 CPU, 4GB Memory, 20GB Disk
- **Medium**: 2 CPU, 8GB Memory, 40GB Disk
- **Large**: 4 CPU, 16GB Memory, 40GB Disk
- **Extra Large**: 8 CPU, 32GB Memory, 80GB Disk

You can optionally assign the management cluster a name and enable machine health checks (on by default) and audit logging (off by default). Machine health check provide health monitoring for control plane and worker nodes. It can also auto-repair nodes if something fails. This can be queried from the tanzu CLI command line after the management cluster is deployed. Audit logging tracks requests to the Kubernetes API server. These are stored in */var/log/audit.log* on the control plane nodes. In the day 2 operations chapter, the use of Fluent Bit to retrieve logs such as this from the cluster will be discussed.

The final setting to consider is how the management cluster is going to get a virtual IP address for the API server. Just like we saw with Cluster API, `kube-vip` can once again be used with a static IP address to provide the virtual IP address to make the control plane highly available. We want to keep things as simple as possible for an initial deployment. Thus, we are going to use `kube-vip` and assign a virtual static IP address to the control plane. The completed form is below, with the instance type for both control plane VMs and worker node VMs set to small (2 CPU, 4GB RAM, 20GB disk).

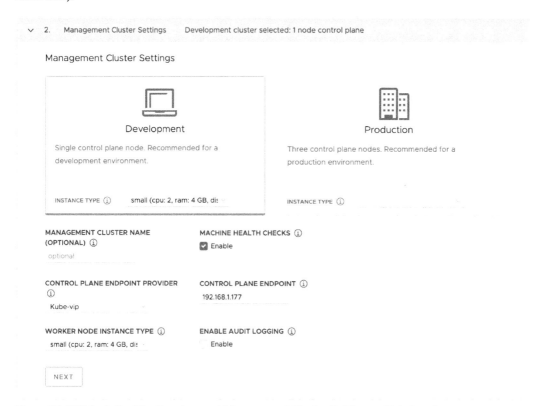

Figure 12: TKG Installer UI – Development Management Cluster Settings with kube-vip

If `kube-vip` is providing an endpoint for the management cluster control plane, all of the fields in the NSX ALB (Advanced Load Balancer) section may be left blank in step 3 of the UI as shown here.

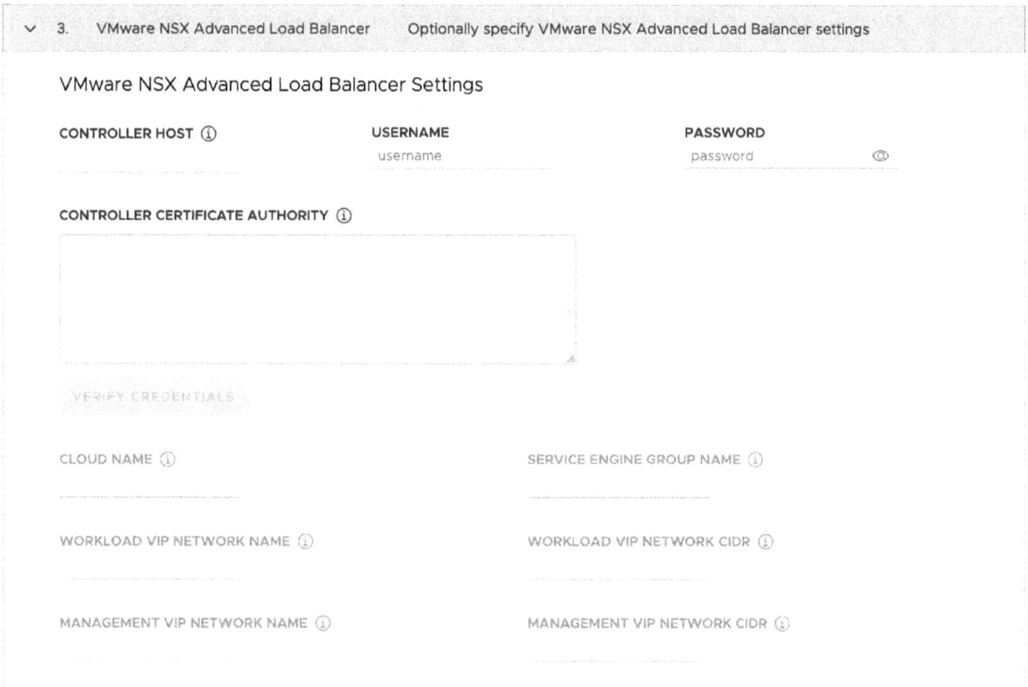

> 3. VMware NSX Advanced Load Balancer   Optionally specify VMware NSX Advanced Load Balancer settings

VMware NSX Advanced Load Balancer Settings

CONTROLLER HOST ⓘ   USERNAME   PASSWORD
                         username   password

CONTROLLER CERTIFICATE AUTHORITY ⓘ

VERIFY CREDENTIALS

CLOUD NAME ⓘ   SERVICE ENGINE GROUP NAME ⓘ

WORKLOAD VIP NETWORK NAME ⓘ   WORKLOAD VIP NETWORK CIDR ⓘ

MANAGEMENT VIP NETWORK NAME ⓘ   MANAGEMENT VIP NETWORK CIDR ⓘ

Figure 13: TKG Installer UI – VMware NSX Advanced Load Balancer – Blank for kube-vip

However, let's take a side-step here and assume that there is an NSX ALB available in the environment where TKG is being deployed. Below is an example of the NSX ALB selection in step 2 of the UI.

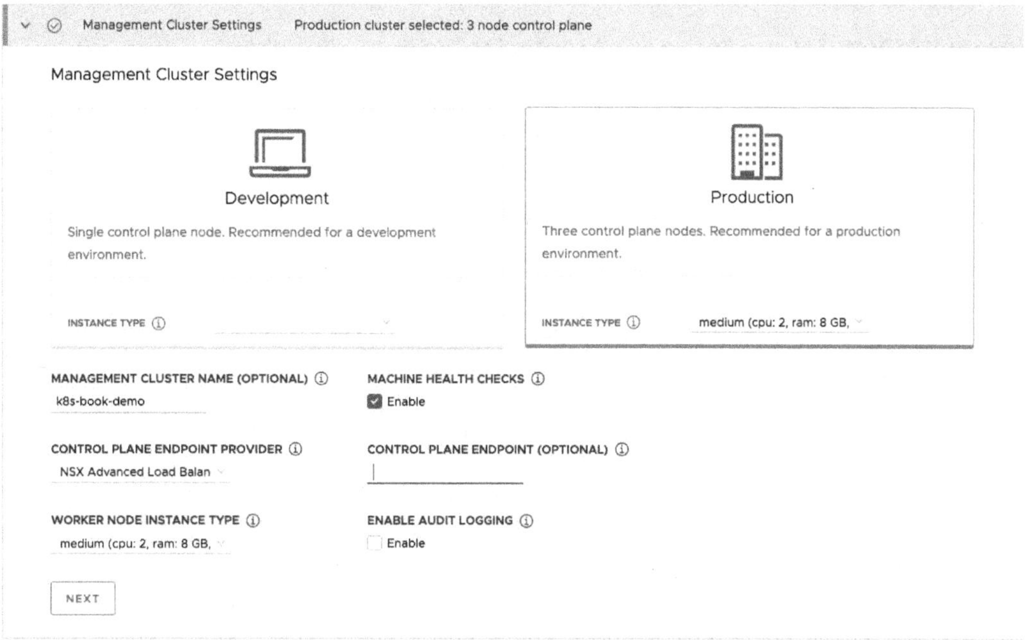

> ⊘ Management Cluster Settings   Production cluster selected: 3 node control plane

Management Cluster Settings

Development
Single control plane node. Recommended for a development environment.

Production
Three control plane nodes. Recommended for a production environment.

INSTANCE TYPE ⓘ

INSTANCE TYPE ⓘ   medium (cpu: 2, ram: 8 GB,

MANAGEMENT CLUSTER NAME (OPTIONAL) ⓘ   MACHINE HEALTH CHECKS ⓘ
k8s-book-demo   ☑ Enable

CONTROL PLANE ENDPOINT PROVIDER ⓘ   CONTROL PLANE ENDPOINT (OPTIONAL) ⓘ
NSX Advanced Load Balan

WORKER NODE INSTANCE TYPE ⓘ   ENABLE AUDIT LOGGING ⓘ
medium (cpu: 2, ram: 8 GB,   ☐ Enable

NEXT

Figure 14: TKG Installer UI – Production Management Cluster Settings with NSX ALB

I have also selected a production instance type for comparison. The setup of the NSX ALB is an advanced topic which we will not be discussing just yet. Instructions on how to deploy the NSX ALB will be discussed later in the book. With NSX ALB option chosen as the Control Plane Endpoint Provider, there is no need to provide an IP address for the control plane endpoint as it will be automatically provisioned from the range of Virtual IP addresses (VIPs) on the NSX ALB.

Click Next to proceed to the VMware NSX Advanced Load Balancer screen. If you decide to use an NSX ALB to provide load balancing functionality, this is where you would provide information about the NSX ALB controller. This includes details such as login credentials, along with the certificate to enable secure communication between the TKG clusters and the Load Balancer. The certificate is retrievable directly from the NSX ALB by logging into the controller, navigating to **Templates > Security > SSL/TLS Certificates** and downloading the certificate created in the controller setup steps. With this information provided, click on '**Verify Credentials**' to establish a connection to the NSX ALB, as follows:

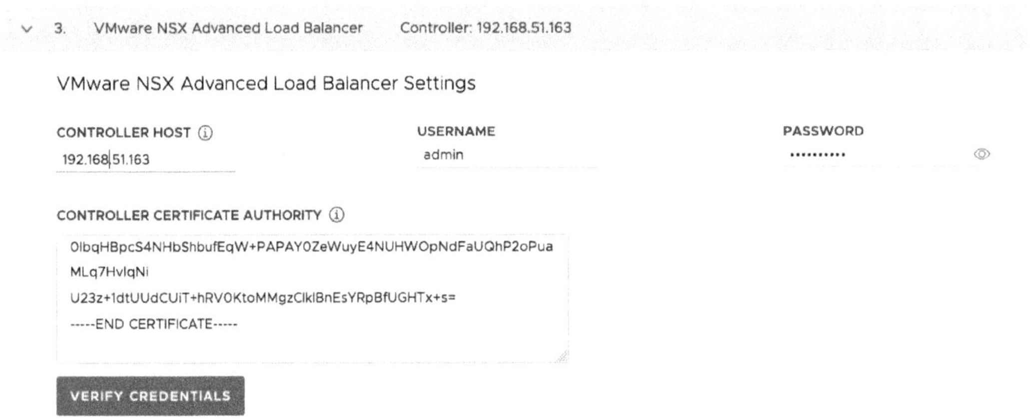

Figure 15: TKG Installer UI – VMware NSX Advanced Load Balancer - Credentials

Once, communication has been established, other information about the NSX ALB must now be added. In the example below, virtual IPs for both the management cluster and the workload cluster(s) are from the same network range.

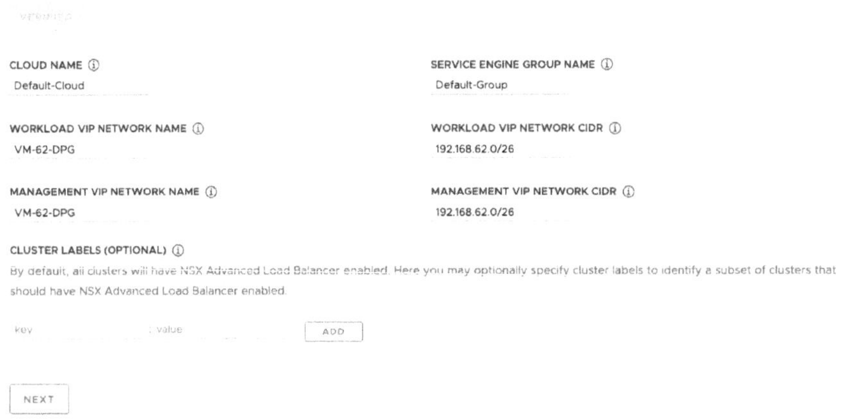

Figure 16: TKG Installer UI – VMware NSX Advanced Load Balancer - Details

However, this was just to show how a configuration with an NSX ALB would look. We will continue the setup with the `kube-vip` option as shown previously. At this point, you can move on to the next stage of the UI. This is the Metadata section. This can be very useful as it allows you to add specific labels to the clusters, which can prove useful in trying to identify them. It is also possible that labels could be used to do specific operations to a group of clusters, or even identify where a particular cluster has been deployed in your infrastructure. We are not going to add any metadata in this deployment.

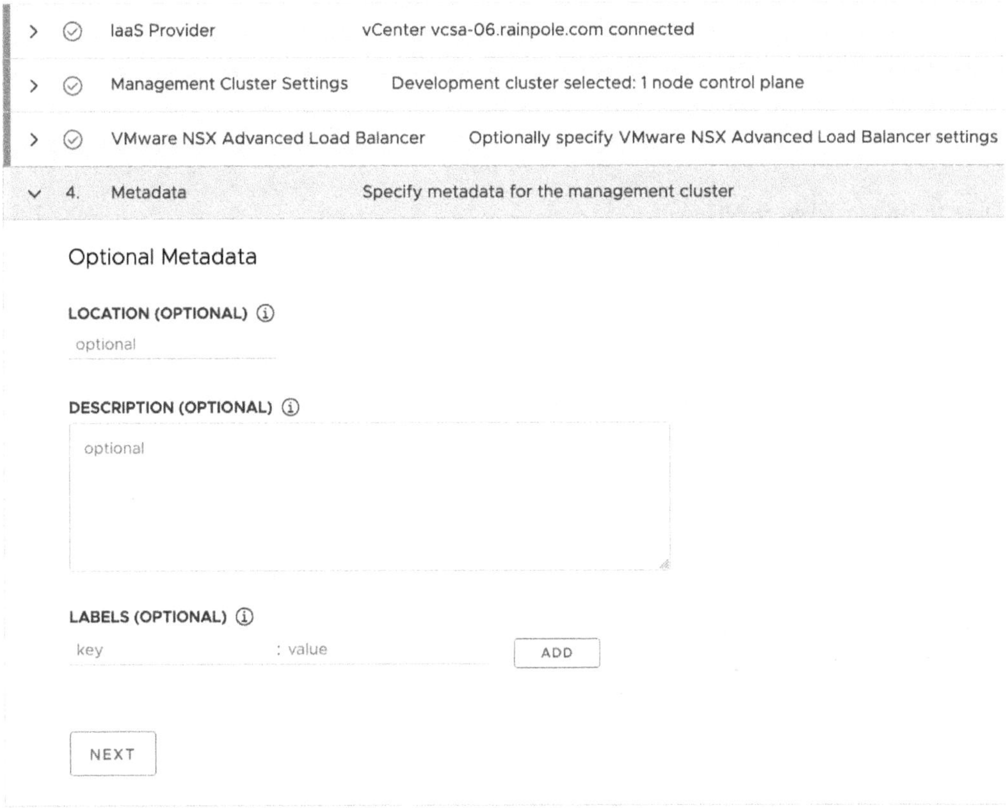

> ⊘ IaaS Provider   vCenter vcsa-06.rainpole.com connected

> ⊘ Management Cluster Settings   Development cluster selected: 1 node control plane

> ⊘ VMware NSX Advanced Load Balancer   Optionally specify VMware NSX Advanced Load Balancer settings

∨ 4.   Metadata   Specify metadata for the management cluster

Optional Metadata

LOCATION (OPTIONAL) ⓘ

optional

DESCRIPTION (OPTIONAL) ⓘ

optional

LABELS (OPTIONAL) ⓘ

key   : value   [ADD]

[NEXT]

Figure 17: TKG Installer UI – Metadata

The next screen after metadata is the Resources screen. This is where the VM Folder to deploy the TKG management cluster VMs is chosen. It is also where the vSphere resources such as datastore and either cluster, host, or resource pool are selected. These are the resources for the TKG VMs. If you have not yet created a VM Folder for the VMs, there is no need to exit the UI. Simply create it on the vSphere Client, then return to this UI and click on the refresh icon (circular arrow). The newly created resource should now appear.

Figure 18: TKG Installer UI – Resources

This now brings us to the networking section of the deployment. Here, the portgroup on which the management cluster VMs are deployed is selected. It must support DHCP to allocate IP addresses to the nodes. You will need to choose a portgroup from the dropdown list. The values for the Service CIDR and the Pod CIDR can be changed from their defaults at this point, if necessary. At this point, you should be aware of the requirement for both a Service network and a Pod network in Kubernetes, and how they are used.

Figure 19: TKG Installer UI – Kubernetes Network

Another configuration option in the Kubernetes Network section is around a Proxy. TKG has a requirement to pull down components from VMware to build the bootstrap and management clusters. In certain organizations, internet access is via a proxy. For this management cluster example, a proxy is not required. If a proxy configuration is a requirement in your environment, this is where it can be configured.

The next section is all around Identity Management and if there is a need to integrate the management cluster with LDAP or OIDC. This allows fine grained control on who can access the management cluster and allow the admin access to be locked down. Again, since the objective is to deploy the simplest management cluster on this occasion, we will leave Identity Management disabled.

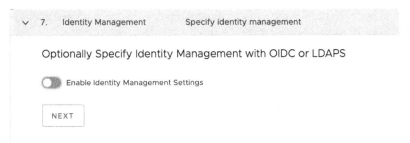

Figure 20: TKG Installer UI – Identity Management

We are almost at the end of our configuration of the TKG management cluster. The next step is to choose an OS image for the Kubernetes nodes. Note that only a select set of images are supported, and these OVAs (virtual appliances) need to be downloaded from the VMware Customer Connect site and uploaded to your vCenter Server. They will then have to be converted to templates in order to be discovered for TKG by the installer.

Any suitable templates will be displayed in the dropdown menu at this point. Note that certain versions of TKG only supports certain versions of Kubernetes distribution. Thus, if deploying TKG v1.5.4, older OVA templates which have earlier distributions of Kubernetes may not be visible. This is expected. Only supported versions of Kubernetes that are supported with TKG v1.5.4 will be displayed. This is also true for earlier versions of TKG. Below, only a single template is available for selection.

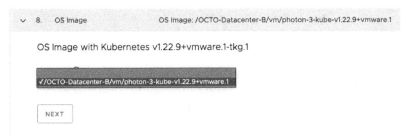

Figure 21: TKG Installer UI – OS Image

If you have arrived at this point of the setup and there is no valid template, there is no need to quit the UI. Simply upload a suitable OVA and convert it to a template. Then click on the refresh icon next to the OS Image and the new template should be available for selection.

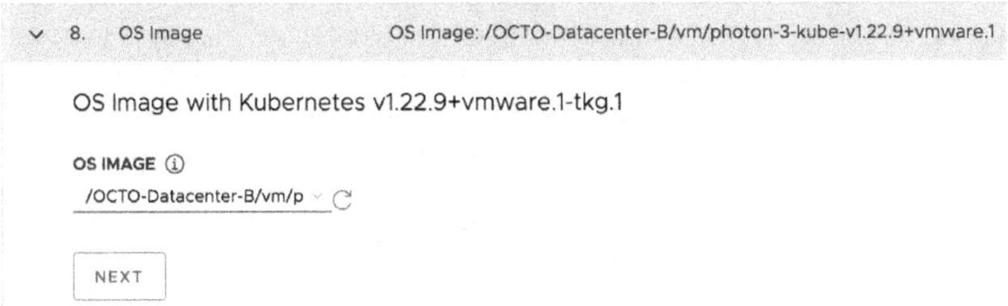

Figure 22: TKG Installer UI – OS Image configured

Once a suitable template image is selected, click next to continue. This will take you to the CEIP section. As this point, you can choose to join the Customer Experience Improvement Program, which allows VMware to gather obfuscated telemetry from your deployment.

Figure 23: TKG Installer UI – CEIP Agreement

And that completes the setup. Although we could certainly configure more than what we have configured in this setup, it is enough information to get a TKG management cluster deployed.

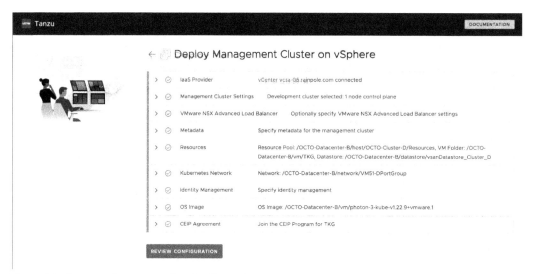

Figure 24: TKG Installer UI – Review Configuration

We can now review the configuration to make sure everything is correct and adjust the configuration should that be necessary. Note that the review window also shows a command line equivalent option for the deployment of the management cluster. At this point, you could drop out of the UI and complete the management cluster deployment from the command line. Even if you decide to continue the deployment from the UI, the configuration file will remain available in the `.config/tanzu/tkg/clusterconfigs` folder for future reference and future use. The management cluster configuration file usually forms the building block for creating your workload clusters.

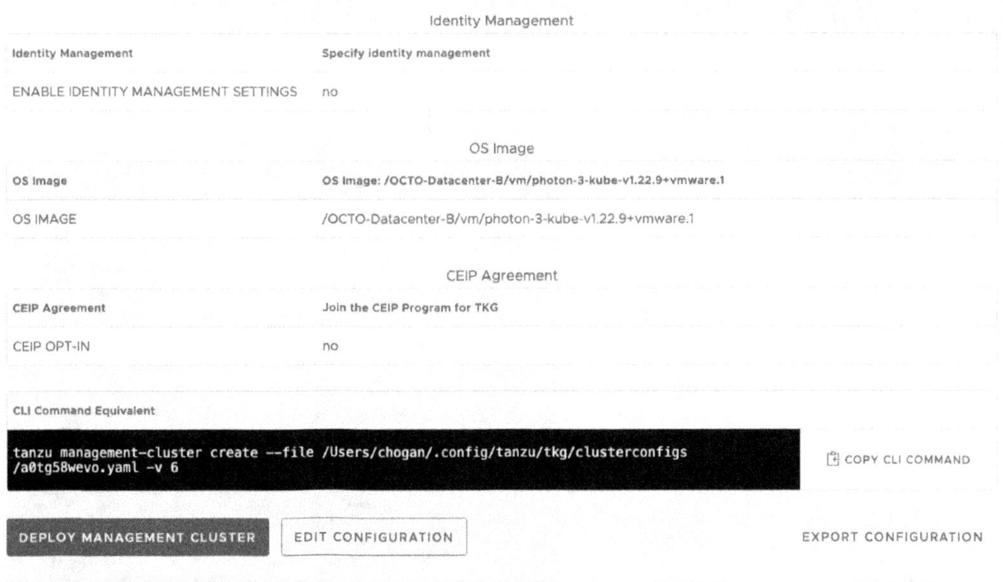

	Identity Management
Identity Management	Specify identity management
ENABLE IDENTITY MANAGEMENT SETTINGS	no
	OS Image
OS Image	OS Image: /OCTO-Datacenter-B/vm/photon-3-kube-v1.22.9+vmware.1
OS IMAGE	/OCTO-Datacenter-B/vm/photon-3-kube-v1.22.9+vmware.1
	CEIP Agreement
CEIP Agreement	Join the CEIP Program for TKG
CEIP OPT-IN	no

CLI Command Equivalent

```
tanzu management-cluster create --file /Users/chogan/.config/tanzu/tkg/clusterconfigs
/a0tg58wevo.yaml -v 6
```
⎘ COPY CLI COMMAND

DEPLOY MANAGEMENT CLUSTER   EDIT CONFIGURATION   EXPORT CONFIGURATION

Figure 25: TKG Installer UI – Deploy Management Cluster

We can now click on the button to "Deploy Management Cluster". This will begin by creating a temporary management 'bootstrap' cluster. This temporary management cluster, which is a kind cluster, that requires docker to be available, will then create the Tanzu Kubernetes Grid management cluster on the vSphere environment. Context then switches to the new management cluster and the temporary bootstrap cluster will be removed. The progress can be monitored from the UI and the command line.

Note: This will now initialize the creation of a kind cluster on the system where tanzu CLI was run. The initial **kind** docker image is approximately 1.3GB in size, so it may take some time to download. However, once it is downloaded and stored locally, it can be used for subsequent management cluster creations without the need to download it again.

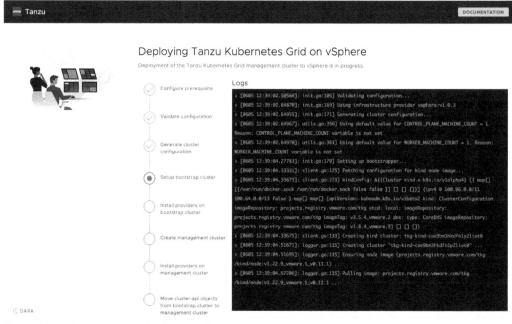

Figure 26: TKG Installer UI – Deployment logs

The status of the kind cluster can be examined using *docker ps* since it is simply a container. Also, if the *kind* binary – see https://kind.sigs.k8s.io/ - is installed on the system where you are running the tanzu CLI command, it can also be used to query the status of the bootstrap cluster.

```
% docker ps
CONTAINER ID    IMAGE
COMMAND              CREATED          STATUS          PORTS
NAMES
42d9f1688bcf    projects.registry.vmware.com/tkg/kind/node:v1.22.9_vmware.1_v0.11.1
"/usr/local/bin/entr…"   18 minutes ago   Up 10 minutes   127.0.0.1:51853->6443/tcp    tkg-
kind-caer4ejhkdfmvg9ft5ag-control-plane

% kind get clusters
tkg-kind-caer4ejhkdfmvg9ft5ag
```

Assuming everything is working as expected, you should begin to see virtual machines corresponding to the TKG management cluster appear in the vCenter Server inventory, under the Data Center and Cluster that was configured in the setup. They should also be placed in the folder that you selected in the Resources section. The control plane node should have its DHCP allocated IP address but should also be configured with the kube-vip, control plane endpoint virtual IP address that was placed in the configuration settings.

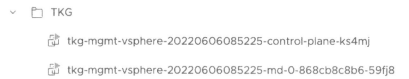

Figure 27: TKG Installer UI – Virtual Machines

The management cluster nodes will then have the necessary Cluster API components (providers) installed on it, so it can subsequently deploy workload clusters onto vSphere. The management cluster will also have some necessary packages installed, such as the vSphere CPI, the vSphere CSI and the Antrea CNI, along with some tanzu management packages. Once all of these are successfully reconciled on the cluster, the management cluster creation is complete. The installer then deletes the kind bootstrap cluster. Instructions on how to access the management cluster, i.e. the KUBECONFIG, are also provided. The installation automatically adds the management cluster context to ~/.kube/config on the local system. Once all activities have a green tick mark in the UI, and the green banner "Installation complete, you can now close the browser ...." appears, the management cluster is up and running and is ready to be used for the creation of a workload cluster.

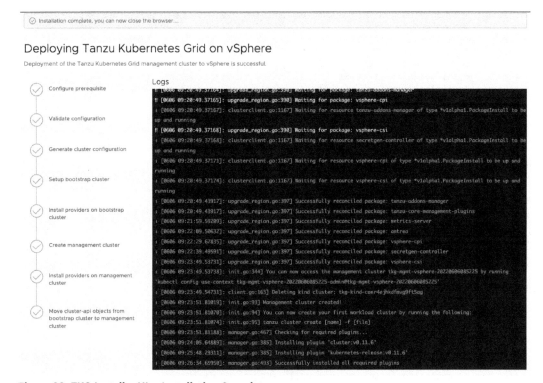

Figure 28: TKG Installer UI – Installation Complete

The UI provides some reasonable logging should something go wrong and you need to troubleshoot. Similarly, on the command line, the following logs appeared during the deployment. They correspond to many of the logs which also appear in the UI.

```
% tanzu mc create --ui

Validating the pre-requisites...
Serving kickstart UI at http://127.0.0.1:8080
Identity Provider not configured. Some authentication features won't work.
Using default value for CONTROL_PLANE_MACHINE_COUNT = 1. Reason:
CONTROL_PLANE_MACHINE_COUNT variable is not set
Using default value for WORKER_MACHINE_COUNT = 1. Reason: WORKER_MACHINE_COUNT variable is
not set
Validating configuration...
web socket connection established
sending pending 2 logs to UI
```

```
Using infrastructure provider vsphere:v1.0.3
Generating cluster configuration...
Using default value for CONTROL_PLANE_MACHINE_COUNT = 1. Reason:
CONTROL_PLANE_MACHINE_COUNT variable is not set
Using default value for WORKER_MACHINE_COUNT = 1. Reason: WORKER_MACHINE_COUNT variable is
not set
Setting up bootstrapper...
Bootstrapper created. Kubeconfig: /Users/chogan/.kube-tkg/tmp/config_pTdRmuBK
Installing providers on bootstrapper...
Fetching providers
Installing cert-manager Version="v1.5.3"
Waiting for cert-manager to be available...
Installing Provider="cluster-api" Version="v1.0.1" TargetNamespace="capi-system"
Installing Provider="bootstrap-kubeadm" Version="v1.0.1" TargetNamespace="capi-kubeadm-
bootstrap-system"
Installing Provider="control-plane-kubeadm" Version="v1.0.1" TargetNamespace="capi-
kubeadm-control-plane-system"
Installing Provider="infrastructure-vsphere" Version="v1.0.3" TargetNamespace="capv-
system"
Start creating management cluster...
[cluster control plane is still being initialized: WaitingForControlPlane, cluster
infrastructure is still being provisioned: WaitingForControlPlane]
cluster control plane is still being initialized: ScalingUp
Saving management cluster kubeconfig into /Users/chogan/.kube/config
Installing providers on management cluster...
Fetching providers
Installing cert-manager Version="v1.5.3"
Waiting for cert-manager to be available...
Installing Provider="cluster-api" Version="v1.0.1" TargetNamespace="capi-system"
Installing Provider="bootstrap-kubeadm" Version="v1.0.1" TargetNamespace="capi-kubeadm-
bootstrap-system"
Installing Provider="control-plane-kubeadm" Version="v1.0.1" TargetNamespace="capi-
kubeadm-control-plane-system"
Installing Provider="infrastructure-vsphere" Version="v1.0.3" TargetNamespace="capv-
system"
Waiting for the management cluster to get ready for move...
Waiting for addons installation...
Moving all Cluster API objects from bootstrap cluster to management cluster...
Performing move...
Discovering Cluster API objects
Moving Cluster API objects Clusters=1
Creating objects in the target cluster
Deleting objects from the source cluster
Waiting for additional components to be up and running...
Waiting for packages to be up and running...
You can now access the management cluster tkg-mgmt-vsphere-20220606085225 by running
'kubectl config use-context tkg-mgmt-vsphere-20220606085225-admin@tkg-mgmt-vsphere-
20220606085225'

Management cluster created!


You can now create your first workload cluster by running the following:

  tanzu cluster create [name] -f [file]

Checking for required plugins...
Installing plugin 'cluster:v0.11.6'
Installing plugin 'kubernetes-release:v0.11.6'
Successfully installed all required plugins
```

One interesting item to note from the log output is the following:

```
Bootstrapper created. Kubeconfig: /Users/chogan/.kube-tkg/tmp/config_pTdRmuBK
```

This is a reference to the KUBECONFIG of the bootstrap kind cluster. This KUBECONFIG can be used to examine the status of the Cluster API components of the bootstrap cluster. These will be named capi and capv, similar to what we saw in the Cluster API section previously. Simply run *kubectl get* and *kubectl describe* commands against the various components using the option --*kubeconfig* and point it to the KUBECONFIG reported in the logs. This can be very useful if there are issues with the bootstrap failing to come online as you can check the status of the nodes and Pods.

```
% kubectl get nodes --kubeconfig .kube-tkg/tmp/config_n7zxrcIu
NAME                                           STATUS ROLES         AGE    VERSION
tkg-kind-cam6bkrhkdfjba8i5ne0-control-plane  Ready  control-plane  48s    v1.22.9+vmware.1

% kubectl get pods -A --kubeconfig .kube-tkg/tmp/config_n7zxrcIu
NAMESPACE            NAME
READY    STATUS                RESTARTS    AGE
cert-manager         cert-manager-cainjector-cc485fcdc-pqxvl
0/1      ContainerCreating     0           7s
cert-manager         cert-manager-d6b468546-5qkqk
0/1      ContainerCreating     0           7s
cert-manager         cert-manager-webhook-dd697458d-xb7bg
0/1      ContainerCreating     0           7s
kube-system          coredns-67c8559bb6-ln8h7
1/1      Running               0           34s
kube-system          coredns-67c8559bb6-tbxjw
1/1      Running               0           34s
kube-system          etcd-tkg-kind-cam6bkrhkdfjba8i5ne0-control-plane
1/1      Running               0           50s
kube-system          kindnet-dvkd6
1/1      Running               0           34s
kube-system          kube-apiserver-tkg-kind-cam6bkrhkdfjba8i5ne0-control-plane
1/1      Running               0           50s
kube-system          kube-controller-manager-tkg-kind-cam6bkrhkdfjba8i5ne0-control-plane
1/1      Running               0           55s
kube-system          kube-proxy-h9kzs
1/1      Running               0           34s
kube-system          kube-scheduler-tkg-kind-cam6bkrhkdfjba8i5ne0-control-plane
1/1      Running               0           53s
local-path-storage   local-path-provisioner-547f784dff-zkbbz
1/1      Running               0           34s
```

Using the KUBECONFIG, it is even possible to check the logs inside of the Pods. This command is examining the logs of the cert-manager Pod in the cert-manager namespace on the bootstrap kind cluster.

```
% kubectl logs cert-manager-d6b468546-5qkqk \
-n cert-manager \
--kubeconfig .kube-tkg/tmp/config_n7zxrcIu
I0617 11:56:31.263639      1 start.go:75] cert-manager "msg"="starting controller"  "git-
commit"="" "version"="canary"
W0617 11:56:31.263994      1 client_config.go:615] Neither --kubeconfig nor --master was
specified.  Using the inClusterConfig.  This might not work.
I0617 11:56:31.266926      1 controller.go:268] cert-manager/controller/build-context
"msg"="configured acme dns01 nameservers" "nameservers"=["100.64.0.10:53"]
I0617 11:56:31.268040      1 controller.go:85] cert-manager/controller "msg"="enabled
controllers: [certificaterequests-approver certificaterequests-issuer-acme
certificaterequests-issuer-ca certificaterequests-issuer-selfsigned certificaterequests-
issuer-vault certificaterequests-issuer-venafi certificates-issuing certificates-key-
manager certificates-metrics certificates-readiness certificates-request-manager
certificates-revision-manager certificates-trigger challenges clusterissuers ingress-shim
issuers orders]"
```

Another very useful option is to use the *-w* flag when examining the Pods as they come online. This keeps a watch on the Pod objects and reports on the changing state of Pods.

```
% kubectl get pods -A --kubeconfig .kube-tkg/tmp/config_n7zxrcIu -w
NAMESPACE               NAME
READY    STATUS          RESTARTS    AGE
capi-system             capi-controller-manager-65c5769c4c-5npnp
0/1      ContainerCreating    0         2s
.
.
.
capi-kubeadm-bootstrap-system    capi-kubeadm-bootstrap-controller-manager-7ffb6dc8fc-gtttm
0/1      Pending         0           1s
capi-kubeadm-bootstrap-system    capi-kubeadm-bootstrap-controller-manager-7ffb6dc8fc-gtttm
0/1      Pending         0           1s
capi-kubeadm-bootstrap-system    capi-kubeadm-bootstrap-controller-manager-7ffb6dc8fc-gtttm
0/1      ContainerCreating    0       1s
capi-kubeadm-control-plane-system    capi-kubeadm-control-plane-controller-manager-
667999fdb8-g6rcx        0/1      Pending         0           0s
capi-kubeadm-control-plane-system    capi-kubeadm-control-plane-controller-manager-
667999fdb8-g6rcx        0/1      Pending         0           0s
capi-kubeadm-control-plane-system    capi-kubeadm-control-plane-controller-manager-
667999fdb8-g6rcx        0/1      ContainerCreating    0       0s
```

The management cluster KUBECONFIG is stored in ~/.kube-tkg/config. This can also be used during start-up to examine the management cluster. Once the management cluster is online, this management cluster KUBECONFIG is merged with the default ~/.kube/config.

Let's now try to access the management cluster using the *kubectl config use-context* command provided in the log output above.

```
% kubectl config use-context tkg-mgmt-vsphere-20..25-admin@tkg-mgmt-vsphere-20220606085225
Switched to context "tkg-mgmt-vsphere-20..25-admin@tkg-mgmt-vsphere-20220606085225".
```

```
% kubectl get nodes
NAME                                STATUS    ROLES              AGE VERSION
tkg-mgmt-vsphere-2022..25-c-p-ks4mj          Ready   control-plane,mstr 21m v1.22.9+vmware.1
tkg-mgmt-vsphere-2022..25-md-0-86..b6-5..8  Ready   <none>             19m v1.22.9+vmware.1
```

The Pods that have been created on the management cluster can be examined to show that there are Cluster API extensions installed. Again, these will be named capi and capv, similar to what we saw in the bootstrap cluster and the earlier Cluster API section. Of course, many other Pods related to CPI, CSI and CNI are also running since this Kubernetes cluster is deployed on vSphere. There are also some Tanzu specific Pods related to TKG (Tanzu Kubernetes Grid) and TKr (Tanzu Kubernetes release) for package handling and release management respectively.

The *tanzu mc* command can also be used to query the state of the management cluster. Since the cluster is built using Cluster API, this output is very similar to the *clusterctl describe* output seen in the previous section.

```
% tanzu mc get
NAME                         NAMESPACE    STATUS   CP  WKS  KUBERNETES        ROLES       PLAN
  tkg-mgmt-vsphere-…85225 tkg-system   running  1/1 1/1  v1.22.9+vmware.1  management  dev


Details:

NAME                                                                            READY  SINCE
/tkg-mgmt-vsphere-20220606085225                                                True   17m
├─ClusterInfrastructure - VSphereCluster/tkg-mgmt-vsphere-20220606085225        True   17m
├─ControlPlane - KubeadmControlPlane/tkg-mgmt-vsphere-…85225-control-plane       True   17m
│ └─Machine/tkg-mgmt-vsphere-20220606085225-control-plane-ks4mj                 True   17m
└─Workers
  └─MachineDeployment/tkg-mgmt-vsphere-20220606085225-md-0                       True   17m
    └─Machine/tkg-mgmt-vsphere-20220606085225-md-0-868cb8c8b6-59fj8             True   17m


Providers:

NAMESPACE                    NAME                    TYPE                   PROVIDERNAME VERSION
capi-kubeadm-bs-system       bootstrap-kubeadm       BootstrapProvider      kubeadm      v1.0.1
capi-kubeadm-cp-system       control-plane-kubeadm   ControlPlaneProvider   kubeadm      v1.0.1
capi-system                  cluster-api             CoreProvider           cluster-api  v1.0.1
capv-system                  infrastructure-vsphere  InfrastructureProvider vsphere      v1.0.3
```

Everything is now in place to use the management cluster to build the first TKG workload cluster on vSphere.

TKG Workload Cluster Creation

You may have noticed the following output in either the UI or the CLI when the management cluster was created previously.

```
You can now create your first workload cluster by running the following:

  tanzu cluster create [name] -f [file]
```

Note that there is no UI option to create a TKG workload cluster. It must be created with a configuration file. Fortunately, the act of creating a management cluster creates a configuration file that can also be used to build a workload cluster. During the setup of the management cluster, we were informed that as well as using the UI, we could manually run a command on the CLI to create the management cluster. The command pointed to a configuration file in `~/.config/tanzu/tkg/clusterconfigs`. This management cluster configuration file can now be used to create the workload cluster configuration file.

Here is a sample copy of the management cluster configuration file which was created in the previous demonstration. This is quite simple. There is no NSX ALB integration or Identity Management configured.

```
% cat .config/tanzu/tkg/clusterconfigs/m323ii59g4.yaml
AVI_CA_DATA_B64: ""
AVI_CLOUD_NAME: ""
AVI_CONTROL_PLANE_HA_PROVIDER: ""
AVI_CONTROLLER: ""
AVI_DATA_NETWORK: ""
AVI_DATA_NETWORK_CIDR: ""
AVI_ENABLE: "false"
AVI_LABELS: ""
AVI_MANAGEMENT_CLUSTER_VIP_NETWORK_CIDR: ""
AVI_MANAGEMENT_CLUSTER_VIP_NETWORK_NAME: ""
AVI_PASSWORD: ""
AVI_SERVICE_ENGINE_GROUP: ""
AVI_USERNAME: ""
CLUSTER_CIDR: 100.96.0.0/11
CLUSTER_PLAN: dev
ENABLE_AUDIT_LOGGING: "false"
ENABLE_CEIP_PARTICIPATION: "false"
ENABLE_MHC: "true"
IDENTITY_MANAGEMENT_TYPE: none
INFRASTRUCTURE_PROVIDER: vsphere
LDAP_BIND_DN: ""
LDAP_BIND_PASSWORD: ""
LDAP_GROUP_SEARCH_BASE_DN: ""
LDAP_GROUP_SEARCH_FILTER: ""
LDAP_GROUP_SEARCH_GROUP_ATTRIBUTE: ""
LDAP_GROUP_SEARCH_NAME_ATTRIBUTE: cn
LDAP_GROUP_SEARCH_USER_ATTRIBUTE: DN
LDAP_HOST: ""
LDAP_ROOT_CA_DATA_B64: ""
LDAP_USER_SEARCH_BASE_DN: ""
LDAP_USER_SEARCH_FILTER: ""
LDAP_USER_SEARCH_NAME_ATTRIBUTE: ""
LDAP_USER_SEARCH_USERNAME: userPrincipalName
OIDC_IDENTITY_PROVIDER_CLIENT_ID: ""
OIDC_IDENTITY_PROVIDER_CLIENT_SECRET: ""
OIDC_IDENTITY_PROVIDER_GROUPS_CLAIM: ""
OIDC_IDENTITY_PROVIDER_ISSUER_URL: ""
OIDC_IDENTITY_PROVIDER_NAME: ""
OIDC_IDENTITY_PROVIDER_SCOPES: ""
OIDC_IDENTITY_PROVIDER_USERNAME_CLAIM: ""
OS_ARCH: amd64
OS_NAME: photon
OS_VERSION: "3"
SERVICE_CIDR: 100.64.0.0/13
TKG_HTTP_PROXY_ENABLED: "false"
TKG_IP_FAMILY: ipv4
VSPHERE_CONTROL_PLANE_DISK_GIB: "20"
VSPHERE_CONTROL_PLANE_ENDPOINT: 192.168.1.177
VSPHERE_CONTROL_PLANE_MEM_MIB: "4096"
VSPHERE_CONTROL_PLANE_NUM_CPUS: "2"
VSPHERE_DATACENTER: /OCTO-Datacenter-B
VSPHERE_DATASTORE: /OCTO-Datacenter-B/datastore/vsanDatastore_Cluster_D
VSPHERE_FOLDER: /OCTO-Datacenter-B/vm/TKG
VSPHERE_INSECURE: "false"
VSPHERE_NETWORK: /OCTO-Datacenter-B/network/VM51-DPortGroup
VSPHERE_PASSWORD: <encoded:Vk13YXJlMTIzIQ==>
VSPHERE_RESOURCE_POOL: /OCTO-Datacenter-B/host/OCTO-Cluster-D/Resources
VSPHERE_SERVER: vcsa-06.rainpole.com
```

```
VSPHERE_SSH_AUTHORIZED_KEY: ssh-rsa xxxJlH cormac@rainpole.com
VSPHERE_TLS_THUMBPRINT: FA:A5:8A:18:82:49:50:40:B9:83:1B:67:88:E2:2C:D9:6A:01:F0:5E
VSPHERE_USERNAME: administrator@vsphere.local
VSPHERE_WORKER_DISK_GIB: "20"
VSPHERE_WORKER_MEM_MIB: "4096"
VSPHERE_WORKER_NUM_CPUS: "2"
```

The VSPHERE fields, as you probably have guessed, relate to the vSphere infrastructure on which the workload cluster will be deployed. The only field that will need to change is the VSPHERE_CONTROL_PLANE_ENDPOINT. This needs to be a different IP address to the one that was used to create the management cluster. Once again, since there is no NSX ALB to provide front-end/load balancer IP addresses (because we are keeping this simple), kube-vip will use this IP Address to provide the virtual IP address for the control plane in the workload cluster. None of the rest of the configuration file needs to change.

Any fields that begin with the label AVI is a reference to the NSX ALB, formerly the product known as Avi Vantage. Since we did not configure a Load Balancer, these fields are empty.

The fields that begin with LDAP and OIDC refer to Identify Management. Once again, since this was not configured on the management cluster, these fields are also empty.

The CLUSTER_PLAN field is set to dev, indicating that this a development environment rather than a prod [production] environment. Thus, it only creates a single control plane and a single worker node, which are the defaults for fields CONTROL_PLANE_MACHINE_COUNT and WORKER_MACHINE_COUNT. You may add these fields to increase the node count if you wish.

The OS fields relate to the image that will be used to build the TKG control plane and worker nodes. This is the Photon image that we uploaded earlier in the process.

To create a TKG workload cluster, make a copy of the management cluster configuration file, change the VSPHERE_CONTROL_PLANE_ENDPOINT to a unique IP address for the control plane on the workload cluster, and run the *tanzu cluster create [name] --file [config]* to create the workload cluster. This will build a new Kubernetes cluster with a single control plane node and a single worker node (dev cluster plan). The VMs for those nodes will be placed in the 'TKG' folder in the vSphere inventory, and will be created with 2 CPU, 4GB RAM, and a 20GB disk. After this task completes, there should be 4 VMs in the TKG folder, 2 for the management cluster, and 2 for the workload cluster.

Let's create the workload cluster. Make a copy of the management cluster, and change the VIP endpoint, as described.

```
% cp .config/tanzu/tkg/clusterconfigs/m323ii59g4.yaml \
.config/tanzu/tkg/clusterconfigs/workload.yaml

% nano .config/tanzu/tkg/clusterconfigs/workload.yaml

% tanzu cluster create workload --file .config/tanzu/tkg/clusterconfigs/workload.yaml
Validating configuration...
Warning: Pinniped configuration not found. Skipping pinniped configuration in workload
cluster. Please refer to the documentation to check if you can configure pinniped on
workload cluster manually
Creating workload cluster 'workload'...
Waiting for cluster to be initialized...
```

```
[cluster control plane is still being initialized: WaitingForControlPlane, cluster
infrastructure is still being provisioned: WaitingForControlPlane]
cluster control plane is still being initialized: ScalingUp
Waiting for cluster nodes to be available...
Waiting for addons installation...
I0606 17:28:37.745541   52303 request.go:665] Waited for 1.1041988s due to client-side
throttling, not priority and fairness, request:
GET:https://192.168.1.178:6443/apis/node.k8s.io/v1beta1?timeout=32s
Waiting for packages to be up and running...


Workload cluster 'workload' created
```

Success! The workload cluster has been created. The next step is to retrieve the KUBECONFIG using the *tanzu cluster kubeconfig get* command and check the status of the workload cluster.

```
% tanzu cluster kubeconfig get workload --admin
Credentials of cluster 'workload' have been saved
You can now access the cluster by running 'kubectl config use-context workload-
admin@workload'

% kubectl config use-context workload-admin@workload
Switched to context "workload-admin@workload".

% kubectl get nodes
NAME                            STATUS    ROLES                   AGE       VERSION
workload-control-plane-vhxqm    Ready     control-plane,master    8m22s     v1.22.9+vmware.1
workload-md-0-7dfb8598cb-hklkn  Ready     <none>                  7m37s     v1.22.9+vmware.1

% kubectl get pods -A
NAMESPACE        NAME                                           READY  STATUS    RES  AGE
kube-system      antrea-agent-68ddk                             2/2    Running   0    4m59s
kube-system      antrea-agent-vwkqq                             2/2    Running   0    4m59s
kube-system      antrea-controller-56c8c84758-8h72v             1/1    Running   0    4m59s
kube-system      coredns-67c8559bb6-9v8db                       1/1    Running   0    8m18s
kube-system      coredns-67c8559bb6-dxqh4                       1/1    Running   0    8m18s
kube-system      etcd-workload-control-plane-vhxqm              1/1    Running   0    8m21s
kube-system      kube-apiserver-workload-control-plane-vhxqm    1/1    Running   0    8m21s
kube-system      kube-ctlr-mgt-workload-control-plane-vhxqm     1/1    Running   0    8m21s
kube-system      kube-proxy-22cfv                               1/1    Running   0    7m42s
kube-system      kube-proxy-gkztt                               1/1    Running   0    8m17s
kube-system      kube-scheduler-workload-control-plane-vhxqm    1/1    Running   0    8m20s
kube-system      kube-vip-workload-control-plane-vhxqm          1/1    Running   0    8m21s
kube-system      metrics-server-cfcbddfc9-jsgs9                 1/1    Running   0    5m8s
kube-system      vsphere-cloud-controller-manager-zs6bk         1/1    Running   0    5m5s
kube-system      vsphere-csi-controller-56f797bddc-kwm9b        6/6    Running   0    4m20s
kube-system      vsphere-csi-node-nrxlw                         3/3    Running   0    4m20s
kube-system      vsphere-csi-node-s2cpc                         3/3    Running   0    4m20s
tanzu-system     secretgen-controller-d47b4fb5f-xtgtr           1/1    Running   0    5m6s
tkg-system       kapp-controller-769d645d4-8kp4h                1/1    Running   0    8m5s
tkg-system       tanzu-capabilities-ctlr-mgr-67...c8f-98gcf     1/1    Running   0    7m53s
```

Success! We have a healthy workload cluster deployed to our vSphere infrastructure. From the Pod listing above, notice that the vSphere CPI, vSphere CSI and the Antrea CNI from VMware are automatically installed on this workload cluster. That's pretty neat, isn't it?

A word about the *tanzu cluster kubeconfig get* command run above. The options provided include the name of the workload cluster and the request to retrieve admin credentials. The name of the workload cluster(s) can be found by running the command *tanzu cluster list*.

```
% tanzu cluster list
  NAME      NAMESPACE  STATUS   CONTROLPLANE  WORKERS  KUBERNETES        ROLES    PLAN
  workload  default    running  1/1           1/1      v1.22.9+vmware.1  <none>   dev
```

If the option `--include-management-cluster` is included, both management and workload
clusters are displayed.

```
% tanzu cluster list --include-management-cluster
  NAME                     NAMESPACE   STATUS   CPL WORK  KUBERNETES        ROLES       PLAN
  workload                 default     running  1/1 1/1   v1.22.9+vmware.1  <none>      dev
  tkg-mgmt-vsphere-202..225 tkg-system  running  1/1 1/1   v1.22.9+vmware.1  management  dev
```

Since we have not configured any LDAP or OIDC identity management on the cluster, the only
access allowed to the cluster in via the admin user. This is why the `--admin` is added to the
command when retrieving the KUBECONFIG. Anyone who has access to this context has admin
privileges to the cluster. In chapter 7, day 2 operations, we will see how management and workload
clusters can be deployed with LDAP integration so that a Platform Operator can control who has
access to the TKG clusters.

There are a lot of tanzu CLI commands that a Platform Operator can now explore in relation to the
TKG management and workload clusters. One issue that a Platform Operator might want to
monitor is the health of the Kubernetes nodes. During the deployment, it was mentioned that there
was an option to enable machine health checks, which was left enabled by default. The tanzu CLI
commands can now be used to examine the health of nodes on both the management and
workload clusters. Here is an example taken from the management cluster control plane.

```
% tanzu cluster machinehealthcheck control-plane get tkg-mgmt-vsphere-20220606085225
[
    {
        "name": "tkg-mgmt-vsphere-20220606085225-control-plane",
        "namespace": "tkg-system",
        "spec": {
            "clusterName": "tkg-mgmt-vsphere-20220606085225",
            "selector": {
                "matchLabels": {
                    "cluster.x-k8s.io/control-plane": ""
                }
            },
            "unhealthyConditions": [
                {
                    "type": "Ready",
                    "status": "Unknown",
                    "timeout": "5m0s"
                },
                {
                    "type": "Ready",
                    "status": "False",
                    "timeout": "12m0s"
                }
            ],
            "maxUnhealthy": "100%",
            "nodeStartupTimeout": "20m0s"
        },
        "status": {
            "expectedMachines": 1,
            "currentHealthy": 1,
            "remediationsAllowed": 1,
            "observedGeneration": 1,
            "targets": [
```

```
            "tkg-mgmt-vsphere-20220606085225-control-plane-ks4mj"
        ],
        "conditions": [
            {
                "type": "RemediationAllowed",
                "status": "True",
                "lastTransitionTime": "2022-06-06T08:20:48Z"
            }
        ]
    }
  }
]
```

The above output is showing some default settings for the remediation of the cluster. If the Ready condition of a machine remains `Unknown` for longer than 5 minutes, or remains `False` for longer than 12 minutes, the Machine Health Check controller running inside of the cluster considers the machine unhealthy and recreates it.

Scaling the cluster can also be achieved through the tanzu CLI. In the following example, I will scale the workload cluster to 2 worker nodes. First, I am going to check the name of the node-pool of the worker nodes in the workload cluster. If there were multiple node-pools, this would be necessary in order to specify which node-pool to scale. In this case, there is only a single node-pool.

```
% tanzu cluster node-pool list workload
  NAME  NAMESPACE  PHASE    REPLICAS  READY  UPDATED  UNAVAILABLE
  md-0  default    Running  1         1      1        0

% tanzu cluster scale -p md-0 -w 2 workload
Workload cluster 'workload' is being scaled
```

Note that the control plane nodes can be scaled by replacing the *-w* for worker option with *-c* for control plane. When scaling the control plane, note that it must always be an odd number of control plane nodes. The control plane cannot be an even number of nodes due to etcd (K/V store) quorum requirements.

```
% tanzu cluster list
  NAME      NAMESPACE  STATUS   CONTROLPLANE  WORKERS  KUBERNETES       ROLES    PLAN
  workload  default    running  1/1           2/2      v1.22.9+vmware.1  <none>   dev

% tanzu cluster get workload
  NAME      NAMESPACE  STATUS   CONTROLPLANE  WORKERS  KUBERNETES       ROLES
  workload  default    running  1/1           2/2      v1.22.9+vmware.1  <none>
```

```
Details:

NAME                                                    READY SEVERITY REASON SINCE MESSAGE
/workload                                               True                  10d
├─ClusterInfrastructure - VSphereCluster/workload       True                  10d
├─ControlPlane - KubeadmControlPlane/workload-c-p       True                  10d
│ └─Machine/workload-control-plane-vhxqm                True                  10d
└─Workers
  └─MachineDeployment/workload-md-0                      True                  2m2s
    └─2 Machines...                                      True                  10d   See
workload-md-0-7dfb8598cb-hklkn, workload-md-0-7dfb8598cb-t2zzm
```

The final item to bring to your attention is the procedure to gain SSH access to the nodes in the TKG cluster.

Way back in step 1 of the UI deployment, an SSH public key was added along with the vCenter credentials. This is the public key of the user who is allowed to access the nodes on the management and workload cluster(s). To gain access, the public key owner uses the **capv** user, e.g. `capv@node_ip_address` to get onto the TKG nodes deployed on vSphere. Below is an example on how to retrieve the IP address of a worker node, and then SSH onto that node. Once on the node, the capv user can do steps such as check the status of the kubelet.

```
% kubectl get nodes -o wide
NAME                                               STATUS ROLES        AGE    VERSION
INTERNAL-IP    EXTERNAL-IP    OS-IMAGE              KERNEL-VERSION   CONTAINER-RUNTIME
tkg-mgmt-vsphere-202..225-control-plane-ks4mj Ready  control-plane 10d    v1.22.9+vmware.1
192.168.51.31    192.168.51.31 VMware Photon OS/Linux 4.19.232-4.ph3    containerd://1.5.11
tkg-mgmt-vsphere-202..225-md-0-868cb8c8b6-59fj8 Ready <none>       10d    v1.22.9+vmware.1
192.168.51.33    192.168.51.33 VMware Photon OS/Linux 4.19.232-4.ph3    containerd://1.5.11
```

```
% ssh capv@192.168.51.31
The authenticity of host '192.168.51.31 (192.168.51.31)' can't be established.
ECDSA key fingerprint is SHA256:EMTid5vSs/otAldpL2fgBQjIQUBK+7ua3m6b5FVIpcs.
Are you sure you want to continue connecting (yes/no/[fingerprint])? yes
Warning: Permanently added '192.168.51.31' (ECDSA) to the list of known hosts.
 07:56:59 up 10 days, 23:46,  0 users,  load average: 1.34, 0.78, 0.77

7 Security notice(s)
Run 'tdnf updateinfo info' to see the details.
capv@tkg-mgmt-vsphere-20220606085225-control-plane-ks4mj [ ~ ]$

capv@tkg-mgmt-vsphere-20220606085225-control-plane-ks4mj [ ~ ]$ systemctl status kubelet
● kubelet.service - kubelet: The Kubernetes Node Agent
   Loaded: loaded (/lib/systemd/system/kubelet.service; enabled; vendor preset: enabled)
  Drop-In: /usr/lib/systemd/system/kubelet.service.d
           └─10-kubeadm.conf
   Active: active (running) since Mon 2022-06-06 08:10:59 UTC; 1 weeks 3 days ago
     Docs: https://kubernetes.io/docs/home/
 Main PID: 1319 (kubelet)
    Tasks: 16 (limit: 4714)
   Memory: 84.7M
   CGroup: /system.slice/kubelet.service
           └─1319 /usr/bin/kubelet --bootstrap-kubeconfig=/etc/kubernetes/bootstrap-
kubelet.conf --kubeconfig=/etc/kubernetes/kubelet.conf
--config=/var/lib/kubelet/config.yaml
--cloud-provider=external
--container-runtime=remote
--container-runtime-endpoint=/var/run/containerd/containerd.sock
--pod-infra-container-image=projects.registry.vmware.com/tkg/pause:3.5
--tls-cipher-suites=TLS_ECDHE_ECDSA_WITH_AES_128_GCM_SHA256,
TLS_ECDHE_RSA_WITH_AES_128_GCM_SHA256,TLS_ECDHE_ECDSA_WITH_CHACHA20_POLY1305,
TLS_ECDHE_RSA_WITH_AES_256_GCM_SHA384,TLS_ECDHE_RSA_WITH_CHACHA20_POLY1305,
TLS_ECDHE_ECDSA_WITH_AES_256_GCM_SHA384
--pod-infra-container-image=projects.registry.vmware.com/tkg/pause:3.5
```

That completes our first look at the deployment of a TKG management cluster, followed by a TKG workload cluster. Similar to what we needed to do with Cluster API, an operating system / kubernetes images needed to first be uploaded as an OVA to the vSphere infrastructure and converted to a template. We also needed to have a Docker container runtime available on the host where the bootstrap kind cluster is deployed. This took a bit of setting up. However, once that was all in place and available, the management cluster could now be deployed either via the UI method or using a prepopulated configuration file. With the management cluster in place, copies of the management cluster configuration file are made. These are then edited so they can be used for deploying the workload cluster(s). Now Platform Operators can very quickly proceed with the creation of workload clusters, all via the tanzu CLI.

We have just built our first, albeit very simple, TKG management cluster and workload cluster. Later on, we will return to TKG so you can see how it integrates with external Load Balancers on vSphere, and also see how to integrate with Pinniped and Dex for Identity Management (LDAP, OIDC). The latter enables a Platform Operators to control access to the cluster, and not have to have a single *admin* account shared by all users.

The last step to demonstrate is how to remove these clusters from vSphere. To delete a workload cluster, the command is simply *tanzu cluster delete <cluster-name>*:

```
% tanzu cluster list
  NAME      NAMESPACE   STATUS    CONTROLPLANE   WORKERS   KUBERNETES        ROLES    PLAN
  workload  default     running   1/1            2/2       v1.22.9+vmware.1  <none>   dev

% tanzu cluster delete workload
Deleting workload cluster 'workload'. Are you sure? [y/N]: y
Workload cluster 'workload' is being deleted
```

To delete the management cluster, use *tanzu mc delete*.

```
% tanzu mc get
  NAME                                    NAMESPACE    STATUS    CONTROLPLANE   WORKERS   KUBERNETES
ROLES         PLAN
  tkg-mgmt-vsphere-20220606085225  tkg-system   running   1/1            1/1
v1.22.9+vmware.1  management   dev
```

Details:

```
NAME                                                                                    READY
SEVERITY   REASON   SINCE   MESSAGE
/tkg-mgmt-vsphere-20220606085225                                                        True
11d
├─ClusterInfrastructure - VSphereCluster/tkg-mgmt-vsphere-20220606085225                True
11d
├─ControlPlane - KubeadmControlPlane/tkg-mgmt-vsphere-20220606085225-control-plane True
11d
│   └─Machine/tkg-mgmt-vsphere-20220606085225-control-plane-ks4mj                       True
11d
└─Workers
  └─MachineDeployment/tkg-mgmt-vsphere-20220606085225-md-0                              True
11d
    └─Machine/tkg-mgmt-vsphere-20220606085225-md-0-868cb8c8b6-59fj8                     True
11d
```

Providers:

```
  NAMESPACE                        NAME                    TYPE
PROVIDERNAME   VERSION   WATCHNAMESPACE
  capi-kubeadm-bootstrap-system    bootstrap-kubeadm       BootstrapProvider
kubeadm        v1.0.1
  capi-kubeadm-control-plane-system  control-plane-kubeadm  ControlPlaneProvider
kubeadm        v1.0.1
  capi-system                      cluster-api             CoreProvider
cluster-api    v1.0.1
```

```
  capv-system                      infrastructure-vsphere  InfrastructureProvider
vsphere       v1.0.3
```

```
% tanzu mc delete tkg-mgmt-vsphere-20220606085225
Deleting management cluster 'tkg-mgmt-vsphere-20220606085225'. Are you sure? [y/N]: y
Verifying management cluster...
Setting up cleanup cluster...
Installing providers to cleanup cluster...
Fetching providers
Installing cert-manager Version="v1.5.3"
Waiting for cert-manager to be available...
Installing Provider="cluster-api" Version="v1.0.1" TargetNamespace="capi-system"
Installing Provider="bootstrap-kubeadm" Version="v1.0.1" TargetNamespace="capi-kubeadm-
bootstrap-system"
Installing Provider="control-plane-kubeadm" Version="v1.0.1" TargetNamespace="capi-
kubeadm-control-plane-system"
Installing Provider="infrastructure-vsphere" Version="v1.0.3" TargetNamespace="capv-
system"
Moving Cluster API objects from management cluster to cleanup cluster...
Performing move...
Discovering Cluster API objects
Moving Cluster API objects Clusters=1
Creating objects in the target cluster
Deleting objects from the source cluster
Waiting for the Cluster API objects to get ready after move...
Deleting management cluster...
Management cluster 'tkg-mgmt-vsphere-20220606085225' deleted.
Deleting the management cluster context from the kubeconfig file
'/Users/chogan/.kube/config'
warning: this removed your active context, use "kubectl config use-context" to select a
different one

Management cluster deleted!
%
```

Again, remember that you need a docker daemon / container runtime available on the system where you delete the management cluster from. This is because it once again spins up a bootstrap kind cluster to remove the management cluster. This might take a while if the kind container image needs was removed and needs to be downloaded once again.

Summary

We have now looked at three methods of deploying Kubernetes clusters onto vSphere. We saw the older *kubeadm* method, then the newer Cluster API method, before finally seeing the tanzu CLI mechanism which deploys TKG clusters onto vSphere. But there is one other product left to examine. This is vSphere with Tanzu and is possibly the best mechanism for deploying Kubernetes onto vSphere platforms. It has also been built with the vSphere administrator in mind. However, it does require an external Load Balancer provider before it can be enabled. For that reason, we will now move on to discussing networking concepts, looking at the Antrea CNI and Load Balancer providers (HA-Proxy, NSX ALB, and NSX-T) in much greater detail. Once those topics have been covered, we will return to the TKG deployment with a Load Balancer, as well as look at vSphere with Tanzu deployments.

04

Kubernetes networking & vSphere integration

In chapter 3, we saw some different techniques to deploy Kubernetes clusters. We saw how an open source product such as `MetalLB` could be used as a provider to requests for a Load Balancer type service. We also saw how both manual Cluster API deployments and TKG cluster deployments both use `kube-vip` to provide a virtual IP address which is used to make the control plane highly available. However, in production environments, Kubernetes clusters deployed on the vSphere networking stack would need to use one of the supported external Load Balancers. In this section, we are going to look at all two types of Load Balancer providers, NSX ALB and HA-Proxy, which work with Kubernetes clusters that are deployed on vSphere networking. Note that the HA-Proxy is only supported on vSphere with Tanzu – it is not supported with stand-alone TKG (multi-cloud version). Guidance is provided on creating an NSX ALB (which can be used for both TKG and vSphere with Tanzu) and guidance on how to deploy the HA-Proxy. In this chapter, we will not discuss using NSX-T which can also be used to provide a networking stack for vSphere with Tanzu. NSX-T provides a Load Balancing service through the NSX Edge, so there is no need to deploy an external provider with NSX-T. Using NSX-T with vSphere with Tanzu will be reviewed later in the book. This chapter begins where container networking left off in chapter 1. We now look at Pod and node networking in Kubernetes.

	vSphere with Tanzu	TKG
HA-Proxy Load Balancer	Supported	Not Supported
NSX Advanced Load Balancer	Supported	Supported
NSX-T Load Balancer	Supported	Supported

Table 1: Supported Load Balancer Providers

Container Network Interface (CNI)

Kubernetes networking is handled by a plugin known as the Container Network Interface, or CNI for short. Two CNIs are supported on TKG clusters – Calico and VMware's own Antrea. The Antrea CNI provides networking and security services for a Kubernetes cluster. It is based on the Open vSwitch project (OVS), which is used as the networking data plane to provide network overlays for Pod-to-Pod communication.

Antrea CNI includes significant network security policies. While Kubernetes does have in-built network policies, Antrea builds on those native network policies to provide more fine-grained network policies of its own. It has a ClusterNetworkPolicy which, as the name implies, operates at the Kubernetes cluster level. It also has NetworkPolicy which limits the scope of a policy to a Kubernetes namespace. The ClusterNetworkPolicy can be thought of as a means for a Kubernetes Cluster Admin to create a security policy for the cluster as a whole. The NetworkPolicy can be thought of as a means for a developer to secure applications in a particular namespace. How these network policies can be used to secure traffic between Pods in the same workload, and between workloads in the same cluster, are beyond the scope of this book however.

Troubleshooting Pod to Pod networking, and how Pods communicate to external entities outside the Kubernetes cluster, may not necessarily be the remit of the vSphere administrator. However, since Pods communicate to the outside world via the network interfaces of the Kubernetes nodes on which they run, vSphere administrators may be expected to assist with networking design or troubleshooting when Kubernetes is running on a vSphere platform. Therefore, an appreciation of how Kubernetes networking works is useful to understand.

Each time a Pod is created on a Kubernetes worker node, it creates what is known as a network namespace on the node. Just like we saw in chapter 1 when container networking was examined, a network namespace can be considered a logical copy of the network stack taken from the node on which it runs. Thus, each network namespace gets its own range of IP addresses, network interfaces, routing tables, and so on. Multiple containers that are created within the same Pod share the same network namespace.

In this example, I have created a simple busybox Pod (single container) on one of my TKG worker nodes. To examine the networking details of a Pod network namespace, the following command can be run after *exec*'ing a shell session onto the Pod/container. You can see the container IP address (192.168.1.3) listed. 192.168.0.0/16 is the default Pods network CIDR that the system creates when deploying TKG cluster using the Antrea CNI plugin.

```
/ # ip a
1: lo: <LOOPBACK,UP,LOWER_UP> mtu 65536 qdisc noqueue qlen 1000
    link/loopback 00:00:00:00:00:00 brd 00:00:00:00:00:00
    inet 127.0.0.1/8 scope host lo
      valid_lft forever preferred_lft forever
    inet6 ::1/128 scope host
      valid_lft forever preferred_lft forever
3: eth0@if7: <BROADCAST,MULTICAST,UP,LOWER_UP,M-DOWN> mtu 1450 qdisc noqueue
    link/ether f6:38:e6:86:d7:69 brd ff:ff:ff:ff:ff:ff
    inet 192.168.1.3/24 brd 192.168.1.255 scope global eth0
      valid_lft forever preferred_lft forever
    inet6 fe80::f438:e6ff:fe86:d769/64 scope link
      valid_lft forever preferred_lft forever
```

The default gateway on the Pod is also query-able. We will see how this relates to the Antrea CNI in a moment.

```
/ # netstat -rn
Kernel IP routing table
Destination     Gateway         Genmask         Flags  MSS Window  irtt Iface
0.0.0.0         192.168.1.1     0.0.0.0         UG       0 0          0 eth0
192.168.5.0     0.0.0.0         255.255.255.0   U        0 0          0 eth0
```

We now switch from the Pod context and into the context of the Kubernetes worker node. This allows us to find the network namespace for the Pod. Note the **cni-** labels in the command below, meaning that network namespaces are being handled by the CNI driver, in this case Antrea. It looks like there is more than one network namespace created in this example, possibly due to other Pods having been deployed. You may observe a number of namespace in your cluster.

```
$ ip netns list
cni-c45cf45b-cff1-f78e-0679-6b3ca1df357e (id: 1)
cni-5d4cf301-70dc-7f21-312c-518fe09d7085 (id: 0)
```

To detect the latest network namespace, which would have been the one created for the busybox Pod, you can list them as follows to see the creation dates. One date should coincide with the Pod creation time. If there are no new networks created since the Pod was created, you may be on the incorrect worker node. Check with *kubectl describe pod* to be sure.

```
$ ls -lt /var/run/netns
total 0
-r--r--r-- 1 root root 0 May 10 10:47 cni-c45cf45b-cff1-f78e-0679-6b3ca1df357e
-r--r--r-- 1 root root 0 May 10 10:30 cni-5d4cf301-70dc-7f21-312c-518fe09d7085
```

Identify the network namespace that corresponds to the Pod. To examine the networking details of a Pod network namespace, the following command can be run. You can see the container IP address (192.168.1.3) listed once again. Note how it corresponds to the IP address reported from within the container/Pod in the previous step.

```
$ sudo ip netns exec cni-c45cf45b-cff1-f78e-0679-6b3ca1df357e ip a
1: lo: <LOOPBACK,UP,LOWER_UP> mtu 65536 qdisc noqueue state UNKNOWN group default qlen
1000
    link/loopback 00:00:00:00:00:00 brd 00:00:00:00:00:00
    inet 127.0.0.1/8 scope host lo
      valid_lft forever preferred_lft forever
    inet6 ::1/128 scope host
      valid_lft forever preferred_lft forever
3: eth0@if7: <BROADCAST,MULTICAST,UP,LOWER_UP> mtu 1450 qdisc noqueue state UP group
default
    link/ether 6e:e6:16:77:94:a6 brd ff:ff:ff:ff:ff:ff link-netnsid 0
    inet 192.168.1.3/24 brd 192.168.1.255 scope global eth0
      valid_lft forever preferred_lft forever
    inet6 fe80::6ce6:16ff:fe77:94a6/64 scope link
      valid_lft forever preferred_lft forever
```

Note that this is the Pod network namespace link. This link from the Pod is connected to an Open vSwitch (OVS) bridge created by the Antrea CNI. To find the other end of the network that is connected to the OVS bridge, we can *grep* for the 7 taken from the interface eth0@if7. As shown in the output below, it is referencing the same network namespace that we saw earlier. This is the **veth** pair connecting the Pod to the OVS bridge. The CNI (in this case the Antrea Agent) creates a veth pair for each Pod, with one end being in the Pod's network namespace and the other connected to the OVS bridge.

```
$ ip link | grep -A1 ^7
7: busybox1-9bdd44@if3: <BROADCAST,MULTICAST,UP,LOWER_UP> mtu 1450 qdisc noqueue master
ovs-system state UP mode DEFAULT group default
    link/ether 7a:42:d4:b4:97:bd brd ff:ff:ff:ff:ff:ff link-netns cni-c45cf45b-cff1-f78e-
0679-6b3ca1df357e
```

```
$ ip a show busybox1-9bdd44
7: busybox1-9bdd44e@if3: <BROADCAST,MULTICAST,UP,LOWER_UP> mtu 1450 qdisc noqueue master
ovs-system state UP group default
    link/ether 7a:42:d4:b4:97:bd brd ff:ff:ff:ff:ff:ff link-netns cni-c45cf45b-cff1-f78e-
0679-6b3ca1df357e
    inet6 fe80::7842:d4ff:feb4:97bd/64 scope link
      valid_lft forever preferred_lft forever
```

Another interesting interface on the worker node is the Antrea gateway. The Antrea gateway matches the default gateway that we saw on the Pod/container previously.

```
$ ip a show antrea-gw0
5: antrea-gw0: <BROADCAST,MULTICAST,UP,LOWER_UP> mtu 1450 qdisc noqueue state UNKNOWN
group default qlen 1000
    link/ether 82:0f:0d:0d:7f:70 brd ff:ff:ff:ff:ff:ff
    inet 192.168.1.1/24 brd 192.168.1.255 scope global antrea-gw0
      valid_lft forever preferred_lft forever
    inet6 fe80::800f:dff:fe0d:7f70/64 scope link
      valid_lft forever preferred_lft forever
```

The following image shows how all of this ties together from within the context of a Pod/container running on a Kubernetes worker node using the Antrea CNI. Consider this worker node as a virtual machine running a guest operation

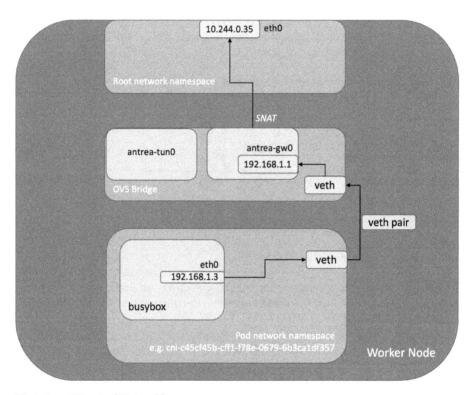

Figure 29: Antrea CNI – Pod Networking

I drew the antrea-tun0 interface as well, even though it is not being used in the above example. This tunnel is used to for Pod-to-Pod communication across TKG worker nodes in the same cluster. It should be quite obvious that for external communication outside of the cluster, Pod traffic is forwarded by the bridge to the gateway and then out on the node interface.

Let's look at Pod to Pod communication next. In the first example, we have a multiple Pods on the same TKG node. In this case, communication between the Pods travels across the veth pairs.

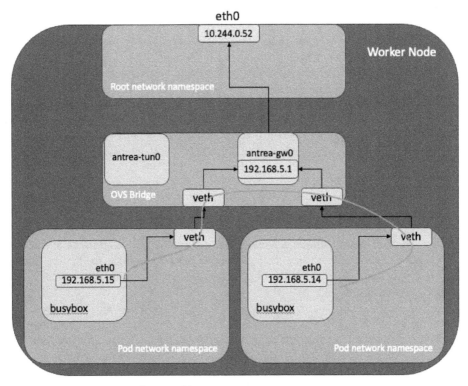

Figure 30: Antrea CNI – Intra-Pod Networking

This final example shows the communication path between Pods that are located on different Kubernetes nodes. In this case, the tunnel on the source node is used to encapsulate and forward traffic from the source Pod to the destination node. Once the traffic arrives on the bridge at the destination node, it is decapsulated and forwarded to the destination Pod on that node.

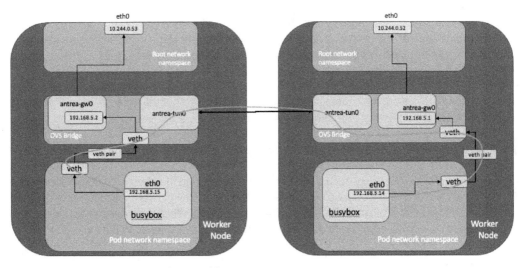

Figure 31: Antrea CNI – Inter-Pod Networking

While this has been far from a complete deep-dive into the workings of a CNI, it has hopefully provided some understanding of Pod networking within Kubernetes. For vSphere administrators, some appreciation of how networking works at the Kubernetes layer is important to understand before packets arrive at the virtual networking layers in vSphere.

At this point, we should mention one additional CNI, the NSX Container Plugin, or NCP for short. NCP provides integration between NSX-T and Kubernetes. NCP monitors and manages networking resources for containers. NSX-T will automatically build networking infrastructure as required by Kubernetes objects. Later, we shall see how it dynamically creates tier-1 gateways, network segments, load balancers, etc. More on this later when NSX-T with vSphere with Tanzu is examined in more detail.

Load Balancer Providers

Let's now move onto something that has come up time and again in this book, the Load Balancer type Service. We mentioned that there is no built in Load Balancer provider in vSphere, and that these have to be manually deployed. In the next couple of sections, options to provide Load Balancer Services are discussed.

One thing to highlight is that there can be some confusing terminology around Load Balancers. One often hears of the Load Balancer providing Virtual IP Address, often referred to VIPs. In other references, one comes across the term FrontEnd network and more commonly the term Load Balancer network. In essence, these are all referring to the same thing.

Setup Steps - HA-Proxy Load Balancer

As mentioned at the beginning of this chapter, the HA-Proxy Load Balancer is only supported with vSphere with Tanzu. It is not supported with TKG. vSphere with Tanzu can use the HA-Proxy appliance to provide virtual IP addresses (VIPs) to its management cluster control plane (referred to as the Supervisor Cluster), as well as the TKG clusters provisioned by the TKG service on the management cluster. It also can provide Load Balancer IP addresses to any Load Balancer services provisioned on the cluster. In the following sections, the steps involved in deploying an HA-Proxy for vSphere with Tanzu are described.

Getting the network configuration correct is the most difficult part of a HA-Proxy deployment. The following table provides some guidance on how to correctly map out the network requirements for a vSphere with Tanzu deployment using the HA-Proxy.

There are three networks to consider with the deployment of the HA-Proxy. The first is the management network, and is where communication between vCenter Server, the Supervisor Cluster nodes and the HA-Proxy occurs. The second is the workload network. Both the Supervisor Cluster nodes and any TKG workload clusters are deployed to this network. The final network is the virtual IP (VIP) network also referred to as the frontend network. This is used to get virtual IP addresses for the control planes for each of the clusters, as well as the Load Balancer IP Address for Load Balancer services.

Management Network	Workload Network	FrontEnd Network
Requires a contiguous range of **5** IP addresses for Supervisor Cluster nodes, as well as unique IP address for HA-Proxy	Requires a range of **N** IP addresses, provided in CIDR format, as well as unique IP address for HA-Proxy	Requires a range of **N** IP addresses, provided in CIDR format
Consumed by the Supervisor Cluster nodes in vSphere with Tanzu, and HA-Proxy	Consumed by the Supervisor Cluster nodes in vSphere with Tanzu, TKG cluster nodes and HA-Proxy	Consumed by the Supervisor Cluster control plane in vSphere with Tanzu and TKG cluster control plane, as well as Load Balancer type services
FQDN, IP address and gateway for HA-Proxy on management network must be specified during HA-Proxy deployment	IP address and gateway for HA-Proxy on workload network must be specified during deployment	Range must be specified during HA-Proxy setup

Table 2: Network Requirements for vSphere with Tanzu

Be aware that the HA-Proxy can be provisioned in 2 modes, known as 2-NIC mode and 3-NIC mode respectively. The former simply means that the workload network used by the TKG clusters shares the same network as the VIP addresses used for control planes and Load Balancer services. The latter method implies that the workload network and the VIP networks are distinct, separate networks. One could visualise the 2-NIC mode as follows.

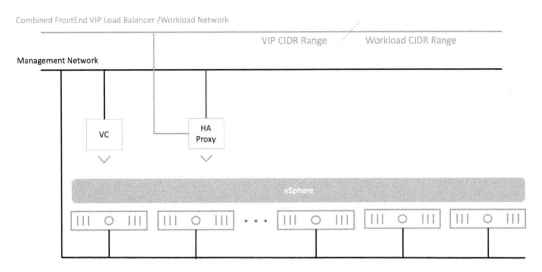

Figure 32: HA-Proxy – 2 NIC setup

Similarly, one could visualise the 3-NIC mode as follows.

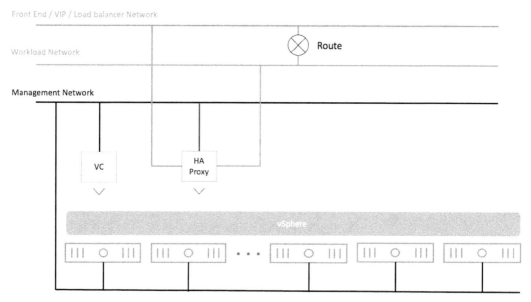

Figure 33: HA-Proxy – 3 NIC setup

As shown in the 3 NIC configuration, there does need to be a route from the workload network to the front-end/VIP network. This is because requests to the VIP addresses need to be routed to the appropriate service running on the Kubernetes nodes on the workload network. Now that we understand the difference between the 2-NIC and 3-NIC approach, lets proceed with the deployment of the HA-Proxy. The latest version of the HA-Proxy (v0.2.0) at the time of writing is available to download from GitHub at https://github.com/haproxytech/vmware-haproxy/blob/main/README.md. Download and deploy the HA-Proxy onto the vSphere environment where you plan to enable vSphere with Tanzu.

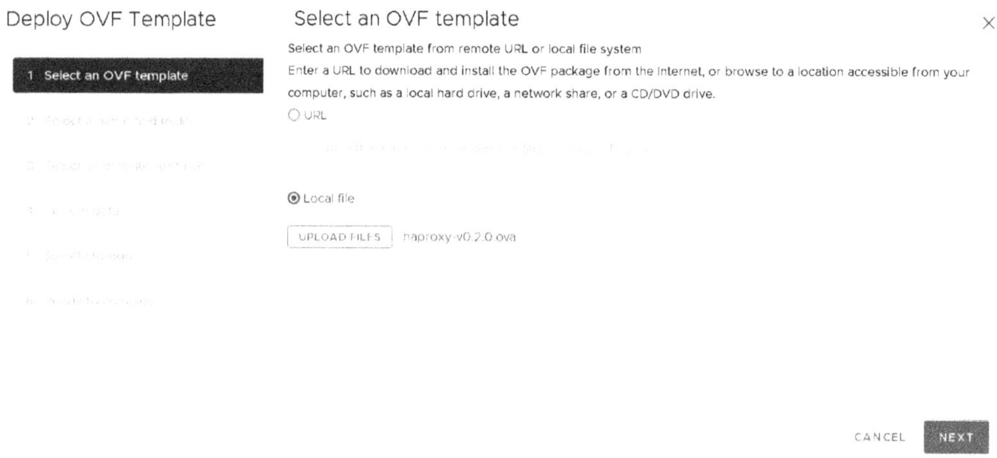

Figure 34: HA-Proxy – OVF Deployment

The rest of the OVF deployment screens should not need much explanation. They cover areas such as where the OVA should be deployed, and which vSphere datastore should be used to provision the HA-Proxy appliance to. It is only once the deployment moves onto the Configuration window that some thought needs to be given to the networking setup. At this point, the administrator is asked to select between the 2-NIC and 3-NIC configuration. The default is to deploy the HA-Proxy with 2 NICs.

Figure 35: HA-Proxy – 2-NIC Configuration

As per the description field, even with the 2-NIC configuration selected, options related to a frontend network continue to appear in the deployment wizard. These should be ignored since Load Balancer IP addresses are assigned on the workload network. For completeness' sake, here is the description from the 3-NIC mode, which includes a dedicated frontend network.

Figure 36: HA-Proxy – 3-NIC Configuration

Once the storage section is completed, the main configuration around selecting networks is displayed. The first step is to select the appropriate portgroups for the Management, Workload and Frontend networks. Note that if you opted for a 2-NIC setup, the Frontend destination network here is irrelevant. If you opted for the 3-NIC setup, you would need to ensure that there is a route from the frontend network to the workload network.

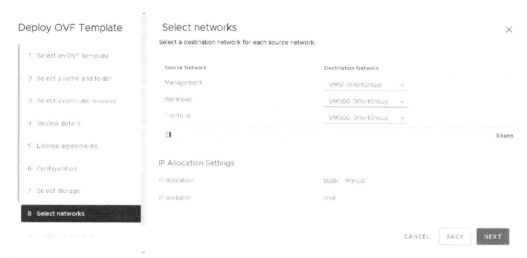

Figure 37: HA-Proxy – Network Configuration

After selecting the appropriate portgroups for the various HA-Proxy, clicking next will take you to the networking configuration screens. Here, the first step is to provide a root password and ensure that SSH is enabled. You will need to be able to SSH onto the appliance during the setup of vSphere with Tanzu to retrieve the CA from the appliance. It is also possible to provide your own certificates at this point if required.

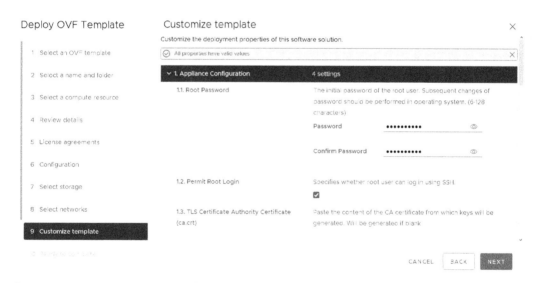

Figure 38: HA-Proxy – Appliance Configuration

A fully qualified domain name for the ha-proxy will need to be provided (default `haproxy.local`). A list of comma-separated list of DNS servers must also be provided so the HA-Proxy hostname can be resolved. Finally, you will need to provide an IP address for the HA-Proxy on the management network as well as specify a gateway for the management network.

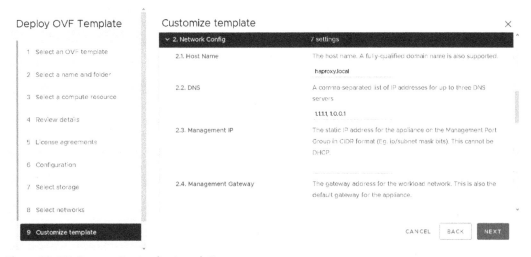

Figure 39: HA-Proxy – Customize template

This brings us to the workload network configuration for the HA-Proxy. The HA-Proxy will have an interface on both the management network and the workload network. The HA-Proxy will need an IP address on this network, as well as a gateway. It is also possible to specify additional workload networks at this point, but these must also be reachable via the workload gateway.

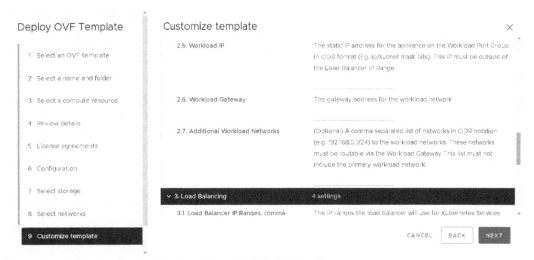

Figure 40: HA-Proxy – Customize Template – Workload Network

The final network configuration is the Load Balancer, VIP network, or Frontend network – all terms to mean the same thing in this context. As the first field mentions, this is the range of IP addresses that will be used to assign a virtual IP address to the various control planes on the Supervisor Cluster and TKG clusters to achieve availability. It is also the range of IP addresses that will be used to provide IP address to Load Balancer type services. The other fields here are the Dataplane API Management Port, which is basically saying that this is the port that vSphere with Tanzu will use to access the HA-Proxy. The only other fields are the HA-Proxy username and password. These will also need to be provided to vSphere with Tanzu when it is configured later.

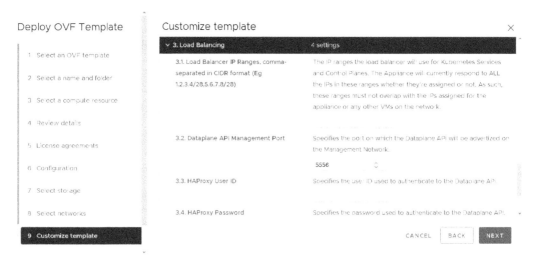

Figure 41: HA-Proxy – Customize Template – Load Balancing

Note that for all 3 networks, the IP requested were requested in CIDR format. Thus, it is very important to verify that the CIDR format that you place in the configuration matches the desired range that you wish to use. While some CIDR formats are easy to understand, e.g., /24, other ranges are not quite so easy. This is essential if you are planning on using the same network for both workload and frontend IP address ranges, but with different CIDRs. I like to use an IP address calculator to ensure the CIDR I use matches the range I want to assign to a network. My preference is the converter found here - https://www.ipaddressguide.com/cidr - but feel free to use any of the other calculators that are available.

That essentially completes the setup of the HA-Proxy.

Here is a sample review screen from a deployment of the HA-Proxy. I am showing this simply to highlight the use of CIDR format in the HA-Proxy configuration. This is a 2-NIC configuration where the Load Balancer IP addresses are on the same network as the management network. Thus, the network is carved up, allocating 16 addresses only to the Load Balancer IP range using a /28 CIDR. However, the full range of the network is only /26 (64 IP addresses), so the workload IP address allocated to the HA-Proxy must include the /26 CIDR as well. Finally, the management IP address for the HA-Proxy is on a full /24 network, so the management IP must have a /24 CIDR. You can see how this gets confusing. Therefore, I would urge you to use an IP Address/CIDR calculator. You may choose a range of IP addresses that do not match a CIDR.

Figure 42: HA-Proxy – Ready to Complete

Verifying the HA-Proxy deployment

There are several ways to verify that the deployment of a HA-Proxy appliance was successful. Now that the HA-Proxy is providing both Control Plane VIPs and Load Balancer IP addresses, it should respond to pings on those IP address ranges. I like to use a freely available tool called `angryip` - https://angryip.org/ - which will send a ping to a range of IP addresses. If the frontend network is working, all addresses should respond to the ping request.

Another verification test is to point a browser at the FQDN of the HA-Proxy on the Dataplane API Management Port, default port 5556. You should receive a login window. Login with the credentials provided during the deployment of the HA-Proxy. If you see the following after logging in, the HA-Proxy is working as expected and you should be all set to deploy vSphere with Tanzu using the HA-Proxy to provide control plane VIPs and IP addresses for Load Balancer services.

Figure 43: HA-Proxy – JSON Test

Setup Steps - NSX Advanced Load Balancer (ALB)

Another option for providing control plane IP addresses and Load Balancer services in vSphere with Tanzu is the NSX Advanced Load Balancer (ALB for short), formerly the Avi Vantage product. Once again, this can provide load balancer/front-end IP addresses to the Supervisor Cluster and the TKG clusters. In the following sections, the steps involved in deploying an NSX ALB are described. The appliance is available for download via the Customer Connect portal. Instructions on how to download it can be found in the following VMware Knowledgebase Article https://kb.vmware.com/s/article/82049. In this example, I am using NSX ALB OVA version 21.1.4-2p3 which has a release date of April 2022.

The one thing to note is that the NSX ALB controller requires considerably more resources than the HA-Proxy appliance. The HA-Proxy requires 2 CPUs, 4GB Memory and a 20GB disk. The NSX ALB requires 8 CPUs, 24GB Memory and a 128GB disk. Note also that the NSX ALB provisions additional appliances known as Service Engine virtual machines to run the virtual services, such as a Load Balancer. These Service Engines are a little more lightweight, with each Service Engine requiring 1 CPU, 2GB Memory and a 15GB disk. Therefore is it important to plan your resource management correctly if you plan to use an NSX ALB.

When the NSX ALB receives a request to create a Load Balancer virtual service, it automatically provisions Service Engine virtual machines. These connect to the workload network and handle the routing of traffic from the virtual IP address to the correct endpoints, such as control plane nodes or Kubernetes Pods.

NSX ALB OVA Deployment

The first step is to locate the downloaded OVF template for the NSX ALB. It usually has a name of controller plus version number, as shown below.

Figure 44: NSX ALB – OVF Deployment

The default virtual machine name for the NSX ALB is `controller`. I have not changed it in this example, but you can do so if you wish. The only other step is to select a location within the vSphere inventory to deploy the appliance.

Figure 45: NSX ALB – Select a name and folder

The 'Review details' screen provides some information about the NSX ALB (albeit it continues to be referred to as the Avi Cloud Controller). Note the size on disk field of 128 GB, which is much larger than the HA-Proxy appliance as mentioned.

Figure 46: NSX ALB – Review details

This brings us to the storage selection. As I have a vSAN available, I am going to choose that along with the appropriate policy. vSAN is a hyperconverged infrastructure solution from VMware. Your storage selection may differ from this, and that is fine. Choose an available storage solution from your infrastructure.

Figure 47: NSX ALB – Select storage

The NSX ALB needs to be able to communicate to the vSphere with Tanzu Supervisor Cluster. Thus it is important that the network chosen as the source management network on which to deploy the NSX ALB is one which is used by other management components in your infrastructure.

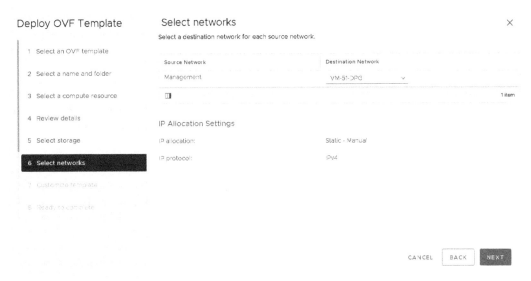

Figure 48: NSX ALB – Select Management Network

We now arrive at the 'Customize template' section. Here is where the main configuration information about the NSX ALB appliance is provided. Information required at this point include a static IP Address on the management network, a subnet mask, a default gateway and especially important, an SSH login authentication key for the user that wishes to securely login to the NSX ALB appliance after deployment. Note that there is no DNS configuration. This will take place after the appliance is online, and additional configuration steps are implemented.

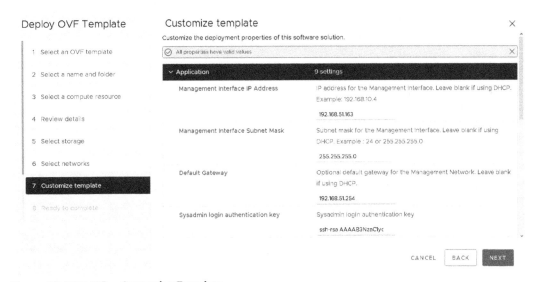

Figure 49: NSX ALB – Customize Template

There are additional fields in this section related to NSX ALB to NSX-T integration, but that procedure is beyond the scope of this book. In this example deployment, these fields are not populated.

Figure 50: NSX ALB – Customize Template – NSX-T

Note that there are also no credentials provided at this point. The credentials for the admin user are provided when the NSX ALB user interface is accessed, and additional configuration steps are implemented, as highlighted for DNS.

The final screen in the NSX ALB OVA deployment is a review screen. Here you can check your deployment details. If everything is correct, click the 'Finish' button.

Figure 51: NSX ALB – Ready to Complete

Once the OVA has been successfully deployed, it can be powered on. Give it a few moments to complete configuring and come online. At that stage, you can open a web browser to the FQDN or IP address of the appliance. Once logged in, the configuration of the NSX ALB can commence. The NSX ALB relies heavily on a component called the Service Engine. It is the Service Engine that takes care of providing the Load Balancer service and can be configured to provide a route from the workload network to the VIP network for the Kubernetes control plane, if one does not already exist. Service Engines are deployed automatically as virtual machines on the vSphere infrastructure, and are connected to both the management network and the VIP network. The Service Engines implement virtual services for Kubernetes. Let's look at the NSX ALB configuration steps in more detail next.

NSX ALB Configuration

Once we have logged into the NSX ALB UI, several configuration tasks need to be implemented in the Load Balancer before it can be used by Workload Management for vSphere with Tanzu. These tasks can be summarized as follows:

- Set the Cloud to VMware vCenter/vSphere ESX
- Modify the Default-Cloud to provide vCenter login details
- Select the vSphere Datacenter in the Default-Cloud
- Define the management network for the Service Engines in the Default-Cloud
- Configure the Service Engine Group if necessary
- Configure the VIP and SE Networks
- Enable Basic Authentication
- Create a Self-Signed SSL/TLS Certificate, used when Workload Management is enabled
- Export the Self-Signed SSL/TLS Certificate, as it is required by vSphere with Tanzu
- Install the License
- Create a new IPAM Profile for assigning VIPs to Virtual Services
- Add new IPAM Profile to Default-Cloud

These steps are now examined in detail.

When the login screen first appears, you are prompted to provide the password for the admin user. This passwords requires confirmation. There is also an option to provide an email address. Be aware that this page can take a number of minutes to come online after initial deployment.

VMware NSX ALB (Avi)
CREATE ACCOUNT

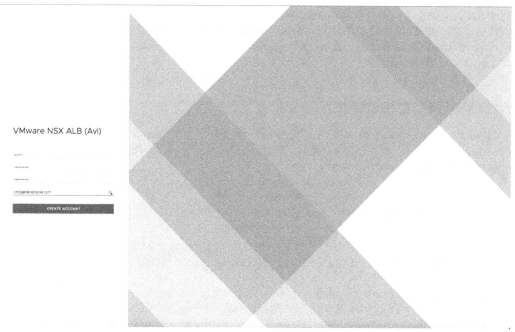

Figure 52: NSX ALB – Initial Login

The welcome page requests information about a passphrase. This must also be confirmed. You can now optionally provide DNS details. However, optionally is probably not highlighting the importance of this setting. If your vCenter Server and ESXi hosts are already in DNS, it is a very good idea to include the DNS resolvers here. If vCenter returns fully qualified domain names (FQDNs) of the ESXi hosts, which it will when the NSX ALB is looking to deploy to Service Engine components, it is important that the NSX ALB is able to resolve these names so it can successfully communicate to those ESXi hosts.

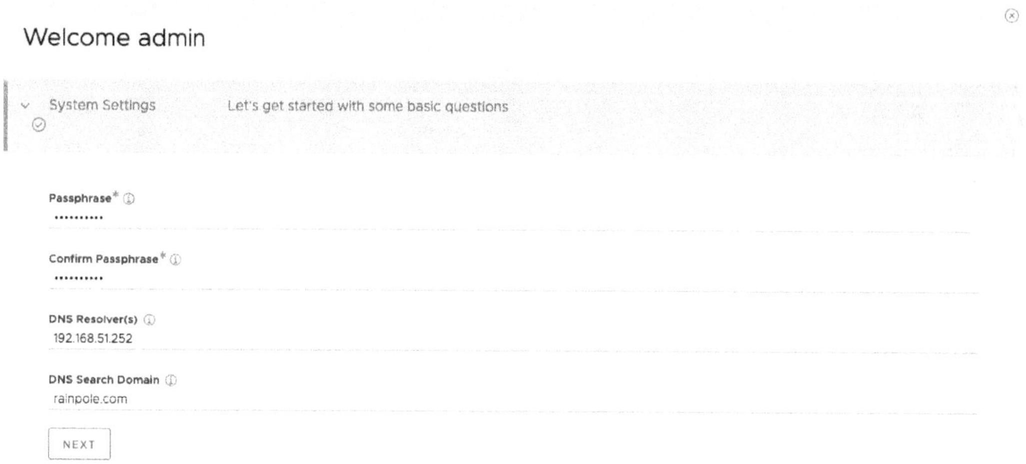

Welcome admin
System Settings
Let's get started with some basic questions
Passphrase*
Confirm Passphrase*
DNS Resolver(s)
192.168.51.252
DNS Search Domain
rainpole.com
NEXT

Figure 53: NSX ALB – System Settings

There are some additional pages on the welcome section that can be modified. You can setup email (SMTP) and some multi-tenancy settings to control the IP route domain and the placement of Service Engines. For the purposes of our setup, these can be left at the default.

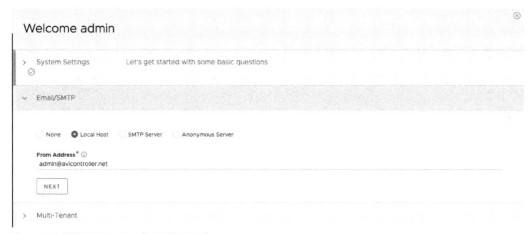

Figure 54: NSX ALB – Email/SMTP Settings

IMPORTANT: At the bottom of the Multi-Tenant window, there is a check-box to `Setup Cloud after 'Save'`. Check this option to go directly to the Default-Cloud configuration.

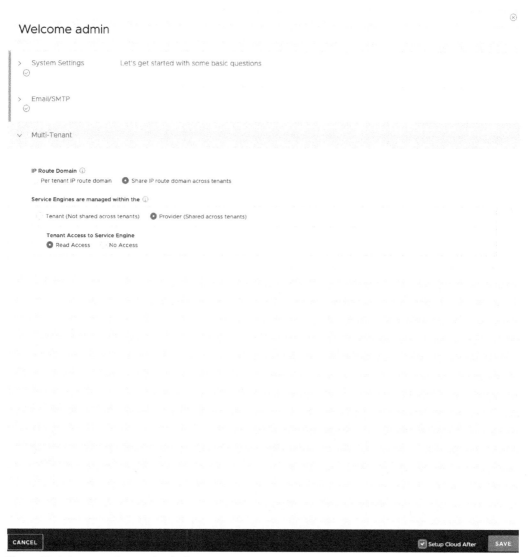

Figure 55: NSX ALB – Setup Cloud After

After clicking on 'Save', the UI will move to the **Infrastructure > Clouds** view, and the Default-Cloud should be visible. Note that there is currently no orchestrator. On the right hand side of the screen, there are a number of icons. The icon which looks like a cog/gear allows you to select the orchestrator type. Click on this icon.

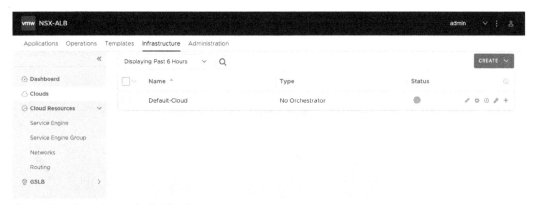

Figure 56: NSX ALB – Default-Cloud

From the list of available clouds types, choose VMware vCenter/vSphere ESX.

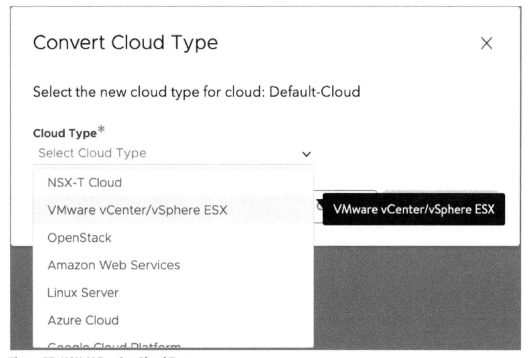

Figure 57: NSX ALB – Set Cloud Type

Once this is selected, click on 'Yes, Continue'. The next step is to edit the Default-Cloud and add our vCenter Server / vSphere information to the Default-Cloud. To edit the settings, click on the icon which looks like a pencil.

The first tab in the Default-Cloud is the Infrastructure tab. In here, details about the vCenter Server, including its IP address and credentials may be added. Don't worry about the IPAM settings for the moment. We have not created an IPAM. Later on in the process, this needs to be done and then we will return to the Default-Cloud and make the relevant updates.

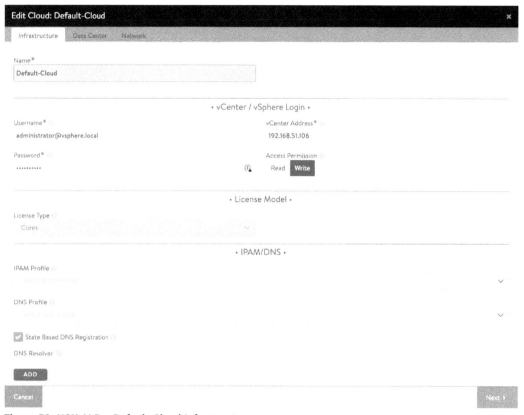

Figure 58: NSX ALB – Default-Cloud Infrastructure

After adding information about the vCenter Server, click on the 'Next' button in the lower right-hand corner to move to the Data Center tab. The only required configuration step in this tab is to select the correct Data Center from the drop-down list of Data Centers discovered on the vCenter Server selected previously

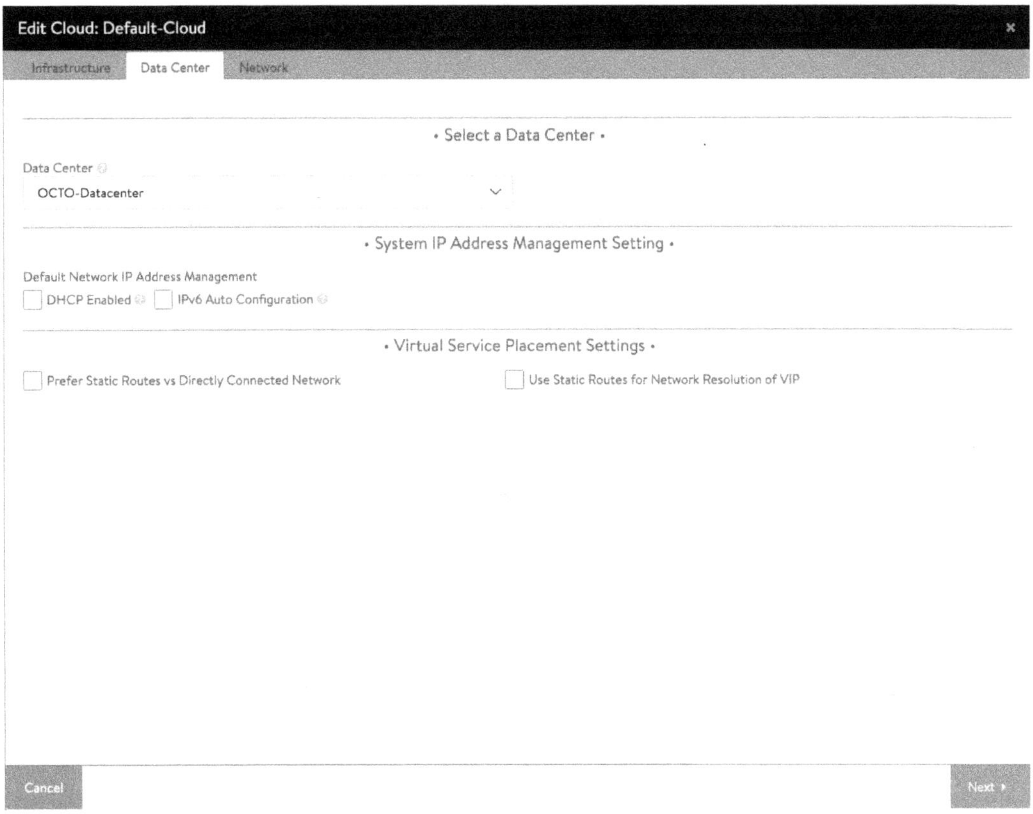

Figure 59: NSX ALB – Default-Cloud Data Center

Prefer Static Routes vs Directly Connect Network in the Virtual Service Placement Settings is left unchecked in this deployment. This is because the Service Engines network interfaces will be plumbed directly onto the management network. If for some reason you do not want to plumb the Service Engines directly onto the management network, but the management network is accessible over layer 3 (routing), then it is still possible to deploy the Service Engines with a static route. Such a step is not necessary in this setup as this configuration connects the SEs directly to the management network. Static Routes for Network Resolution of VIP is unused in vSphere with Tanzu.

Note: The management network must allow communication between the NSX ALB controller and the vSphere environment and vSphere with Tanzu Supervisor Cluster. If there is a communication issue, the Default-Cloud status will report that it cannot communicate to vSphere, and this will prevent the successful deployment of Service Engines onto the vSphere infrastructure. The Default-Cloud status should report this as an issue, however.

After clicking next to move to the Network tab, the following is displayed. Here, the management network for the Service Engines must be selected along with the Service Engine Group template.

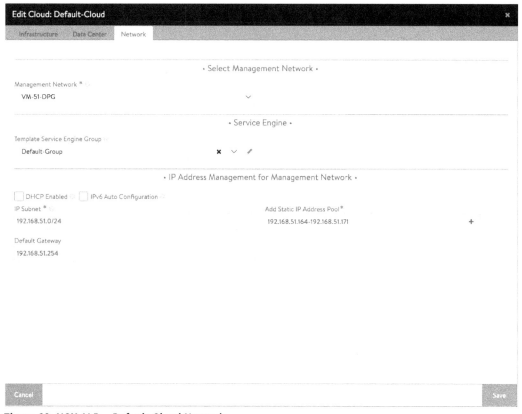

Figure 60: NSX ALB – Default-Cloud Network

The Service Engine Group defines the size of Service Engines, where they should be placed in the vSphere infrastructure, and how to make them highly available. Details regarding the range of IP addresses that are available to Service Engines are added here so that they can be plumbed up onto the management network. An existing Service Engine Group template called Default-Group may be chosen for the Service Engines. In the example here, a static address range is chosen though DHCP is another option, if it is available on the management network. Any virtual services created on the NSX ALB, such as those that will provide Load Balancer services, will use Service Engines from the default SE group.

Save the management network settings for the Service Engines to complete the configuration of the Default-Cloud. After a moment, the status of the Default-Cloud should flip from yellow to green.

Figure 61: NSX ALB – Default-Cloud Status

By clicking on the green circle, any issues with reaching any of the ESXi hosts in the Data Center are reported.

The next major task on our list is complete the network configuration, particularly the configuration of the network that is to be used for the Virtual IP (VIP) network. This is often referred to as the Data network in some of the official documentation. The Service Engines connect to the VIP network. In the menu bar on the left hand side, under Cloud Resources, choose Networks. The Service Engine management network that was configured in the Default-Cloud should already be a visible network. In order for the NSX ALB (or specifically, for the Service Engines) to be able to provide virtual IP addresses for control planes and load balancer service types, select the appropriate port group from the list of port groups in the network view. This second interface of the Service Engine connects to the VIP network. On the right hand side of this network is a pencil icon that allows the network to be edited. Click on this to launch the wizard to define the correct network for VIPs.

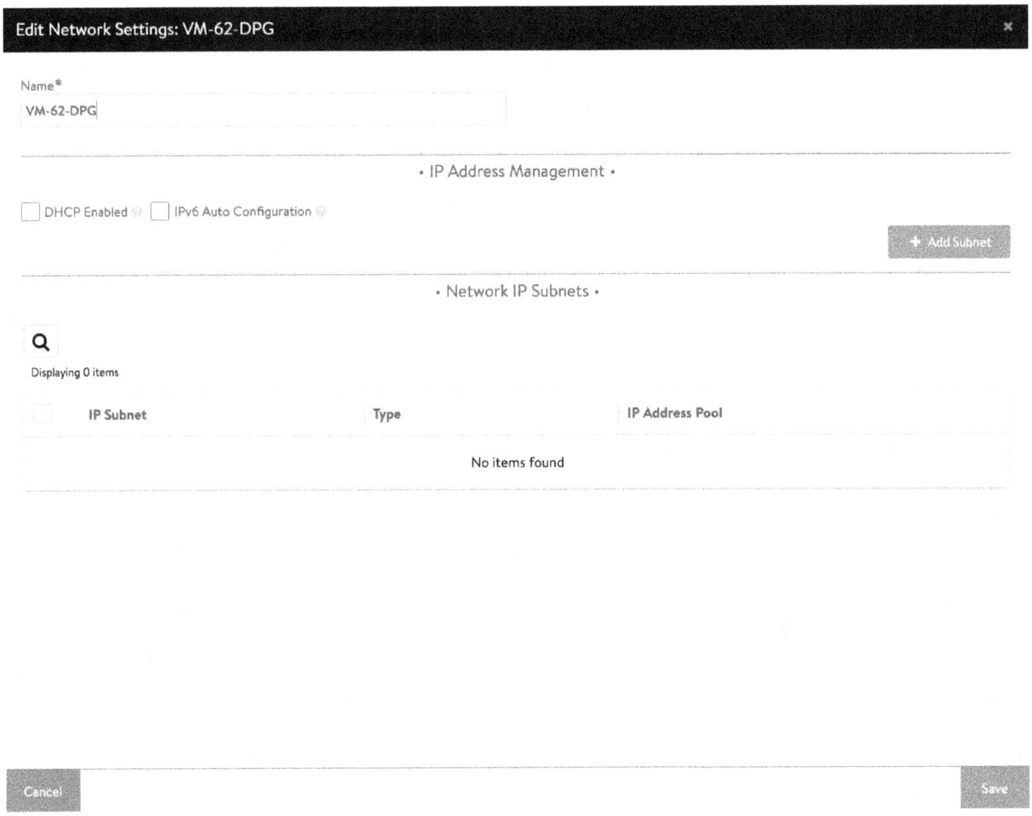

Edit Network Settings: VM-62-DPG   ✕

Name*

VM-62-DPG

· IP Address Management ·

☐ DHCP Enabled   ☐ IPv6 Auto Configuration

➕ Add Subnet

· Network IP Subnets ·

🔍

Displaying 0 items

☐	IP Subnet	Type	IP Address Pool
		No items found	

Cancel   Save

Figure 62: NSX ALB – SE/VIP Network Setup

Next, under IP Address Management, click on the '+ Add Subnet' button. This will allow a range of addresses to be specified for VIPs. Note that this can be set for both Service Engines and VIPs. For more complex network setup, a network can be allocated to just Service Engines or to just VIPs. Note in the example below that I have chosen both Service Engines and VIPs so the SE and load balancer network is shared. Next, provide the IP subnet, along with the range of IP addresses. In this example, 16 addresses are selected.

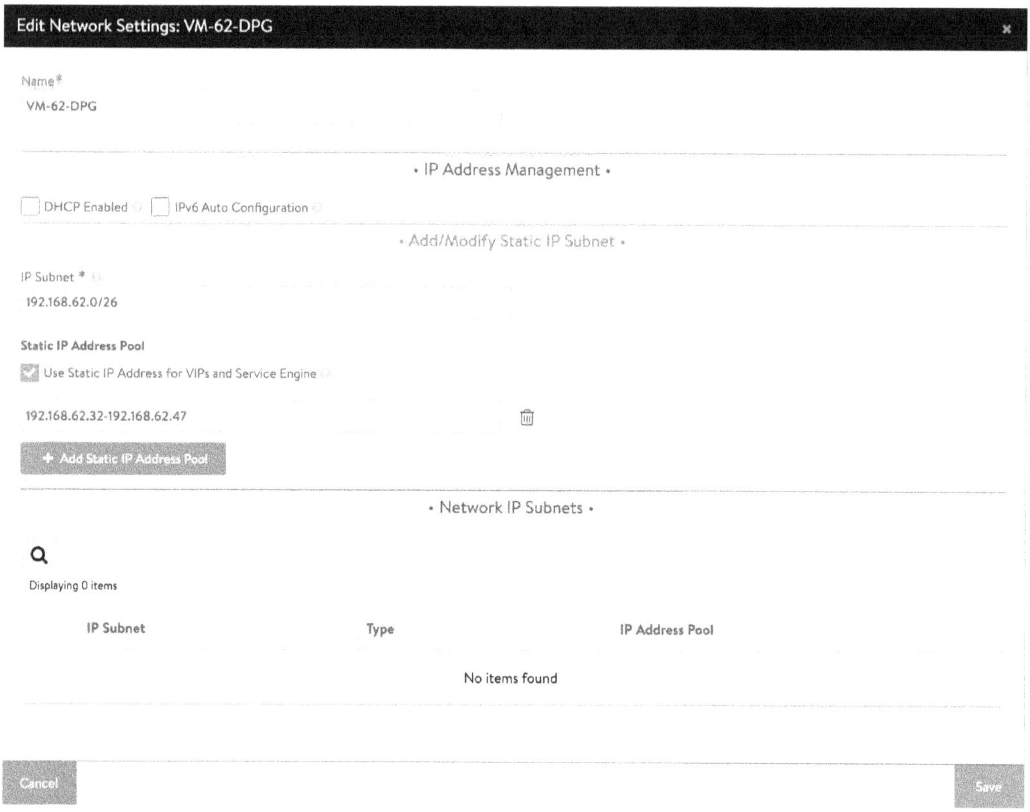

Figure 63: NSX ALB – Add Static IP Address Pool

Click 'Save' to save the network configuration. It is not a requirement to share the same range for both Service Engines and VIPs. Separate subnets can be used for both, as we have already setup a network for the Service Engines. However, as we are creating a setup that is as simple as possible, a single network for both SEs and VIPs can be specified.

The Service Engines do not need a connection to the Workload network. The Service Engines routes the load balanced traffic to the workload network endpoints. However, if the Load Balancer/VIP network and the workload network are separate, you may need to add a static route to tell the Service Engine how to route the load balancer traffic to the workload network. The NSX ALB has a mechanism for creating static routes which we shall see shortly.

That completes most of the setup tasks. There are still a few to complete however, such as certificate management and IPAM configuration. Let's look at those next.

The first item is that you may wish to introduce Basic Authentication on the NSX ALB. Select Administration from the list of menu options. Next, select **Settings** > **Access Settings**. This should display the System Access Settings. On the right hand side, you should find a pencil icon. Click on that to edit the System Access Settings. Finally check on the "**Allow Basic Authentication**" checkbox, as shown below.

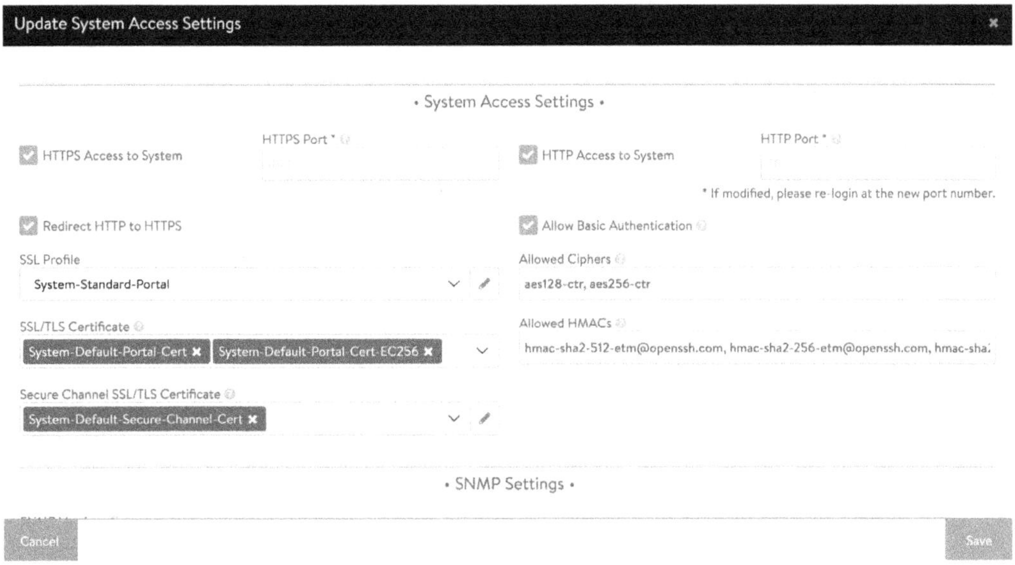

Figure 64: NSX ALB – Update System Access Settings

Note that allowing basic authentication is an optional setting, and you may wish to leave it disabled for security purposes. Staying in the System Access Settings, a new self-signed certificate can be created. You could of course import your own signed certificates, but in this case, a self-signed certificate is being created for convenience. This certificate will need to be provided later, when setting up Workload Management in vSphere.

Under the SSL/TLS Certificate section, delete any certificates that already exist from the installation. By default there are two, called System-Default-Portal-Cert and System-Default-Portal-Cert-EC256 (as shown above). The, from the drop-down list in the SSL/TLS section, select the option to Create Certificate.

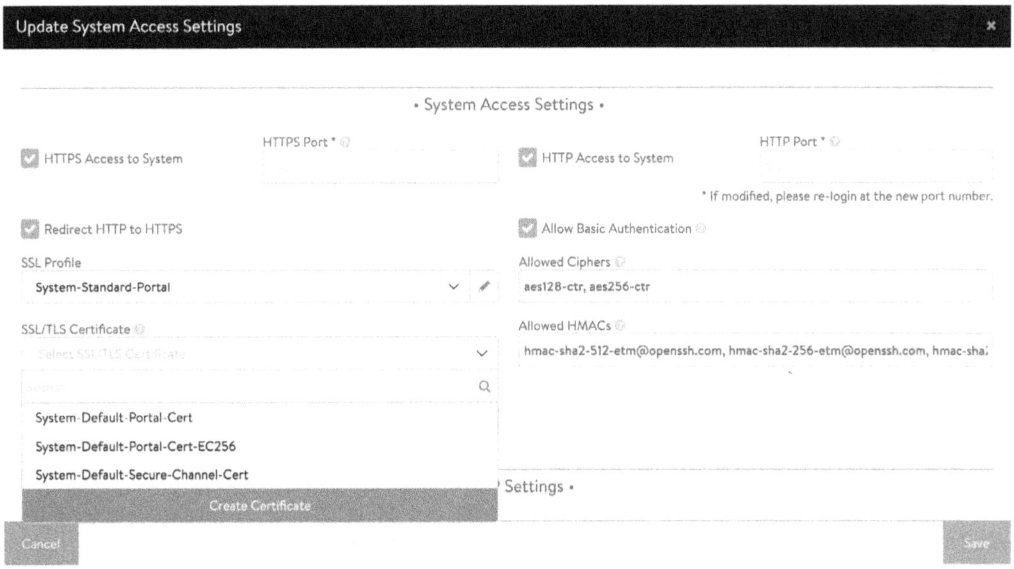

Figure 65: NSX ALB – Create Certificate

Provide a Name, ensure that the Type is set to Self-Signed, give it a Common Name which should be the FQDN of the NSX ALB.

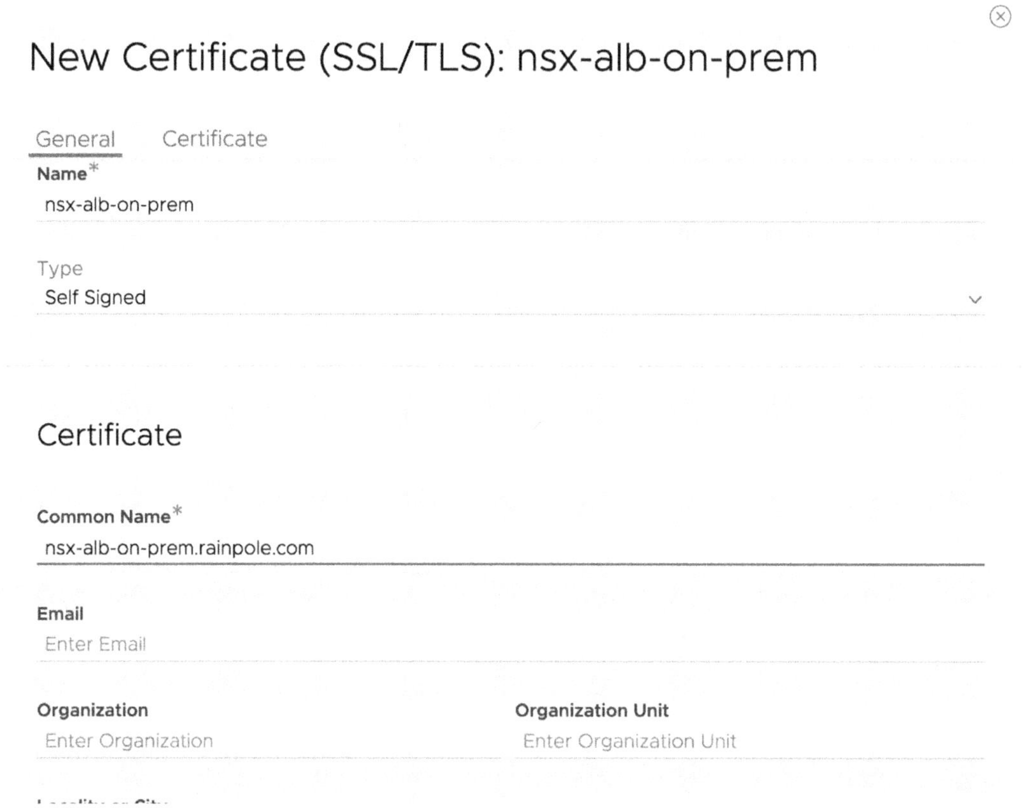

New Certificate (SSL/TLS): nsx-alb-on-prem

ⓧ

General   Certificate

Name＊
nsx-alb-on-prem

Type
Self Signed   ⌄

Certificate

Common Name＊
nsx-alb-on-prem.rainpole.com

Email
Enter Email

Organization   **Organization Unit**
Enter Organization   Enter Organization Unit

Figure 66: NSX ALB – Create a self-signed certificate

Finally provide it with a Subject Alternate Name (SAN) which is the same as the IP address of the NSX ALB. You do this by clicking on the Add button under the SAN section. The Algorithm, Key Size and Days Until Expiry can be left at the default.

Subject Alternate Name (SAN) (1) ⓘ

ADD

Name

192.168.51.163

Items per page   10 ⌄

Figure 67: NSX ALB – Certificate SAN

Once the self-signed cert has been created, you can Save it, and then Save the updated System Access Settings. After changing the self-signed certificate, you will need to refresh your browser, and log back into the NSX ALB UI.

After logging back in, the certificate can be downloaded from the NSX ALB UI by navigating to Templates, then under Security, select SSL/TLS Certificates. The down-arrow icon on the far right of the certificate is the download option. This allows you to copy the certificate to your clipboard, so that you can paste into, for example, vSphere with Tanzu Workload Management.

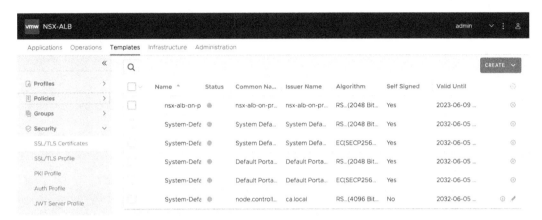

Figure 68: NSX ALB – Certificate Download

Next, add a license. The Licensing section is also found in the **Administration** > **Settings** section. First, you will need to select the license type from the list of available licenses. Click on the icon that looks like a cog wheel next to Licensing. Next, add the license for the version of NSX ALB that you are using. You can install it via a key, or upload it as a file. As soon as the license is added, it should be reported as successfully applied, as follows:

Licensing ⚙

> ⊘ License key successfully applied.   ✕

ADD LICENSE		🔍 LICENSE	Enterprise
● Enter a License Key ◯ Upload a License File (.lic)		**Service Units Usage**	
License Key* ⓘ			
XXXXX-XXXXX-XXXXX-XXXXX-XXXXX APPLY KEY			
		Used Service Units 0	

Figure 69: NSX ALB – Licensing

We now revisit IPAM. IPAM is used to assign Virtual IP addresses to Virtual Services, such as the Kubernetes control planes and Load Balancer type services mentioned previously. Click on Templates, then under Profiles select the IPAM/DNS Profiles. Click on the blue Create button on the right and select IPAM Profile. Set the name of the profile to Default-IPAM, and leave the type set to Avi Vantage IPAM. While both native IPAM and external IPAM provider are available, AVI native IPAM is the one that is used. Next, click on the + Add Usable Network. Here, set the Cloud for Usable Network to Default-Cloud and set the Usable Network to the port group used for the VIPs earlier, in my case VLAN-62-DPG.

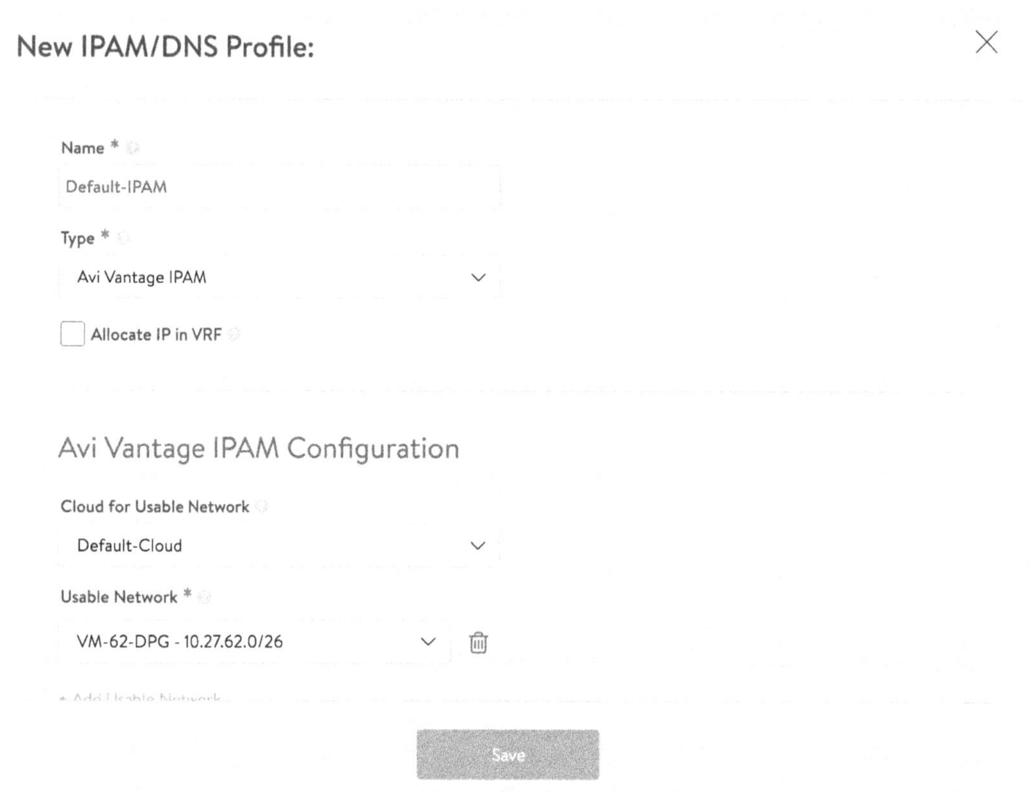

New IPAM/DNS Profile: ✕

Name *

Default-IPAM

Type *

Avi Vantage IPAM   ∨

☐ Allocate IP in VRF

Avi Vantage IPAM Configuration

Cloud for Usable Network

Default-Cloud   ∨

Usable Network *

VM-62-DPG - 10.27.62.0/26   ∨   🗑

+ Add Usable Network

[Save]

Figure 70: NSX ALB – IPAM Profile

The penultimate configuration step is to modify the Default-Cloud and add the IPAM Profile. Navigate back to Infrastructure, and click the edit (pencil) icon again the Default-Cloud. In the first screen, under IPAM Profile, select the new Default-IPAM from the drop-down menu. It should be the only one available.

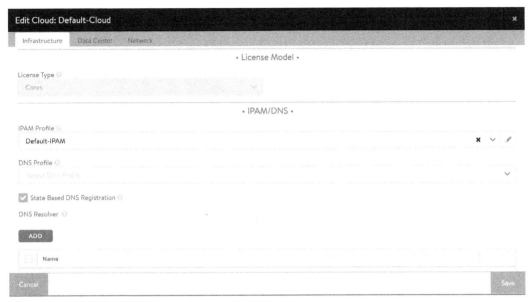

Figure 71: NSX ALB – Add IPAM Profile to Default-Cloud

Save the changes to the Default-Cloud. The final thing to check before we leave the configuration of the NSX ALB is to check that the Default-Cloud orchestrator is still showing a green status.

Figure 72: NSX ALB – Default-Cloud Status

If it is, it is a good indicator that all is well with the deployment and configuration. Click on the green status indicator to make sure. It should report that the configuration is completed.

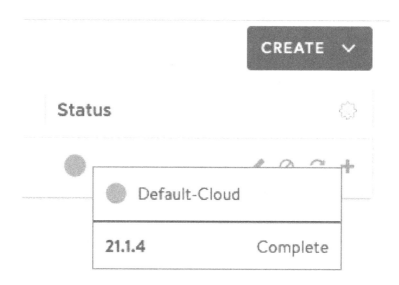

Figure 73: NSX ALB – Default-Cloud Status - Complete

If it is not green, then navigate to Cloud Resources, select Controller and check the logs to see what it is complaining about. The common issue is that there are some duplicate portgroups in the vSphere environment using the same VLAN, so could potentially overlap the range of IP addresses allocated to the SEs and VIPs. This is usually after a migration to a vSphere Distributed Switch, and some standalone virtual switches with VM portgroups are still on the system. Another issue is that the networking chosen as the management network in the Default-Cloud configuration cannot connect to the vSphere infrastructure. Another possibility is that DNS is not configured correctly on the NSX ALB controller, so it is unable to resolve the names of the ESXi hosts (it need to choose one when deploying Service Engines). These issues will need to be resolved before the status of the Default-Cloud turns green.

Now, when there is a request for a control plane VIP or a Load Balancer type Service from Kubernetes, Service Engine VMs are automatically created and connected to the VIP network previously configured. The SEs then take care of the routing of traffic to the nodes of the Kubernetes nodes and Load Balancer services. This is achieved by a component called the Avi Kubernetes Operator (AKO). This is an operator which performs specific functions in a Kubernetes environment which uses the NSX ALB. The AKO makes the necessary API calls to NSX ALB to setup virtual services on behalf of the Kubernetes, specifically load balancing.

I did not make an changes to the default SE Group. The default configuration is enough to allow this setup to complete. However, if you wish to change the settings within the default SE Group, such as the high availability mode, please refer to the official documentation for details on how to do this.

Note: I did not create any static routes between the VIP network and the workload network since these are sharing the same network segment in this simple setup. If you do have distinct networks for both workload and VIP, which is definitely possible in production environments, the NSX ALB has a section under **Infrastructure** > **Cloud Resources** > **Routing** that enables Static Routes between the workload and VIP network to be configured. This will allow the Service Engine to route load balancer traffic to the workload network and vice versa.

The Static Route configuration only has two fields to populate. The first field, Gateway subnets, takes the subnet of the workload subnet, and the Next Hop field is the gateway of the VIP network. Save it off, and the static route is configured. The Service Engines now know how to route the VIP traffic to the endpoints.

That now completes the setup of the NSX ALB. This Load Balancer can now be used by TKG or vSphere with Tanzu. In chapter 6, during the deployment of vSphere with Tanzu, where to make the selection of the NSX Advanced Load Balancer is shown

A word on NSX-T

I suspect most vSphere administrators will be aware of NSX-T, the software based networking platform from VMware. NSX-T can also be used to provide a Load Balancing service (amongst other services) to Kubernetes. NSX-T by itself is a massive topic to try and cover, which would be impossible to do in this single volume book. Instead, we will look at the requirements to configure NSX-T to a point to where it can provide the networking infrastructure for vSphere with Tanzu. While it is also possible to use NSX-T with TKG, the focus of this book is Kubernetes for vSphere administrators. Thus, we will concentrate on configuring NSX-T with the vSphere with Tanzu product as that has been specifically designed with vSphere administrators in mind.

One other item to mention in relation to NSX-T is the NSX Container Plugin, the NCP. The NCP Container Network Interface (CNI) runs on the Supervisor Cluster nodes and builds the necessary NSX-T network infrastructure for containers requiring network components that are running in the Supervisor Cluster.

However, it is not possible to plan an NSX-T deployment without first understanding the requirements associated with vSphere with Tanzu. This is because there is some significant correlation between NSX-T objects and the vSphere with Tanzu installer UI. Since we have not yet covered vSphere with Tanzu deployments, we will defer this discussion to chapter 6, when we look at vSphere with Tanzu in detail.

Summary

As a vSphere administrator, you may not be expected to know the intricacies of container networking. However, since Pods leverage the CNI installed in the Kubernetes nodes to get their network configuration, having some understanding of how all of this works is certainly useful to the vSphere administrator. At the very least, it may help in troubleshooting to isolate some issues when the finger is being pointed at the vSphere network layer. The other important aspect that the vSphere administrator may need to involve themselves with is the provisioning of a Load Balancer provider. We have seen how to deploy the HA-Proxy and the NSX ALB. Now that networking has been covered, let's take a closer look at storage, and the vSphere CSI.

05

Kubernetes storage and vSphere integration

We have already discussed why we need the vSphere Container Storage Interface (CSI) driver in Kubernetes distributions that are deployed on top of vSphere. In this chapter, this is explored a little further and how vSphere datastores can store data from Kubernetes applications is explored. We will show integration with upstream Kubernetes distributions, as well as integrations with VMware's own Tanzu branded Kubernetes distributions.

Persistent Storage in Kubernetes

In chapter 2, we learned how to build Kubernetes Persistent Volumes on vSphere datastores, and we saw some examples showing how a containerized application running in a Pod can consume those volumes. Let's do a recap. In its simplest form, a Pod is a Kubernetes compute construct comprising of one or more containers. All containers within the Pod share storage and network resources. In this chapter, the only aspect of a Pod that we are interested in is how it can consume external storage. Thus, the parts of a Pod manifest that should be configured are `spec.volumes` which references a Persistent Volume Claim (PVC), and `spec.containers.volumeMounts` which mounts the volume into the Pods. The `spec.containers.volumeMounts.name` mounts the volume which matches `spec.volumes.name` from the same Pod manifest.

It is probably also a good point to recap on the different volume access modes available for volumes. The two most common volume access modes are read-write-once (RWO) and read-write-many (RWX). RWO access mode implies that a persistent volume can only be accessed from a single Kubernetes Pod. With the vSphere CSI driver, this volume type is a block volume. The vSphere CSI driver is used to dynamically create RWO (read-write-once) volumes on any vSphere datastore. This is true for vSAN, VMFS, vVols and NFS. These volumes are instantiated as special VMDKs on a vSphere datastore.

RWX access mode implies that a persistent volume can be accessed from multiple Pods. The vSphere CSI driver can also be used to dynamically create RWX (read-write-many) volumes. However, the creation of RWX volumes via the vSphere CSI driver is only supported with vSAN File Service. To achieve this, the vSphere CSI driver dynamically creates NFS file shares using vSAN File Service. The volumes can then be mounted by multiple Pods.

A common question relates to dynamically creating volumes for Kubernetes on third party storage arrays. As discussed, third party storage arrays are supported when they present their storage as volumes to vSphere, and vSphere formats them as datastores (vVols, VMFS, NFS). This storage can then be consumed by the vSphere CSI driver. A follow on question relates to whether it is possible to dynamically create storage objects directly on the storage array, allowing storage array volumes to be consumed for Kubernetes Persistent Volumes. Yes, this is possible. Both RWO block volumes or RWX file shares may be built on the third party storage array. These would then be presented to the Kubernetes node, then formatted and mounted to the Kubernetes Pods. However to achieve this, a CSI driver from the third party would need to be installed on the Kubernetes cluster. This is not something that the vSphere CSI driver can deliver. The Platform Operator would then need to build appropriate storage classes which use this third party CSI provider from external storage vendor. Note that there may be support implications with installing third party CSI drivers on TKG clusters, since these clusters are built and signed by VMware for support. I'd recommend checking the VMware Support before installing any third party CSI drivers in a TKG cluster to be safe.

With that said, let's look at some vSphere CSI driver examples. What follows is a manifest of a Pod with a single *busybox* container that is claiming a Persistent Volume from the PVC `vsan-claim`. As mentioned, his container provides a number of Unix utilities in a single executable.

```
apiVersion: v1
kind: Pod
metadata:
  name: vsan-block-pod
spec:
  containers:
  - name: busybox
    image: busybox
    volumeMounts:
    - name: block-vol
      mountPath: "/demo"
    command: [ "sleep", "1000000" ]
  volumes:
    - name: block-vol
      persistentVolumeClaim:
        claimName: vsan-claim
```

Referencing the PVC via `volumes.persistentVolumeClaim.claimName`, this creates a request for a 2GB read write once (RWO) block volume matching the StorageClass `vsan-sc`. Here is the relevant PVC manifest.

```
apiVersion: v1
kind: PersistentVolumeClaim
metadata:
  name: vsan-claim
spec:
  storageClassName: vsan-sc
  accessModes:
    - ReadWriteOnce
  resources:
    requests:
      storage: 2Gi
```

Within Kubernetes, this request is sent to the vSphere CSI driver components, which in turn talks to other components in vCenter Server, which we could refer to as CNS (Cloud Native Storage). After applying the various YAML manifests, this should result in a 2GB volume being instantiated on a vSAN datastore. It is created with a configuration that matches the default vSAN storage policy as this is what was placed in the StorageClass.

```
kind: StorageClass
apiVersion: storage.k8s.io/v1
metadata:
  name: vsan-sc
```

```
  annotations:
    storageclass.kubernetes.io/is-default-class: "true"
provisioner: csi.vsphere.vmware.com
allowVolumeExpansion: true
parameters:
  storagepolicyname: "vSAN Default Storage Policy"
  csi.storage.k8s.io/fstype: "ext4"
```

If successful, the volume will be formatted as an `ext4` filesystem and mounted onto the folder `/demo` in the busybox Pod.

The following manifest is another example of a Pod deployment. However, in this case, we are deploying 2 Pods. Both of which will attempt to mount the same read write many (RWX) volume. The PVC is again as described in the `volume.persistentVolumeClaim.claimName` attribute. This also sends a request to the vSphere CSI driver to instantiate a volume on the vSAN datastore. Since it is RWX, this will be sent to the vSAN File Service to create a file share for the volume and export it as NFS. If this operation is successful, the volume will appear as an NFS mount on both Pods created with this PVC, and accessible in the busybox container on the `/nfsvol` folder. This PVC should therefore be a 2GB file share. Note that the next manifest creates 2 Pods. Multiple manifests can reside in the same YAML file if they are separated with `---` to indicate a different kind of Kubernetes object.

```
apiVersion: v1
kind: Pod
metadata:
  name: file-pod-a
spec:
  containers:
  - name: busybox
    image: busybox
    volumeMounts:
    - name: file-vol
      mountPath: "/nfsvol"
    command: [ "sleep", "1000000" ]
  volumes:
    - name: file-vol
      persistentVolumeClaim:
        claimName: vsan-file-claim

---

apiVersion: v1
kind: Pod
metadata:
  name: file-pod-b
spec:
  containers:
  - name: busybox
    image: busybox
    volumeMounts:
    - name: file-vol
      mountPath: "/nfsvol"
    command: [ "sleep", "1000000" ]
  volumes:
    - name: file-vol
      persistentVolumeClaim:
        claimName: vsan-file-claim
```

vSphere CSI in action – block volume

To demonstrate the creation of a block PV via a PVC, and then accessing the resulting volume from a Pod, I will use a small Kubernetes cluster made up of 1 control plane node and 2 worker nodes. Suffice to say that this Kubernetes cluster is deployed on vSphere infrastructure, and already has the vSphere CSI driver installed.

Let's check the nodes in the cluster. One of the nodes is the "control-plane, master" as per the role. The others are the workers. The Kubernetes version that has been deployed to this cluster is v1.23.3.

```
% kubectl get nodes
NAME           STATUS   ROLES                 AGE   VERSION
csisnap-cp0    Ready    control-plane,master  20d   v1.23.3
csisnap-wk0    Ready    <none>                20d   v1.23.3
csisnap-wk1    Ready    <none>                20d   v1.23.3
```

Next, we will show the CSI driver components. There is a CSI controller Pod, and a CSI node Pod for all 3 nodes. We will go into further detail regarding the different CSI components that make up the controller Pod shortly. In this version of Kubernetes, which is an upstream, vanilla, Kubernetes, the CSI driver components are placed in the `vmware-system-csi` namespace. Therefore, we need to specify the namespace when querying for Pods. Note that vSphere CSI driver version 2.5.x, shown here, has a total of 7 containers in the controller Pod. Other, older versions of the vSphere CSI driver may show fewer containers in the controller Pod.

```
% kubectl get pods -n vmware-system-csi
NAME                                         READY   STATUS    RESTARTS      AGE
vsphere-csi-controller-5b6dfc6799-lmphc      7/7     Running   7 (11d ago)   19d
vsphere-csi-node-ggkng                       3/3     Running   0             19d
vsphere-csi-node-r6pfh                       3/3     Running   5 (11d ago)   19d
vsphere-csi-node-tsd4r                       3/3     Running   3 (11d ago)   19d
```

To create a sample application, we are going to work in the `default` namespace. Thus, it is not necessary to specify this namespace when we create, query, or delete the objects. Some objects, such as StorageClass and PV, are not namespace scoped, but PVCs and Pods are. At present, there are no StorageClasses, PVCs, PVs, or Pods on this cluster.

```
% kubectl get pods,pvc,pv,sc
No resources found
```

Next, apply a manifest that contains a StorageClass, a PVC, and a Pod. As mentioned, these can all be added to the same file so long as they are separated with --- on their own line in the file. Thus, a single file can create multiple Kubernetes objects. Here is the contents of the file.

```
kind: StorageClass
apiVersion: storage.k8s.io/v1
metadata:
  name: vsan-sc
  annotations:
    storageclass.kubernetes.io/is-default-class: "true"
provisioner: csi.vsphere.vmware.com
allowVolumeExpansion: true
parameters:
  storagepolicyname: "vSAN Default Storage Policy"
  csi.storage.k8s.io/fstype: "ext4"
```

```
---
apiVersion: v1
kind: PersistentVolumeClaim
metadata:
  name: vsan-claim
spec:
  storageClassName: vsan-sc
  accessModes:
    - ReadWriteOnce
  resources:
    requests:
      storage: 2Gi
---
apiVersion: v1
kind: Pod
metadata:
  name: vsan-block-pod
spec:
  containers:
  - name: busybox
    image: busybox
    volumeMounts:
    - name: csisnaps-vol
      mountPath: "/demo"
    command: [ "sleep", "1000000" ]
  volumes:
    - name: csisnaps-vol
      persistentVolumeClaim:
        claimName: vsan-claim
```

```
% kubectl apply -f demo-sc-pvc-pod-rwo.yaml
storageclass.storage.k8s.io/vsan-sc created
persistentvolumeclaim/vsan-claim created
pod/vsan-block-pod created
```

Check if the objects were created successfully. Let's check the StorageClass, the PVC, the PV that should have been created with the PVC, and finally the Pod.

```
% kubectl get sc
NAME      PROVISIONER              RECLAIMPOLICY  VOLUMEBINDINGMODE  ALLOWVOLUMEEXPANSION  AGE
vsan-sc csi.vsphere.vmware.com Delete          Immediate          true                  12s
```

```
% kubectl get pvc
NAME          STATUS VOLUME       CAPACITY ACCESS MODES  STORAGECLASS  AGE
vsan-claim  Bound  pvc-e086a59e….  2Gi      RWO           vsan-sc       15s
```

```
% kubectl get pv
NAME            CAPACITY ACCESS MODES RECLAIM STATUS CLAIM       STORAGECLASS REASON AGE
pvc-e086a59e…   2Gi       RWO          Delete  Bound  vsan-claim  vsan-sc             16s
```

```
% kubectl get pod
NAME             READY  STATUS   RESTARTS  AGE
vsan-block-pod  1/1    Running  0         20s
```

It would appear that all objects have been created successfully. One final check is to open a shell to the Pod and check to see if a 2GB volume has been formatted and mounted to the *busybox* container within the Pod. Since the Pod only contains a single container, we do not need to explicitly specify the container, but if the Pod held more than one container, the container name would need to be also specified on the command line.

```
% kubectl exec -it vsan-block-pod -- sh
/ # df -h
Filesystem              Size  Used Available Use% Mounted on
overlay                77.7G 12.1G    61.6G  16% /
tmpfs                  64.0M     0    64.0M   0% /dev
/dev/sdb                1.9G  6.0M     1.8G   0% /demo
/dev/sda3              77.7G 12.1G    61.6G  16% /dev/termination-log
/dev/sda3              77.7G 12.1G    61.6G  16% /etc/resolv.conf
/dev/sda3              77.7G 12.1G    61.6G  16% /etc/hostname
/dev/sda3              77.7G 12.1G    61.6G  16% /etc/hosts
shm                    64.0M     0    64.0M   0% /dev/shm
tmpfs                  15.5G 12.0K    15.5G   0%
/var/run/secrets/kubernetes.io/serviceaccount
tmpfs                   7.8G     0     7.8G   0% /proc/acpi
tmpfs                  64.0M     0    64.0M   0% /proc/kcore
tmpfs                  64.0M     0    64.0M   0% /proc/keys
tmpfs                  64.0M     0    64.0M   0% /proc/timer_list
tmpfs                   7.8G     0     7.8G   0% /proc/scsi
tmpfs                   7.8G     0     7.8G   0% /sys/firmware
/ # cd /demo
/demo # ls
lost+found
/demo # mount | grep "/dev/sdb"
/dev/sdb on /demo type ext4 (rw,relatime)
```

A 2GB volume has now been successfully attached (/dev/sdb) as requested by the PVC manifest, formatted as ext4 as requested in the StorageClass manifest, and then mounted to /demo as requested in the Pod manifest.

Cloud-Native Storage (CNS) – block volume

One of the primarily goals of VMware when running Kubernetes on vSphere is to provide as much information as possible to the vSphere administrator. This is to help with monitoring, capacity planning, troubleshooting, etc. To that end, VMware added a Cloud-Native Storage (CNS) UI to provide this visibility. Please note that the examples below are taken from a vSphere 7.0U3 environment. If you are using a different environment, some of the views and some of the functionality may not be present or may be superseded.

Since a persistent volume has now been created in a Kubernetes cluster running on vSphere and consuming vSAN storage, CNS now displays information about the PV in the vSphere UI. Below is what is visible in the UI for the volume created in the previous steps. The information displayed includes the name of the PV, whether it is a block or file type, any labels associated with the volume, which datastore it is provisioned on, the storage policy used for the volume, whether the storage policy is compliant or not, a volume ID, volume health, which Kubernetes cluster the PV is on (since there can be many Kubernetes clusters running on the same vSphere infrastructure), and then the Capacity Quota of the volume.

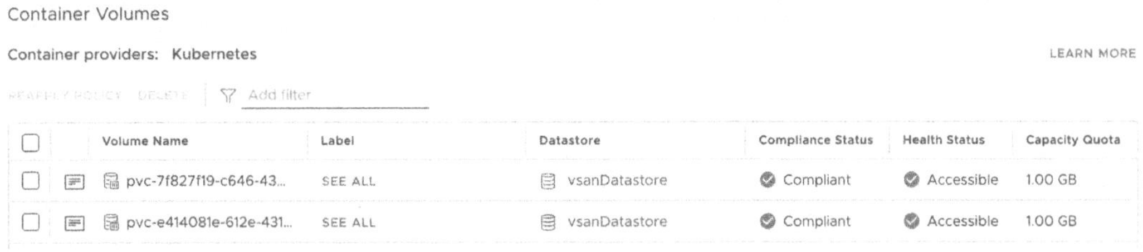

Container Volumes
Container providers: Kubernetes
LEARN MORE
Add filter
Volume Name
Label
Datastore
Compliance Status
Health Status
Capacity Quota
pvc-7f827f19-c646-43...
SEE ALL
vsanDatastore
Compliant
Accessible
1.00 GB
pvc-e414081e-612e-431...
SEE ALL
vsanDatastore
Compliant
Accessible
1.00 GB

Figure 74: Cloud-Native Storage

The second column in the output above contains a "Details" icon. Clicking this icon reveals even more information about the persistent volume, with several different views. The first view is the Basics view, which provides a lot of vSphere specific information about the volume, but of particular interest is the VM which has the volume attached. This VM is, of course, one of the Kubernetes worker nodes. This view also provides the full path to the VMDK object on the vSAN datastore which is backing this persistent volume.

Container Volumes
pvc-e086a59e-8961-400c-b303-e2485d81662d
Basics
Kubernetes objects
Physical Placement
Performance

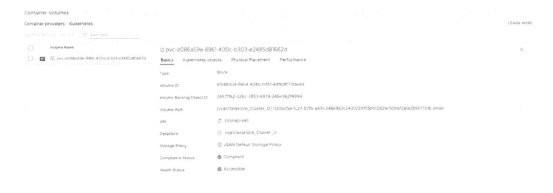

Figure 75: Cloud-Native Storage - Basic View

The next view gives additional information about the Kubernetes objects, including the name of the persistent volume claim, the namespace where the PVC was created, and any Pods that are currently using the volume. Since we did not specify any labels in the manifests of the PVC, these are not populated. This view is a great way to determine which applications are using which volumes in Kubernetes without having to do manual mappings of Kubernetes objects to vSphere datastore objects.

Figure 76: Cloud-Native Storage - Kubernetes Objects View

The next view is of particular interest to vSphere administrators who are also responsible for vSAN storage. It displays the physical placement of the volume. If you recall, we placed a storage policy as a parameter in the StorageClass. The policy chosen at the time was the vSAN Default Storage Policy, which is a RAID-1 configuration, mirroring the data and using a witness component for a quorum. We can now see that the volume has been built using this policy. The three vSAN components are visible below; 2 data components (replicas) and 1 witness component.

Figure 77: Cloud-Native Storage - Physical Placement View

The very last view is a performance view, which means you can get visibility into the performance of individual persistent volumes. This is invaluable for a vSphere administrator when developers begin to complain about poorly performing applications and allows vSphere administrators to quickly assess if the poor performance is storage-related.

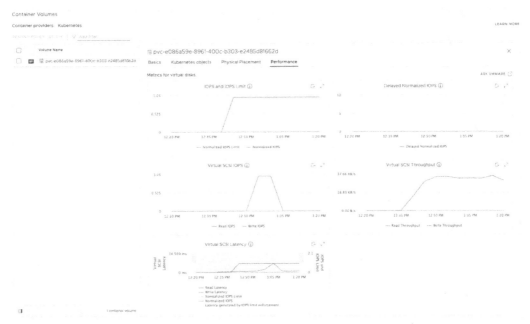

Figure 78: Cloud-Native Storage - Performance View

vSphere CSI in action – file volume

In this section, we turn our attention to a read-write-many file volume. As mentioned, the vSphere CSI driver has been developed to include the ability to dynamically provision NFS file volumes on vSAN. There is a requirement to have vSAN File Service enabled, however, and the details on how to do this are beyond the scope of this book. Using standard Kubernetes manifests, requests to create an RWX persistent volume are sent to the vSphere CSI provider. This results in a dynamically provisioned file share that is automatically exported and can be NFS mounted onto multiple Pods simultaneously. When creating this file volume, the previously created block volume is left in place. Thus, when we query Kubernetes objects for this new file volume, the block volume objects will also be displayed.

Once more, we begin by deploying a manifest that contains the StorageClass, the PVC and the Pods that will share the volume, as defined earlier in this chapter. Again, all objects can be defined in a single manifest and separated using the --- divider. The difference this time is that two Pods are created that share access to the same volume, the access mode is set to RWX, and the fstype in the StorageClass is set to nfs4.

```
kind: StorageClass
apiVersion: storage.k8s.io/v1
metadata:
  name: vsan-file-sc
provisioner: csi.vsphere.vmware.com
parameters:
  storagepolicyname: "vSAN Default Storage Policy"
  csi.storage.k8s.io/fstype: nfs4
---
apiVersion: v1
kind: PersistentVolumeClaim
metadata:
```

```
    name: vsan-file-claim
spec:
  storageClassName: vsan-file-sc
  accessModes:
    - ReadWriteMany
  resources:
    requests:
      storage: 3Gi
---
apiVersion: v1
kind: Pod
metadata:
  name: file-pod-a
spec:
  containers:
  - name: busybox
    image: busybox
    volumeMounts:
    - name: file-vol
      mountPath: "/nfsvol"
    command: [ "sleep", "1000000" ]
  volumes:
    - name: file-vol
      persistentVolumeClaim:
        claimName: vsan-file-claim
---
apiVersion: v1
kind: Pod
metadata:
  name: file-pod-b
spec:
  containers:
  - name: busybox
    image: busybox
    volumeMounts:
    - name: file-vol
      mountPath: "/nfsvol"
    command: [ "sleep", "1000000" ]
  volumes:
    - name: file-vol
      persistentVolumeClaim:
        claimName: vsan-file-pvc-claim
```

```
% kubectl apply -f demo-sc-pvc-pod-rwx.yaml
storageclass.storage.k8s.io/vsan-file-sc created
persistentvolumeclaim/vsan-file-claim created
pod/file-pod-a created
pod/file-pod-b created
```

The StorageClass, PVC, PV and Pods can be queried as before, but now the outputs report
Kubernetes objects for both block and file. Note that the access mode for the new PVC and PV is
RWX, read write many.

```
% kubectl get sc
```

NAME	PROVISIONER	RECLAIMPOLICY	VOLUMEBINDINGMODE	ALLOWVOLUMEEXPANSION	AGE
vsan-file-sc	csi.vsphere…	Delete	Immediate	false	13s
vsan-sc	csi.vsphere…	Delete	Immediate	true	74m

```
% kubectl get pvc
```

NAME	STATUS	VOLUME	CAPACITY	ACCESS MODES	STORAGECLASS	AGE
vsan-claim	Bound	pvc-e086a59e…	2Gi	RWO	vsan-sc	74m

```
vsan-file-claim    Bound    pvc-13d1015d...    2Gi         RWX              vsan-file-sc    22s
```

```
% kubectl get pv
NAME            CAPACITY  ACCESS  RECLAIM  STATUS  CLAIM            STORAGECLASS REASON  AGE
pvc-13d1015d... 2Gi       RWX     Delete   Bound   vsan-file-claim  vsan-filesc          24s
pvc-e086a59e... 2Gi       RWO     Delete   Bound   vsan-claim       vsan-sc              75m
```

```
% kubectl get pods
NAME            READY  STATUS   RESTARTS  AGE
file-pod-a      1/1    Running  0         36s
file-pod-b      1/1    Running  0         36s
vsan-block-pod  1/1    Running  0         75m
```

On this occasion, the same volume is mounted to both Pods. The following steps will verify that the same volume is mounted on both Pods and that both Pods can read and write to the volume. First, exec into file-pod-a, and create a directory and file on the file volume that is mounted on /nfsvol. Then repeat the operation via file-pod-b.

```
% kubectl exec -it file-pod-a -- sh
/ # df -h
Filesystem                      Size        Used Available Use% Mounted on
overlay                         77.7G      12.1G    61.6G   16%  /
tmpfs                           64.0M          0    64.0M    0%  /dev
vsan-fs1-b.rainpole.com:/52290524-f5a9-9415-2175-4bfa51e0a6fa
                                2.0G           0     2.9G    0%  /nfsvol
/dev/sda3                       77.7G      12.1G    61.6G   16%  /dev/termination-log
/dev/sda3                       77.7G      12.1G    61.6G   16%  /etc/resolv.conf
/dev/sda3                       77.7G      12.1G    61.6G   16%  /etc/hostname
/dev/sda3                       77.7G      12.1G    61.6G   16%  /etc/hosts
shm                             64.0M          0    64.0M    0%  /dev/shm
tmpfs                           15.5G      12.0K    15.5G    0%
/var/run/secrets/kubernetes.io/serviceaccount
tmpfs                           7.8G           0     7.8G    0%  /proc/acpi
tmpfs                           64.0M          0    64.0M    0%  /proc/kcore
tmpfs                           64.0M          0    64.0M    0%  /proc/keys
tmpfs                           64.0M          0    64.0M    0%  /proc/timer_list
tmpfs                           7.8G           0     7.8G    0%  /proc/scsi
tmpfs                           7.8G           0     7.8G    0%  /sys/firmware
```

```
/ # cd /nfsvol
/nfsvol # mkdir POD1
/nfsvol # cd POD1
/nfsvol/POD1 # echo "Pod1 was here" >> sharedfile
/nfsvol/POD1 # cat sharedfile
Pod1 was here
/nfsvol POD1 # exit
```

OK – we have been able to successfully read and write to the file share from file-pod-a. Let's see if the same thing is possible from file-pod-b.

```
% kubectl exec -it file-pod-b -- sh
/ # df -h
Filesystem                      Size        Used Available Use% Mounted on
overlay                         77.7G      12.1G    61.6G   16%  /
tmpfs                           64.0M          0    64.0M    0%  /dev
vsan-fs1-b.rainpole.com:/52290524-f5a9-9415-2175-4bfa51e0a6fa
                                2.0G           0     2.9G    0%  /nfsvol
/dev/sda3                       77.7G      12.1G    61.6G   16%  /dev/termination-log
/dev/sda3                       77.7G      12.1G    61.6G   16%  /etc/resolv.conf
/dev/sda3                       77.7G      12.1G    61.6G   16%  /etc/hostname
```

```
/dev/sda3                77.7G    12.1G    61.6G   16%  /etc/hosts
shm                      64.0M        0    64.0M    0%  /dev/shm
tmpfs                    15.5G    12.0K    15.5G    0%
/var/run/secrets/kubernetes.io/serviceaccount
tmpfs                     7.8G        0     7.8G    0%  /proc/acpi
tmpfs                    64.0M        0    64.0M    0%  /proc/kcore
tmpfs                    64.0M        0    64.0M    0%  /proc/keys
tmpfs                    64.0M        0    64.0M    0%  /proc/timer_list
tmpfs                     7.8G        0     7.8G    0%  /proc/scsi
tmpfs                     7.8G        0     7.8G    0%  /sys/firmware
/ # cd /nfsvol
/nfsvol # ls
POD1
/nvfvol # cd POD1
/nfsvol/POD1 # ls
sharedfile
/nfsvol/POD1 # cat sharedfile
Pod1 was here
/nfsvol/POD1 # echo "Pod2 was also here" >> sharedfile
/nfsvol/POD1 # cat sharedfile
Pod1 was here
Pod2 was also here
/nfsvol/POD1 # exit
```

As shown above, the files created via file-pod-a are visible on the same volume from file-pod-b, and both Pods can write to the volume. It seems that the read-write-many file share volume is working as expected.

Cloud-Native Storage (CNS) – file volume

File volumes are also visible in the vSphere UI, providing some detailed information about how a vSAN file share is being used by Kubernetes. Much the same information is displayed as seen previously, with the Basics and Physical Placement views providing very similar information. One interesting view is the Kubernetes Objects view. Two Pods are now shown sharing the same volume.

Figure 79: Cloud-Native Storage – RWX Object View

There is also a Performance view as seen with RWO block volumes. The focus of the file volume performance charts is IOPS, Latency, and Throughput.

Before leaving RWX volumes, the **Cluster > Configure > vSAN > File Shares** view can be visited in the vSphere Client UI to check that a vSAN File Share was indeed dynamically created to provide the backing for this Kubernetes volume.

		Name	▼	Deployment type	Protocol	▼	Storage Policy	Usage/Quota	Actual Usage
☐	⊡	▯ 52f518fa-a52f-95cb-4896-32f5e9d7ab…		Container File Volume	NFS 4.1 and NFS 3		🗋 vSAN Default Storage Policy		0% 0.00 B

File Shares
File service domain: vsancns
Share deployment type: All
ADD

Figure 80: vSAN File Shares — Container File Volume (RWX)

If the "Details" view is opened by clicking on the icon in the second column, much of the same information observed in the Container Volumes view is also available in this vSAN File Shares view. One thing to note is that there are two types of file shares; one is vSAN File Shares and the other is Container File Volumes. If the view is left at vSAN File Shares, dynamically created file shares which back Kubernetes RWX persistent volumes will not be visible. That is why the **Share deployment type** is set to ALL in the previous screenshot, as this will show both vSAN File Shares and Container File Volumes.

vSphere CNS CSI Architecture

In this section, the major components of the vSphere CSI driver and the CNS component that resides on the vCenter Server are discussed. We also examine first class disks (FCDs) which are also known as independent virtual disks (IVDs). These are special vSphere storage volumes used to back Kubernetes PVs. We can think of the CNS component in vCenter Server as the storage control plane, handling the lifecycle operations of container volumes, e.g., create, delete, etc., as well as other functions around metadata retrieval. It is this volume metadata that enables the vSphere Client UI to display such detailed information regarding Kubernetes volumes. With the release of vSphere CSI v2.5, CSI snapshots are also supported in the vSphere CSI driver. This added an additional sidecar container to the CSI controller Pod to watch for snapshot requests, bringing the total number of containers in the CSI controller to 7 at the time of writing.

To put it simply, in the Kubernetes cluster, the vSphere CSI driver is the component that communicates to vSphere and handles the volume create and delete requests, as well as the attach and detach of a volume to a Kubernetes node which is a virtual machine. It communicates with the *kubelet* for the formatting of the volume, as well as the mounting and unmounting of the volume to a Pod running in the Kubernetes node. Another major component of the CSI driver is the CSI syncer. This component is what pushes the Kubernetes metadata regarding the volume to CNS on the vCenter Server so that it can be displayed in the vSphere Client UI.

First, let's look at the Pods that are deployed in a vanilla, upstream Kubernetes cluster by the vSphere CSI driver. This is using a cluster that has vSphere CSI driver v2.5 installed. This version was released in March 2022. This driver uses the namespace `vmware-system-csi` to deploy its components. The two Pods that we see deployed are the vsphere-csi-controller Pod and several vsphere-csi-node Pods.

```
% kubectl get pods -n vmware-system-csi
NAME                                      READY   STATUS    RESTARTS     AGE
vsphere-csi-controller-7b87c8b9bc-fg8c4   7/7     Running   0            87m
vsphere-csi-node-ggkng                    3/3     Running   0            20d
vsphere-csi-node-r6pfh                    3/3     Running   5 (12d ago)  20d
vsphere-csi-node-tsd4r                    3/3     Running   3 (12d ago)  20d
```

vsphere-csi-controller Pod

The vSphere CSI controller Pod handles multiple activities when it comes to volume lifecycle management within Kubernetes. First and foremost, it provides the communication from the Kubernetes Cluster API server to the CNS component on the vCenter Server for volume lifecycle operations and metadata syncing. It listens for Kubernetes events related to volume lifecycle, such as create, delete, attach, and detach. This functionality is implemented by several distinct containers within the Pod. Let's take a closer look at the containers which make up the vSphere CSI driver in Kubernetes. This is using a cluster that has vSphere CSI driver v2.5. The following command will return all the container names that exist in a Pod.

```
% kubectl get pod vsphere-csi-controller-7b87c8b9bc-fg8c4 \
-n vmware-system-csi \
-o jsonpath='{.spec.containers[*].name}'
```

This command should return the following 7 Pods:

- csi-snapshotter
- csi-attacher
- csi-resizer
- vsphere-csi-controller
- liveness-probe
- vsphere-syncer
- csi-provisioner

There are 7 containers (sometimes referred to as sidecars) in the Pod. Separating the distinct features of the vSphere CSI driver into their separate sidecar containers means that the development and deployment of CSI drivers are simplified. Different parts of the driver can be worked on independently of other parts. This is why developers like containers so much, something we discussed in chapter 1. The following is a brief description of each container within the vSphere CSI controller Pod.

csi-snapshotter

This is a new sidecar container introduced with the vSphere CSI driver v2.5 in March 2022. The purpose of this container is to watch the Kubernetes API server for VolumeSnapshot objects. It works with the snapshot controller which watches for Kubernetes VolumeSnapshotContent objects.

csi-attacher

This container monitors the Kubernetes API server for VolumeAttachment objects. If any are observed, it informs the vsphere-csi-controller that a new volume should be attached to a specified node. Similarly, if it observes that the object is removed, then informs the vsphere-csi-controller that a volume should be detached from a specified node.

csi-resizer

This container was added to the vSphere CSI driver v2.2, which was released around April 2021. This is the component that watches for online volume extend operations.

vsphere-csi-controller

This provides the communication from the Kubernetes Cluster API server to the CNS component on the vCenter Server for persistent volume lifecycle operations.

liveness-probe

Monitors the overall health of the vSphere CSI controller Pod. The kubelet (agent) that runs on the Kubernetes nodes uses this liveness-probe to determine if a container needs to be restarted. This helps to improve the availability of the vSphere CSI controller Pod.

vsphere-syncer

Send metadata information back to the CNS component on the vCenter Server so that it can be displayed in the vSphere Client UI in the Container Volumes view.

csi-provisioner

Watches the Kubernetes API server for Persistent Volume Claim objects. If any are observed, it informs the vsphere-csi-controller that a new volume should be created. Similarly, if it observes that the PVC is removed, then it informs the vsphere-csi-controller that the volume should be deleted.

vsphere-csi-node Pod

Each node gets its own vsphere-csi-node Pod. Within each Pod are 3 containers. This output is once again using a cluster that has vSphere CSI driver v2.5, released in March 2022

```
% kubectl get pod vsphere-csi-node-ggkng \
-n vmware-system-csi \
-o jsonpath='{.spec.containers[*].name}'
node-driver-registrar vsphere-csi-node liveness-probe
```

node-driver-registrar

This container establishes communication with the node's kubelet (which can be thought of as the Kubernetes agent that runs on the node). Once established, the kubelet can make volume operation requests, such as mount, unmount, format, etc.

vsphere-csi-node

This container performs volume operations associated with Pod access, e.g., operations such as format, mount, and unmount.

liveness-probe

Monitors the overall health of the vSphere CSI node Pod. The kubelet (agent) that runs on the Kubernetes nodes used this liveness-probe to determine if a container needs to be restarted. This helps to improve the availability of the vSphere CSI node Pod.

Examining vSphere CSI logs

To assist in troubleshooting CSI issues, which you might be called upon in your role as a vSphere administrator, it is useful to be able to examine the logs of the various vSphere CSI driver components. To look at the logs, simply use the *kubectl logs* command against the vSphere CSI controller Pod, specifying which of the containers you wish to see the logs from. Here is a snippet from the beginning of the CSI controller container logs in the CSI controller Pod. Note that how the container name needs to be specified with the *-c* option. Note also that the logs command is a shortcut to displaying the names of all the containers with a Pod.

```
% kubectl logs vsphere-csi-controller-7b87c8b9bc-fg8c4 -n vmware-system-csi
error: a container name must be specified for pod vsphere-csi-controller-7b87c8b9bc-fg8c4,
choose one of: [csi-snapshotter csi-attacher csi-resizer vsphere-csi-controller liveness-
probe vsphere-syncer csi-provisioner]

% kubectl logs vsphere-csi-controller-7b87c8b9bc-fg8c4 \
-n vmware-system-csi \
-c vsphere-csi-controller | more
{"level":"info","time":"2022-03-
03T11:11:28.949237576Z","caller":"logger/logger.go:41","msg":"Setting default log level to
:\"PRODUCTION\""}
{"level":"info","time":"2022-03-03T11:11:28.949619487Z","caller":"vsphere-
csi/main.go:56","msg":"Version : v2.4.0","TraceId":"5f825313-af3f-4f5e-911d-213a75293ec6"}
{"level":"info","time":"2022-03-
03T11:11:28.950847344Z","caller":"logger/logger.go:41","msg":"Setting default log level to
:\"PRODUCTION\""}
{"level":"info","time":"2022-03-
03T11:11:28.950891699Z","caller":"k8sorchestrator/k8sorchestrator.go:152","msg":"Initializ
ing k8sOrchestratorInstance","TraceId":"5f825313-af3f-4f5e-911d-
213a75293ec6","TraceId":"71509a5d-52fd-4a1a-82fd-dd6037a23fa8"}
{"level":"info","time":"2022-03-
03T11:11:28.950965495Z","caller":"kubernetes/kubernetes.go:85","msg":"k8s client using in-
cluster config","TraceId":"5f825313-af3f-4f5e-911d-213a75293ec6","TraceId":"71509a5d-52fd-
4a1a-82fd-dd6037a23fa8"}
{"level":"info","time":"2022-03-
03T11:11:28.951741025Z","caller":"kubernetes/kubernetes.go:352","msg":"Setting client QPS
to 100.000000 and Burst to 100.","TraceId":"5f825313-af3f-4f5e-911d-
213a75293ec6","TraceId":"71509a5d-52fd-4a1a-82fd-dd6037a23fa8"}
```

Lastly, you may want to follow the logs in real-time. You can use the -f option to follow the log stream for new events.

```
% kubectl logs vsphere-csi-controller-7b87c8b9bc-fg8c4 \
-n vmware-system-csi \
-c vsphere-csi-controller -f
.
.
.
{"level":"info","time":"2022-06-
11T11:11:58.67532959Z","caller":"cnsvolumeoperationrequest/cnsvolumeoperationrequest.go:40
7","msg":"Clean up of stale CnsVolumeOperationRequest complete.","TraceId":"48091c29-07a4-
4b28-a754-2397cb6a1567"}
```

vSphere CSI Snapshots

The vSphere CSI driver version 2.5 introduces support for CSI snapshots. This feature enables snapshots to be taken of block-based persistent volumes, as well as the ability to restore snapshots to persistent volumes. There are two additional CSI driver components which enable snapshot support. The first is a new snapshot controller. When a snapshot is created, two new objects are created; a VolumeSnapshot and a VolumeSnapshotContent. Simply put, one can consider a VolumeSnapshot to be something akin to a Persistent Volume Claim and a VolumeSnapshotContent object as being something akin to a Persistent Volume. The snapshot controller is responsible for the dynamic creation and deletion of snapshots, and binding VolumeSnapshot requests with its VolumeSnapshotContent in the backed. The second component is a new sidecar that has been added to the CSI controller Pod called csi-snapshotter. This triggers the CreateSnapshot and DeleteSnapshot operations.

VMware has provided a scripted mechanism (see the official VMware documentation) which checks that the snapshot feature has been enabled in your current Kubernetes cluster. If it is not, the script pulls the necessary manifest to install the necessary snapshot components, deploys the snapshot controller, and finally updates the CSI driver with the additional snapshot sidecar. Here is a sample output from an upstream, vanilla Kubernetes cluster when the deployment bash script is run. I've taken the liberty of removing some of the 'waiting' outputs to reduce the output length.

```
% wget https://raw.githubusercontent.com/kubernetes-sigs/vsphere-csi-
driver/v2.4.0/manifests/vanilla/deploy-csi-snapshot-components.sh

% bash deploy-csi-snapshot-components.sh
No existing snapshot-controller Deployment found, deploying it now..
Start snapshot-controller deployment...
customresourcedefinition.apiextensions.k8s.io/volumesnapshotclasses.snapshot.storage.k8s.i
o created
Created CRD volumesnapshotclasses.snapshot.storage.k8s.io
customresourcedefinition.apiextensions.k8s.io/volumesnapshotcontents.snapshot.storage.k8s.
io created
Created CRD volumesnapshotcontents.snapshot.storage.k8s.io
customresourcedefinition.apiextensions.k8s.io/volumesnapshots.snapshot.storage.k8s.io
created
Created CRD volumesnapshots.snapshot.storage.k8s.io
✅ Deployed VolumeSnapshot CRDs
serviceaccount/snapshot-controller unchanged
clusterrole.rbac.authorization.k8s.io/snapshot-controller-runner unchanged
clusterrolebinding.rbac.authorization.k8s.io/snapshot-controller-role unchanged
role.rbac.authorization.k8s.io/snapshot-controller-leaderelection unchanged
rolebinding.rbac.authorization.k8s.io/snapshot-controller-leaderelection unchanged
✅ Created  RBACs for snapshot-controller
deployment.apps/snapshot-controller created
deployment.apps/snapshot-controller image updated
deployment.apps/snapshot-controller patched
deployment.apps/snapshot-controller patched
Waiting for deployment spec update to be observed...
Waiting for deployment "snapshot-controller" rollout to finish: 0 out of 2 new replicas
have been updated...
Waiting for deployment "snapshot-controller" rollout to finish: 1 out of 2 new replicas
have been updated...
Waiting for deployment "snapshot-controller" rollout to finish: 1 of 2 updated replicas
are available...
deployment "snapshot-controller" successfully rolled out

✅ Successfully deployed snapshot-controller
```

```
No existing snapshot-validation-deployment Deployment found, deploying it now..
creating certs in tmpdir /var/folders/31/y77ywvzd6lqc0g60r4xnfyd80000gp/T/tmp.HmdOwrGg7f
Generating a 2048-bit RSA private key
.............................................................................
...+++
........................+++
writing new private key to
'/var/folders/31/y77ywvzd6lqc0g60r4xnfyd80000gp/T/tmp.HmdOwrGg7f/ca.key'
-----
Generating RSA private key, 2048 bit long modulus
...........................................................+++
................................................................+++
e is 65537 (0x10001)
Signature ok
subject=/CN=snapshot-validation-service.kube-system.svc
Getting CA Private Key
secret "snapshot-webhook-certs" deleted
secret/snapshot-webhook-certs created
service "snapshot-validation-service" deleted
  % Total    % Received % Xferd  Average Speed   Time    Time     Time  Current
                                 Dload  Upload   Total   Spent    Left  Speed
100  2238  100  2238    0     0   9060      0 --:--:-- --:--:-- --:--:--  9024
service/snapshot-validation-service created
validatingwebhookconfiguration.admissionregistration.k8s.io/validation-
webhook.snapshot.storage.k8s.io configured
deployment.apps/snapshot-validation-deployment created
deployment.apps/snapshot-validation-deployment image updated
deployment.apps/snapshot-validation-deployment patched
Waiting for deployment spec update to be observed...
Waiting for deployment spec update to be observed...
Waiting for deployment "snapshot-validation-deployment" rollout to finish: 0 out of 3 new
replicas have been updated...
Waiting for deployment "snapshot-validation-deployment" rollout to finish: 1 out of 3 new
replicas have been updated...
Waiting for deployment "snapshot-validation-deployment" rollout to finish: 2 out of 3 new
replicas have been updated...
Waiting for deployment "snapshot-validation-deployment" rollout to finish: 2 out of 3 new
replicas have been updated...
Waiting for deployment "snapshot-validation-deployment" rollout to finish: 1 old replicas
are pending termination...
deployment "snapshot-validation-deployment" successfully rolled out

☑ Successfully deployed snapshot-validation-deployment

csi-snapshotter side-car not found in vSphere CSI Driver Deployment, patching..
creating patch file in tmpdir
/var/folders/31/y77ywvzd6lqc0g60r4xnfyd80000gp/T/tmp.GiMDimfZdq
Scale down the vSphere CSI driver
deployment.apps/vsphere-csi-controller scaled
Patching vSphere CSI driver..
deployment.apps/vsphere-csi-controller patched
Scaling the vSphere CSI driver back to original state..
deployment.apps/vsphere-csi-controller scaled
Waiting for deployment spec update to be observed...
Waiting for deployment spec update to be observed...
Waiting for deployment "vsphere-csi-controller" rollout to finish: 0 out of 3 new replicas
have been updated...
Waiting for deployment "vsphere-csi-controller" rollout to finish: 0 of 3 updated replicas
are available...
Waiting for deployment "vsphere-csi-controller" rollout to finish: 1 of 3 updated replicas
are available...
Waiting for deployment "vsphere-csi-controller" rollout to finish: 2 of 3 updated replicas
are available...
deployment "vsphere-csi-controller" successfully rolled out
```

☑ Successfully deployed all components for CSI Snapshot feature!

If the update has been successful, you should observe 7 containers in the vSphere CSI controller Pod. This is an upstream Kubernetes, so the Pods are in the `vmware-system-csi` namespace.

```
% kubectl get pod -n vmware-system-csi vsphere-csi-controller-5b6dfc6799-lmphc
NAME                                        READY  STATUS    RESTARTS   AGE
vsphere-csi-controller-5b6dfc6799-lmphc     7/7    Running   0          20d
```

To demonstrate CSI snapshots in the vSphere CSI driver, take an existing StorageClass, PVC, PV and Pod. Take a snapshot of the volume, convert the snapshot to a new volume, and then mount the snapshot volume to another Pod. Lastly, the data on the volume is verified and checked to make sure that it is present and available.

In the following test, a Pod, PVC, PV and StorageClass were already created. The Pod is our old friend, the very simple busybox which has some basic Unix utilities incorporated.

```
% kubectl get sc
NAME          PROVISIONER             RECLAIMPOLICY  VOLUMEBINDINGMODE ALLVOLEXPANSION  AGE
csisnaps-sc   csi.vsphere.vmware.com  Delete         Immediate         true            10s


% kubectl get pod
NAME            READY  STATUS    RESTARTS  AGE
csisnaps-pod    1/1    Running   0         9s


% kubectl get pvc
NAME                       STATUS VOLUME                        CAP ACC MODES  SC           AGE
csisnaps-pvc-vsan-claim    Bound. pvc-ca1960f2-…-6aab0f506e7a  2Gi RWO        csisnaps-sc. 9s


% kubectl get pv
NAME                CAP  ACCESS RECPOL STATUS CLAIM                    SC          REASON AGE
pvc-ca1960f2-..6e7a 2Gi  RWO    Delete Bound  csisnaps-pvc-vsan-claim  csisnaps-sc        9s
```

Let's add some simple data to the volume mounted to the busybox Pod by 'exec'ing onto it and creating a directory with a file with some contents.

```
% kubectl exec -it csisnaps-pod -- sh
/ # df -h
Filesystem              Size    Used  Available  Use% Mounted on
overlay                77.7G   12.1G     61.6G    16% /
tmpfs                  64.0M       0     64.0M     0% /dev
/dev/sdb                1.9G    6.0M      1.8G     0% /demo
/dev/sda3              77.7G   12.1G     61.6G    16% /dev/termination-log
/dev/sda3              77.7G   12.1G     61.6G    16% /etc/resolv.conf
/dev/sda3              77.7G   12.1G     61.6G    16% /etc/hostname
/dev/sda3              77.7G   12.1G     61.6G    16% /etc/hosts
shm                    64.0M       0     64.0M     0% /dev/shm
tmpfs                  15.5G   12.0K     15.5G     0%
/var/run/secrets/kubernetes.io/serviceaccount
tmpfs                   7.8G       0      7.8G     0% /proc/acpi
tmpfs                  64.0M       0     64.0M     0% /proc/kcore
tmpfs                  64.0M       0     64.0M     0% /proc/keys
tmpfs                  64.0M       0     64.0M     0% /proc/timer_list
tmpfs                   7.8G       0      7.8G     0% /proc/scsi
tmpfs                   7.8G       0      7.8G     0% /sys/firmware

/ # cd /demo

/demo # ls
lost+found

/demo # mkdir Special-Data

/demo # cd Special-Data/

/demo/Special-Data # echo "my-special-data" >> special-data-file

/demo/Special-Data # cat special-data-file
my-special-data
```

Next, take a snapshot of this volume. These are the manifests used to first make a CSI snapshot class. The first manifest defines which provider should be used to create snapshots, and what to do when a snapshot is deleted. The second manifest is used to make the snapshot. Note that the snapshot manifest contains a `spec.source.persistentVolumeClaimName` which determines which volume should have the snapshot taken. In this example, it matches the PVC called `csisnaps-pvc-vsan-claim`, as shown above.

```
% cat csi-snapshot-class.yaml
apiVersion: snapshot.storage.k8s.io/v1
kind: VolumeSnapshotClass
metadata:
  name: block-snapshotclass
driver: csi.vsphere.vmware.com
deletionPolicy: Delete

% cat dynamic-vol-snap.yaml
apiVersion: snapshot.storage.k8s.io/v1
kind: VolumeSnapshot
metadata:
  name: block-snapshotvol
spec:
  volumeSnapshotClassName: block-snapshotclass
  source:
    persistentVolumeClaimName: csisnaps-pvc-vsan-claim
```

Apply the manifests, and check the VolumeSnapshot and the VolumeSnapshotContent. The output is rather long, and has wrapped which makes it a bit difficult to read. However, hopefully you can see what is happening.

```
% kubectl apply -f dynamic-vol-snap.yaml
volumesnapshot.snapshot.storage.k8s.io/block-snapshotvol created

% kubectl get volumesnapshot
NAME                READYTOUSE    SOURCEPVC            SOURCESNAPSHOTCONTENT    RESTORE
SIZE    SNAPSHOTCLASS          SNAPSHOTCONTENT                          CREATIONTI
ME    AGE
block-snapshotvol    true          csisnaps-pvc-vsan-
claim                 2Gi              block-snapshotclass    snapcontent-2471e409-
7e7e-4fed-8d7a-95a73b097abf    24s               30s

% kubectl get volumesnapshotcontents
NAME                                            READYTOUSE    RESTORESIZE    DELETIONPOLI
CY    DRIVER            VOLUMESNAPSHOTCLASS    VOLUMESNAPSHOT        VOLUMESNAPSHOTNAME
SPACE    AGE
snapcontent-2471e409-7e7e-4fed-8d7a-
95a73b097abf    true          2147483648      Delete              csi.vsphere.vmware.com    block-
snapshotclass    block-snapshotvol    default                        34s
```

Success! It looks like a snapshot of the volume has been successfully taken. The next step is to restore that snapshot. This will instantiate a new persistent volume. Once that step is successful, the volume can then be mounted to a Pod where we can check its contents. We should be able to verify that the volume data was indeed captured by the snapshot. First, I have to construct a snapshot restore manifest which is basically a PVC that includes a `spec.datasource.kind` set to `VolumeSnapshot`, along with the name of the snapshot we wish to instantiate the volume from. Note also that this manifest uses the same StorageClass as the original volume, and also has the same size and access mode as the original volume.

```
apiVersion: v1
kind: PersistentVolumeClaim
metadata:
  name: block-snapshot-restore
spec:
  storageClassName: csisnaps-sc
  dataSource:
    name: block-snapshotvol
    kind: VolumeSnapshot
    apiGroup: snapshot.storage.k8s.io
  accessModes:
    - ReadWriteOnce
  resources:
    requests:
      storage: 2Gi
```

Now apply this manifest, and check to see if we get a new volume for the restored snapshot.

```
% kubectl apply -f snapshot-restore.yaml
persistentvolumeclaim/block-snapshot-restore created

% kubectl get pvc,pv
NAME                                            STATUS    VOLUME
         CAPACITY   ACCESS MODES    STORAGECLASS    AGE
persistentvolumeclaim/block-snapshot-restore    Bound     pvc-343fdfd7-e32d-4e0e-94c9-
9a4e88c4999a    2Gi          RWO            csisnaps-sc     5s
```

```
persistentvolumeclaim/csisnaps-pvc-vsan-claim   Bound    pvc-ca1960f2-6a86-43d6-80e4-
6aab0f506e7a  2Gi         RWO              csisnaps-sc      30m

NAME                                                     CAPACITY  ACCESS
MODES  RECLAIM
POLICY  STATUS   CLAIM                          STORAGECLASS   REASON  AGE
persistentvolume/pvc-343fdfd7-e32d-4e0e-94c9-
9a4e88c4999a  2Gi         RWO              Delete        Bound    default/block-snapshot-
restore    csisnaps-sc            3s
persistentvolume/pvc-ca1960f2-6a86-43d6-80e4-
6aab0f506e7a  2Gi         RWO              Delete        Bound    default/csisnaps-pvc-
vsan-claim    csisnaps-sc            30m
```

It appears to have worked. There is a new volume available. The final part of the exercise is to create a Pod which uses the newly restored snapshot. Once that is complete, it will then be possible to verify that the data that was placed on the original volume was indeed captured as part of the snapshot. Here is a new Pod manifest which will mount the volume to the /snapshot folder.

```
apiVersion: v1
kind: Pod
metadata:
  name: csisnaps-restore-pod
spec:
  containers:
  - name: busybox
    image: busybox
    volumeMounts:
    - name: csisnaps-snap
      mountPath: "/snapshot"
    command: [ "sleep", "1000000" ]
  volumes:
    - name: csisnaps-snap
      persistentVolumeClaim:
        claimName: block-snapshot-restore
```

Create the Pod and check the contents of the volume.

```
% kubectl apply -f snapshot-restore-pod.yaml
pod/csisnaps-restore-pod created

% kubectl get pods -w
NAME                    READY  STATUS             RESTARTS  AGE
csisnaps-pod            1/1    Running            0         38m
csisnaps-restore-pod    0/1    ContainerCreating  0         11s
csisnaps-restore-pod    1/1    Running            0         12s
^C%

% kubectl exec -it csisnaps-restore-pod -- sh

/ # df -h
Filesystem              Size    Used Available Use% Mounted on
overlay                 77.7G   12.1G  61.6G    16% /
tmpfs                   64.0M       0  64.0M     0% /dev
/dev/sdc                 1.9G    6.0M   1.8G     0% /snapshot
/dev/sda3               77.7G   12.1G  61.6G    16% /dev/termination-log
/dev/sda3               77.7G   12.1G  61.6G    16% /etc/resolv.conf
/dev/sda3               77.7G   12.1G  61.6G    16% /etc/hostname
/dev/sda3               77.7G   12.1G  61.6G    16% /etc/hosts
shm                     64.0M       0  64.0M     0% /dev/shm
tmpfs                   15.5G   12.0K  15.5G     0%
/var/run/secrets/kubernetes.io/serviceaccount
```

```
tmpfs                    7.8G        0      7.8G    0% /proc/acpi
tmpfs                   64.0M        0     64.0M    0% /proc/kcore
tmpfs                   64.0M        0     64.0M    0% /proc/keys
tmpfs                   64.0M        0     64.0M    0% /proc/timer_list
tmpfs                    7.8G        0      7.8G    0% /proc/scsi
tmpfs                    7.8G        0      7.8G    0% /sys/firmware
```

```
/ # ls /snapshot/
Special-Data   lost+found
```

```
/ # cat /snapshot/Special-Data/special-data-file
my-special-data
```

Everything looks good. We have successfully taken a snapshot of a volume, restored that volume to a PVC, and the resulting PV has our backed up data. While this might be somewhat useful to do on a manual basis, it will be extremely useful to VMware backup partners. At the time of writing, my understanding was that there were a number of conversations underway with these backup partners to integrate their backup/restore products with vSphere CSI snapshots. This will allow their products to backup/restore modern applications running on Kubernetes, which in turn is running on vSphere. Check with your preferred backup vendor to see how those conversations are progressing.

vSphere CSI Online Volume Grow

The vSphere CSI driver can hot extend block volumes while the Pods remain online. This feature first became available in CSI driver version 2.2 and required vSphere 7.0U2. To use this feature, the StorageClass manifest requires an entry called allowVolumeExpansion set to true. Here is a sample manifest:

```
kind: StorageClass
apiVersion: storage.k8s.io/v1
metadata:
  name: vol-exp-sc
provisioner: csi.vsphere.vmware.com
allowVolumeExpansion: true
parameters:
    storagePolicyName: "vsan-b"
```

The Persistent Volume Claim manifest does not need any particular setting to allow volume grow. It simply needs to use the previously created StorageClass. Here is a PVC manifest where the initial size of the volume is set to 1 GB.

```
apiVersion: v1
kind: PersistentVolumeClaim
metadata:
  name: vol-exp-pvc
spec:
  storageClassName: vol-exp-sc
  accessModes:
    - ReadWriteOnce
  resources:
    requests:
      storage: 1Gi
```

To prove that it is an online volume expansion, a simple busybox Pod is also created. This is the

Pod where the expanding volume will be attached and mounted. The Pod mounts it to
/mnt/volume1.

```
apiVersion: v1
kind: Pod
metadata:
  name: vol-exp-busybox
spec:
  containers:
  - image: "k8s.gcr.io/busybox"
    command:
      - sleep
      - "3600"
    imagePullPolicy: Always
    name: busybox
    volumeMounts:
    - name: vol-exp
      mountPath: "/mnt/volume1"
  restartPolicy: Always
  volumes:
  - name: vol-exp
    persistentVolumeClaim:
      claimName: vol-exp-pvc
      readOnly: false
```

After applying the manifests, *exec* onto the Pod and copy the contents of /etc onto the volume.

```
$ kubectl exec -it pod/vol-exp-busybox -- sh

/ # mount | grep volume1
/dev/sdd on /mnt/volume1 type ext4 (rw,relatime)

/ # df -h | grep volume1
/dev/sdd                 975.9M      2.5M     906.2M   0% /mnt/volume1

/ # cd /mnt/volume1/

/mnt/volume1 # ls
lost+found

/mnt/volume1 # mkdir demo-folder

/mnt/volume1 # cd demo-folder/

/mnt/volume1/demo-folder # cp /etc/* .

/mnt/volume1/demo-folder # ls
fstab          hostname      inittab         issue     mtab        os-release
profile        random-seed   securetty       shadow    group       hosts
inputrc        ld.so.conf    nsswitch.conf   passwd    protocols   resolv.conf
services
```

Next, grow the volume from 1GB to 2GB, online using the *kubectl patch* command.

```
$ kubectl get pvc
NAME          STATUS   VOLUME                                       CAP   ACC   STOCLASS    AGE
vol-exp-pvc   Bound    pvc-59eeb319-658a-4fb5-a09c-dc91bedfbc1a   1Gi   RWO   vol-exp-sc  10m

$ kubectl patch pvc vol-exp-pvc \
-p '{"spec": {"resources": {"requests": {"storage": "2Gi"}}}}'
persistentvolumeclaim/vol-exp-pvc patched
```

```
$ kubectl get pvc
NAME         STATUS   VOLUME                                        CAP  ACC  STOCLASS    AGE
vol-exp-pvc  Bound    pvc-59eeb319-658a-4fb5-a09c-dc91bedfbc1a      2Gi  RWO  vol-exp-sc  12m
```

It appears that the PVC capacity has successfully grown. Let's now check the Pod to see if the new volume size is also reflected on the mount.

```
/mnt/volume1/demo-folder # mount | grep volume1
/dev/sdd on /mnt/volume1 type ext4 (rw,relatime)

/mnt/volume1/demo-folder # df -h | grep volume1
/dev/sdd                  1.9G      3.1M      1.8G    0% /mnt/volume1

/mnt/volume1/demo-folder # ls
fstab          hostname      inittab       issue         mtab            os-
release        profile       random-seed   securetty     shadow
group          hosts         inputrc       ld.so.conf    nsswitch.conf   passwd
protocols      resolv.conf   services
```

The volume has been successfully grown whilst remaining online.

Role of vSphere CSI in Multi-AZ / Topology

There are also several different vSphere topologies that are support for Kubernetes deployment. For example, a single Kubernetes cluster could be deployed across multiple vSphere Clusters, often referred to as a multi-AZ deployment, AZ short for Availability Zones.

Note: Multi-AZ/Topology cannot be enabled on an existing Kubernetes cluster. It can only be installed on new Kubernetes clusters.

CSI Topology can be used to provide another level of availability to your Kubernetes cluster and applications. The objective is to deploy Kubernetes Pods with their own Persistent Volumes (PVs) to the same zone. Thus, if a StatefulSet is deployed across multiple zones using CSI Topology, and one of the zones fail, it does not impact the overall application. vSphere Tags are utilized to define Regions and Zones. Regions and Zones are topology constructs used by Kubernetes. To achieve this, administrators must associate a Region Tag (k8s-region) at the Data Centre level and a unique Zone Tag (k8s-zone) to each of the Clusters in the Data Centre. Since this involves vSphere Tags, a vSphere administrator will certainly be involved, at the very least coordinating the tagging of different Data Centres and providing this to whomever is responsible for configuring the vSphere CSI Driver configuration.

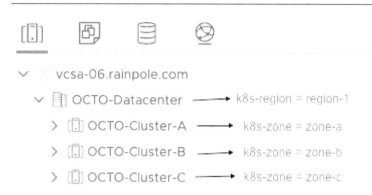

Figure 81: vSphere Tags in Multi-AZ/Topology deployments

To achieve a multi-AZ, some additional entries must be added to the vSphere CSI driver configuration file. We saw how to manually installed the vSphere CSI driver in vanilla Kubernetes back when we looked at installing Kubernetes using *kubeadm*. The CSI driver discovers each Kubernetes node/virtual machine topology, and through the `kubelet`, adds them as labels to the nodes. In this configuration, the vSphere CSI driver continues to have a dependency on the vSphere Cloud Provider Interface (CPI). As long as all of the nodes have a `ProviderID` after the Cloud Provider has initialized, you can proceed with the CSI driver deployment. Here is a reminder on how to check the ProviderID after the CPI has been deployed.

```
$ kubectl get nodes
NAME                   STATUS   ROLES                 AGE     VERSION
k8s-controlplane-01    Ready    control-plane,master  4h35m   v1.21.1
k8s-worker-01          Ready    <none>                4h33m   v1.21.1
k8s-worker-02          Ready    <none>                4h32m   v1.21.1
k8s-worker-03          Ready    <none>                4h31m   v1.21.1

$ kubectl describe nodes | grep ProviderID
ProviderID:            vsphere://42247114-0280-f5a1-0e8b-d5118f0ff8fd
ProviderID:            vsphere://42244b45-e7ec-18a3-8cf1-493e4c9d3780
ProviderID:            vsphere://4224fde2-7fae-35f7-7083-7bf6eaafd3bb
ProviderID:            vsphere://4224e557-2b4f-61d3-084f-30d524f97238
```

The `csi-vsphere.conf` file is located on the Kubernetes control plane node in `/etc/kubernetes`. It now has two additional entries. These are the labels for region and zone, k8s-region and k8s-zone. These are the same tags that were used on the vSphere inventory objects.

```
[Global]
cluster-id = "k8s"
[VirtualCenter "192.168.51.1"]
insecure-flag = "true"
user = "administrator@vsphere.local"
password = "VMware123!"
port = "443"
datacenters = "Datacenter"

[Labels]
topology-categories = "k8s-region, k8s-zone"
```

We can now proceed with the deployment of the vSphere CSI driver. Since multi-AZ is only available in vSphere CSI driver version 2.5 or later, this is the version that will be installed. First, download the vSphere CSI driver, but before applying it, ensure that the following feature gates are uncommented in the CSI controller deployment manifest:

```
- "--feature-gates=Topology=true"
- "--strict-topology"
```

Now, create a secret out of the configuration file, and deploy the vSphere CSI driver manifest, as we saw in the *kubeadm* section of chapter 3.

```
$ kubectl create secret generic vsphere-config-secret \
--from-file=csi-vsphere.conf --namespace=vmware-system-csi
secret/vsphere-config-secret created

$ kubectl get secret vsphere-config-secret --namespace=vmware-system-csi
NAME                     TYPE     DATA   AGE
vsphere-config-secret    Opaque   1      7s

$ kubectl apply -f https://raw.githubusercontent.com/kubernetes-sigs/vsphere-csi-
driver/v2.5.1/manifests/vanilla/vsphere-csi-driver.yaml
```

Using the following commands, it should be possible to verify that the `csinodes` objects have `topologyKeys` set, and that the Kubernetes nodes have the correct topology labels assigned.

```
$ kubectl get csinodes -o jsonpath='{range .items[*]}{.metadata.name} {.spec}{"\n"}{end}'
k8s-controlplane-01 {"drivers":[{"name":"csi.vsphere.vmware.com","nodeID":"k8s-control-
1","topologyKeys":["topology.csi.vmware.com/k8s-region","topology.csi.vmware.com/k8s-
zone"]}]}
k8s-worker-01 {"drivers":[{"name":"csi.vsphere.vmware.com","nodeID":"k8s-worker-
01","topologyKeys":["topology.csi.vmware.com/k8s-region","topology.csi.vmware.com/k8s-
zone"]}]}
k8s-worker-02 {"drivers":[{"name":"csi.vsphere.vmware.com","nodeID":"k8s-worker-
02","topologyKeys":["topology.csi.vmware.com/k8s-region","topology.csi.vmware.com/k8s-
zone"]}]}
k8s-worker-03 {"drivers":[{"name":"csi.vsphere.vmware.com","nodeID":"k8s-worker-
03","topologyKeys":["topology.csi.vmware.com/k8s-region","topology.csi.vmware.com/k8s-
zone"]}]}

$ kubectl get nodes --show-labels
NAME                  STATUS   ROLES                 AGE   VERSION   LABELS
k8s-controlplane-01   Ready    control-plane,master  1h    v1.21.1
topology.csi.vmware.com/k8s-region=region-1,topology.csi.vmware.com/k8s-zone=zone-a
k8s-worker-01         Ready    <none>                1h    v1.21.1
topology.csi.vmware.com/k8s-region=region-1,topology.csi.vmware.com/k8s-zone=zone-a
k8s-worker-02         Ready    <none>                1h    v1.21.1
topology.csi.vmware.com/k8s-region=region-1,topology.csi.vmware.com/k8s-zone=zone-b
k8s-worker-03         Ready    <none>                1h    v1.21.1
topology.csi.vmware.com/k8s-region=region-1,topology.csi.vmware.com/k8s-zone=zone-c
```

Everything looks good. Let's now look at ways to make use of this topology for applications.

Deploying to Multi-AZ/Topology enabled clusters

To deploy a Pod and PV to a particular zone, in this example zone-a, note the existence of a topology references in the StorageClass, which imply that volumes will only be created on available storage in this region (region-1) and this zone (zone-a).

```
kind: StorageClass
apiVersion: storage.k8s.io/v1
metadata:
  name: zone-a-sc
provisioner: csi.vsphere.vmware.com
parameters:
  storagepolicyname: vsan-a
allowedTopologies:
  - matchLabelExpressions:
      - key: topologies.csi.vmware.com/zone
        values:
          - zone-a
      - key: topologies.csi.vmware.com/region
        values:
          - region-1
```

Note that this manifest does not need to include a storage policy. If it did not, the persistent volume could be created on any of the available storage at this zone. Using a storage policy means that it will pick a particular datastore in this region / zone. In this case, the policy matches a vSAN datastore, and there is a vSAN datastore available in this region / zone.

The PVC manifest simply references the StorageClass above. Pod manifests do not need any special entries either. The Pod will be instantiated in the same region / zone where the PV exists, and will thus will be scheduled on the worker node (or nodes) in that zone. The PV will be attached to same worker node and the kubelet process running in the worker will mount it onto the Pod.

Let's look at a more complex example, such as a StatefulSet. This is where each replica in the set has its own Pod and PV, and as the set is scaled, a new Pod and PV are instantiated for each replica. As mentioned, each zone has its own vSAN datastore, and so that each PV ends up on a vSAN datastore and not any other storage, I am creating a common policy across all vSAN clusters. This policy is RAID0 since availability will be provided by replication from within the application, thus I do not need to do any protection at the infrastructure layer. I am also using a `volumeBindingMode` of `WaitForFirstConsumer` instead of the default `Immediate`, as discussed in chapter 2. This means that the PV will not be instantiated until the Pod has first been scheduled on a worker node. Therefore we do not need the explicit topology statements in the StorageClass that we saw earlier. The PV will be instantiated and attached to the Kubernetes node where the Pod has been scheduled, so that the kubelet can format and mount it into the Pod. Thus, it is the Pod which will drive the topology deployment in this case.

This is the StorageClass manifest which will be used by the StatefulSet. This is where the `volumeBindingMode` is specified.

```
apiVersion: v1
kind: StorageClass
apiVersion: storage.k8s.io/v1
metadata:
  name: wffc-sc
provisioner: csi.vsphere.vmware.com
volumeBindingMode: WaitForFirstConsumer
parameters:
  storagePolicyName: RAID0
```

The sample application is made up of a single container, called web, which has two volumes, www and logs. The container image is Nginx, our familiar web server. The volumes are created based on the StorageClass defined previously. Of particular interest are the `affinity` statements in the StatefulSet manifest. There is a `nodeAffinity` and a `podAntiAffinity`.

The `nodeAffinity` defines which nodes your Pods are allowed to be scheduled on, based on the node labels. In this case, I have allowed my Pods to be scheduled on all 3 zones, in other words, on any of the three vSphere Clusters.

The `podAntiAffinity` also deals with Pod placement, again based on labels. It states that this Pod cannot be scheduled on a node if a Pod with the same label (nginx) is already scheduled here. Thus, Pods in this StatefulSet will be scheduled in different zones, and afterwards, the PVs will then be instantiated in the same zone as the Pod since we have set the `volumeBindingMode` to `WaitForFirstConsumer`, i.e. wait for the Pod. For Affinity and anti-Affinity to work in Kubernetes, all nodes in the Kubernetes cluster must be labelled appropriately and correctly with the label described in `topologyKey`. We have already verified that this is the case. Here is the complete StatefulSet manifest.

```
apiVersion: apps/v1
kind: StatefulSet
metadata:
  name: web
spec:
  replicas: 3
  selector:
    matchLabels:
      app: nginx
  serviceName: nginx
  template:
    metadata:
      labels:
        app: nginx
    spec:
      affinity:
        nodeAffinity:
          requiredDuringSchedulingIgnoredDuringExecution:
            nodeSelectorTerms:
              - matchExpressions:
                  - key: topologies.csi.vmware.com/zone
                    operator: In
                    values:
                      - zone-a
                      - zone-b
                      - zone-c
        podAntiAffinity:
          requiredDuringSchedulingIgnoredDuringExecution:
            - labelSelector:
                matchExpressions:
                  - key: app
                    operator: In
                    values:
                      - nginx
              topologyKey: topologies.csi.vmware.com/zone
      containers:
        - name: nginx
          image: gcr.io/google_containers/nginx-slim:0.8
          ports:
            - containerPort: 80
              name: web
          volumeMounts:
            - name: www
```

```
                mountPath: /usr/share/nginx/html
          - name: logs
            mountPath: /logs
  volumeClaimTemplates:
    - metadata:
        name: www
      spec:
        accessModes: [ "ReadWriteOnce" ]
        storageClassName: wffc-sc
        resources:
          requests:
            storage: 5Gi
    - metadata:
        name: logs
      spec:
        accessModes: [ "ReadWriteOnce" ]
        storageClassName: wffc-sc
        resources:
          requests:
            storage: 1Gi
```

After applying the StatefulSet, the rollout of the web server can be verified. Remember, we are looking to make sure that each Pod/PV combinations in the StatefulSet has been placed in its own unique vSphere Cluster in our environment.

```
$ kubectl get sts
NAME   READY   AGE
web    3/3     49m

$ kubectl get pods web-0 web-1 web-2
NAME    READY   STATUS    RESTARTS   AGE
web-0   1/1     Running   0          49m
web-1   1/1     Running   0          49m
web-2   1/1     Running   0          49m

$ kubectl get pods web-0 web-1 web-2 -o json | egrep "hostname|nodeName|claimName"
                        "f:hostname": {},
                                    "f:claimName": {}
                                    "f:claimName": {}
            "hostname": "web-0",
            "nodeName": "k8s-worker-02",
                        "claimName": "www-web-0"
                        "claimName": "logs-web-0"
                            "f:hostname": {},
                                        "f:claimName": {}
                                        "f:claimName": {}
            "hostname": "web-1",
            "nodeName": "k8s-worker-01",
                        "claimName": "www-web-1"
                        "claimName": "logs-web-1"
                            "f:hostname": {},
                                        "f:claimName": {}
                                        "f:claimName": {}
            "hostname": "web-2",
            "nodeName": "k8s-worker-03",
                        "claimName": "www-web-2"
                        "claimName": "logs-web-2"
```

Let's remind ourselves of which K8s nodes are in which zones:

```
$ kubectl get nodes -L topologies.csi.vmware.com/zone -L topologies.csi.vmware.com/region
NAME                    STATUS    ROLES                    AGE    VERSION    ZONE      REGION
k8s-controlplane-01     Ready     control-plane,master     22h    v1.21.1    zone-a    region-1
k8s-worker-01           Ready     <none>                   22h    v1.21.2    zone-a    region-1
k8s-worker-02           Ready     <none>                   22h    v1.21.2    zone-b    region-1
k8s-worker-03           Ready     <none>                   22h    v1.21.1    zone-c    region-1
```

And we can also check with zone the various PVs were deployed to by using the JSON output to display certain fields. Unfortunately, the wrapping of the output makes it a little difficult to decipher, but this output is displaying where the PVs that are associated with the Pods reside.

```
$ kubectl get pv -o=jsonpath='{range .items[*]}{.metadata.name}{"\t"}\
{.spec.claimRef.name}{"\t"}{.spec.nodeAffinity}{"\n"}{end}'
pvc-12c9b0d4-e0a5-48b5-8e5d-479a8f96715b    logs-web-
0     {"required":{"nodeSelectorTerms":[{"matchExpressions":[{"key":"failure-
topologies.csi.vmware.com/zone","operator":"In","values":["zone-b"]},{"key":"failure-
topologies.csi.vmware.com/region","operator":"In","values":["region-1"]}]}]}}
pvc-2d8dfb98-966d-4006-b731-1aedd0cffbc5    logs-web-
1     {"required":{"nodeSelectorTerms":[{"matchExpressions":[{"key":"failure-
topologies.csi.vmware.com/zone","operator":"In","values":["zone-a"]},{"key":"failure-
topologies.csi.vmware.com io/region","operator":"In","values":["region-1"]}]}]}}
pvc-590da63c-1839-4848-b1a1-b7068b67f00b    logs-web-
2     {"required":{"nodeSelectorTerms":[{"matchExpressions":[{"key":"failure-
topologies.csi.vmware.com/zone","operator":"In","values":["zone-c"]},{"key":"failure-
topologies.csi.vmware.com/region","operator":"In","values":["region-1"]}]}]}}
pvc-5ea98c4d-70ef-431f-9e87-a52a2468a515    www-web-
1     {"required":{"nodeSelectorTerms":[{"matchExpressions":[{"key":"failure-
topologies.csi.vmware.com/zone","operator":"In","values":["zone-a"]},{"key":"failure-
topologies.csi.vmware.com/region","operator":"In","values":["region-1"]}]}]}}
pvc-b23ba58a-3275-4bf5-835d-bf41aefa148d    www-web-
2     {"required":{"nodeSelectorTerms":[{"matchExpressions":[{"key":"failure-
topologies.csi.vmware.com/zone","operator":"In","values":["zone-c"]},{"key":"failure-
topologies.csi.vmware.com/region","operator":"In","values":["region-1"]}]}]}}
pvc-b8458bef-178e-40dd-9bc0-2a05f1ddfd65    www-web-
0     {"required":{"nodeSelectorTerms":[{"matchExpressions":[{"key":"failure-
topologies.csi.vmware.com/zone","operator":"In","values":["zone-b"]},{"key":"failure-
topologies.csi.vmware.com/region","operator":"In","values":["region-1"]}]}]}}
```

This looks good. Pod web-0 in on k8s-worker-02 which is in zone-b, and the two PVs — www-web-0 and logs-web-0 — are also in zone-b. Likewise for the other Pods and PVs. Topology placement is working as designed.

vSAN Stretched Cluster Considerations

A frequently requested topology on which to deploy a Kubernetes cluster is a vSAN Stretched Cluster. This requires some careful consideration since a vSAN Stretched Cluster has only two availability zones/data sites and Kubernetes always has an odd number of control plane nodes, either 1, 3, 5, or 7. Thus you will always have a situation where one of the vSAN Stretched Cluster sites has more control plane nodes than the other. If the site with the most control plane nodes fails, then the control plane will not be available until vSphere HA has had time to restart the failed nodes on the remaining site and the control plane components such as the Kubernetes key-value store (etcd) has recovered. These are some of the factors that should be considered if you plan to deploy a Kubernetes cluster on vSAN Stretched Cluster. Support for vSAN Stretched Cluster appeared in the official vSAN 7.0U3 release notes in January 2022. However, there was a significant issue uncovered whereby if the data sites partitioned, persistent volume information could be lost from the CNS. When volume metadata is not present in the CNS, you cannot create, delete, or re-schedule Pods with CNS volumes since the vSphere CSI Driver must access volume information from CNS to perform these operations. It seems that this issue was addressed in the 7.0U3d release which became available in April 2022. This is vCenter Server build number 19480866 so ensure you are using this release at a minimum if planning to use vSAN Stretched Cluster topologies for Kubernetes clusters.

The official VMware documentation provides additional guidance such as enabling vSphere HA, DRS, Host and VM Affinity Groups, etc. However, when it comes to PV provisioning, the advice given in the official documentation is that the same storage policy should be used for all node VMs, including the control plane and worker, as well as all Persistent Volumes (PVs). This single, standardized storage policy in vSphere equates to the Kubernetes administrator creating a single, standard StorageClass for all storage objects in the Kubernetes cluster.

The other major limitation at the time of writing (June 2022) is that currently only block based read-write-once (RWO) volumes are supported. There is no support for Kubernetes read-write-many (RWX) vSAN File Service based file volumes in vSAN Stretched Cluster.

Network Permissions for vSAN based RWX Volumes

As a security precaution, a vSphere administrator may be asked to assist in locking down network access to certain read-write-many volumes that can be dynamically created on vSAN File Service. You may be asked to control which networks could access a volume, what access permissions were allowed from that network and whether we could squash root privileges when a root user accesses a volume? All of these options are configurable from the vSphere Client and are very visible when creating file shares manually in the vSphere UI. But how does one configure these when dynamically provisioning vSAN file share read-write-many PVs in Kubernetes. This section will show how to accomplish this task.

Assume that the vSphere CSI (Container Storage Interface) driver has already been deployed with no considerations given for vSAN File Service network permissions. Therefore, any PVs backed by file shares will be read-write accessible from any IP address by default. We can verify this by starting an ssh session to the Kubernetes cluster control plane node and displaying the current contents of the `vsphere-config-secret`. As seen a number of times already, this holds the vSphere CSI driver configuration file located in `/etc/kubernetes/csi-vsphere.conf`. This time, instead of displaying the outputs in column format or in JSON format, the *-o yaml* displays the output in YAML format.

```
$ kubectl get secret vsphere-config-secret -n kube-system
NAME                    TYPE     DATA  AGE
vsphere-config-secret   Opaque   1     72d


$ kubectl get secret vsphere-config-secret -n kube-system -o yaml
apiVersion: v1
data:
  csi-vsphere.conf: CltHbG9iYWxdCmNsd<<<--snip--->>>4cy16b251Cg==
kind: Secret
metadata:
  creationTimestamp: "2021-04-28T10:09:00Z"
  managedFields:
  - apiVersion: v1
    fieldsType: FieldsV1
    fieldsV1:
```

```
    f:data:
      .: {}
      f:csi-vsphere.conf: {}
    f:type: {}
  manager: kubectl-create
  operation: Update
  time: "2021-04-28T10:09:00Z"
name: vsphere-config-secret
namespace: kube-system
resourceVersion: "2502"
uid: 1fa17219-0d91-437c-831b-094710723f56
type: Opaque
```

Since the secret is encoded in base64, let's decode it.

```
$ echo "CltHbG9iYWxdCmNsd<<<--snip--->>>4cy16b251Cg==" | base64 -d
[Global]
cluster-id = "cormac-upstream"
cluster-distribution = "native"

[VirtualCenter "192.168.51.1"]
user = "administrator@vsphere.local"
password = "******"
port = "443"
insecure-flag = "1"
datacenters = "OCTO-Datacenter"

[Labels]
topology-categories = "k8s-region, k8s-zone"
```

As can be seen, there is no information about network permissions in this configuration file. Let's assume there is a requirement to provide read-write access to networks A (VLAN 51), but provide read-only access to a different network B (VLAN62). The steps to achieve this are:

- Build a new `csi-vsphere.conf` file or modify the current one if it already exists
- Delete the existing vsphere-config-secret
- Create a new vsphere-config-secret with the new `csi-vsphere.conf` contents
- Create a new RWX PV backed by vSAN File Service and verify that it has new network permissions

Here is the contents of my new `csi-vsphere.conf`, located in `/etc/kubernetes` on the Kubernetes control plane node. Note the additional of two additional `NetPermissions` stanzas and the quotes around the names "VLAN51" and "VLAN62". Strings are expected here, and so quote them to get them recognized. The contents of each stanza is pretty straight-forward. Access from network 51 is given read-write permissions while access from network 62 has read-only permissions. Note that "VLAN51" and "VLAN62" are simply identifiers here – I could have called them anything so long as the string is unique. The identifiers do not have any bearing on the underlying network topology, or anything important like that. For the sake of security, I have hidden the password.

```
$ cat csi-vsphere.conf
[Global]
cluster-id = "cormac-upstream"
cluster-distribution = "native"

[VirtualCenter "192.168.51.1"]
user = "administrator@vsphere.local"
password = "*********"
```

```
port = "443"
insecure-flag = "1"
datacenters = "OCTO-Datacenter"

[NetPermissions "VLAN51"]
ips = "192.168.51.0/24"
permissions = "READ_WRITE"
rootsquash = false

[NetPermissions "VLAN62"]
ips = "192.168.62.0/26"
permissions = "READ_ONLY"
rootsquash = false

[Labels]
topology-categories = "k8s-region, k8s-zone"
```

Now I need to delete the current secret and create a new one with the new contents of the `csi-vsphere.conf`. I am doing this operation from the `/etc/kubernetes` folder on the control plane nodes in my Kubernetes cluster.

```
$ kubectl delete secret vsphere-config-secret --namespace=kube-system
secret "vsphere-config-secret" deleted

$ kubectl create secret generic vsphere-config-secret \
--from-file=csi-vsphere.conf \
--namespace=kube-system
secret/vsphere-config-secret created
```

It is possible to display the secret in YAML format and decode it once again to make sure the contents have been updated successfully. Assuming the secret is successfully created, there is no need to do anything further with the vSphere CSI driver. It will automatically use the updated secret and CSI configuration.

The next step is to create a new application which uses dynamic, RWX PV backed by the vSAN File Service file share. This application is getting deployed onto a Kubernetes cluster that resides on VLAN51, the network which has full access to the file shares. The StorageClass manifest, while referencing a storage policy that resolves to a vSAN datastore, it is the inclusion of the line `csi.storage.k8s.io/fstype: nfs4` that indicates that this volume should be build using a file share rather than block storage on vSAN.

```
kind: StorageClass
apiVersion: storage.k8s.io/v1
metadata:
  name: vsan-file-netperms
provisioner: csi.vsphere.vmware.com
parameters:
  storagepolicyname: "vsanfs-octo-c"
  csi.storage.k8s.io/fstype: nfs4
```

With the StorageClass in place, it is now possible to create the Persistent Volume Claim.

```
apiVersion: v1
kind: PersistentVolumeClaim
metadata:
  name: file-pvc-netperms
spec:
  accessModes:
```

```
  - ReadWriteMany
  resources:
    requests:
      storage: 3Gi
  storageClassName: vsan-file-netperms
```

Next, create two busybox Pods which share access to the resulting Persistent Volume. Each Pod runs a command that simply writes a message into a file on the file share/NFS. If the Pods have read-write access, then they should both be able to successfully write to the file on the share.

```
apiVersion: v1
kind: Pod
metadata:
  name: app-1-netperm
spec:
  containers:
  - name: test-container
    image: gcr.io/google_containers/busybox:1.24
    command: ["/bin/sh", "-c", "echo 'hello from app1' >> /mnt/volume1/index.html && while
true ; do sleep 2 ; done"]
    volumeMounts:
    - name: file-volume-netp
      mountPath: /mnt/volume1
  restartPolicy: Always
  volumes:
  - name: file-volume-netp
    persistentVolumeClaim:
      claimName: file-pvc-netperms

---

apiVersion: v1
kind: Pod
metadata:
  name: app-2-netperm
spec:
  containers:
  - name: test-container
    image: gcr.io/google_containers/busybox:1.24
    command: ["/bin/sh", "-c", "echo 'hello from app2' >> /mnt/volume1/index.html && while
true ; do sleep 2 ; done"]
    volumeMounts:
    - name: file-volume-netp
      mountPath: /mnt/volume1
  restartPolicy: Always
  volumes:
  - name: file-volume-netp
    persistentVolumeClaim:
      claimName: file-pvc-netperms
```

There is one final test to do, and that is to make sure that I cannot write to these volumes if I try to access them from a network that has read-only permissions. Thus, if I deploy my application once again, but to a Kubernetes cluster that exists on "VLAN 62", the Pods on this cluster have read-only access:

```
% kubectl get pods
NAME                 READY   STATUS            RESTARTS   AGE
app-1-netperm        0/1     CrashLoopBackOff  3          78s
app-2-netperm        0/1     Error             3          78s
```

207

```
% kubectl logs app-1-netperm
/bin/sh: can't create /mnt/volume1/index.html: Read-only file system
```

Something is preventing the Pods from coming online in this last example, but it looks like it is behaving as expected. The Pods are unable to write to this volume since the network has been granted read-only permissions. Hopefully this exercise has given you (the vSphere administrator) some insight into how you can manage network access to RWX Kubernetes Persistent Volumes backed by vSAN File Service file shares.

vSphere CSI Metrics

This feature, introduced in version 2.5 of the vSphere CSI driver, enables the exposing of CSI metrics. This allows third party metric collecting products, such as Prometheus, to gather and store CSI metrics as time series data. Using the information captured in Prometheus, monitoring dashboards such as those provided by Grafana, make it easy to monitor the health and stability of the CSI driver.

In the vSphere CSI controller Pod, there are two containers that expose metrics. The first is the **vsphere-csi-controller** container which provides the communication from the Kubernetes Cluster API server to the CNS component on vCenter Server. This handles volume lifecycle operations, as we have seen earlier. The second is the **vsphere-syncer** container. This sends metadata information about persistent volumes to the CNS component on vCenter Server so that it can be displayed in the vSphere Client UI in the Container Volumes view. The vsphere-csi-controller container exposes Prometheus metrics from port **2112**, while the vsphere-syncer container exposes Prometheus metrics from port **2113**.

Setting up Prometheus and Grafana to gather and display TKG cluster metrics will be discussed in the Day 2 Operations chapter.

Summary

In this chapter, we delved much deeper into the vSphere CSI driver. This is an area that a vSphere administrator should definitely get some insight, as allowing Kubernetes to consume vSphere storage for Persistent Volumes is an area which is very popular. In this chapter, we looked at many features of the CSI driver. We saw considerations around different topologies, such as multi-AZ and vSAN Stretched Cluster. Note that for vanilla, upstream Kubernetes, the vSphere CSI driver must be manually installed. We saw how to do this in chapter 02, and in this chapter we saw how to modify the configuration for various use cases. For TKG and vSphere with Tanzu, the CSI driver are installed automatically without any user intervention required. However, there are some special considerations when it comes to the CSI on vSphere with Tanzu which will be discussed in the next chapter. In a nutshell, different features and functionalities may be supported depending on whether the Kubernetes distribution is upstream/vanilla, TKG (multi-cloud) or a TKG deployed through the TKG service in vSphere with Tanzu.

This GitHub page, maintained by the vSphere CSI engineering team, is a good starting point for details about vSphere CSI driver versions and supported features: https://github.com/kubernetes-sigs/vsphere-csi-driver

06

vSphere with Tanzu

Architectural Overview

VMware announced vSphere with Tanzu, formerly known as Project Pacific, at VMworld 2019 in Barcelona. This is a product that was specifically designed for vSphere administrators who are managing vSphere infrastructure which is being used to host developer platforms. In many cases, the developer platform is Kubernetes, but it could be much more than that. It is important to keep in mind that this platform was designed so that vSphere administrators could work closely and collaborate with Platform Operators, those people who are responsible for creating infrastructure for developers. Thus, the goal here is for vSphere administrators to be able to carve out resources for the Platform Operators to consume as they build platforms for the developers. Not only that, but it offers full visibility to vSphere administrators into resource usage so that the vSphere administrator can monitor usage and forecast future resources requirements. This will become clearer as the vSphere UI enhancements for vSphere with Tanzu will be examined.

To begin however, let's review some of the architectural details of the platform.

Supervisor Clusters

Let's start with an overview of the Supervisor Cluster. Since this is a book designed for vSphere administrators, most readers will understand the concept of a vSphere Cluster, which is essential a group of ESXi hosts for running virtual machine workloads. While vSphere with Tanzu continues to allow administrators to run traditional VM workloads on a vSphere Cluster, it also extends the cluster to allow container workloads to run natively on it. One way to think about this is that vSphere with Tanzu is making a vSphere Cluster behave like a Kubernetes Cluster. That might be stretching the point a little, but we can certainly think of the Supervisor Cluster as a set of three virtual machines running a Kubernetes control plane, while at the same time allowing ESXi hosts to behave similar to Kubernetes worker nodes and running container workloads. This is all configured and managed through the vSphere Client by a vSphere administrator when vSphere with Tanzu is enabled. The Supervisor Cluster leverages core vSphere features such as vSphere Distributed Resource Scheduler (DRS) and its anti-affinity rules to make sure the Supervisor Cluster nodes are placed on different ESXi hosts for availability. vSphere High Availability (HA) is also leveraged so that in the event of an ESXi host failure, the Supervisor node on the failing ESXi host can be started on another host, in accordance with the anti-affinity rules, so long as there are enough available resources. Even if there is no way to schedule the failed Supervisor node on another ESXi host, having a quorum of nodes available will allow the API server and etcd KV store on the Supervisor Cluster to remain available.

Supervisor Cluster Deployment

vCenter Server now includes several new components to enable vSphere with Tanzu and the creation of a Supervisor Cluster. The first of these components is a Supervisor Control Plane image, which is used to deploy the Supervisor Cluster control plane nodes as a set of VMs on the ESXi hosts. This is essentially Kubernetes. It is provisioned as an odd number of control plane nodes (3) and is responsible for maintaining `etcd`, the KV (key-value) store that is essentially the Kubernetes configuration database. These nodes are integrated with vSphere DRS and are deployed with anti-affinity rules to ensure that any failure or maintenance on an ESXi host in the vSphere Cluster does not bring down the control plane. These control plane VMs, as well as running the traditional Kubernetes API server, also have a bunch of vSphere extensions around networking (Container Network Interface/CNI), storage (Container Storage Interface/CSI), scheduling and authentication, the latter enabling users to log in to vSphere Namespaces and TKG guest/workload clusters using their vSphere single sign-on (SSO) credentials.

Another significant part is the Spherelet Bundle, which is the component that allows an ESXi host to behave as a Kubernetes worker node. A service called the Workload Platform Service (WCP) on vCenter installs a Spherelet daemon on every ESXi host in the cluster when vSphere with Tanzu is enabled. It also exposes a REST API that enables the management of vSphere Namespaces which we will read about shortly. Note that the Spherelet is only deployed and enables ESXi hosts to behave as worker nodes only when NSX-T is available. Without NSX-T, some of the features are not available. These will be highlighted later in the chapter.

Finally, there is the Token Exchange Service. This authentication service takes vSphere SSO Service SAML credentials and converts them to JSON Web Tokens (JWT) for use with systems like Kubernetes. This is what allows a vSphere SSO user to login to a Kubernetes Guest Cluster. The login mechanism utilizes Kubernetes Role-Based Access Control (RBAC). This means that customized Kubernetes Role Bindings can also be created for users who are not part of the vCenter SSO. RBAC and cluster access with be discussed in chapter 7, day 2 operations.

With all of this in mind, let's look at some on the major building blocks that make up vSphere with Tanzu.

vSphere Namespaces

vSphere Namespaces are how we are achieving multi-tenancy and isolation in vSphere with Tanzu.

For those readers who have a Kubernetes background, the first thing to mention is that vSphere Namespaces in a Supervisor Cluster are very different to namespaces in Kubernetes. Namespaces in the context of a Supervisor Cluster can be thought of as an extension to the vSphere concept known as Resource Pools. At a basic level, it is used to isolate a set of CPU, Memory and Storage resources for a given application or a given user, although it can do much more than that. The vSphere administrator will be required to setup and modify attributes of the vSphere Namespace to determine who can access it. A vSphere administrator can also configure which storage policies are visible to the vSphere Namespace which in turn determines which datastores the vSphere Namespace has access to. vSphere Namespaces are also used to control which virtual machine images can be used for create TKG cluster nodes, as well as standalone virtual machines. This is done by associating content libraries with the vSphere Namespace, and only the images that are stored in the content library are available within the vSphere Namespace. Content library creation, image management and association with vSphere Namespaces is again the tole of the vSphere administrator.

vSphere namespaces can be created for the running of traditional VMs, the running of Native Pods, the deployment of a complete Tanzu Kubernetes Cluster (TKC), or all of the above.

Spherelet/Spherelet Agent

It was previously highlighted that ESXi hosts can now work as Kubernetes worker nodes. How exactly is that achieved? Well, in vanilla Kubernetes, the worker nodes run a Kubernetes agent, called the `kubelet`. It manages Pods and manage containers in those Pods. We talked about the function of the `kubelet` already. The `kubelet` watches the API server on the control plane for new Pods that need to be scheduled on its node, as well as taking care of configuring and mounting external storage to the node on behalf of containers. It also configures networking for the Pods and nodes, creating pseudo NICs and putting in place all of the bridging required by a container.

Once the `kubelet` determines that the node is fully configured and is ready to run containers, it informs the container run-time to say that it can now start containers. The `kubelet` continuously probes the Pod and Container health and monitors the communication endpoints. It also handles the killing and restarting of Pods when necessary – taking care of the life-cycle management of the Pods and Containers on that node. It constantly polls the Kubernetes API server to see if there are new Pods that have been scheduled on its node.

To make an ESXi host into a Kubernetes node, we introduce the concept of a `spherelet`. The `spherelet` runs on the ESXi host and just like the `kubelet`, monitors the API server for new Native Pod requests, etc. The `spherelet` is only responsible for the Native Pods on that ESXi host/node. The concept of Native Pods has not yet been introduced, but we will come to this directly. Suffice to say that Native Pods are like Kubernetes Pods in that they group containers into a single unit of management. But there are some difference which we will cover in a moment. Once the `spherelet` on the ESXi host has determined that networking and storage has been configured correctly, and that the Native Pod is now ready to run containers, it passes control over the `spherelet agent` which runs inside of the Native Pod. This takes care of the container disk mounts, any network bridging and running the containers. Once a container is launched, the responsibility for the container stays with the `spherelet agent` in the Native Pod – it is no longer the responsibility of the `spherelet` on the node. The `spherelet agent` will issue all of the probes for necessary for container health, provide the interactive endpoint for container communication (shell access, retrieve logs) and also deciding whether or not a container should be killed or restarted and so on.

Native Pods / PodVMs / vSphere Pods

When discussing the `spherelet` and the `spherelet agent` in the previous section, it covered most of the concepts around the Native Pod. Sometimes these objects are referred to as PodVMs, but we will use the term Native Pods here. Since the ESXi host is now a Kubernetes node, it has the ability to run Pods, and those Pods are what we are calling Native Pods. The Native Pod can be thought of as a virtual machine, but a very light-weight, optimized, highly opinionated and fast booting virtual machine which in turn can run containers.

Be aware that the Native Pod feature has a requirement on NSX-T at this time. The author believes there are plans to remove this restriction at some point in the future, but no details or timelines are available to share at the time of going to press.

At its core, a Native Pod is really just a flavour of what we call a CRX instance. A CRX instance is a very special form of VM which provides a Linux Application Binary Interface (ABI) through a very isolated environment. Let's take a closer look at **CRX** next.

CRX – Container Run-time for ESXi

When the CRX instance starts, it also launches a single controlling process. This is what makes it very similar to containers and why we called it the Container Run-time for ESXi. VMware provides the Linux Kernel image used by CRX instances. It is packaged with ESXi and maintained by VMware. When a CRX instance is brought up, ESXi will push the Linux image directly into the CRX instance.

CRX instances have a `CRX init` process which is responsible for providing the endpoint to allow communication with ESXi, and allow the environment running inside of the CRX instance to be managed.

CRX instances have 2 personalities or modes. The `spherelet` is responsible for injecting the personality of the CRX instance when it starts up. The first, called managed mode, which is what a Native Pod is. A CRX instance in managed mode means that the instance is visible to vCenter Server as a virtual machine. Its resource usage can be examined, its IP address can be checked, etc. An un-managed CRX instance means that the instance is treated as an application or daemon, and is not visible to vCenter Server. The image service in vSphere with Tanzu, which provides images to the containers running in a Native Pod, is an example of the unmanaged mode instance. It only exists for the duration of downloading and extracting an image. The job of the image service is to download and extract images to a location where they can be mounted by Pods. The personalities for CRX instances are provided by ESXi VIBs and are injected into the CRX Instance. The `spherelet agent` manages the containers in the Native Pod.

When using CRX and Native Pods for applications, it is important to consider availability. Kubernetes has no concept of vMotion or of moving a Pod from one node to another in an orchestrated fashion. If a Kubernetes node fails, the node gets drained and the Native Pods get rescheduled on another node elsewhere in the cluster, assuming it is part of a highly available construct like a Deployment or StatefulSet. If it is a Standalone Pod, then it is deleted. If this is a stateless application, then anything that was written in the Pod is lost. The same is true during upgrade scenarios. Users of Native Pods need to understand that their applications need to be deployed as highly available, either as ReplicaSets/Deployments or as StatefulSets, same as for standard Kubernetes.

TKG Service

The TKG Service is a service on the Supervisor Cluster to provide life-cycle management of guest Kubernetes cluster. This means that by using a vSphere Namespace and, using the resources allocated within it, a TKG Guest or Workload cluster can be created. The TKG clusters are upstream aligned, fully conformant Kubernetes cluster. As a vSphere administrator, your role is to isolate a set of resources through the vSphere namespaces. Within the namespace, the vSphere administrator assigns storage policies which will be converted to StorageClasses so that developers can create persistent volumes. The vSphere administrator can also control who has access to the cluster. This will probably be a Platform Operator who creates developer infrastructure or it could be developer(s).

Now there is very much a layered approach to how Guest Clusters are deployed in a namespace in vSphere with Tanzu. We have introduced a number of custom resources within the Supervisor Cluster to simplify the deployment of Kubernetes as much as possible. And while there are many ways to deploy the cluster, the aim here was to make it as simple as possible and to hide the complexity of some of the lower layers.

At the top-most layer, we have the TKG Service, and the concept of a Guest Cluster Manager. With a simple YAML manifest file, a platform operator with the appropriate Namespace credentials can request the creation of a Guest Cluster with X number of control plane nodes and Y number of worker nodes. As well as specifying the number of nodes, vSphere administrators can control the size of these nodes through a concept called the VM Class. A VM Class is a description of the amount of resources that a VM is allowed to use, and this includes Kubernetes nodes deployed by the TKG Service. There are a total of 16 built-in VM Classes, and as part of creating a vSphere Namespace, a vSphere administrator controls which of these VM Classes can be used within the Namespace. Thus, a Platform Operator can only build TKG manifests using these VM Classes. This prevents them from building clusters with unnecessarily large nodes, and prevents them from consuming their allocated resources needlessly. Note that while there are 16 pre-canned VM Classes in vSphere with Tanzu, vSphere administrators can also create their own custom VM Classes.

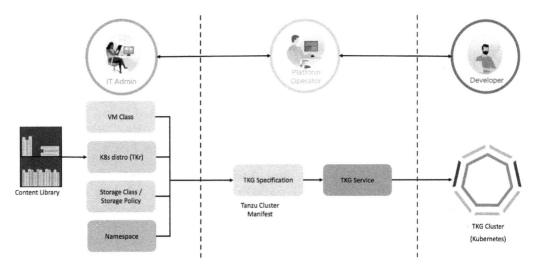

Figure 82: Controlling TKG Service Resources

Platform Operators can also specify which distribution of Kubernetes they wish to have deployed. However, the distribution is also controlled by the vSphere administrator. The Kubernetes images are held in a Content Library which the vSphere administrator associates with the vSphere Namespace. Only the images that are available in the Content Library can be used for creating TKG cluster.

The Platform Operator completes the YAML manifest with the node and image information, and alongside some other basic information about networking, a simple *kubectl apply* against the YAML manifest will send the request to the TKG Service to begin the deployment of the cluster.

The Guest Cluster Manager then produces specifications that can be consumed by Cluster API. This mechanism has already been covered in detail in chapter 2, and it is a similar mechanism that we saw being used by the TKG management cluster. This information from the YAML manifest is now passed to Cluster API controllers in the Supervisor Cluster which knows how to create new Kubernetes clusters. This is responsible for the deployment of the Tanzu Kubernetes guest/workload cluster.

The Cluster API controllers now provides a set of VM resources. These resources are consumed by a component in the Supervisor cluster called the VM Operator. This in turn communicates with vSphere to achieve the desired state of our TKG Guest Cluster, e.g. create the specified number and type of control plane nodes, create the specified number and type of worker nodes.

It should be noted that anyone that has been provided with 'edit' access on the vSphere namespace where the TKG cluster is deployed automatically gets cluster admin privileges on a Guest Cluster provisioned in that namespace – this means they have full control over Kubernetes cluster RBAC after that. This topic of controlling access to the TKG cluster will be revisited in more detail later when we look at day 2 operations in chapter 7.

vSphere VM Service

The vSphere VM Service enables Platform Operators to create virtual machines on vSphere Infrastructure via Kubernetes YAML manifests, just like they would create Tanzu Kubernetes clusters via the TKG service, or Native Pods via the Pod service. Since VMware feels that many applications will be comprised of both containers and VMs, this service allows Platform Operators and developers to create Virtual Machines through simple YAML manifests.

This feature became available with vSphere 7.0 U2a which released on April 27th, 2021. This coincided with version v1.19.1+vmware.2-vsc0.0.9-17882987 of the Supervisor Cluster. Note that there is no dependency on NSX-T to use this feature, unlike Native Pods.

In the Workload Management view, under Services, there is a link to Manage the VM Service. This is where a vSphere administrator can manage and monitor two items related to the VM Service, namely VM Classes and Content Libraries. A VM Class defines the resources that are allocated to a virtual machine provisioned by the VM service, and whether or not these should be reserved resources such as CPU and Memory, or whether the resources should be shared with other objects that require similar resources. A vSphere admin will need to give careful consideration as to how resources are allocated to VMs provisioned by Platform Operators via the VM Service, taking into account any potential conflicts that might arise due to excessive VM provisioning by Platform Operators overloading the system.

A Content Library is used to store the images of the guest operating system that will be installed in the virtual machine by the VM Service. At the time of writing, there are two guest OS supported, a Centos and an Ubuntu distribution. VMware provides these images. These can be downloaded from the VMware Cloud Marketplace - https://marketplace.cloud.vmware.com/. Search for VM

Service in the portal. Then download and add the images you require to a Content Library that has been created for your VM Service images.

When navigating the VM Service in the vSphere Client UI, the Overview section will show the 16 VM Classes that are available for use when creating the VirtualMachine YAML manifests. These are the same VM Classes available for creating TKG cluster nodes. However, a vSphere administrator can also create their own bespoke classes for the VM Service if required.

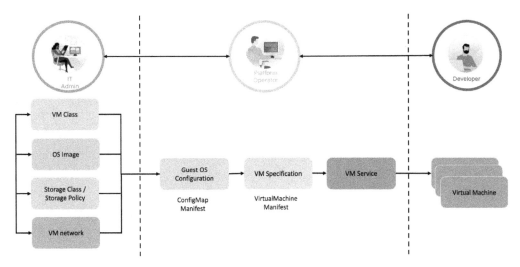

Figure 83: Controlling VM Service Resources

The VM Classes view shows more details about the classes, and how to create new ones. Each class has a Manage drop-down associated with it, which allows you to Edit or Delete the class. I recommend not editing the existing classes but rather create your own new, well-named VM classes.

The final view in the VM Service section is the Content Library view. This shows if there is a Content Library associated with any namespaces for the purposes of the VM Service. Note that it will not report on a Content Library that has been associated with a namespace for the purposes of deploying TKG clusters through the TKG Service. It only reports Content Libraries that have been associated for the purposes of deploying Virtual Machines through the VM Service. You can also create a new Content Library from this view.

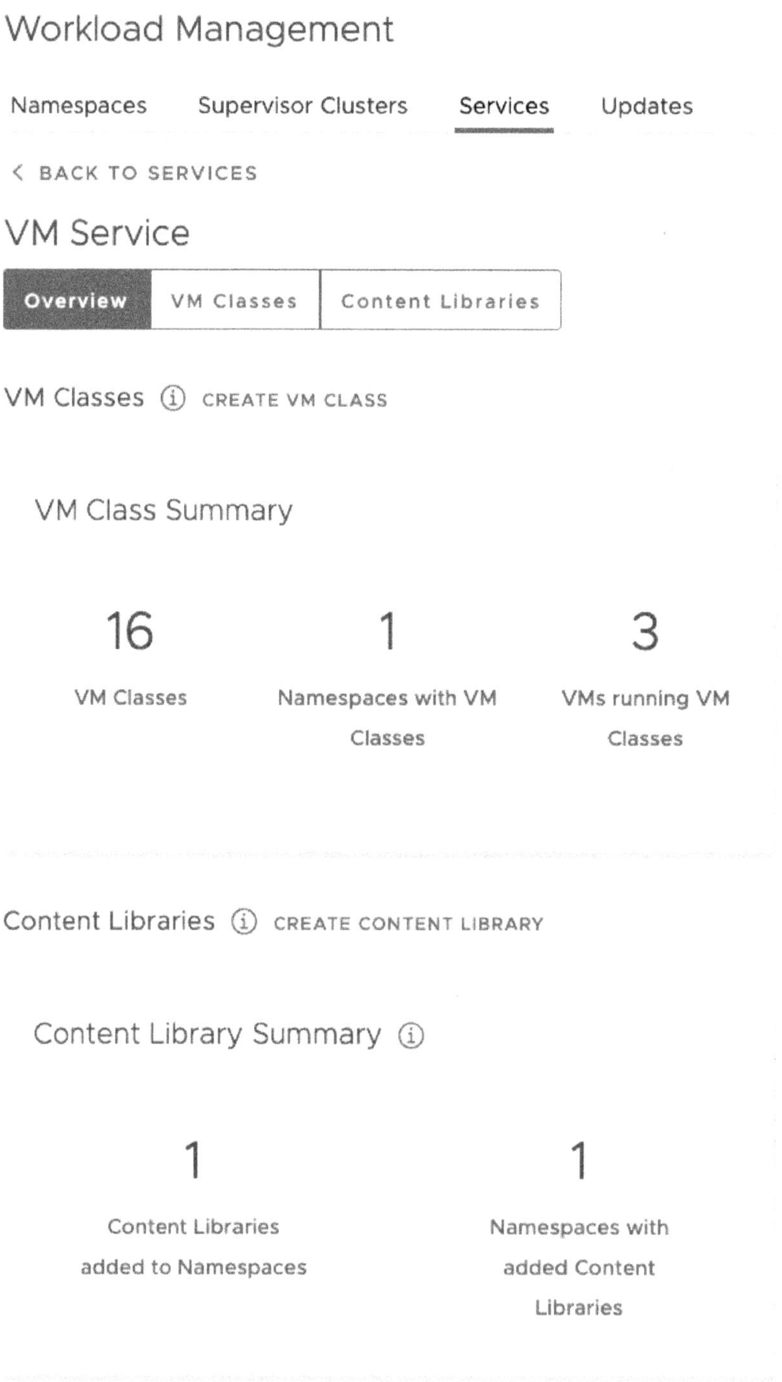

Workload Management

Namespaces   Supervisor Clusters   **Services**   Updates

< BACK TO SERVICES

VM Service

| **Overview** | VM Classes | Content Libraries |

VM Classes (i) CREATE VM CLASS

VM Class Summary

16	1	3
VM Classes	Namespaces with VM Classes	VMs running VM Classes

Content Libraries (i) CREATE CONTENT LIBRARY

Content Library Summary (i)

1	1
Content Libraries added to Namespaces	Namespaces with added Content Libraries

Figure 84: vSphere with Tanzu – VM Service

Namespace Service

The Namespace Service enables Platform Operators to create their own Supervisor Namespaces through the command line via *kubectl*, rather than continuously opening tickets to have the vSphere administrator do this on their behalf. In vSphere 7.0U3c, this feature was extended to allow the Platform Operators to add their own Kubernetes labels and annotations.

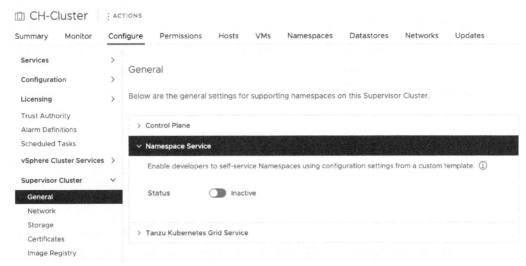

Figure 85: vSphere with Tanzu – Namespace Service

To enable the Supervisor Namespace self-service feature, navigate to **Cluster** > **Configure** > **Supervisor Cluster** > **General** and toggle the Status button show above. This will launch the following wizard where the vSphere administrator can control the amount of CPU and Memory resources that can be consumed within a namespace.

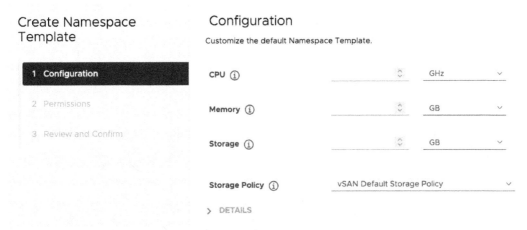

Figure 86: vSphere with Tanzu – Namespace Service Resources

After setting the resources, the next step is to specify who can create namespaces. This is typically the Platform Operator responsible for building developer infrastructure. This person also needs to have vSphere SSO credentials so that the permissions can be added to the vSphere

Namespace Service. This Platform Operator now has self-service to create vSphere Namespaces via *kubectl* when the Kubernetes context is set to the Supervisor Cluster. The important point here however is that the vSphere administrator is in complete control of the Namespace Services, and is responsible for giving permissions to the appropriate Platform Operators.

Embedded Harbor Image Registry

One of the most useful built-in features in vSphere with Tanzu is the ability to create an Image Registry with the click of a button. The Image Registry can be used as an on-premises registry for your developer teams to store and retrieve container images. The Image Registry is automatically integrated with vSphere single sign-on, and every vSphere Namespace gets its own private project area in the registry. Note that the Image Registry is built using Native Pods. Therefore, it does have a dependency on NSX-T. The feature is not available with vSphere networking.

There will be examples on how to enable and use the Harbor Image Registry later in this chapter.

vSphere Services with vSAN Data Persistence platform

Many cloud-native applications implement what is known as a "shared nothing" architecture. These applications do not require shared storage as they are designed with built-in replication/protection features. A feature available on vSphere with Tanzu which enables vSphere administrators to provide these services to developers is vSphere Services.

vSphere Services have been integrated with an earlier product called vSAN Data Persistence platform. Applications deployed to DPp have the built-in smarts to understand what action needs to be taken when there is an event on the underlying vSphere infrastructure, e.g., maintenance mode, upgrade, patching, etc.

Note that both NSX-T and vSAN are a requirement for DPp based vSphere Services. Since these applications have built-in protection, it implies that vSAN does not need to provide protection at the underlying layer. Therefore, the storage objects for the cloud-native application may be provisioned with no protection. vSAN can hand off storage services to the application if the application already has those capabilities built-in (replication, encryption, erasure-coding, etc.). This means that vSAN does not duplicate these features at the infrastructure layer and avoids consuming more storage capacity than necessary. However, if these features are not available in the application, vSAN may still be leveraged to provide these capabilities.

There is also another deployment option from a storage perspective. To facilitate a high-performance data path for these cloud-native applications, the Data Persistence platform also introduces a new construct for storage called vSAN-Direct. vSAN-Direct allows applications to consume the local storage devices on a vSAN host directly. However, these local storage devices are still under the control of HCI management, so that health, usage, and other pertinent information about the device is bubbled up to the vSphere Client. The primary goal here is to allow cloud-native applications to be seamlessly deployed onto vSAN whilst leveraging the native device speed with minimum overhead, but at the same time have those applications understand infrastructure operations such as maintenance mode, upgrades, and indeed host failures. Note that at the time of writing (June 2022), if a decision is reached to use vSAN-Direct for DPp, then the whole of the vSAN cluster must be dedicated to vSAN-Direct. It is not supported to run traditional vSAN workloads and vSAN-Direct workloads side-by-side. As per the official documentation from

VMware, "Use vSAN Direct if you are creating a dedicated hardware cluster for the shared nothing cloud-native services". Before embarking on a project with this feature, the author recommends checking the official VMware documentation for vSphere Services with vSAN DPp to see if this guidance has changed.

This is another option if considering the vSAN Data Persistence platform for cloud-native applications. You may opt to use DPp without vSAN-Direct and implement vSAN objects with *failures to tolerate* set to 0 since the application is handling the replication. This option is also fully supported but may not deliver on the performance and speed that can be achieved with vSAN-Direct.

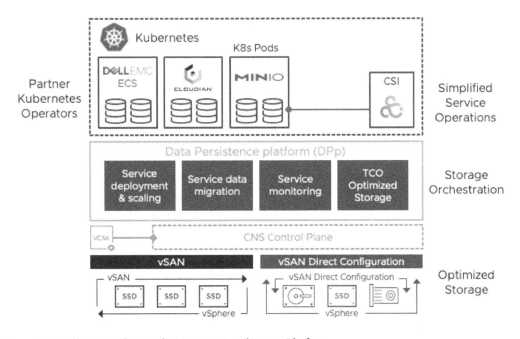

Figure 87: vSphere Services and vSAN Data Persistence Platform

As mentioned, we have partnered with several cloud-native application vendors who will create bespoke Kubernetes operators that will work with the Data Persistence platform. Partners can then define how their application should behave (e.g., re-shard, evacuate, delete and reschedule Pods, etc.) when a vSphere operation is detected. Partners can also create their own vCenter UI plugins so that operations (e.g., resize, scale in and out) that are specific to their application can be added to vCenter.

Now that we have discussed the major architectural details, let's look at how to deploy vSphere with Tanzu. Before this can be done, we need to setup an external load balancer provider. This can be provided in one of three ways, which we've already setup. The provider can be (i) an HA-Proxy appliance, (ii) a NSX ALB or (iii) it can also be provided by NSX-T which has an L4 Load Balancer built into the NSX-T Edge.

vSphere with Tanzu Limits

VMware provided an excellent Configuration Maximums tool located online at
https://configmax.esp.vmware.com/home. To see the configuration maximums for vSphere with
Tanzu and the TKG Service, navigate to **vSphere > vSphere 7.0 > vSphere with Kubernetes** and
click on the **View Limits** button. You may also select **VMware Tanzu Kubernetes Grid Service for
vSphere** to see limits associated with the TKG Service.

Workload Management Setup with HA-Proxy

The next section is going to walk through the steps of enabling workload management with the
HA-Proxy which we configured in chapter 4. Workload Management can be found in the shortcuts
section of the vSphere Client, as shown below.

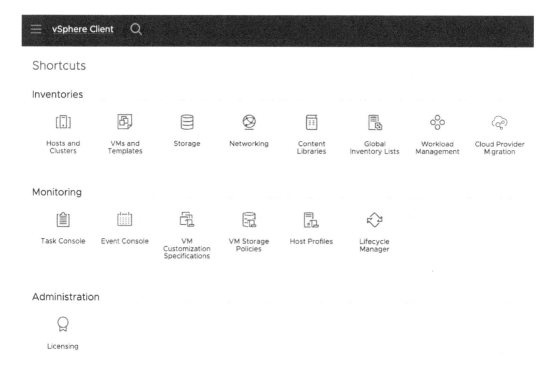

Figure 88: vSphere with Tanzu – Workload Management

Clicking on the Workload Management icon will take you to the getting started page for Workload
Management. Here, all the prerequisites for enabling Workload Management are explained. From a
vSphere infrastructure perspective, DRS and HA will need to be enabled. DRS is used to place the
nodes of the Supervisor Clusters onto separate hosts for availability purposes.

Another consideration is that the TKG service requires access to Kubernetes images in order to be
able to deploy workload clusters. This requires the setup of a content library which has a
subscription URL which will download available OVF and OVA templates for the different
Kubernetes versions supported by TKGS.

The main consideration for Workload Management is around networking, which has been discussed in detail in chapter 4. Both NSX-T and vSphere networking are supported. However, if vSphere networking is chosen, a vSphere Distributed Switch must be configured, the ESXi hosts participating in Workload Management must be added to it, and distributed portgroups for the management network, workload network and Load Balancer network should be configured. We must also setup a load balancer instance, which we have already done. For this configuration, a HA-Proxy will be used so we can see the configuration steps.

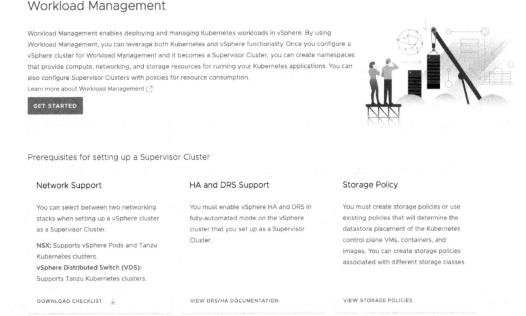

Figure 89: vSphere with Tanzu – Workload Management - Prerequisites

After clicking 'Get Started', select the correct vCenter Server and network stack. VDS is automatically selected since there is no NSX-T on this cluster.

Figure 90: vSphere with Tanzu – Workload Management – vSphere Distributed Switch

In the Cluster section, compatible clusters are displayed. These are vSphere Clusters which meet the requirements to enable Workload Management. Clusters which are not compatible are placed in the Incompatible view, and a reason for their incompatibility is displayed.

Figure 91: vSphere with Tanzu – Workload Management – Cluster Details

Another prerequisite is the selection of a storage policy. If vSAN is available as a storage solution on you cluster, then there will be some default storage policies automatically available, as shown below. If you are using some other sort of storage, then you are required to create a policy (tag based) in order to be able to select this storage type.

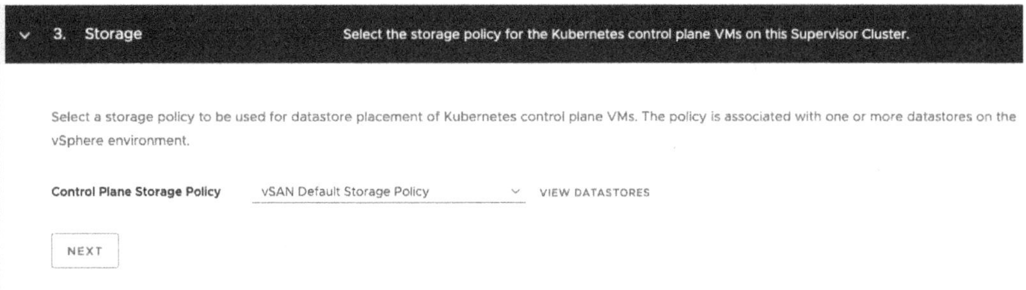

∨	3.	Storage	Select the storage policy for the Kubernetes control plane VMs on this Supervisor Cluster.

Select a storage policy to be used for datastore placement of Kubernetes control plane VMs. The policy is associated with one or more datastores on the vSphere environment.

Control Plane Storage Policy   vSAN Default Storage Policy   ∨   VIEW DATASTORES

[NEXT]

Figure 92: vSphere with Tanzu – Workload Management – Control Plane Storage Policy

Next step is where the Supervisor Cluster is informed about the HA-Proxy appliance. The name of the HA-Proxy should be a very simple name – don't specify the fully qualified domain name, and don't use any special characters. From the Type dropdown menu, select `HAProxy`. The only other option available for vSphere distributed switch networking from the dropdown is NSX ALB. We will look at that configuration next.

The management IP address is that of the HA Proxy on the management network plus the Dataplane API management port (default 5556) so in this setup, this is `192.168.51.134:5556`. Username and password are the same as what was provided when the HA-Proxy appliance was initially deployed.

The Virtual IP Ranges are the range of Load Balancer IP addresses we provided when configuring the HA-Proxy – `192.168.62.32/28` – which provides 16 load balancer IP addresses ranging from `192.168.62.32-192.168.62.47`. Note you must now provide the range and not a CIDR, which is what was provided when we deployed the HA-Proxy initially.

Lastly, we need the Server Certificate Authority. This can be found by SSH'ing as root to the HA-Proxy appliance, and copying the contents of the `/etc/haproxy/ca.crt` file to here. The CA is used to sign the actual certificate (server.crt) that the HAProxy will serve. With all of this information provided, we can proceed to the next step.

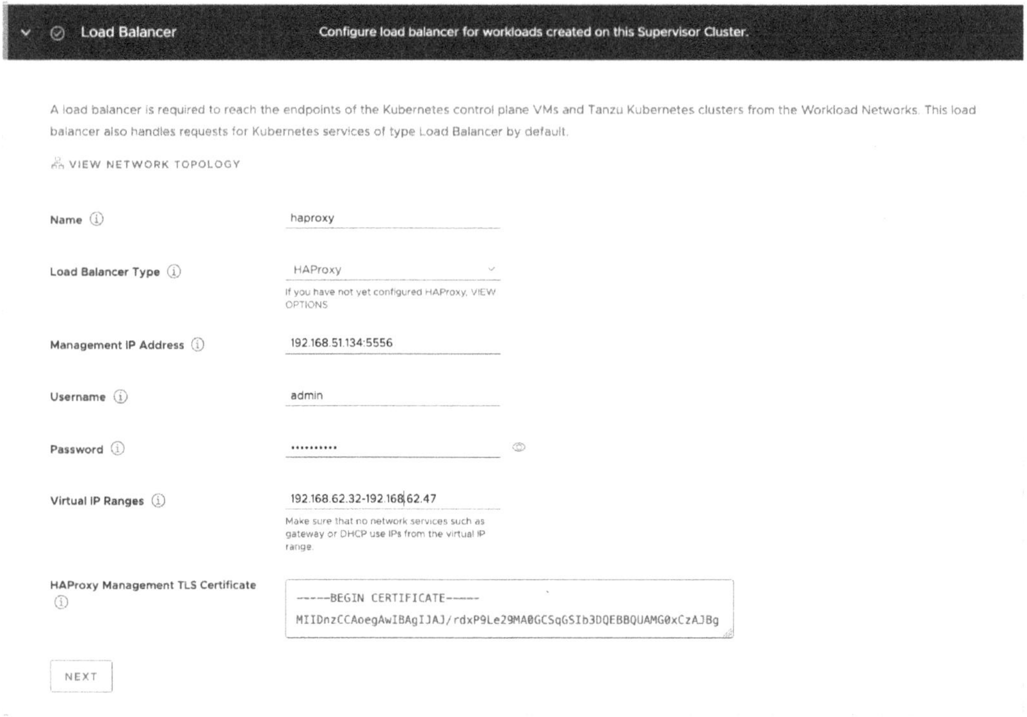

Figure 93: vSphere with Tanzu – Workload Management – Load Balancer with HA-Proxy

Now that the Load Balancer network is configured, we can move on to configuring the management and workload network. This is where the IP addresses that will be used by the Supervisor Control Plane VMs are added. A starting IP address needs to be provided, but you should set aside a minimum of 5 contiguous IP addresses for the Supervisor Control Plane VMs. Each node gets an IP address, and one of the nodes also uses the IP address for the control plane frontend. Another IP address is required for the cluster to be able to do successful rolling upgrades. The rest of the fields here, such as NTP, DNS and Gateway, are self-explanatory. Note that the management network supports both static IP address configuration as well as DHCP. Both configuration screens are shown below.

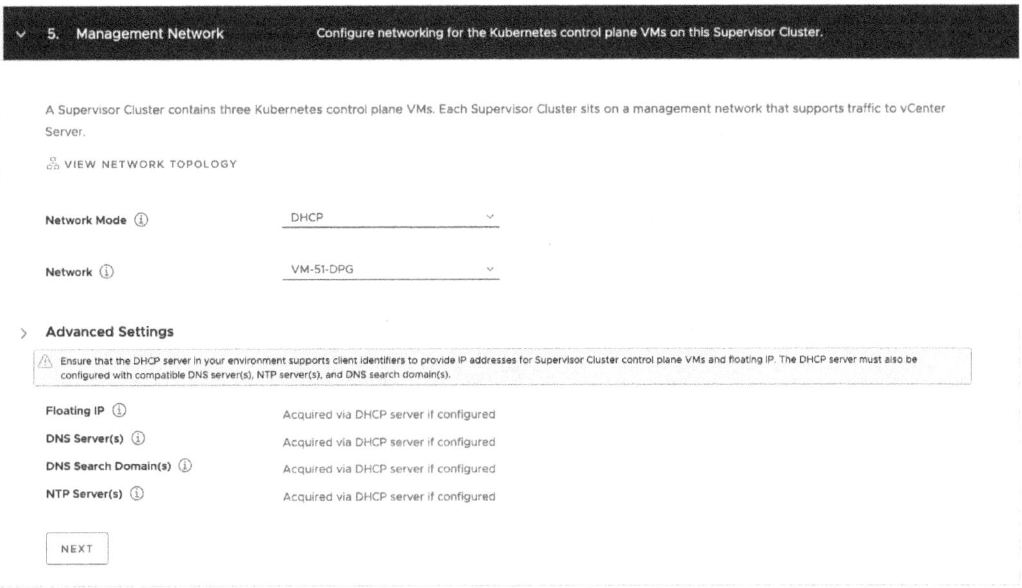

5. Management Network — Configure networking for the Kubernetes control plane VMs on this Supervisor Cluster.

A Supervisor Cluster contains three Kubernetes control plane VMs. Each Supervisor Cluster sits on a management network that supports traffic to vCenter Server.

VIEW NETWORK TOPOLOGY

Network Mode (i)   DHCP

Network (i)   VM-51-DPG

> Advanced Settings

⚠ Ensure that the DHCP server in your environment supports client identifiers to provide IP addresses for Supervisor Cluster control plane VMs and floating IP. The DHCP server must also be configured with compatible DNS server(s), NTP server(s), and DNS search domain(s).

Floating IP (i)   Acquired via DHCP server if configured
DNS Server(s) (i)   Acquired via DHCP server if configured
DNS Search Domain(s) (i)   Acquired via DHCP server if configured
NTP Server(s) (i)   Acquired via DHCP server if configured

NEXT

Figure 94: vSphere with Tanzu – Workload Management – Management Network (DHCP)

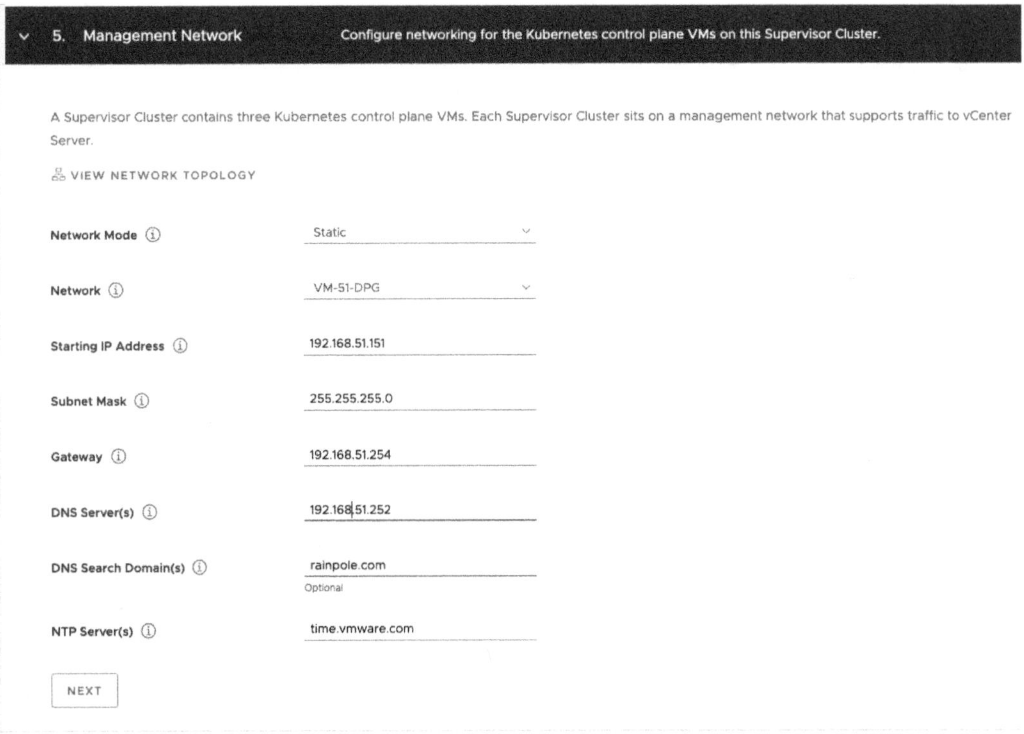

5. Management Network — Configure networking for the Kubernetes control plane VMs on this Supervisor Cluster.

A Supervisor Cluster contains three Kubernetes control plane VMs. Each Supervisor Cluster sits on a management network that supports traffic to vCenter Server.

VIEW NETWORK TOPOLOGY

Network Mode (i)   Static

Network (i)   VM-51-DPG

Starting IP Address (i)   192.168.51.151

Subnet Mask (i)   255.255.255.0

Gateway (i)   192.168.51.254

DNS Server(s) (i)   192.168.51.252

DNS Search Domain(s) (i)   rainpole.com
                           Optional

NTP Server(s) (i)   time.vmware.com

NEXT

Figure 95: vSphere with Tanzu – Workload Management – Management Network (Static)

This brings us to the final network configuration, the workload network. This can once again be configured with DHCP or with Static IP addresses. Both are once again shown below. This network will be consumed by both Supervisor Cluster nodes (multi-homed with management network) and

TKG cluster nodes. With DHCP, the only parameter that needs to be chosen is the port group where the workload entities will be connected.

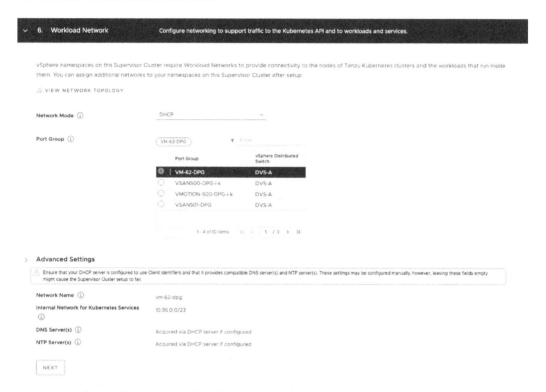

Figure 96: vSphere with Tanzu – Workload Management – Workload Network (DHCP)

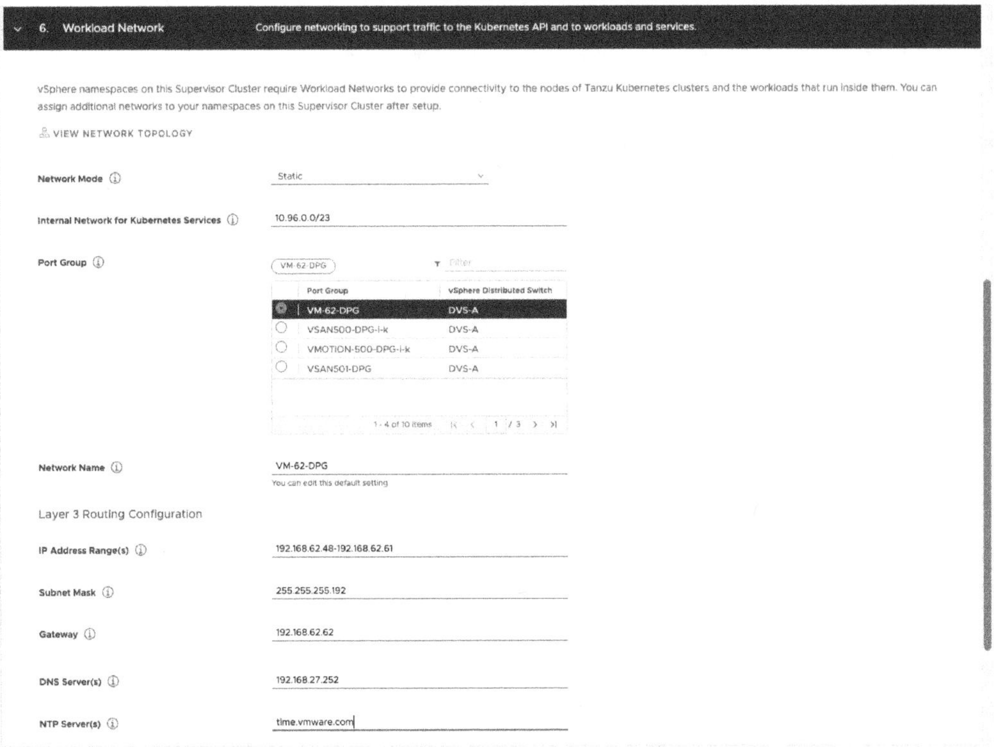

Figure 97: vSphere with Tanzu – Workload Management – Workload Network (Static)

I have used the example of a 2-NIC HA-Proxy where the workload network and load balancer network share a network segment. For this reason, I have added some more complex ranges and CIDRs to show what can be achieved. In the above example, I have a /26 segment giving me 64 IP addresses in total. I have given a range of 16 IP addresses to the load balancer network and a range of 16 IP addresses to the workload network, by way of a proof of concept. The same range of load balancer IP addresses needed to be added to the HA-Proxy at deployment time (check back to chapter 4). However, in the HA-Proxy deployment, these were added as a CIDR. Here they are added as a range. Note that because this is consuming only /26, the subnet mask must also match. This may be more complex than what is provisioned in your environment, but hopefully, it enforces the importance of getting the network configuration validated before deployment.

The next screen is where the Content Library which has the subscription URL is selected. This is for the TKG Service. The TKG Service build TKG clusters using these images.

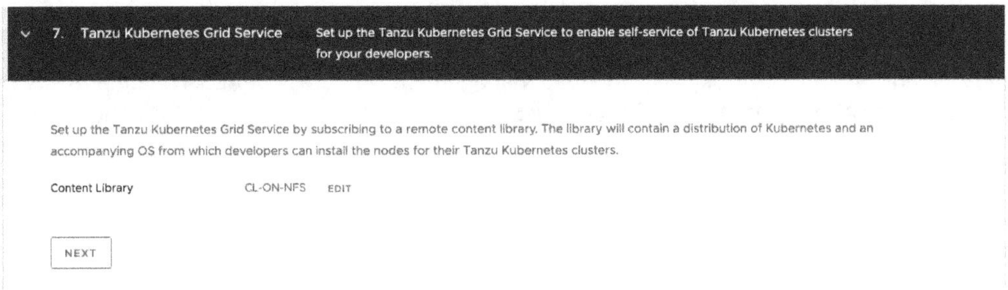

Figure 98: vSphere with Tanzu – Workload Management – TKG Service

The final screen allows the administrator to select the control plane size, which defines the size of the Supervisor VMs. The final field is an optional field where the administrator can enter the FQDN of the API server endpoint.

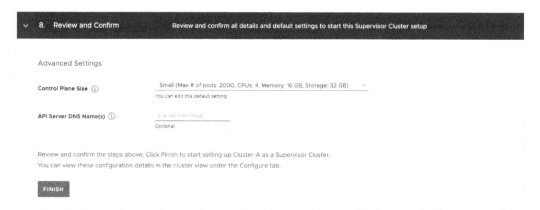

Figure 99: vSphere with Tanzu – Workload Management – Review and Confirm

This completes the configuration of Workload Management with the HA-Proxy. At this point, if you click 'Finish', the Supervisor Cluster will get deployed and will deploy Supervisor nodes which will be multi-homed on both the management network and the workload network. It will also be assigned a front-end VIP address from the load balancer network to provide for a highly available Kubernetes API server. This VIP is how Platform Operators interact with vSphere with Tanzu.

Workload Management Setup with NSX ALB

The enabling workload management using the NSX ALB is identical to the steps just described by the HA-Proxy, but rather than selecting the HA-Proxy as the Load Balancer, the NSX Advanced Load Balancer (ALB) is now chosen. Just like the HA-Proxy, once the NSX ALB controller is configured, it provides load balancing endpoints to Kubernetes services.

Note that all the same vSphere networking requirements apply to the NSX ALB as well. The ESXi hosts that are part of the vSphere Cluster that will have Workload Management enabled need to be on the same vSphere Distributed switch, and have distributed portgroups created for the necessary networks.

We saw how to configure the NSX ALB in chapter 4. Since we have seen the steps to launch workload management earlier in the shortcuts section of the vSphere Client, we will skip straight to the configuration section relevant to networking. This time, rather than selecting HA-Proxy from the drop-down list, we will select NSX ALB. That is the only difference between setting up workload management with the HA-Proxy and workload management with the NSX ALB. Note that the NSX ALB uses port 443, whereas the HA-Proxy uses 5556. This is also an important distinction in the setups.

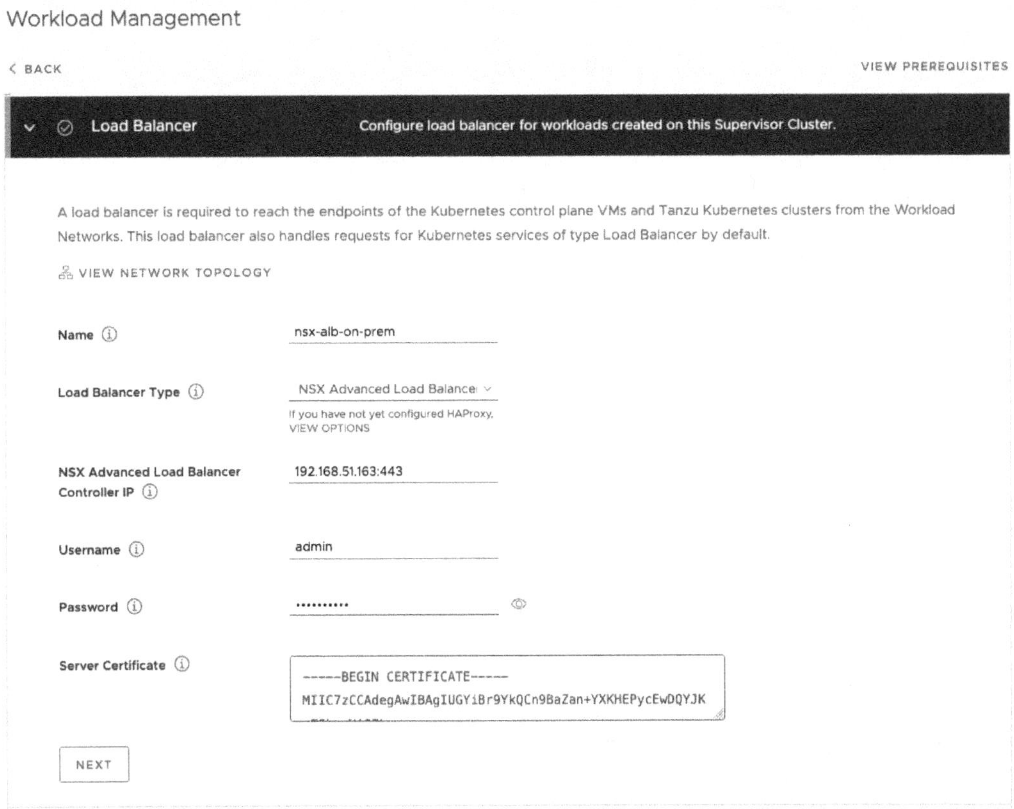

Workload Management

< BACK   VIEW PREREQUISITES

∨ ⊘ Load Balancer   Configure load balancer for workloads created on this Supervisor Cluster.

A load balancer is required to reach the endpoints of the Kubernetes control plane VMs and Tanzu Kubernetes clusters from the Workload Networks. This load balancer also handles requests for Kubernetes services of type Load Balancer by default.

⛓ VIEW NETWORK TOPOLOGY

Name ⓘ   nsx-alb-on-prem

Load Balancer Type ⓘ   NSX Advanced Load Balance ∨

                                If you have not yet configured HAProxy,
                                VIEW OPTIONS

NSX Advanced Load Balancer   192.168.51.163:443
Controller IP ⓘ

Username ⓘ   admin

Password ⓘ   •••••••••

Server Certificate ⓘ
                                -----BEGIN CERTIFICATE-----
                                MIIC7zCCAdegAwIBAgIUGYiBr9YkQCn9BaZan+YXKHEPycEwDQYJK

NEXT

Figure 100: vSphere with Tanzu – Workload Management – Load Balancer with NSX ALB

After completing the setup, and allowing the configuration of workload management to proceed, the Service Engine VMs which provide the virtual IP address/load balancer addresses on the load balancer network should be automatically deployed. The networking of these VMs can be viewed to see the multi-homed nature of the Service Engines. It should be possible to see at least 2 uplinks on the SE VM, one on the management network and the other on the VIP network.

NSX Advanced Load Balancer (Under the covers)

HA-Proxy operations are easy to understand since all networks are statically configured up-front with all the necessary IP address ranges. However, how the NSX ALB allocates VIPs and Load Balancer IP addresses is a little more complex, especially with the use of Service Engines. The nice thing about the Service Engines is that they dynamically allow the NSX ALB to scale on demand. To try to clarify what is happening 'under the covers', let's try to show the deployment through a series of diagrams. The vSphere administrator will probably be involved with the initial setup and future troubleshooting of the NSX ALB.

Let's begin with the deployment of the NSX ALB appliance, which is deployed to the management network so it can communicate with vSphere infrastructure components and the vSphere with Tanzu Supervisor Cluster. Note that in the diagrams below, I am showing different options for the Workload network and the VIP network. Just like we saw with the HA-Proxy setup, these could also be the same network, containing a unique CIDR for the workload segment and a unique CIDR for the VIP segment. In the HA-Proxy setup, there had to be a route between the VIP and workload network. With the NSX ALB, this route can be provided by the Service Engines.

In this first diagram, I am going with a very simple setup. In this setup, a single network provides ranges for the VIPs, the Workload network, and the Service Engines. No routes need to be added since components on each of the networks can communicate with one another. Also, note that the NSX ALB controller needs to be able to communicate to the vSphere infrastructure components.

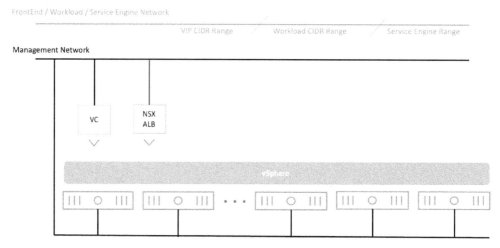

Figure 101: NSX ALB - Simple Network Setup

It is possible to create some more complex setups of course, but then there is the additional onus of making sure that communication is available between the various networks. For example, if the workload network and VIP network are separated, there needs to be a route configured between the VIP and workload networks so that packets sent to the VIP front-end network can be routed to the nodes and Pods on the workload network.

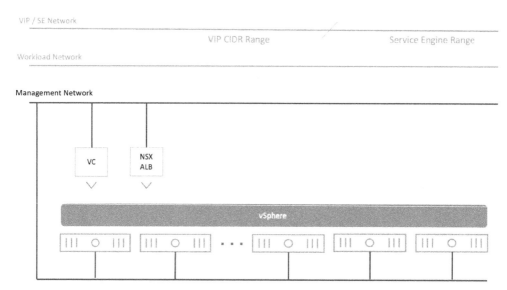

Figure 102: NSX ALB - Separate Workload Network Setup

The NSX ALB allows even more complex network configurations. Here, the VIP and SE networks are separated. Now, not only do you need to make sure that there is a route between the workload and VIP network for the reasons stated earlier but there must also be a route between the management network and the Service Engines. An explanation for this is mentioned back in chapter 4 when the setup of the NSX ALB was discussed in details. At this point, we should also be cognisant of the fact that the Service Engines need to be able to route the load balancer traffic to the appropriate workload network endpoints. Fortunately, the NSX ALB allows static routes to be created between the Service Engines and the Workload network.

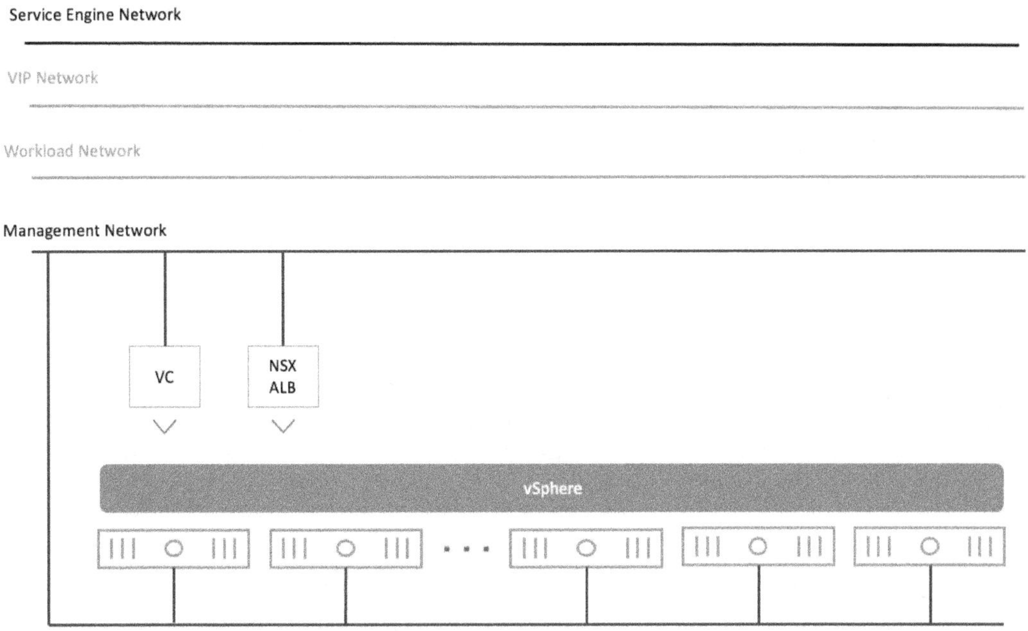

Figure 103: NSX ALB - Separate Workload and Service Engine Network Setup

As seen earlier, when vSphere with Tanzu is enabled, it deploys the Supervisor Cluster. The Supervisor is made up of 3 nodes / virtual machines, which are multi-homed onto the management network and the workload network. Once that network configuration has been completed, it requests a VIP for its control plane. This is a VIP to sit in front of the interfaces that were configured on the workload network. Using the most simplified network example above, this can be viewed as something similar to the following.

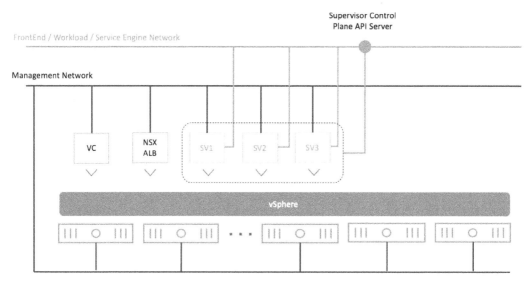

Figure 104: NSX ALB - Network Setup with Supervisor deployment

At present, the NSX ALB controller has not yet deployed any Service Engines that can meet the request for a VIP (load balancer virtual service). This is when the Service Engines get deployed. The Service Engines are configured to sit on both the management network as well as the VIP / Load Balancer network. The SE networks were defined during the NSX ALB setup in chapter 4.

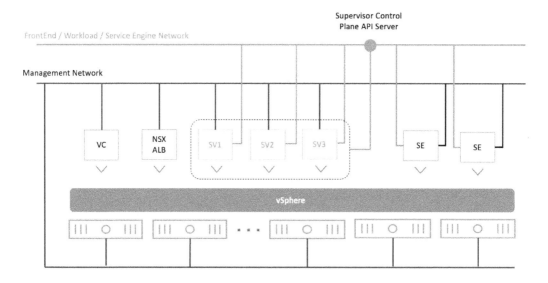

Figure 105: NSX ALB - Network Setup with Supervisor deployment and Service Engines

Two Service Engines are deployed in a highly available pair by default. Now the Service Engines can satisfy the Supervisor Cluster's requests for VIPs. The Service Engines do the Load Balancing work. If we examine the Service Engine Virtual Machines deployed on the vSphere infrastructure, it is possible to observe the networks on which they were placed.

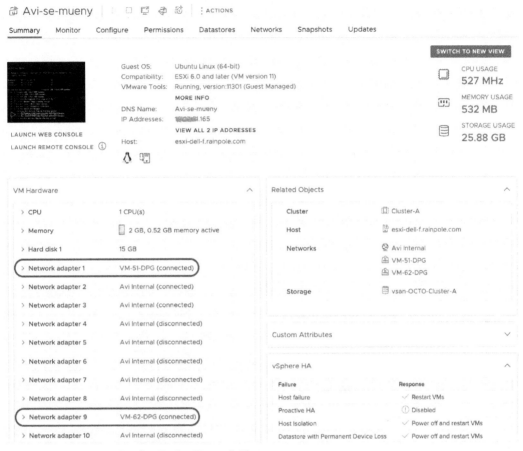

Figure 106: NSX ALB - Service Engine Network Placement

In the above figure, it is visible that the Service Engine has been multi-homed, with one network connection to VM-51-DPG, a management network where the vCenter, ESXi hosts and the NSX ALB controller resides. The other network, VM-62-DPG, is used by the workload network, the VIP network, and the Service Engines in this setup.

It is now interesting to look at the final configuration on the NSX ALB controller. Under Applications, there should be 2 virtual services. One is used by the API Server on the Supervisor, whilst the other is used by vSphere CSI Metrics. Using the View VS Tree option, we can see which IP addresses are the endpoints for the VIPs.

Figure 107: NSX ALB - Service Engine Dashboard

The upper of the two virtual services is for the API Server. It has all 3 Supervisor nodes on the workload network as its endpoints. There are two distinct ports for this service, 443 and 6443. The lower service is the CSI metrics service. This only has a single node endpoint- the node where the CSI metric component is deployed. Again, there are two ports, 2112 and 2113. By clicking on the Virtual Services view, the VIP addresses allocated to the virtual services can be observed, as well as the service ports.

	Name ^	Health	Address	App Do...	Service P...	Pools	Total Ser...	RPS	CPS	Open Co...	Through...	
☐	domain-c22-...	100	32	N/A	443, 6443	domain-c...	1		0.0 /sec	0	0.7 bps	✎
☐	domain-c22-...	100	33	N/A	2112, 2113	domain-c...	1		0.0 /sec	0	0.0 bps	✎

Displaying Past 6 Hours ∨   Average Values ∨   Q

CREATE VIRTUAL SERVICE ∨

Figure 108: NSX ALB - Service Engine Virtual Services

At this point, the role of the NSX ALB should be well understood. As mentioned, as a vSphere administrator you may need to stand up either the NSX ALB, or the HA-Proxy, or even NSX-T as a way of providing virtual IP addresses for the control planes and load balancer services for the Supervisor Cluster, and its workload clusters deployed by the TKG service.

Assuming the configuration has gone as expected, navigate to Workload Management on the vSphere Client. Under the Supervisors Clusters section, the Config Status of the cluster should now display a Running (green tick) status. The Control Plane Node Address should match the VIP Plumbed up for this service in the NSX ALB seen in the previous figure. It should also match the very first IP address in the Load Balancer range which was added as part of the Workload Management configuration.

Workload Management

Namespaces   Supervisor Clusters   Services   Updates

ADD CLUSTER   ▼ Filter

Supervisor Cluster ↑	Namespaces	Hosts	Services	Config Status	Control Plane Node Address	CPU for namespaces	Memory for namespaces
○ Cluster-A	0	4	--	✓ Running	████.32	0	0

Figure 109: vSphere with Tanzu - Supervisor Cluster Running

At this point, vSphere with Tanzu is up and running. Let's see what the next steps for the vSphere administrator are in this environment.

Create a vSphere Namespace

We have now seen two ways to set up Workload Management. We've seen how to deploy it using an HA-Proxy and the NSX Advanced Load Balancer. While the setup of these Load Balancers was quite different, enabling Workload Management was quite similar for each. With Workload Management now enabled, the next step is to create a Namespace. By navigating to **Workload Management > Namespaces**, you should see the following landing page on the vSphere Client.

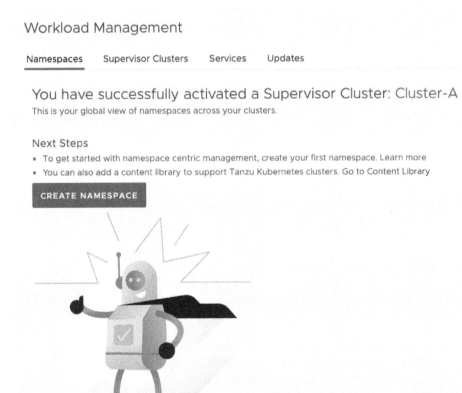

Workload Management

Namespaces   Supervisor Clusters   Services   Updates

You have successfully activated a Supervisor Cluster: Cluster-A
This is your global view of namespaces across your clusters.

Next Steps
- To get started with namespace centric management, create your first namespace. Learn more
- You can also add a content library to support Tanzu Kubernetes clusters. Go to Content Library

CREATE NAMESPACE

Figure 110: vSphere with Tanzu – Create Namespace

Click on the button to 'Create Namespace'. This will open up a wizard to begin the creation of a vSphere Namespace. In the following example which used an environment built with the NSX ALB, a vSphere Cluster which has workload management enablement must first be selected. A name.for the namespace must then be provided, and finally, the workload network must be chosen. If there is only a single workload network, this will be automatically selected. There is also the ability to provide an optional description for the namespace.

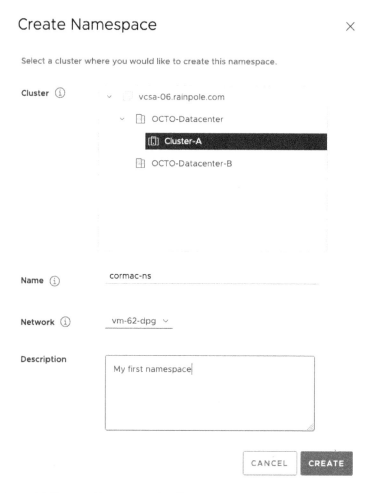

Figure 111: vSphere with Tanzu – Namespace details

After clicking on the 'Create' button, a new namespace object is created in the vSphere inventory. Several cards are displayed to show the various attributes of the namespace. These cards are:

- Status – Details about Supervisor Cluster status, and links to download tools
- Permissions – Where to configure access to the Namespace
- Storage – Which storage is available to the cluster
- Capacity and Usage – CPU, Memory & Storage Limits and Usage
- Tanzu Kubernetes Grid Service – Details about TKG deployments and Content Library
- VM Service – Details about VM Classes, VM deployments and Content Library

The tasks that a vSphere administrator should consider at this point are the following:

- Add Permissions to the Namespace, granting access to certain users.
- Add Storage to the Namespace, through storage policies. The vSphere administrator may also need to consider creating new storage policies before this step.
- Decide what limits should be put in place around CPU, Memory, and Storage usage, if any.
- Decide which VM Classes should be available to the TKG and VM Services.
- If a Content Library has not yet been set up with TKG images, set one up. If it was not added during the setup of Workload Management, add it to the TKG Service card.
- If vSphere VM Service is planned, set up another Content Library for VM images, and add it to the VM Service card.

Let's examine these tasks in more detail.

Add Permissions

By default, there are two identity sources for Namespace permissions, `localos` and `vsphere.local`. Next step is to select the user. A list of users available in the identity sources is provided. Lastly, choose a role for the user from one of Owner, 'Can edit' and 'Can view'.

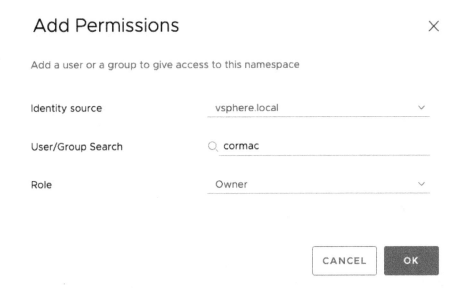

Figure 112: vSphere with Tanzu — Namespace — Add Permissions

Add Storage

This is possibly the biggest difference between standard Kubernetes and vSphere with Tanzu. Through the Storage card in the vSphere Namespace, the vSphere administrators choose storage policies to associate with the namespace. These storage policies are automatically converted to StorageClasses. There is no manual creation of StorageClasses in vSphere with Tanzu — it is all automated. Making storage available to a namespace is a simple as choosing the appropriate storage policies available on the vSphere environment. These storage policies will map to a back-end vSphere storage, such as vSAN, vVols, VMFS or NFS. For VMFS and NFS, tag-based policies will need to be created so that they can be selected in the vSphere Namespace. In this example, vSAN is available so the vSAN Default Storage Policy. This is converted to a Kubernetes StorageClass and made available within the Namespace to the Platform Operator. This StorageClass can then be used by the Platform Operator to create TKG clusters or Virtual Machines inside of the Namespace, with any persistent storage requirements being mapped back to the vSphere datastore by the policy. You can of course select multiple policies and consume multiple different vSphere datastores for persistent volumes requested from within a Namespace.

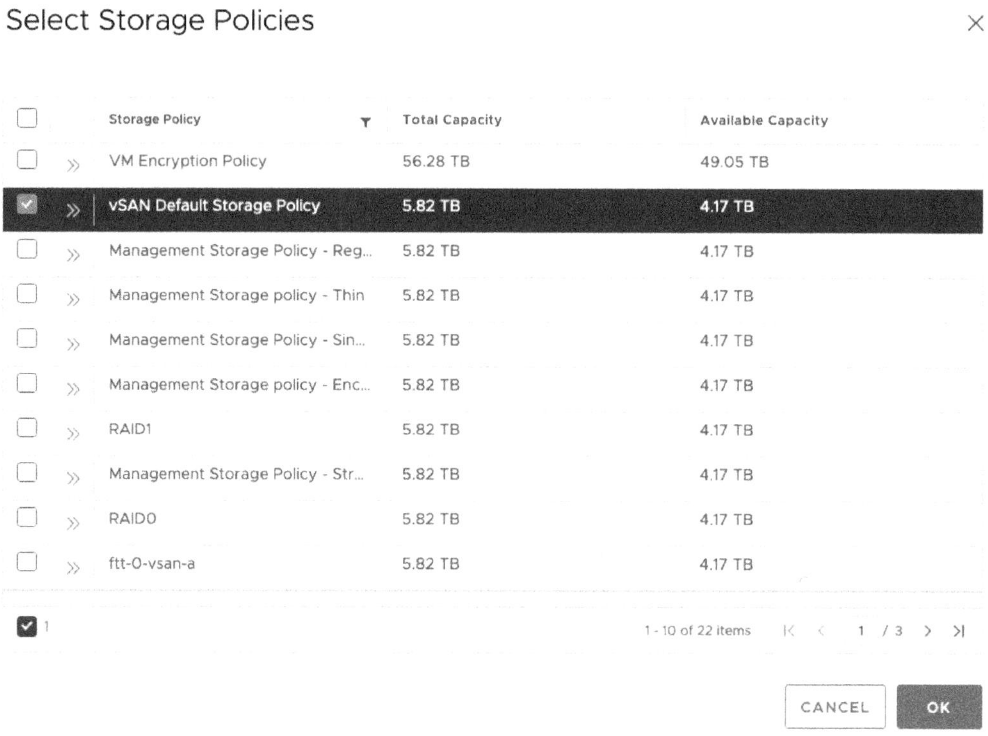

Select Storage Policies

		Storage Policy	Total Capacity	Available Capacity
☐	»	VM Encryption Policy	56.28 TB	49.05 TB
☑	»	**vSAN Default Storage Policy**	**5.82 TB**	**4.17 TB**
☐	»	Management Storage Policy - Reg...	5.82 TB	4.17 TB
☐	»	Management Storage policy - Thin	5.82 TB	4.17 TB
☐	»	Management Storage Policy - Sin...	5.82 TB	4.17 TB
☐	»	Management Storage policy - Enc...	5.82 TB	4.17 TB
☐	»	RAID1	5.82 TB	4.17 TB
☐	»	Management Storage Policy - Str...	5.82 TB	4.17 TB
☐	»	RAID0	5.82 TB	4.17 TB
☐	»	ftt-0-vsan-a	5.82 TB	4.17 TB

☑ 1   1 - 10 of 22 items |<   <   1 / 3   >   >|

CANCEL   OK

Figure 113: vSphere with Tanzu – Namespace – Select Storage Policies

Capacity and Usage

This card in the Namespace allows limits to be set of CPU, Memory and Storage. This enables a vSphere administrator to control the resources that a Platform Operator can consume when building out developer environments. By default there are no limits, meaning that Platform Operators can consume all available resources on the vSphere infrastructure. This may not be such a good idea in a multi-tenanted environment where there are multiple end-users, developers or applications running. Therefore, setting some overarching resource limits on a vSphere Namespace is desirable. Note that storage limits can be set on a very granular level. Since you can associate multiple storage policies and multiple datastores to a vSphere Namespace, this allows you to control the amount that can be consumed from each. For example, you may have a lot of NFS capacity but only limited vSAN capacity. Thus you might grant the Platform Operator a large amount of NFS, but only a small amount of vSAN. This card allows you to do just that.

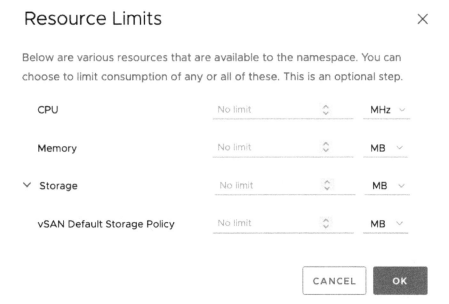

Figure 114: vSphere with Tanzu – Namespace – Resource Limits

Add VM Class

Resource Limits allow a vSphere administrator to control the overall resource consumption by a Namespace. However, a Platform Operator could still build a TKG cluster made up of some unnecessarily very large VMs, consuming the available resources within a Namespace very quickly. Once again, the vSphere administrator has the ability to control this. Through the concept of a VM Class, the vSphere administrator can control the size of virtual machine that can be built within a Namespace, both by the TKG Service when creating Kubernetes clusters and the VM Service building virtual machines. There are 16 built-in classes, which can be selected from within the VM Service card. However, it is also possible to create bespoke VM Classes.

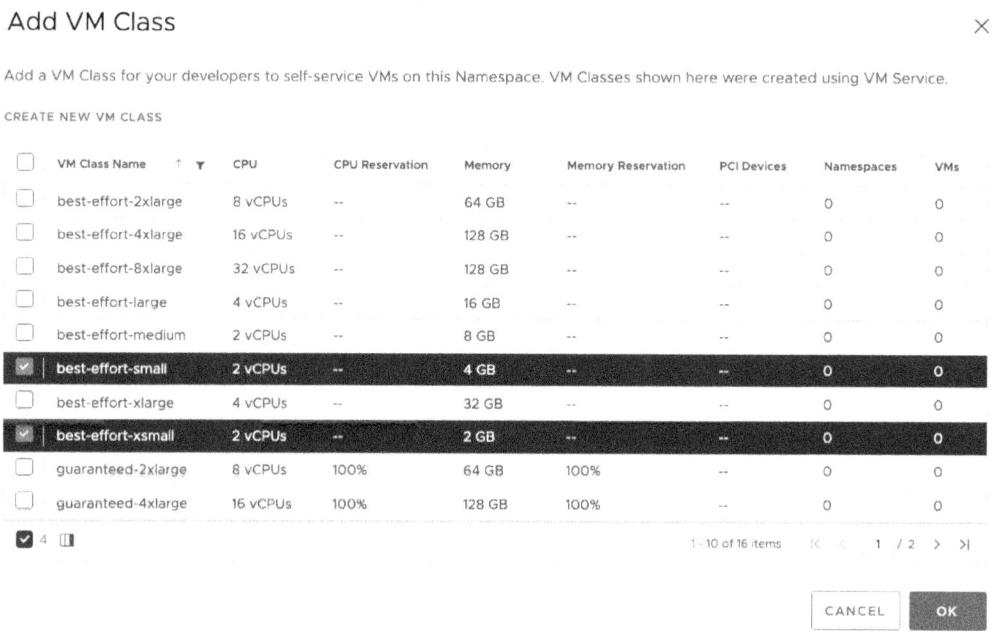

Figure 115: vSphere with Tanzu – Namespace – Add VM Class

One item to highlight here is the difference between best-effort and guaranteed. This is related to the resources allocated to the virtual machine. Guaranteed fully reserves resources whereas a best effort class edition does not reserve resources, thus allowing resources to be overcommitted. This is something to keep in mind as a vSphere administrator. It is possible that you will allow guaranteed VM Classes for production instances, but maybe best-effort instances for test environments. And of course, you will need to do some amount of additional capacity planning and review the limit settings when deploying with guaranteed VM Classes.

Content Libraries

Content libraries play an extremely important role for vSphere with Tanzu. Both the TKG Service and the VM Service rely on content libraries for their respective images. Thus, a content library for TKG node images should be configured with a subscription URL – https://wp-content.vmware.com/v2/latest/lib.json at the time of writing – to download the available Tanzu Kubernetes releases (TKrs). This will automatically sync with the VMware registry holding these images and download them to the content library. At the time of writing (July, 2022), there were 29 images available, ranging from Kubernetes v1.16.8 to v1.22.9. Images are available on both Photon OS and Ubuntu.

The content library for the vSphere VM Service does not have a subscription URL. Instead, the OS images need to be downloaded from the VMware Cloud Marketplace - https://marketplace.cloud.vmware.com/. To locate compatible VM images, search for VM Service in the portal. Download the image or images, and add them to the VM Service Content Library. These images can now be used by the Platform Operator to create virtual machines that have been requested by developers.

That completes the setup of the namespace. It may now look something similar to the following:

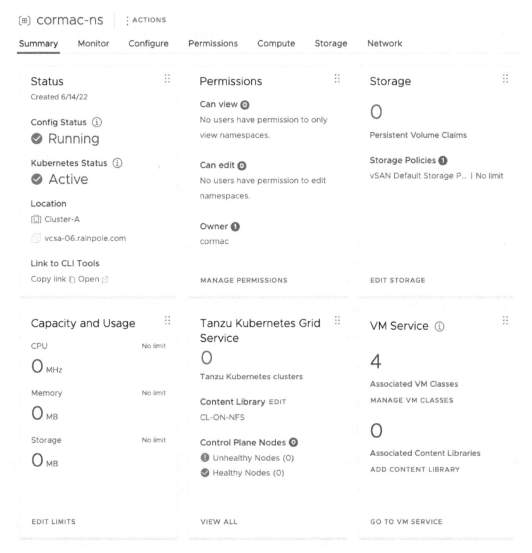

Figure 116: vSphere with Tanzu – Configured vSphere Namespace

You are probably now wondering how does a Platform Operator get access to the resources so that they can go ahead and build the developer platform, provisioning entities like TKG clusters and VMs through the various vSphere with Tanzu services. Let's look at that next.

vSphere with Tanzu and the Platform Operator Role

The Platform Operator is that person responsible for using vSphere resources to create developer infrastructure such as Kubernetes clusters to their developer team. The very first step that any Platform Operator must take with vSphere with Tanzu is to download the appropriate tooling so that they can interact with the Namespace. Note that the very first card has a `Link to CLI tools`. If a Platform Operator clicks on this, they are brought to a landing page which allows them to download the necessary tools to 'login' to the Supervisor Cluster and select the appropriate Namespace context for them to start creating the necessary objects to build a developer platform.

There are two sets of tools. The first are the Kubernetes CLI tools that enable the Platform Operator to login and manage their Namespaces. Here is a look at the landing page.

Kubernetes CLI Tools
Kubectl + vSphere plugin

Download the CLI tools package to view and control namespaces in vSphere.   LEARN MORE

SELECT OPERATING SYSTEM

DOWNLOAD CLI PLUGIN MAC OS ↓

Checksum CLI plugin Mac OS ↓

Get started with CLI Plugin for vSphere

Kubernetes CLI tool lets you manage your namespaces. Below are a few steps that will help you get started.

1. Verify that the SHA256 checksum of `vsphere*-plugin.zip` matches the checksum in the provided file sha256sum.txt. Run command `shasum --algorithm 256 --check sha256sum.txt < vsphere*-plugin.zip` and look for "OK" in the results

2. Put the contents of the .zip file in your OS's executable search path

3. Run command `kubectl vsphere login --server=<IP_or_master_hostname>` to log in to server

4. Run command `kubectl config get-contexts` to view a list of your Namespaces

5. Run command `kubectl config use-context <context>` to choose your default context

vSphere Docker Credential Helper

Download the vSphere Docker Credential Helper to securely pull and push image to the embedded Harbor registry in vSphere.

SELECT OPERATING SYSTEM

DOWNLOAD FOR MAC OS ↓

Checksum for Docker Credential Helper Mac OS ↓

VIEW INSTALL INSTRUCTIONS ∨

Figure 117: vSphere with Tanzu – Kubernetes CLI tools

There is another set of tools available at the bottom of the page. These tools allow a Platform Operator to interact with the embedded Harbor Registry available on vSphere with Tanzu deployments that use NSX-T. This has not yet been covered, so we will skip it for the moment. Later on, we will show an example of how to pull an image from an external registry, and push it to this local embedded Harbor registry.

Supervisor Cluster and vSphere Namespace contexts

At this point, Workload Management is up and running, and the first Namespace is created. The tools to access the environment have been downloaded. The next step is to access the environment so that the various services (TKG, VM) can be accessed, and developer infrastructure can be deployed. It is possible that these are the instructions that you as the vSphere administrator will provide to your Platform Operator. However, you will probably want to test it out in advance of handing it off to the Platform Operator, so in the following examples, the Namespace context will be accessed, a TKG cluster will be provisioned, and then context will be shifted over to the TKG cluster so we can check that it is working as expected. Here is the *kubectl vsphere* command output. You may use this or *kubectl-vsphere*. They provide the same functionality.

```
% kubectl vsphere
vSphere Plugin for kubectl.

Usage:
  kubectl-vsphere [command]

Available Commands:
  help       Help about any command
  login      Authenticate user with vCenter Namespaces
  logout     Destroys current sessions with all vCenter Namespaces clusters.
  version    Prints the version of the plugin.

Flags:
  -h, --help                        help for kubectl-vsphere
      --request-timeout string      Request timeout for HTTP client.
  -v, --verbose int                 Print verbose logging information.

Use "kubectl-vsphere [command] --help" for more information about a command.
```

As you can see, it takes login and logout as arguments. Let's look at the login options.

```
% kubectl vsphere login -h
Authenticate user with vCenter Namespaces:
To access Kubernetes, you must first authenticate against vCenter Namespaces.
You must pass the address of the vCenter Namespaces server and the username of
the user to authenticate, and will be prompted to provide further credentials.

Usage:
  kubectl-vsphere login [flags]

Examples:
kubectl vsphere login --vsphere-username user@domain --server=https://10.0.1.10

Flags:
  -h, --help                                      help for login
      --insecure-skip-tls-verify                  Skip verification (this is insecure).
      --server string                             Server to authenticate against.
      --tanzu-kubernetes-cluster-name string      Tanzu Kubernetes cluster to login to.
      --tanzu-kubernetes-cluster-namespace string Namespace in which the cluster resides.
  -u, --vsphere-username string                   Username to authenticate.

Global Flags:
      --request-timeout string      Request timeout for HTTP client.
  -v, --verbose int                 Print verbose logging information.
```

There is a sample login provided. Let's try to connect. Note that the server address is not the vCenter Server. This is the address of the Supervisor control plane API server, which was assigned by the Load Balancer provider. Also, I do not have a TLS setup, so I am going to include the insecure flag. Note that the command is using a resolvable name `supervisor` to access the server. You could also use the IP address. The login command is as follows (the use of '\' simply means that the command continues on the next line).

```
% kubectl vsphere login \
--vsphere-username administrator@vsphere.local \
--server=https://supervisor \
--insecure-skip-tls-verify

KUBECTL_VSPHERE_PASSWORD environment variable is not set. Please enter the password below
Password: ******
Logged in successfully.

You have access to the following contexts:
   cormac-ns
   supervisor

If the context you wish to use is not in this list, you may need to try
logging in again later, or contact your cluster administrator.

To change context, use `kubectl config use-context <workload name>`
```

Success! The login has succeeded. I can also see the `cormac-ns` namespace context. Some observations can be made here. It would appear that the Supervisor Cluster is the only Kubernetes cluster in the environment. The KUBECONFIG for the Supervisor will be added to the `.kube/config` in the home folder. Since no other contexts are displayed, we can assume that there is no access to other Kubernetes instances. I am also logging in as the `administrator@vsphere.local` SSO. You may wish to try the Platform Operator credentials to ensure they have the correct permissions to do the operations you are about to test. Lastly, to save time from repetitively typing in the same password repeatedly, you could set the environment variable KUBECTL_VSPHERE_PASSWORD to the password value. This means that no password needs to be provided when logging in. Set this in your .profile or .bash_profile to have it configured each time you open a shell. It is a time-saver, but also a security concern – use with caution!

OK – now we are in. Let's switch contexts to the correct namespace and check what resources are available. Let's begin with the nodes.

```
% kubectl get nodes
NAME                                STATUS  ROLES                 AGE  VERSION
4224010ae4399578af7d5df4e7e80f1f    Ready   control-plane,master  14h  v1.21.0+vmware.wcp.2
42243f72ad9460bd8636d41ebcbc6abb    Ready   control-plane,master  14h  v1.21.0+vmware.wcp.2
422450f331929273e040fdfa576b1621    Ready   control-plane,master  14h  v1.21.0+vmware.wcp.2
```

There are 3 nodes in total, each one representing one of the supervisor virtual machines deployed as part of workload management. You might ask why there are no worker nodes. It is a good question. The reason is that NSX-T is required to install the spherelet component on the ESXi hosts and in turn, allow Native Pods to run. This is not available with vSphere networking using one of the Load Balancers described earlier (HA-Proxy, NSX ALB). Thus, when this is the deployment type, no worker nodes are configured. Later on, when we look at NSX-T, you will also see worker nodes representing ESXi hosts listed.

Let's now look at the first major building block for developer infrastructure, the VM Classes.

```
% kubectl get vmclass
NAME                  CPU  MEMORY  AGE
best-effort-small     2    4Gi     38m
best-effort-xsmall    2    2Gi     38m
guaranteed-small      2    4Gi     38m
guaranteed-xsmall     2    2Gi     38m
```

```
% kubectl get vmclassbinding
NAME                 AGE
best-effort-small    39m
best-effort-xsmall   39m
guaranteed-small     39m
guaranteed-xsmall    39m
```

Now you might ask what is the difference between the two commands above? The first one displays all the VM Classes that have been allocated to any of the vSphere Namespaces in the cluster. The second reports on the VM Classes that have been assigned to this current vSphere Namespace, `cormac-ns`. So it is important to use the latter command to verify what VM Classes that this namespace can use. This matches the four VM Classes that we selected in the VM Service card in the UI.

Let's now look at the available StorageClasses. Remember once again that only one was chosen, the vSAN Default Storage Policy.

```
% kubectl get storageclass
NAME                        PROVISIONER            RECLAIM  VOLBINDMODE ALLOWVOLEXP AGE
vsan-default-storage-policy csi.vsphere.vmware.com Delete   Immediate   true        39m
```

You might recall that we also setup a content library with a subscription URL in the VM Service card in the UI. The content libraries can also be queried through the `contentsource` query, and checked to make sure that they are associated with the Namespace through the `contentsourcebinding` query.

```
% kubectl get contentsource
NAME                                   AGE
cd1db9ed-ff30-4820-b299-78c01a6d4ed0   18h
fd3aca87-ae2a-4d63-a79f-cf67d1049358   71m
```

```
% kubectl get contentsourcebinding
NAME                                   AGE
cd1db9ed-ff30-4820-b299-78c01a6d4ed0   4h32m
fd3aca87-ae2a-4d63-a79f-cf67d1049358   72m
```

The images within the content libraries can also be queried from *kubectl*. Since there are 29 images available at the time of writing, I've snipped the output to shorten it.

```
% kubectl get vmimage
NAME                                                    CONTENTSOURCENAME
VERSION                          OSTYPE          FORMAT   AGE
ob-15957779-photon-3-k8s-v1.16.8---vmware.1-tkg.3.60d2ffd    cd1db9ed-ff30-4820-b299-
78c01a6d4ed0   v1.16.8+vmware.1-tkg.3.60d2ffd   vmwarePhoton64Guest  ovf     14h
ob-16466772-photon-3-k8s-v1.17.7---vmware.1-tkg.1.154236c    cd1db9ed-ff30-4820-b299-
78c01a6d4ed0   v1.17.7+vmware.1-tkg.1.154236c   vmwarePhoton64Guest  ovf     14h
ob-16545581-photon-3-k8s-v1.16.12---vmware.1-tkg.1.da7afe7   cd1db9ed-ff30-4820-b299-.
.
.--snip--

ob-18903450-photon-3-k8s-v1.20.12---vmware.1-tkg.1.b9a42f3   cd1db9ed-ff30-4820-b299-
78c01a6d4ed0   v1.20.12+vmware.1-tkg.1.b9a42f3  vmwarePhoton64Guest  ovf     14h
ob-19344082-tkgs-ova-ubuntu-2004-v1.21.6---vmware.1-tkg.1    cd1db9ed-ff30-4820-b299-
78c01a6d4ed0   v1.21.6+vmware.1-tkg.1           ubuntu64Guest        ovf     14h
```

One more thing to check is which workload networks are available to build development infrastructure.

```
% kubectl get network
NAME         AGE
vm-62-dpg    57m
```

Where is this network coming from? This is the workload network that was provided in the Workload Network section when enabling Workload Management. Multiple workload networks can be created. They can also be modified. This will be examined when we return to the vSphere UI shortly, and see what additional controls are available to a vSphere administrator.

At this point, it would appear that everything is in place to allow us to build our first TKG – Tanzu Kubernetes Grid – guest / workload cluster.

Deploying a TKG cluster via the TKG Service

Platform Operators leverage the TKG Services in vSphere with Tanzu by creating a YAML manifest describing the attributes of the cluster that they wish to have deployed. Below is an example of such a manifest.

```
apiVersion: run.tanzu.vmware.com/v1alpha2
kind: TanzuKubernetesCluster
metadata:
 name: tkg-cluster-01
 namespace: cormac-ns
spec:
 topology:
   controlPlane:
     replicas: 1
     vmClass: guaranteed-small
     storageClass: vsan-default-storage-policy
     tkr:
       reference:
         name: v1.20.7---vmware.1-tkg.1.7fb9067
   nodePools:
   - name: worker-pool-1
     replicas: 2
     vmClass: guaranteed-small
     storageClass: vsan-default-storage-policy
     tkr:
       reference:
         name: v1.20.7---vmware.1-tkg.1.7fb9067
```

At this point, it should be possible to appreciate what this is manifest is requesting. We can see that it is of kind `TanzuKubernetesCluster`, so this request will be routed to the TKG Service, which will create the cluster using ClusterAPI through the Guest Cluster Manager in the Supervisor Cluster. It is also requesting that this TKG cluster is built in the `cormac-ns` namespace. In `spec.topology` there is both a `controlPlane` section and a `nodePool` section. These are specifying the number of nodes, the size of the nodes (using `VM Class`), and the Tanzu Kubernetes release (`TKr`) image to use from the local content library, in this case v1.20.7. There is a request for a single control plane node using class guaranteed-small, as well as 2 worker nodes, using the same VM Class and the same TKr. Finally, persistent storage to the nodes will be provisioned using the default vSAN policy `StorageClass`.

Several additional settings have been omitted so the default values are used. These can also be specified if necessary. These include:

- spec.settings.network.cni.name: antrea
- spec.settings.network.pods.cidrBlocks: 192.168.0.0/16
- spec.settings.network.services.cidrBlocks: 10.96.0.0/12
- spec.settings.network.serviceDomain: cluster.local

Antrea is the default CNI, but Calico is also supported. Using the above manifest entries, administrators or Platform Operators can change a TKG cluster to use Calico instead of Antrea.

It is also possible to specify volume attributes for the etcd database on the control plane node, as well as container images on the worker nodes if necessary. This is done via manifest entries:

- spec.topology.controlPlane.volumes
- spec.topology.nodePool.volumes

e.g.

```
spec:
 topology:
  controlPlane:
   replicas: 1
   vmClass: guaranteed-small
   storageClass: vsan-default-storage-policy
   tkr:
    reference:
      name: v1.20.7---vmware.1-tkg.1.7fb9067
   volumes:
    - name: etcd
      mountPath: /var/lib/etcd
      capacity:
        storage: 4Gi
```

The above may be necessary to tune for TKG clusters that are expected to have very large configurations, and lots of Pods and containers running.

Many other configuration options are available, such as how to deploy a TKG cluster with a Proxy Server and how to include custom certificates for TLS. However, in this example, the simplified TKG manifest shown above is used. The creation of the cluster object is the same as any other Kubernetes object – *kubectl* is used.

```
% kubectl apply -f tanzucluster-v1alpha2-v1.20.7.yaml
tanzukubernetescluster.run.tanzu.vmware.com/tkg-cluster-01 created

% kubectl get cluster
NAME            PHASE
tkg-cluster-01  Provisioned

% kubectl get tanzukubernetescluster
NAME             CONTROL PLANE   WORKER    TKR NAME                          AGE   READY
TKR COMPATIBLE   UPDATES AVAILABLE
tkg-cluster-01   1               2         v1.20.7---vmware.1-tkg.1.7fb9067  62s   False
True             [1.21.6+vmware.1-tkg.1.b3d708a 1.20.12+vmware.1-tkg.1.b9a42f3]

% kubectl get virtualmachines
NAME                               POWERSTATE   AGE
tkg-cluster-01-control-plane-zgf86              54s
```

Querying the `tanzukubernetescluster` object (or 'tkc' for short) has wrapped the text to two lines, but hopefully it is still eligible. Note that the Ready state is False. At this time, only the control plane node is being provisioned. The workers are not yet deployed. This can be seen by querying the `virtualmachine` object. On the vSphere Client UI, several tasks are taking place. A new object to represent the TKG cluster is being created in the `cormac-ns` namespace. There are also 'Deploy OVF Template' tasks taking place to create the cluster nodes. Initially, the cluster only contains the control plane node, as observed from *kubectl*.

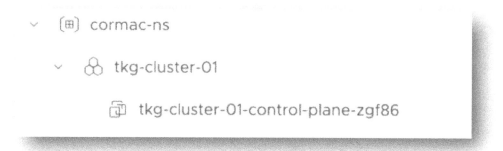

Figure 118: TKG cluster creation

Once the control plane node has been deployed, it gets reconfigured and powered on. During this reconfiguration, it is allocated an IP address from the workload range of IP addresses provided during the configuration of vSphere with Tanzu Workload Management. Of course, this control plane is also allocated a front-end VIP for its API Server. Once all of the various components that are required for the control plane to function are online, additional OVF deployment tasks take place for the rolling out of the worker node VMs. Soon afterwards, the cluster should be online. The status can be monitored using the kubectl commands seen earlier, or monitored from the vSphere Client. Select the **Namespace > Compute > Tanzu Kubernetes clusters**. At present, it is still creating.

Figure 119: TKG cluster status - Creating

Eventually, the cluster should fully form when all the necessary add-ons are installed and running on the TKG cluster. Note how the naming convention of the nodes adheres to the names used in the manifest.

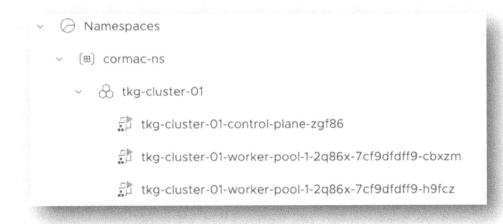

Figure 120: TKG cluster control plane and worker nodes

The status can again be checked from the command line. This time the cluster Ready state is set to True, and all 3 nodes (1 x control plane and 2 x workers) are powered on.

```
% kubectl get tkc
NAME             CONTROL PLANE   WORKER   TKR NAME                            AGE   READY
TKR COMPATIBLE   UPDATES AVAILABLE
tkg-cluster-01   1               2        v1.20.7---vmware.1-tkg.1.7fb9067    19m   True
True             [1.21.6+vmware.1-tkg.1.b3d708a 1.20.12+vmware.1-tkg.1.b9a42f3]

% kubectl get virtualmachines
NAME                                              POWERSTATE   AGE
tkg-cluster-01-control-plane-zgf86                poweredOn    19m
tkg-cluster-01-worker-pool-1-2q86x-7cf9dfdff9-cbxzm   poweredOn   9m25s
tkg-cluster-01-worker-pool-1-2q86x-7cf9dfdff9-h9fcz   poweredOn   9m25s
```

And of course, the status can also be verified from the UI.

Figure 121: TKG cluster status - Running

Success! We have just built our first TKG cluster on vSphere with Tanzu. However, how does a vSphere administrator or Platform Operator find the context of this TKG cluster so they can give access to a developer? At present, I only see the following contexts, which are what was reported when we logged in initially.

```
% kubectl config get-contexts
CURRENT   NAME          CLUSTER        AUTHINFO                                          NAMESPACE
*         cormac-ns     192.168.62.32  wcp:192.168.62.32:administrator@vsphere.local     cormac-ns
          supervisor    supervisor     wcp:supervisor:administrator@vsphere.local
```

There is no context added for the newly created TKG cluster. Let's see how to do this next.

Switching context to a TKG cluster

While there are different ways of switching contexts, my preference is to log out of the current supervisor context and log back into the TKG cluster context. This is how to do that. Begin by logging out.

```
% kubectl-vsphere logout
Your KUBECONFIG context has changed.
The current KUBECONFIG context is unset.
To change context, use `kubectl config use-context <workload name>`
Logged out of all vSphere namespaces.

% kubectl config get-contexts
CURRENT   NAME    CLUSTER   AUTHINFO   NAMESPACE
```

Now, log back in but include additional parameters which specify the namespace where the TKG cluster has been deployed (cormac-ns) and the name of the TKG cluster (tkg-cluster-01).

```
% kubectl vsphere login \
--vsphere-username administrator@vsphere.local \
--server=https://supervisor \
--insecure-skip-tls-verify \
--tanzu-kubernetes-cluster-namespace cormac-ns \
--tanzu-kubernetes-cluster-name tkg-cluster-01

KUBECTL_VSPHERE_PASSWORD environment variable is not set. Please enter the password below
Password: *****
Logged in successfully.

You have access to the following contexts:
   cormac-ns
   supervisor
   tkg-cluster-01

If the context you wish to use is not in this list, you may need to try
logging in again later, or contact your cluster administrator.

To change context, use `kubectl config use-context <workload name>`
```

Note now that there is a new context listed, `tkg-cluster-01`. Let's switch to that context and verify that it has placed us in the context of our newly deployed TKG cluster.

```
% kubectl config use-context tkg-cluster-01
Switched to context "tkg-cluster-01".

% kubectl get nodes
NAME                                   STATUS   ROLES           AGE   VERSION
tkg-cluster-01-control-plane-zgf86     Ready    control-plane   23m   v1.20.7+vmware.1
tkg-cluster-01-worker-pool-1-...-cbxzm Ready    <none>          15m   v1.20.7+vmware.1
tkg-cluster-01-worker-pool-1-...-h9fcz Ready    <none>          15m   v1.20.7+vmware.1
```

Looks good. This appears to show the control plane node and the two worker nodes. Now any kubectl commands will apply to this cluster, and not the Supervisor Cluster. This context can now be handed off to the developers so they can use this cluster to do their development work.

Alternatively, the Platform Operator might want to use this for some testing of code that has already been created, or indeed put an application into production.

One final item to highlight – this TKG cluster control plane has been allocated a VIP by the NSX ALB, which is what is providing VIPs in this deployment. Logging back onto the NSX ALB UI should reveal the Virtual Service created for this cluster, as well as the backend IP address associated with the TKG control plane, which in this case is only a single node and not the three nodes which we saw with the Supervisor.

First, here is the VIP, as reported in the Virtual Service. Note that the health is currently yellow and not green because it has not been up long enough. However, the health will continue to increase over time and the service should eventually turn green.

	Name ^	Health	Address	App D...	Servic...	Pools	Total...	RPS	CPS	Open...	Throughp...	
	domain-c22--cormac-ns-tkg-cluster-01-control-plane-...	73	...2.34	N/A	6443	doma...	1		0.0 /sec	6	30.0 Kbps	
	domain-c22--kube-system-kube-apiserver-lb-svc	100	...2.32	N/A	443, 6...	doma...	1		0.0 /sec	1	9.5 Kbps	
	domain-c22--vmware-system-csi-vsphere-csi-controll...	100	...2.33	N/A	2112, 2...	doma...	1		0.0 /sec	0	0.0 bps	

Figure 122: TKG VIP – NSX ALB Virtual Services view

The address for the TKG control plane VIP is once again taken from the Load Balancer range which was defined when Workload Management was initially configured. Let's now look at the endpoint.

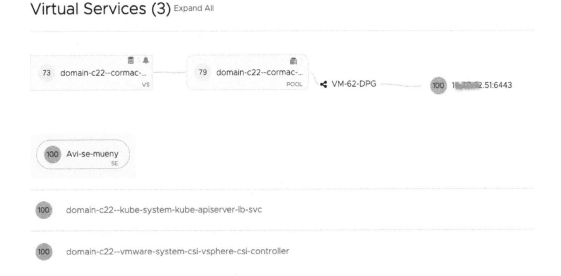

Virtual Services (3) Expand All

Figure 123: TKG VIP – NSX ALB Dashboard view

The endpoint here is the IP address allocated to the control plane node from the workload network address range. Only one endpoint is displayed since the TKG cluster was deployed with a single control plane node. If it was deployed with 3 or 5 control plane nodes, these would all show up here as endpoints since the VIP load balances in front of all control plane nodes.

All is good, and in working order. Let's now try to build something within the TKG workload cluster.

Pod Security Policies

Now that the TKG workload cluster has been deployed via TKG Service (TKGS), it should be possible to allow your developers to create and build applications. However, an important consideration for the TKG workload cluster is the Pod Security Policy or PSP for short. There are two predefined PSPs on TKG workload clusters that have been deployed by the TKGS, `vmware-system-privileged` and `vmware-system-restricted`. These can be queried as follows.

```
% kubectl get psp
NAME                     PRIV    CAPS  SELINUX   RUNASUSER          FSGROUP    SUPGROUP
  READONLYROOTFS  VOLUMES
vmware-system-
privileged  true    *     RunAsAny RunAsAny            RunAsAny   RunAsAny   false
       *
vmware-system-
restricted  false         RunAsAny MustRunAsNonRoot MustRunAs   MustRunAs  false
     configMap,emptyDir,projected,secret,downwardAPI,persistentVolumeClaim
```

You could of course also create your own PSP if you so wish. However, a PSP is important for TKG workload clusters since Service Accounts require a PSP to get privileges to carry out certain tasks, e.g. create, delete, etc. Typically, service accounts are used by in-cluster objects, such as Pods, to authenticate to the Kubernetes API server. Once authenticated, they can get on and do work. Many applications leverage service accounts, so the first step after a TKG cluster has been created is to make sure Service Accounts have privileges. Here, one of the predefined PSPs, `vmware-system-privileged`, is used. It is included as a resource to a new ClusterRole, and then this new ClusterRole is bound to the Service Accounts through a new ClusterRoleBinding, as follows:

```
% cat securityPolicy.yaml
apiVersion: rbac.authorization.k8s.io/v1
kind: ClusterRole
metadata:
 name: psp:privileged
rules:
- apiGroups: ['policy']
 resources: ['podsecuritypolicies']
 verbs: ['use']
 resourceNames:
 - vmware-system-privileged

---

apiVersion: rbac.authorization.k8s.io/v1
kind: ClusterRoleBinding
metadata:
 name: all:psp:privileged
roleRef:
 kind: ClusterRole
 name: psp:privileged
 apiGroup: rbac.authorization.k8s.io
subjects:
- kind: Group
 name: system:serviceaccounts
 apiGroup: rbac.authorization.k8s.io


% kubectl apply -f securityPolicy.yaml
clusterrole.rbac.authorization.k8s.io/psp:privileged created
clusterrolebinding.rbac.authorization.k8s.io/all:psp:privileged created
```

This new ClusterRole and ClusterRoleBinding now grant Service Accounts privileges to be able to do tasks on the cluster. Role and RoleBinding will be discussed in more detail in chapter 7.

Creating applications on the TKG workload cluster

Now that the TKG cluster is set up, we can deploy a simple application to make sure it is working. This is a very simple nginx web server deployment, with 3 replicas. It is also using a load balancer service type, so it should be possible to reach this web server landing page through a VIP that the NSX ALB allocates to the application. Here is the manifest for the deployment and service:

```
apiVersion: apps/v1
kind: Deployment
metadata:
  name: nginx-deployment
spec:
  selector:
    matchLabels:
      app: nginx
  replicas: 3 # tells deployment to run 3 Pods matching the template
  template:
    metadata:
      labels:
        app: nginx
    spec:
      containers:
      - name: nginx
        image: nginx:latest
        ports:
        - containerPort: 80
---
apiVersion: v1
kind: Service
metadata:
  labels:
    app: nginx
  name: nginx-svc
spec:
  type: LoadBalancer
  ports:
    - name: http
      port: 80
      targetPort: 80
      protocol: TCP
  selector:
    app: nginx
```

After kubectl applying the manifest, we should see a new virtual service on the NSX ALB. You might wonder why there are only 2 endpoints since the web server was been deployed with 3 replicas. This is due to the fact that the TKG cluster only has 2 workers nodes. Therefore 2 of the Pods are on the same worker node. If the cluster was scaled out to the 3 worker nodes, then it is plausible that there would be 3 endpoints associated with the VIP.

Virtual Services (4) Expand All

Figure 124: Load Balancer App VIP – NSX ALB Dashboard view

And by opening a browser and point it to the load balancer VIP allocated to the service, we should see the default nginx landing page.

Let's now leave the TKG Service and look at another service available on vSphere with Tanzu that vSphere administrators should familiarize themselves with.

Deploying a Virtual Machine via the VM Service

Creating a virtual machine via the VM Service is very similar in approach to creating a TKG cluster via the TKG Service seen previously. vSphere administrators or Platform Operators again create a YAML manifest with the details about the VM that they wish to have created and send it to the VM Service via *kubectl*. Once again, the resources that can be used are bound by the vSphere Namespace, so they need to check VM Class, StorageClass, and network. However, this time rather than specifying a Kubernetes image, a VM Image must be specified. The VM images are also made available to the vSphere Namespace through a Content Library.

For this exercise, a content library has been created and OVA for both a CentOS image and an Ubuntu image have been stored in it. Details about where to get the images was described in the introduction to this chapter, when the VM Service was discussed. To recap, these images are available from the VMware Customer Connect portal. Login and search for VM Service images.

Figure 125: VM Service – Content Library

This content library should now be associated with the VM Service card in the Namespace. To do this, simply click on the Add Content Library link in the VM Service card, select the content library with the VM image, and click OK. The VM Service should now show a content library associated with it. Below is a figure showing the VM Service card from before and after adding the content library.

Figure 126: VM Service – Add Content Library to VM Service

In order to create a VM through the VM Service, we need to make sure our context is in the Supervisor Cluster namespace and not in the TKG guest/workload cluster context. Once there, we can check that the new VM images are available.

```
% kubectl get vmimage
NAME                                                        CONTENTSOURCENAME
VERSION                         OSTYPE             FORMAT   AGE
centos-stream-8-vmservice-v1alpha1-1638306496810            fd3aca87-ae2a-4d63-a79f-
cf67d1049358                    centos8_64Guest    ovf      11m
ob-15957779-photon-3-k8s-v1.16.8---vmware.1-tkg.3.60d2ffd   cd1db9ed-ff30-4820-b299-
78c01a6d4ed0    v1.16.8+vmware.1-tkg.3.60d2ffd   vmwarePhoton64Guest   ovf   17h
.
.--snip--
.
ob-19344082-tkgs-ova-ubuntu-2004-v1.21.6---vmware.1-tkg.1   cd1db9ed-ff30-4820-b299-
78c01a6d4ed0    v1.21.6+vmware.1-tkg.1   ubuntu64Guest   ovf   17h
ubuntu-20-1633387172196                                     fd3aca87-ae2a-4d63-a79f-
cf67d1049358                    ubuntu64Guest      ovf      11m
```

Now what we see here are images from both the content library associated with the TKG Service and the content library associated with the VM Service. I snipped out most of the output from the above command, but the Centos image and Ubuntu images are clearly visible. I'm also not going to add more VM Classes. I will work with the same small VM Classes that I added to this Namespace in the TKG section previously. You can also assume that the same StorageClass and workload network are still available in the Namespace.

While the deployment of virtual machines from the YAML manifest sounds great, it is not going to be of much use if we cannot customize the image. To facilitate the customization of the VM images, `cloud-init` is used. This has become one of the most common mechanisms to customize OS images, and there is a wealth of documentation available here - https://cloudinit.readthedocs.io/en/latest/.

In VM Service, `cloud-config` is a simple way to do customization by providing what is known as `user-data`. To demonstrate, a simple `user-data` file will be built which contains some simple entries that grant the user authority to ssh from his/her desktop to the VM as user **centos.** The customization is also going to enable DHCP on the VM, so the assumption is that there is a DHCP server available on the workload network where this VM is going to be deployed. One final step is to run a command to update the `/etc/motd` (message of the day) file so that a message is displayed when the user logs in to the VM.

Here is a sample cloud-config with an obfuscated ssh-rsa, is stored in a file called centos-user-data:

```
#cloud-config
ssh_pwauth: yes
users:
  - default
  - name: centos
    ssh_authorized_keys:
      - ssh-rsa AAAAB3NzaC1...xxxxxxxxxx
    sudo: ALL=(ALL) NOPASSWD:ALL
    groups: sudo
    shell: /bin/bash
network:
  version: 2
  ethernets:
      ens192:
          dhcp4: true
runcmd:
  - "echo -e 'Centos VM built by VM Operator on '`date` >> /etc/motd"
```

The ssh_authorized_keys entry comes from the `~/.ssh/id_pub.rsa` on the users own desktop. To use this user data with cloud-init, the data needs to be rendered to a base64 format.

```
% base64 < centos-user-data
I2N...xxxxxxxxxx...CIK
```

This output should now be included in the VM YAML manifest. Here is an example of a manifest which a Platform Operator might create to deploy a virtual machine. It is written in YAML. It has two objects, a VirtualMachine and a ConfigMap, separated with the `---` line. The ConfigMap holds the base64 user-data for cloud-init customization that was created previously.

```
apiVersion: vmoperator.vmware.com/v1alpha1
kind: VirtualMachine
metadata:
  name: centos-vm
  namespace: cormac-ns
spec:
  networkInterfaces:
```

```
    - networkName: vm-62-dpg
      networkType: vsphere-distributed
    className: best-effort-small
    imageName: centos-stream-8-vmservice-v1alpha1-1619529007339
    powerState: poweredOn
    storageClass: vsan-default-storage-policy
    vmMetadata:
      configMapName: centos-vm-cfm
      transport: OvfEnv
---
apiVersion: v1
kind: ConfigMap
metadata:
    name: centos-vm-cfm
    namespace: cormac-ns
data:
  user-data: |
    I2N...xxxxxxxxxx...CIK
  hostname: centos-vm
```

This virtual machine is being provisioned in the `cormac-ns` vSphere Namespace. In the `spec` section, the networking has entries for the name of the network, `vm-62-dpg`, and the type of network, `vsphere-distributed`. There is no NSX-T in this deployment, but VM Service is also supported with NSX-T.

We already saw how only VM Classes added to this vSphere Namespace can be selected. We also saw that the Centos 8 image is available in the content library. Both of these items are added to the manifest. The storage class refers to the storage policy that was added to the namespace by the vSphere administrator. The `user-data` is the base64 encoded data generated in the previous step. The final interesting piece is the `hostname` in the ConfigMap. Everything is in place to deploy the VM.

```
% kubectl apply -f centos-vm.yaml
virtualmachine.vmoperator.vmware.com/centos-vm created
configmap/centos-vm-cfm created
```

If all has gone as expected, it should be possible to query the newly created virtual machines from *kubectl*. Note that since I already have a Tanzu Kubernetes cluster deployed, these VMs will also be listed.

```
% kubectl get vm
NAME                                              POWERSTATE   AGE
centos-vm                                         poweredOn    9m16s
tkg-cluster-01-control-plane-zgf86                poweredOn    101m
tkg-cluster-01-worker-pool-1-2q86x-7cf9dfdff9-cbxzm   poweredOn    92m
tkg-cluster-01-worker-pool-1-2q86x-7cf9dfdff9-h9fcz   poweredOn    92m
```

It should also be possible to see it in the Namespace via the UI.

Figure 127: VM Service – VM visible in Namespace

It should also be possible to query the virtual machine's IP address. However, this requires the output to be in a particular JSON format so the status field for the VM IP address can be retrieved.

```
% kubectl get vm centos-vm -o jsonpath='{.status.vmIp}'
192.168.1.54
```

A developer should now be able to *ssh* to that IP address, and not have to provide any password since we have provided the developer's public key to as part of the `user-data`. Other things that were specified included a message added to the `/etc/motd`, that the developer / user should be able to `sudo`, and that the hostname of the VM should be set to `centos-vm`. Let's check if these worked.

```
% ssh centos@192.168.1.54
The authenticity of host '192.168.1.54 (192.168.1.54)' can't be established.
ECDSA key fingerprint is SHA256:80Mx2li6CNDouvD0vpuSmrEbSdjOgJz1QleE71oddb0.
Are you sure you want to continue connecting (yes/no/[fingerprint])? yes
Warning: Permanently added '192.168.1.54 (ECDSA) to the list of known hosts.
Centos VM built by VM Operator on Wed May 5 06:14:04 EDT 2021

[centos@centos-vm ~]$ sudo su -
Last login: Tue Feb 23 16:03:20 EST 2021 on tty1

[root@centos-vm ~]# hostname
centos-vm
```

Success! Everything appears to be working as expected. Note that at the time of writing, only Centos and Ubuntu distributions were supported by the VM Service. It is the authors understanding that work is underway to support additional OS distributions going forward, so long as they support the cloud_init customization specification.

vSphere with Tanzu and NSX-T

We briefly touched on NSX-T as a network platform for vSphere with Tanzu towards the end of chapter 4. At the time, we had not yet looked at the vSphere with Tanzu architecture, and at that point little was revealed around concepts such as the Supervisor Cluster, vSphere Namespace, Native Pods, etc. Now that we have discussed those major components of vSphere with Tanzu, we can turn our attention to deploying it with NSX-T, the virtualized networking platform from VMware. Once NSX-T has been successfully deployed and configured, the steps to enable Workload Management with NSX-T will also be reviewed.

Before beginning with the configuration, the following requirements must be in place.

NSX-T Requirements

Object	Number	Details
vSphere Distributed Switch	1	A vSphere distributed switch across all ESXi hosts in the cluster where NSX-T will be deployed.
VLANs	3	The tunnel endpoints (TEPs) for the ESXi hosts and the NSX-T Edge controller require their own VLANs. These VLANS must be routable however, and the ESXi hosts must be able to communicate with the Edge on the TEP interfaces. This enables East-West network traffic. If the Host TEP and Edge TEP are using different physical NICs, they can use the same VLAN. A VLAN is also required for North-South traffic, allowing the Tier-0 Gateway to communicate externally. Use VLANs in the range 1-4094 for both ESXi host overlay and Edge overlay. Set MTU to 1600 or more on any network that carries overlay traffic.
vSphere Pod CIDR range	/23 CIDR	A dedicated CIDR range for vSphere Native Pods and Tanzu Kubernetes cluster nodes.
Kubernetes Services CIDR range	/16 CIDR	A dedicated CIDR range for Kubernetes Services.
Egress CIDR range	/27 CIDR	A dedicated CIDR range for Egress. Every vSphere Namespace on the Supervisor Cluster is allocated an Egress IP address. This SNAT address is used to communicate with the various services (TKG, vSphere Pods) in that vSphere Namespace.
Ingress CIDR range	/27 CIDR	A dedicated CIDR range for Ingress and Load Balancer Services consumed by applications deployed in vSphere Namespaces in vSphere with Tanzu.

Table 3: NSX-T Requirements for vSphere with Tanzu

In the following deployment scenario, the following versions of products is used. The versions are included as future versions of the products may have a slightly different approach to configurations. Always check future versions of official documentation and release notes for newer approaches.

- vCenter Server 7.0.3c, build 19480866
- VMware vSphere ESXi, 7.0.3c, build 19193900
- NSX-T Data Center version 3.2.0.1.0.19232597
- vSAN 7.0.3 for shared storage, along with a storage policy
- Distributed Switch 7.0.0

Note for VMware Cloud Foundation (VCF) customers: At the time of writing, there is a requirement for the management overlay network to have the Host and Edge TEPs on separate VLANs. Again, the VLANs must be routable to one another. However, it seems that they cannot be on the same VLAN, even if different physical NICs are used. Therefore, if you are a VCF user, you are still required to place the Host and Edge on separate VLANs. As per the VCF 4.4 Network Design Guide, (found at https://docs.vmware.com/en/VMware-Cloud-Foundation/4.4/vcf-44-management-domain-design.pdf), continue to "Use a dedicated VLAN for the edge overlay network that is segmented from the host overlay VLAN".

NSX-T Manager Deployment

Begin by deploying the OVA for the NSX Manager. This can now be done from the vSphere Client. First, download the OVA. It can be retrieved from the VMware Customer Connect Download Site. Note that there are two NSX Manager OVAs. The first NSX Manager is the unified appliance which does not have vCenter integration. The second includes an integrated vCenter plugin to enable the deployment and configuration of NSX directly from within the vCenter UI. Either can be used. Once the OVA is downloaded, you can proceed with the installation. From the drop-down menu at the top left of the vSphere Client, select NSX. This will bring you to the following landing page.

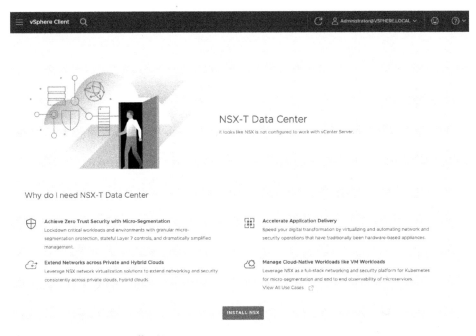

Figure 128: NSX-T– Install NSX

Click on the Install NSX button to begin the OVA deployment. Select the downloaded NSX Manager OVA. Populate the deployment wizard with the appropriate details, such as IP Addresses, passwords, enabling SSH and storage policies.

Once the appliance is deployed and powered on, it should now be possible to connect to the NSX Manager UI via a browser and log in as the `admin` user. Navigate to **System** > **Fabric** > **Compute Managers** in the NSX Manager UI and click on **New Compute Manager**. The next step is to provide details about the vCenter Server which is managing your vSphere infrastructure. This will be the same vCenter that manages the vSphere with Tanzu deployment. If successful, the Compute Manager entry should look similar to the following, with registration and connection status both green:

Compute Managers

	Compute Manager ↑	ID	FQDI	Type	Version	Registration Status	Connection Status	Last Inventory Update	Alarms
	vcsa-cormac	f9fe...67...	1...	vCenter	7.0.3	● Registered	● Up	Jul 5, 2022 1:07:34 ...	0

Figure 129: NSX-T Compute Managers

In its present state, the NSX Manager is a single appliance. The recommendation is to scale this out to three appliances with a virtual IP address front-end so that the NSX Manager is highly available. Navigate to **System** > **Appliances** > **NSX Manager** in the NSX Manager UI, and then click on Add NSX Appliance. Populate with the appropriate information (name, IP address, gateway, etc). Once the additional NSX Manager appliances have been deployed, the status is visible within the UI. When the deployment is complete, the NSX Manager will now be highly available.

Configure NSX-T on ESXi hosts

Before we can configure NSX on the ESXi hosts, several additional configuration steps need to be implemented. This is because the "Host Transport Node" configuration step requires a "Transport Node Profile" before starting the configuration. Therefore this step must be done in advance of configuring NSX on the ESXi hosts.

First, navigate to **System > Fabric > Profile** in the NSX Manager UI, and select **Uplink Profiles**, then select **Add Profile**. This profile defines which ESXi host uplinks will be used for the ESXi host overlay network. The ESXi hosts in this environment are using VLAN 3002 for their host overlay (TEP) network. Note that the teaming settings here are just labels and not references to the actual uplinks. I have used the labels "uplink5" and "uplink6" to remind me that these are the actual uplinks that I need to map when the "Transport Node Profile" gets created later on.

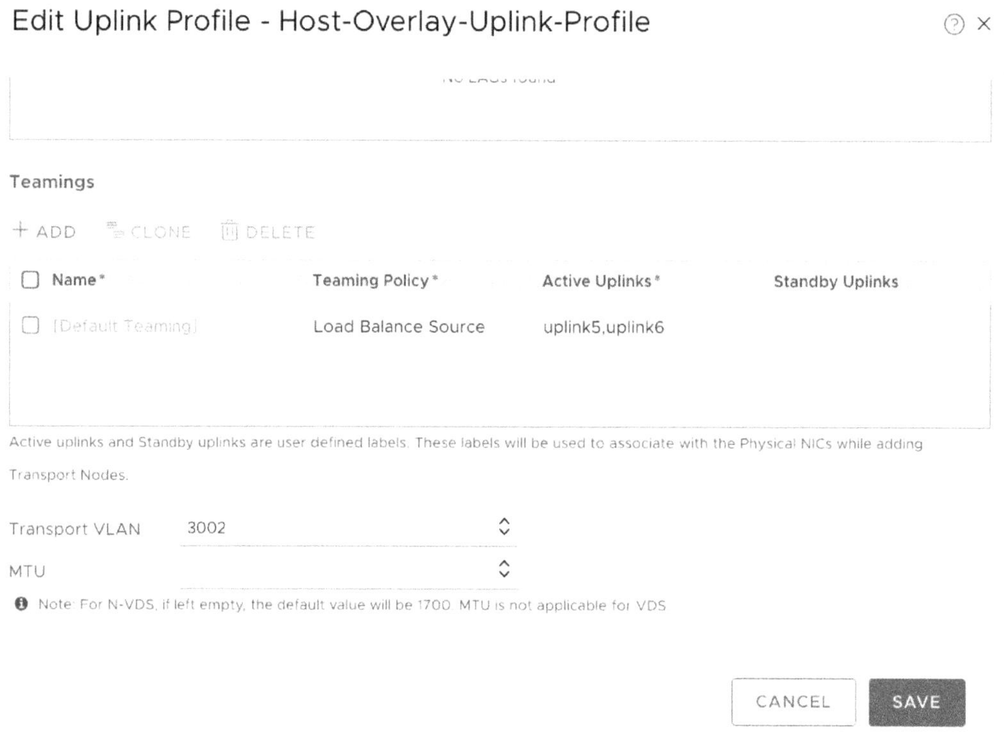

Edit Uplink Profile - Host-Overlay-Uplink-Profile   ⑦ ✕

Teamings

+ ADD   CLONE   DELETE

☐ Name*	Teaming Policy*	Active Uplinks*	Standby Uplinks
☐ (Default Teaming)	Load Balance Source	uplink5,uplink6	

Active uplinks and Standby uplinks are user defined labels. These labels will be used to associate with the Physical NICs while adding Transport Nodes.

Transport VLAN   3002   ⌄

MTU   ⌄

ⓘ Note: For N-VDS, if left empty, the default value will be 1700. MTU is not applicable for VDS

CANCEL   SAVE

Figure 130: NSX-T Host Overlay Uplink Profile

The next step is to create a transport zone for the overlay. A transport zone will define who can communicate on a particular network. This will be the management overlay network. This overlay transport zone will initially contain just the ESXi hosts, but later on, the overlay will be extended to include the Edge nodes. Navigate to **System > Fabric > Transport Zones** in the NSX Manager UI to add the Zone. Note that the traffic type for the zone is set to Overlay and not VLAN.

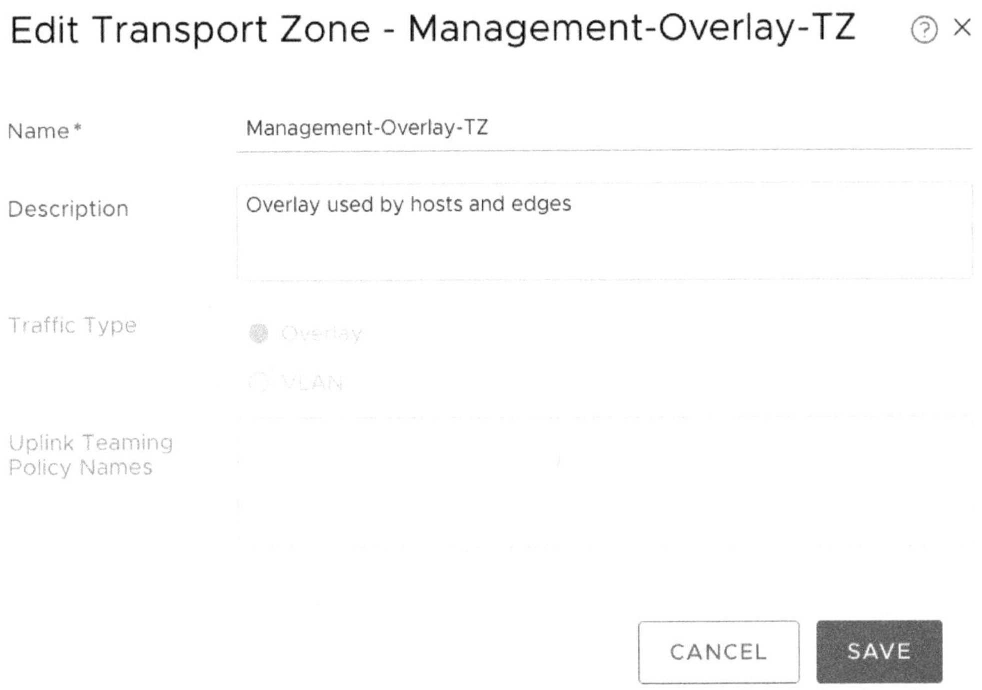

Edit Transport Zone - Management-Overlay-TZ ⑦ ×

Name*   Management-Overlay-TZ

Description   Overlay used by hosts and edges

Traffic Type   ● Overlay
                ○ VLAN

Uplink Teaming
Policy Names

CANCEL   SAVE

Figure 131: NSX-T Management Overlay Transport Zone

There are several ways in which IP addresses can be allocated to the tunnel endpoints (TEPs) on the ESXi hosts. For this example, an IP Pool is used. Navigate to **Networking** > **IP Address Pools**, under **IP Management**. Add a subnet of IP address that can be used for the host TEPs. With this information in place, a transport node profile for the ESXi hosts may now be created.

A Transport Node Profile requires a Transport Zone, an Uplink Profile, and the IP Pool created previously. At this point, the actual uplinks from the ESXi hosts to the uplink mappings are also assigned, e.g. uplink5 and uplink6. Navigate to **System** > **Fabric** > **Profiles**, selected **Transport Node Profiles**, and add a profile for the ESXi hosts.

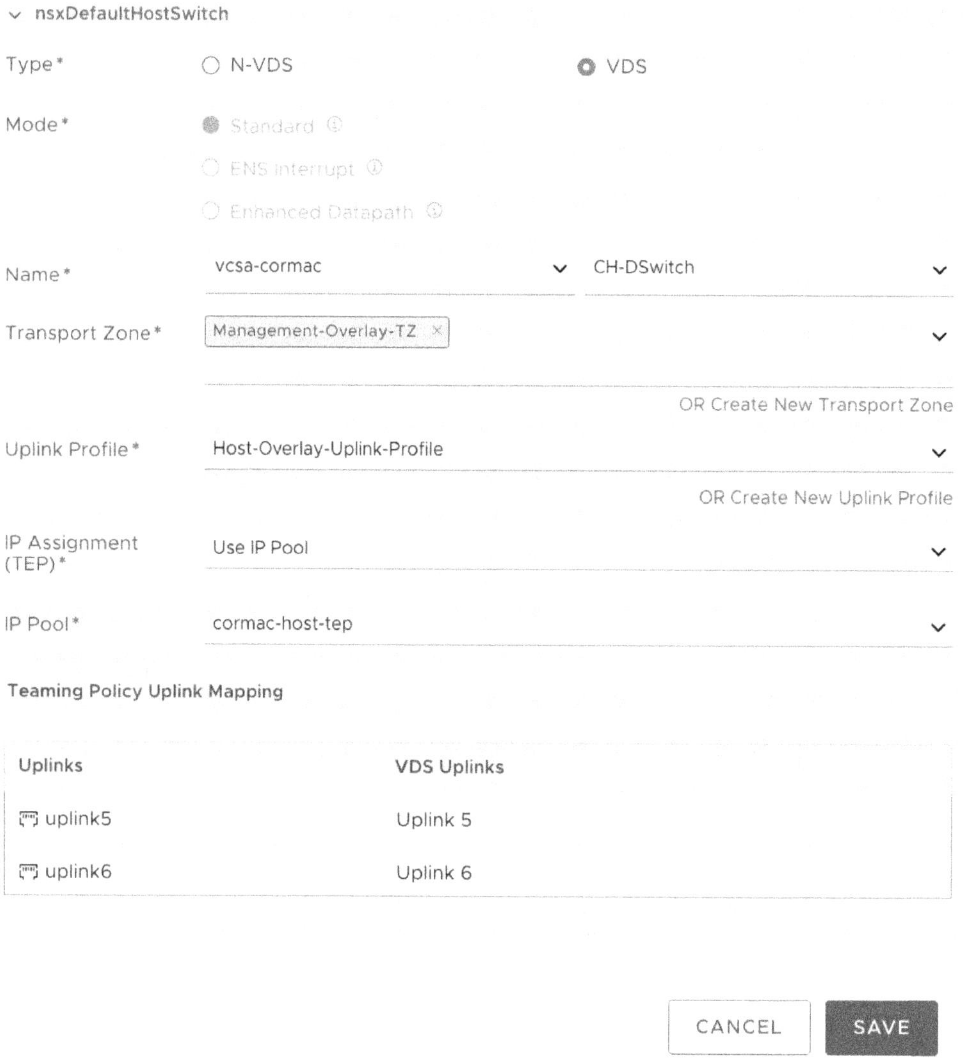

﹀ nsxDefaultHostSwitch

Type*	○ N-VDS	◉ VDS

Mode* ● Standard ⓘ
○ ENS Interrupt ⓘ
○ Enhanced Datapath ⓘ

Name* vcsa-cormac ﹀   CH-DSwitch ﹀

Transport Zone* [Management-Overlay-TZ ✕] ﹀

OR Create New Transport Zone

Uplink Profile* Host-Overlay-Uplink-Profile ﹀

OR Create New Uplink Profile

IP Assignment (TEP)* Use IP Pool ﹀

IP Pool* cormac-host-tep ﹀

Teaming Policy Uplink Mapping

Uplinks	VDS Uplinks
uplink5	Uplink 5
uplink6	Uplink 6

CANCEL   SAVE

Figure 132: NSX-T Transport Node Profile

With the Transport Node Profile created, the configuration of the ESXi hosts as transport nodes can finally proceed.

To complete the host configuration as transport nodes, navigate to **System** > **Fabric** > **Nodes** > **Host Transport Nodes** in the NSX Manager UI. In the "Managed by" section, select the vCenter Server that was configured as the Compute Manager. Select the cluster, and click on **Configure NSX**. This will prompt for a Transport Node Profile, as this is where the newly created Transport Node Profile is added. This will now begin the configuration of NSX on the ESXi hosts. If everything is successfully deployed, the status of the host transport nodes should be shown as UP when the configuration completes. Note that at this point there are no tunnels shown for the hosts – the status is not available. They will remain like this until a virtual machine uses the tunnel. Later on, when we get around to provisioning the vSphere with Tanzu Supervisor Cluster, the Tunnels field in the host transport node view populate with information. In other words, this view showing no tunnels is normal at this point in the proceedings.

To validate the NSX-T configuration on the ESXi hosts, several additional VMkernel adapters should now be visible. Included in the list should be the overlay interfaces that were configured in the host transport node as well as an additional interface on vmk50, the `nsx-hyperbus`. This latter interface is the network used by Kubernetes and container creation logic. One final test is to be able to ping between the different hosts on the overlay network. This can be done by logging onto one of the ESXi hosts, and pinging a remote host using the *++netstack=vxlan* option to the *vmkping* commands:

```
[root@w4-hs4-i1501:~] vmkping ++netstack=vxlan 192.168.101.1
PING 192.168.101.1 (192.168.101.1): 56 data bytes
64 bytes from 192.168.101.1: icmp_seq=0 ttl=63 time=0.877 ms
64 bytes from 192.168.101.1: icmp_seq=1 ttl=63 time=0.362 ms
64 bytes from 192.168.101.1: icmp_seq=2 ttl=63 time=0.318 ms

--- 192.168.101.1 ping statistics ---
3 packets transmitted, 3 packets received, 0% packet loss
round-trip min/avg/max = 0.318/0.519/0.877 ms

[root@w4-hs4-i1501:~]
```

At this point, NSX-T is providing a networking platform with a policy engine, management plane and control plane, e.g. distributed router/firewall for overlay/tunnels for east-west traffic. The next step in the NSX-T configuration is to deploy an Edge appliance which will provide us with additional services for north-south traffic, e.g. firewall, NAT, load balancers, etc.

Build NSX-T Edge Cluster

When this setup is complete, the management overlay network should extend to include the Edge nodes for east-west (E-W) traffic. The Edge nodes will also be configured to have uplinks to allow for north-south (N-S) traffic, which will connect it to an upstream physical router. This setup will be done in two parts. First, the Edge nodes will be built and added to the management overlay network created earlier with the hosts (E-W). The VLAN uplinks for upstream connectivity will be added as a second step (N-S).

Note that the methodology chosen here is simply one way of configuring the Edge, i.e. since the Edge has 4 interfaces in total, we will configure 1 x management interface, 1 x overlay interface and 2 x VLAN interfaces. In this example, the VLANs are being tagged at the distributed portgroup layer which means that VLAN tags are not needed nor added from within NSX. You may choose an alternate approach and trunk your portgroups, then add the VLAN tags to them from within NSX. Like I said, there are many ways to approach this. The choice is yours.

The first step is to create an IP Pool for the Edge Tunnel Endpoints (TEPs). This is almost identical to the step carried out earlier for the host TEPs. This IP Pool will provide the IP addresses for the Edge TEPs. Navigate to **Networking > IP Address Pools**, under **IP Management**. Add a subnet of IP addresses that can be used for the Edge TEPs.

Again, very similar to the host configuration, an Uplink Overlay Profile must be created for the Edge. The purpose this time is to create a profile for the uplink of the NSX Edge appliance so it can participate in the overlay / tunnel with the ESXi hosts. Note that on this occasion, there is only a single teaming uplink. This is because the edge appliance has a maximum of 4 interfaces, with one allocated for management, one for the overlay uplink (east/west traffic) and the remaining 2 for VLAN uplinks (north/south traffic) which connect to an upstream router.

Navigate to **System > Fabric > Profile** in the NSX Manager UI. Select **Uplink Profile**, then **Add Profile**. Note that the Transport VLAN is set to 0. This is because the VLANs are tagged on the distributed portgroups on the vSphere distributed switch. If you do not want to use this approach, maybe because your distributed portgroup are trunked, you should set the Transport VLAN ID appropriately at this point. Lastly, if no MTU is provided, it defaults to 1700.

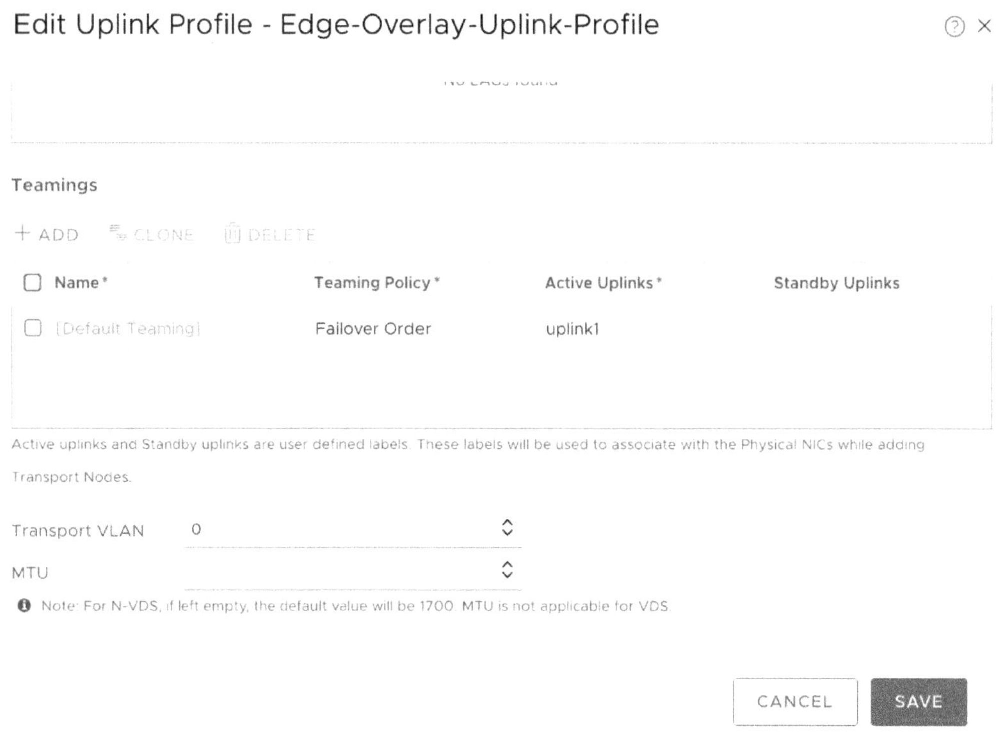

Edit Uplink Profile - Edge-Overlay-Uplink-Profile

Teamings

+ ADD   CLONE   DELETE

Name*	Teaming Policy*	Active Uplinks*	Standby Uplinks
[Default Teaming]	Failover Order	uplink1	

Active uplinks and Standby uplinks are user defined labels. These labels will be used to associate with the Physical NICs while adding Transport Nodes.

Transport VLAN   0

MTU

Note: For N-VDS, if left empty, the default value will be 1700. MTU is not applicable for VDS

CANCEL   SAVE

Figure 133: NSX-T Edge Uplink Profile

Repeating the pattern on how the host transport node was created, a similar process is followed to create an Edge transport node. Navigate to **System > Fabric > Nodes** and select **Add Edge Node**. This will launch the wizard to begin populating information about the Edge node. The first window requests a name and FQDN of the node. An optional description can also be added. You are also asked to provide the form factor for the Edge. The recommendation for production environments is to select a Large configuration. For smaller lab environment, the default setting of Medium may be chosen for the Edge appliances.

The next Edge Transport Node window is 'Credentials', which prompts for various passwords for the NSX Edge node logins. At this point it may be useful to enable SSH, since the ability to login to the Edge appliance to run some commands can be very useful when troubleshooting.

In the 'Configure Deployment' section, the vCenter Server that was set up as the Compute Manager is selected. You must also select the vSphere Cluster and a datastore.

In the 'Configure Node Settings' the management interface for the Edge node is configured. Remember that the Edge node can have a maximum of 4 uplinks. One of those uplinks is for the management network, and that is what is being configured in this step. Choose between DHCP or a static management IP assignment, and provide a CIDR format IP address and a default gateway. In the management interface field, choose the distributed portgroup to attach the interface to. Search Domain Names, DNS Servers and NTP Servers should also be populated at this point.

Finally, the 'Configure NSX' section is the part where the overlay and uplink networks are selected. In this section, the Edge is added to the same management overlay network as the ESXi hosts. When configuring NSX for the ESXi hosts, a Transport Node was first required to be created. The step of creating a Transport Node for the Edge can be done directly whilst creating the Edge node. Similar attributes need to be added as before, such as an uplink profile and the IP Pool created earlier. Finally, the Teaming Policy Uplink Mapping requires the selection of a distributed portgroup to attach the Edge node uplink to. This portgroup must be able to communicate to the ESXi hosts via the uplinks that is being used for the overlay network.

Click on Finish to complete the creation of the Edge node. The Edge nodes are instantiated as virtual machines on the vSphere Infrastructure. The 'Configure NSX' configuration could have been extended to include the VLAN Uplinks to provide the north-south traffic for this environment. However, to keep things a little simpler, this will be done separately to the initial creation of the Edge node. Therefore, after creating the Edge Transport Node, the next step is to create another Uplink Profile for the Edge VLANs. As before, navigate to **System > Fabric > Profile** in the NSX Manager UI. It is created with a single uplink, and as before the Transport VLAN is set to 0 (since it is tagged at the distributed portgroup level) and with no MTU set, the default is 1700.

Two VLAN Transport Zones, one for each VLAN uplink on the Edge nodes, should now be created. Navigate to **System > Fabric > Transport Zones** in the NSX Manager UI. These are simple to create, as we've already seen. This time however the Traffic Type is VLAN rather than Overlay.

Next, modify the Edge node, which currently only has a management interface and an overlay interface, with the newly created VLAN Uplink Profile and VLAN Transport Zones. The remaining two interfaces will now be added for VLAN uplinks to provide north-south traffic. Navigate once more to **System > Fabric > Nodes,** select **Edge Transport Nodes**, select one of the existing Edge node and click on **Edit**. You can modify the existing switch to add the uplinks, or add new switches. one for each uplink. Add the Transport Zone and Uplink Profile for the VLAN uplinks. Chose the distributed port group which is on the correct VLAN for communicating upstream. In the figure shown below, there are 3 switches configured. The first switch is used for the overlay (east-west) traffic whilst the other two are used for VLAN (north-south) traffic. Note that the nsxHostSwitch3 for VLAN has the Transport Zone, Uplink Profile and distributed portgroup selected as described.

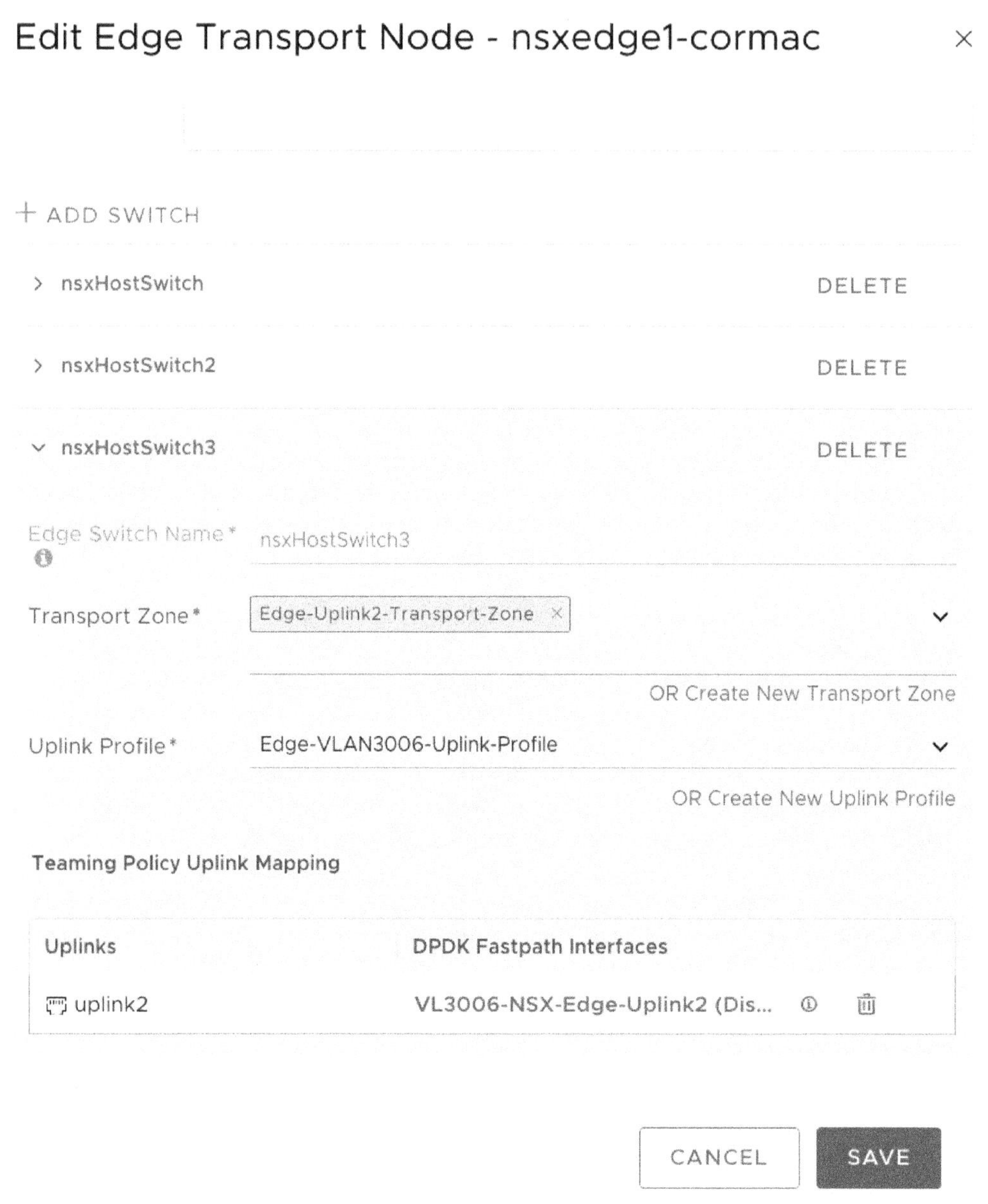

Edit Edge Transport Node - nsxedge1-cormac   ×

+ ADD SWITCH

> nsxHostSwitch   DELETE

> nsxHostSwitch2   DELETE

∨ nsxHostSwitch3   DELETE

Edge Switch Name *   nsxHostSwitch3
ⓘ

Transport Zone *   [Edge-Uplink2-Transport-Zone ×]   ∨

                                            OR Create New Transport Zone

Uplink Profile *   Edge-VLAN3006-Uplink-Profile   ∨

                                            OR Create New Uplink Profile

Teaming Policy Uplink Mapping

Uplinks	DPDK Fastpath Interfaces		
🖧 uplink2	VL3006-NSX-Edge-Uplink2 (Dis...	ⓘ	🗑

CANCEL   SAVE

Figure 134: NSX-T Edge Transport Node

This configuration should now be repeated for the other Edge node. The final step is to add the newly configured Edge nodes to an Edge cluster. Navigate to **System > Fabric > Profile** in the NSX Manager UI. Select **Edge Cluster Profiles**, click on **Add Profile** and create a new profile for the Edge cluster. The default settings for the cluster are fine.

Navigate once more to **System > Fabric > Nodes,** select **Edge Cluster**, click on **Add Edge Cluster**. Select the Edge Cluster Profile created just now, and add both Edge transport nodes to the cluster by selecting them in the Available pane, and clicking on the arrow to move them to the Selected pane, as shown below.

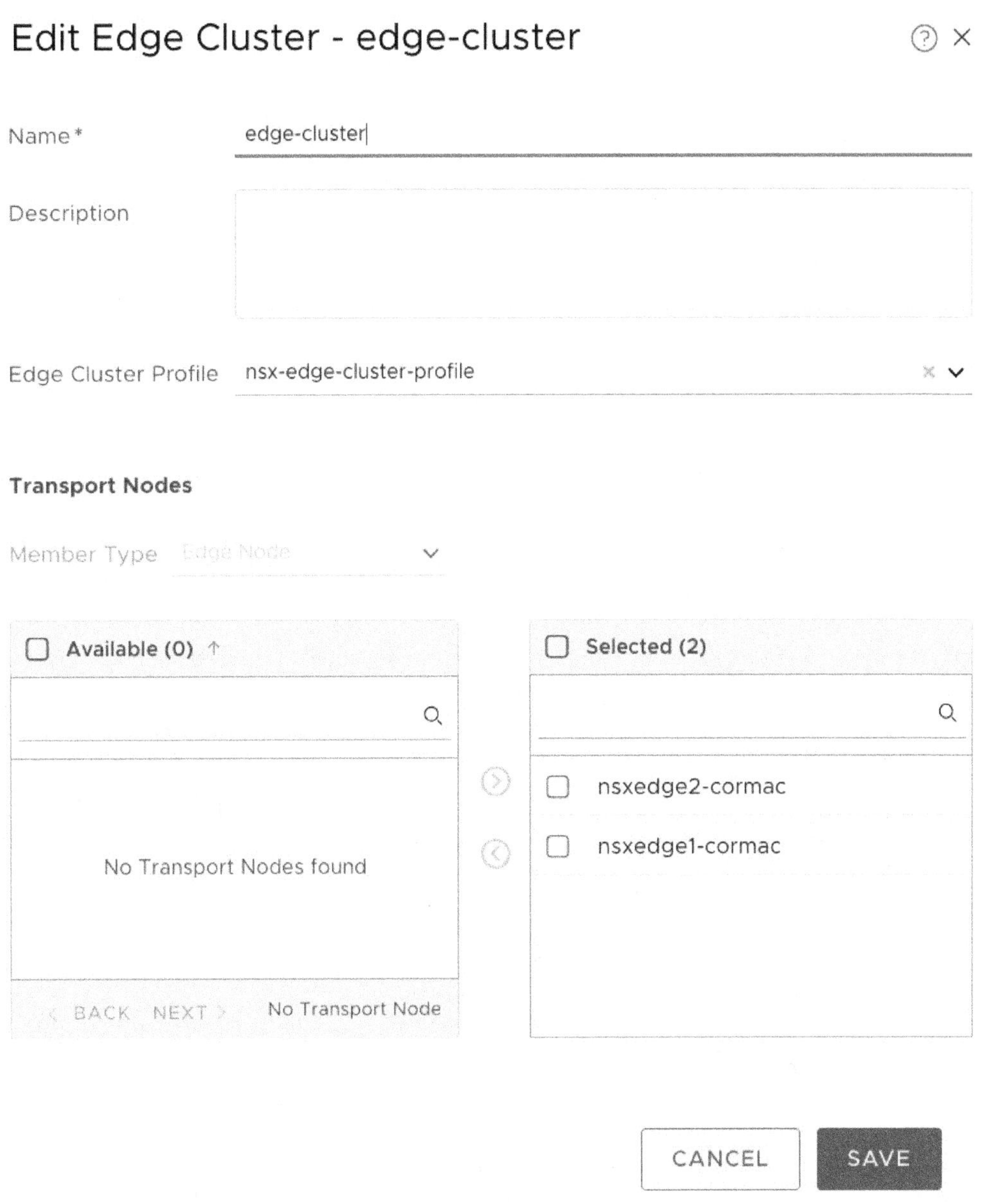

Edit Edge Cluster - edge-cluster ⊘ ×

Name *   edge-cluster|

Description

Edge Cluster Profile   nsx-edge-cluster-profile   × ∨

Transport Nodes

Member Type   Edge Node   ∨

Available (0) ↑	Selected (2)
🔍	🔍
No Transport Nodes found	☐ nsxedge2-cormac
	☐ nsxedge1-cormac
< BACK NEXT > No Transport Node	

CANCEL   SAVE

Figure 135: NSX-T Edge Cluster

To validate that the NSX-T Edge Cluster has deployed correctly, navigate to the Edge Transport Nodes view. Under tunnels, you should notice that the Edge nodes now have a tunnel. It should also be possible to examine the Edge node virtual machines via the vSphere Client. Each Edge node should now have 4 interfaces based on the configuration we provided here. Going by the example setup here, there should be one management interface, one overlay interface (E-W) and 2 VLAN interfaces (N-S). At the risk of repeating myself, this is only one way of implementing the Edge configuration, and other configurations are possible.

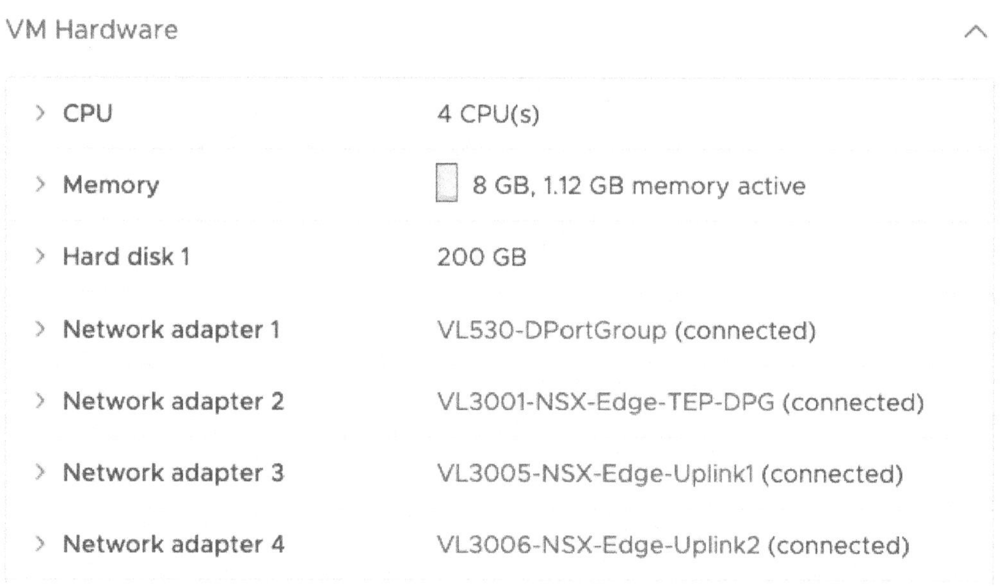

VM Hardware

> CPU	4 CPU(s)
> Memory	8 GB, 1.12 GB memory active
> Hard disk 1	200 GB
> Network adapter 1	VL530-DPortGroup (connected)
> Network adapter 2	VL3001-NSX-Edge-TEP-DPG (connected)
> Network adapter 3	VL3005-NSX-Edge-Uplink1 (connected)
> Network adapter 4	VL3006-NSX-Edge-Uplink2 (connected)

Figure 136: NSX-T Edge VM Uplinks

Finally, we should be able to do some ping tests to verify connectivity between the Edge nodes and the ESXi hosts on the overlay network. This is similar to what we did with the host overlay, where we made sure the ESXi hosts were able to ping each other. Now we repeat this test, but this time ensuring that communication is working between the ESXi hosts and the Edge nodes, e.g.

```
[root@w4-hs4-i1501:~] vmkping ++netstack=vxlan 192.168.102.1
PING 192.168.102.1 (192.168.102.1): 56 data bytes
64 bytes from 192.168.102.1: icmp_seq=0 ttl=64 time=0.343 ms
64 bytes from 192.168.102.1: icmp_seq=1 ttl=64 time=0.177 ms
64 bytes from 192.168.102.1: icmp_seq=2 ttl=64 time=0.186 ms

--- 192.168.102.1 ping statistics ---
3 packets transmitted, 3 packets received, 0% packet loss
round-trip min/avg/max = 0.177/0.235/0.343 ms

[root@w4-hs4-i1501:~]
```

At this point, everything looks good. We have successfully created the Edge cluster, and it can communicate with the hosts via the overlay network. We are now ready to setup our Tier-0 Gateway

Create Tier-0 Gateway

This is the final step in preparing an NSX-T environment for vSphere with Tanzu. It involves the creation and configuring of a tier-0 gateway. Networks that are created for Kubernetes workloads in vSphere with Tanzu will connect to this tier-0 gateway and subsequently allow external connectivity. This might be developers connecting to the API server of a TKG cluster, or end-users accessing Kubernetes based applications. Once the initial tier-0 gateway is created, additional configuration steps, such as setting up BGP (Border Gateway Protocol) and Route Distribution to integrate with upstream routers, are explored.

The first step in setting up the tier-0 gateway is to create an external segment. Navigate to **Networking > Segments** in the NSX Manager UI. Under NSX, click on Add Segment. The information that should be provided at this point are the segment name and the transport zone. This is the Edge uplink transport zone created earlier. At this point, there is no need to add the tier-0 as a connected gateway, or the gateway IP address – this will be done when we create the interfaces on the tier-0 shortly.

Now that the segment is created, we can create the tier-0. Navigate to **Networking > Tier-0 Gateways** in the NSX Manager UI. Click on **Add Gateway**, and select Tier-0 from the drop-down list. Initially, there are only a handful of items to configure. The first is the name of the tier-0 gateway. Then decide on the HA Mode, which can be Active-Active or Active-Standby. The only other options are to add the Edge cluster and select the Fail Over mode if the HA mode is set to Active-Standby. Then click Save so that other options can be configured.

After saving the initial configuration of the tier-0, additional configuration steps can now be carried out. The next step is to add external interfaces to the tier-0. Click on the **Set link** next to **External and Service Interfaces**, then click on **Add Interface**. To create External interfaces, the required settings are (i) provide a name for the interface, (ii) provide an IP Address in CIDR format, (iii) choose which segment to use, i.e. one which was just created and finally (iv) select the Edge node. The remaining entries can be left at the default. Click Save once again, but do not close the editing as we still have more configuration settings to make. Note that the IP addresses that these interfaces are assigned allow connection to an upstream, external router. If your environment allows similar, BGP can be configured. BGP allows the upstream router to learn about the virtual networks that NSX-T is creating, and vice-versa. This will be especially important for Load Balancer IP addresses used for both Kubernetes applications and API servers. Repeat this step for any additional interfaces that you wish to create.

Configure HA VIP on the Tier-0 Gateway

To add an HA VIP Configuration on the Tier-0, it requires an IP address in CIDR format, along with the two interfaces that were created previously. Add the new highly available IP address, then select both interfaces. Click Add, then Apply the HA VIP configuration, and continue to edit the tier-0.

Configure BGP on the Tier-0 Gateway

There are two parts to configuring BGP on the Tier-0 Gateway. The first step is to configure the local BGP attributes, and then configure the attributes of the remote BGP neighbor, i.e. the upstream router. For the local (tier-0) BGP, the only setting need is the Local AS, in this example *64512*.

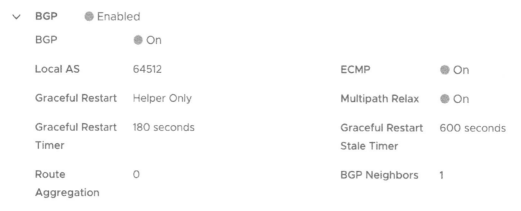

Figure 137: NSX-T BGP Configuration

For the BGP Neighbor, click on the BGP Neighbors Set link, Click on **Add BGP Neighbor** and add the appropriate information. In the previous figure, it is already showing a neighbor as configured. This information to add about the neighbor includes (i) the IP Address of the remote upstream physical router, (ii) the remote AS number and (iii) a route filter. You may also need to set a password to connect to the upstream router. The password can be configured in this window, under Timers and Password. Click on the "Set" link next to Password.

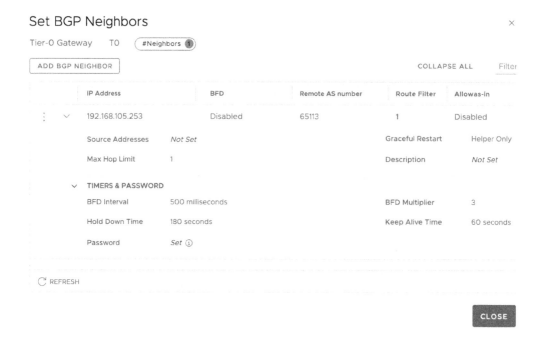

Figure 138: NSX-T BGP Neighbor Configuration

A Route Filter is required when configuring the BGP Neighbor. Simply click on the Route Filter "Set" link, then Add Route Filter to add it. In the previous figure, it is already shown as configured. Leave the IP address family to IPv4 and Enabled. No other settings are required. Click Add then Apply to set the route filter, and then Save to save the BGP Neighbor configuration.

Configure Route Re-distribution on the Tier 0 Gateway

There is one final configuration step and that is to setup Route Re-distribution. This defines which of the traffic sources that the BGP Neighbor should learn about from the Tier 0, and vice-versa. Click on the **Set link** for **Route Re-distribution**, then **Add Route Re-Distribution**. Provide (i) a name which I set to *default*, (ii) leave the destination protocol to *BGP* and then (iii) click on the Route Re-distribution Set link to select the traffic sources to share.

In this setup, the following sources are selected to be re-distributed. **Apply** the selection, then **Add** the Route Re-distribution configuration. **Apply**, then **Save** the tier-0 configuration, and you can now close the editing of the tier-0 gateway editor.

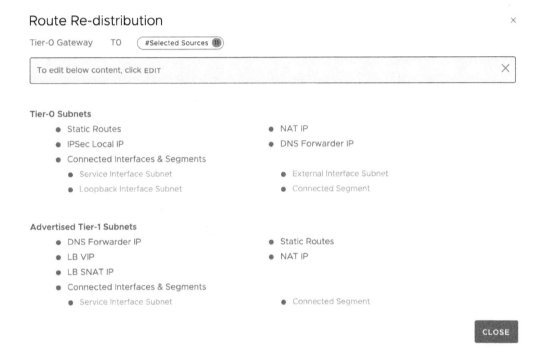

Figure 139: NSX-T Route Re-distribution Sources

That now completes the setup of the tier-0 gateway. With the tier-0 gateway now created and configured to connect to physical infrastructure, it should be possible to see the Service Router and the Distributed Router (DR) when the logical routers are displayed in the NSX CLI. The Distributed Router (DR) takes care of routing the east-west traffic (E-W), whilst the Service Router (SR) takes care of routing the north-south traffic (N-S), and provide connectivity to physical infrastructure such as upstream routers. The DR is instantiated across all transport nodes (Host and Edge nodes). The SR is instantiated on the Edge nodes. As we have seen, the Edge nodes are able to send/receive overlay traffic to/from the ESXi hosts. Thus, traffic from a VM hosted on an ESXi host goes through the Edge node on the overlay network, to connect to a device in physical infrastructure. Login to the NSX Edge command line interface, and check various settings as shown here.

```
nsxedge1-cormac> get logical-routers
Tue Apr 26 2022 UTC 07:43:23.542
Logical Router
UUID                                 VRF LR-ID Name   Type                   Ports Neighbors
736a80e3-23f6-5a2d-81d6 bbefb2786666 0   0     TUNNEL                        3 2/5000
9b92534f-c329-415d-95a3-241ac7501684 22  2050  SR-T0 SERVICE_ROUTER_TIER0     5 1/50000
c61e7ecf-be14-4f10-bec1-f22785920b60 24  14    DR-T0 DISTRIBUTED_ROUTER_TIER0 6 3/50000
```

The NSX Edge CLI also provides the ability to query the BGP information and status. By selecting the Service Router VRF from the list of logical routers, the BGP neighbor can be queried as well as the routes provided by BGP. In this setup, the default route of 0.0.0.0/0 is provided through the upstream router, so all traffic is routed there.

```
nsxedge1-cormac> vrf 22

nsxedge1-cormac(tier0_sr[22])> get bgp neighbor 192.168.105.253
BGP neighbor is 192.168.105.253, remote AS 65113, local AS 64512, external link
  BGP version 4, remote router ID 192.168.255.0, local router ID 192.168.105.1
  BGP state = Established, up for 1d23h12m
  Last read 00:00:50, Last write 00:00:48
  Hold time is 180, keepalive interval is 60 seconds
  Configured hold time is 180, keepalive interval is 60 seconds
  Neighbor capabilities:
.
.--snip--
.

nsxedge1-cormac(tier0_sr[22])> get route bgp

Flags: t0c - Tier0-Connected, t0s - Tier0-Static, b - BGP, o - OSPF
t0n - Tier0-NAT, t1s - Tier1-Static, t1c - Tier1-Connected,
t1n: Tier1-NAT, t1l: Tier1-LB VIP, t1ls: Tier1-LB SNAT,
t1d: Tier1-DNS FORWARDER, t1ipsec: Tier1-IPSec, isr: Inter-SR,
> - selected route, * - FIB route

Total number of routes: 1

b  > * 0.0.0.0/0 [20/0] via 192.168.105.253, uplink-435, 21:56:30
Tue Apr 26 2022 UTC 07:43:42.269
nsxedge1-cormac(tier0_sr[22])>
```

This all looks good, and we now have an NSX-T network infrastructure that we can use for vSphere with Tanzu.

Workload Management Setup with NSX-T

When enabling Workload Management with NSX-T, the networking is a little different to enabling Workload Management with vSphere networking using either the HA-Proxy or NSX ALB. The first thing to observe is that there is no Load Balancer network. Instead, a bunch of information related to the NSX-T networking stack is requested, such as the name of the Edge cluster and the tier-0 gateway. Other information required are the Ingress and Egress CIDRs. Every vSphere Namespace created within vSphere with Tanzu using NSX-T is isolated through these Ingress and Egress settings, as we shall see shortly.

This is a review of the management network settings. Some of the IP addresses have been deliberately obfuscated.

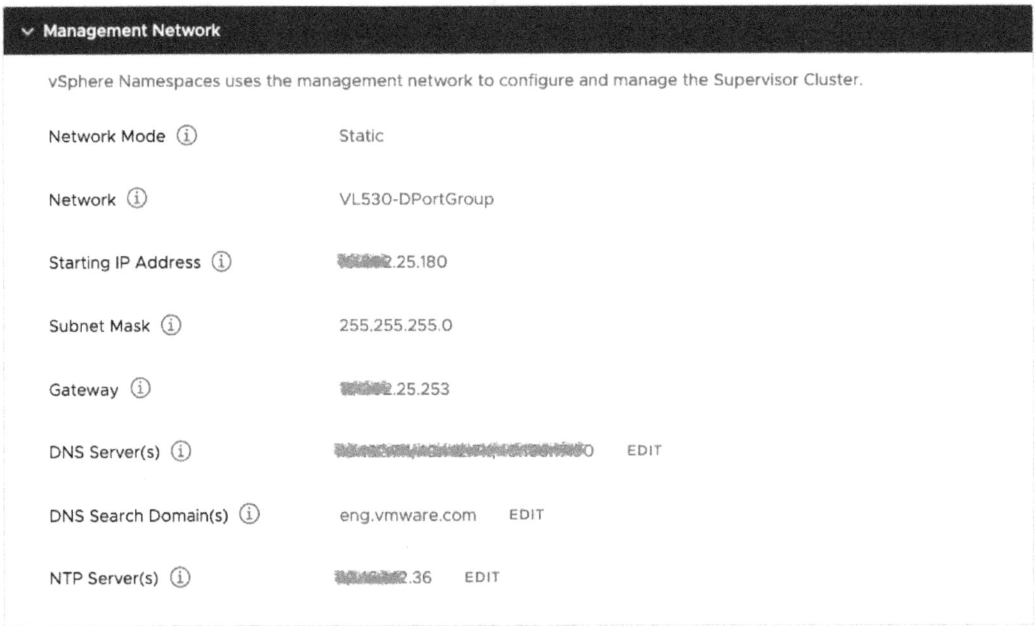

Management Network

vSphere Namespaces uses the management network to configure and manage the Supervisor Cluster.

Network Mode (i)   Static

Network (i)   VL530-DPortGroup

Starting IP Address (i)   ███████.25.180

Subnet Mask (i)   255.255.255.0

Gateway (i)   █████.25.253

DNS Server(s) (i)   ████████████████████0   EDIT

DNS Search Domain(s) (i)   eng.vmware.com   EDIT

NTP Server(s) (i)   ████████.36   EDIT

Figure 140: Workload Management with NSX-T – Management network

Whilst the management network may not look much different to deployments with either the HA-Proxy or NSX ALB Load Balancers, the workload network looks very different with NSX-T. Note the inclusion of an Edge cluster, the Tier-0 Gateway, a Namespace Network, as well as the Ingress and Egress entries. Each of these will be explained in more detail in the next section.

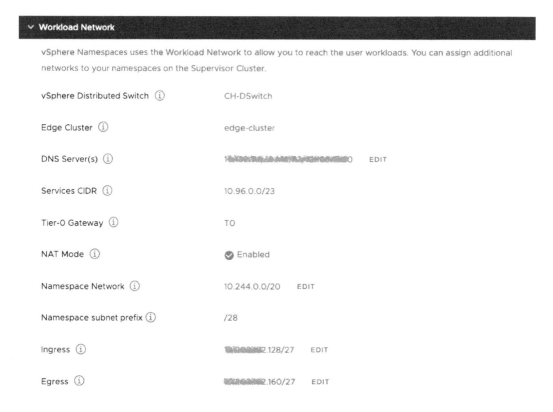

Figure 141: Workload Management with NSX-T – Workload network

One of the most interesting observations, when vSphere with Tanzu is deployed with NSX-T, is the fact that the ESXi hosts in the cluster now appear as nodes.

```
% kubectl get nodes
NAME                                STATUS   ROLES                 AGE   VERSION
42251773574d7864ce30fb6af26f7faf    Ready    control-plane,master  48d   v1.22.6+vmware.wcp.2
4225925c2ebd965766e35132241a888d    Ready    control-plane,master  48d   v1.22.6+vmware.wcp.2
42259a6824d75fcf410b580a023500a9    Ready    control-plane,master  48d   v1.22.6+vmware.wcp.2
w4-hs4-i1501.eng.vmware.com         Ready    agent                 48d   v1.22.6-sph-2d0356d
w4-hs4-i1502.eng.vmware.com         Ready    agent                 48d   v1.22.6-sph-2d0356d
w4-hs4-i1503.eng.vmware.com         Ready    agent                 48d   v1.22.6-sph-2d0356d
w4-hs4-i1504.eng.vmware.com         Ready    agent                 48d   v1.22.6-sph-2d0356d
```

This is different from the list of nodes when vSphere with Tanzu is deployed with either NSX ALB or HA-Proxy. The ESXi hosts are not listed since the spherelet process is not installed without NSX-T.

NSX-T (Under the covers)

At this point, quite a number of NSX-T system objects are setup in advance of enabling vSphere with Tanzu Workload Management. This includes the Compute Manager and Edge Cluster. Some network objects are also created such as IP Address Pools for the Host and Edge TEPs, Network Segments, and a Tier-0 gateway associated with the Edge Cluster for external network access. These items altogether are consumed by what is commonly referred to as the system namespace, and is essential for a correctly functioning Supervisor Cluster. This sections examines the network objects and services that are automatically created once the Supervisor Cluster is deployed. Let's begin with *Network Overview,* found under the Networking tab in the NSX Manager. This is what is displayed when vSphere with Tanzu has been enabled and the Supervisor Cluster has been deployed.

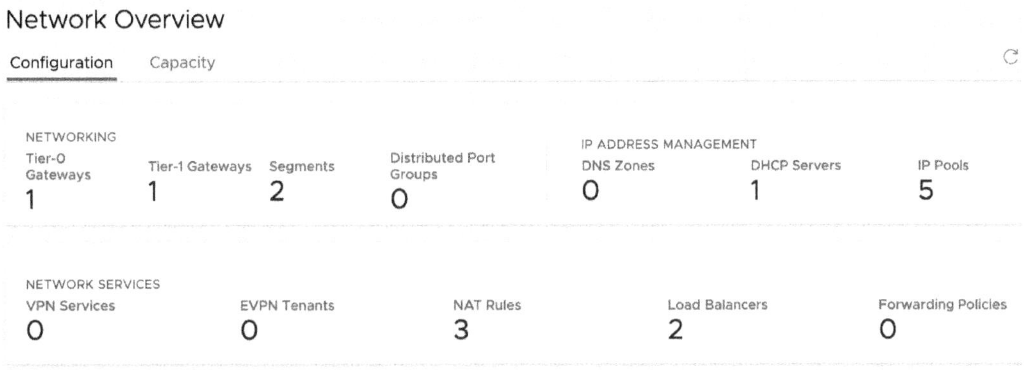

Network Overview

Configuration   Capacity

NETWORKING				IP ADDRESS MANAGEMENT		
Tier-0 Gateways	Tier-1 Gateways	Segments	Distributed Port Groups	DNS Zones	DHCP Servers	IP Pools
1	1	2	0	0	1	5

NETWORK SERVICES				
VPN Services	EVPN Tenants	NAT Rules	Load Balancers	Forwarding Policies
0	0	3	2	0

Figure 142: NSX-T Configuration Overview

The following are the new objects and services created after enabling vSphere with Tanzu:

- **1 x Tier-1 Gateway**
- **1 x Segment** (1 existed already – the segment for external access)
- **1 x DHCP Server**
- **3 x IP Pools** (2 existed already – the IP Pools for Host TEPs and Edge TEPs)
- **3 x NAT Rules** (1 x SNAT, 2 x No SNAT)
- **2 x Load Balancers**

Let's now take a look at the *Network Topology* view from NSX-T to see how all of this ties together.

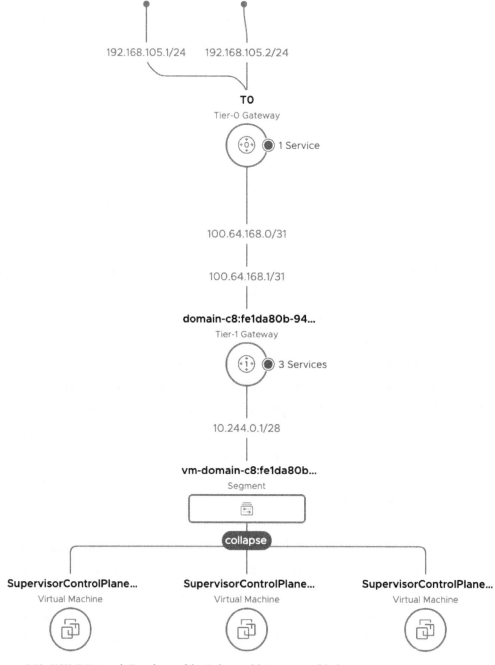

Figure 143: NSX-T Network Topology with vSphere with Tanzu enabled

The three virtual machines that make up the Supervisor Cluster are visible in the lower part of the diagram above. These are all on the same newly-created segment, and are connected to the same newly-created Tier-1 gateway. This gateway is then connected to the already existing Tier-0 Gateway, which provides external access via the Edge Cluster (not shown). Note that the Tier-1 has 3 Services, while the Tier-0 has a single Service.

Let's look at the newly created segment next. By clicking on the segment in the *Network Topology* view above, more details can be learnt about it.

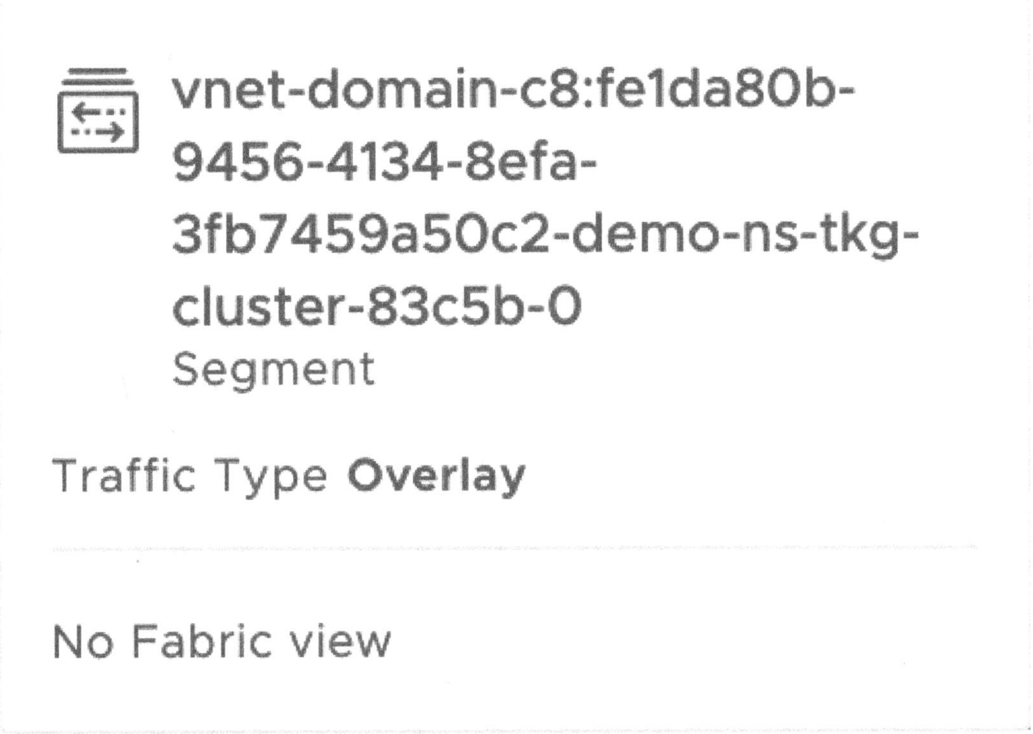

 vnet-domain-c8:fe1da80b-9456-4134-8efa-3fb7459a50c2-demo-ns-tkg-cluster-83c5b-0
Segment

Traffic Type **Overlay**

No Fabric view

Figure 144: NSX-T Segment

As shown here, we get the full name of the segment and also that is of type `Overlay`. If we navigate to the Segment view (**Networking > Connectivity > Segments**), we can learn more details about it. The two items of particular interest are shown below. The first is the number of ports consumed on the segment. There are 3, one for each of the Supervisor nodes / virtual machines. The second item of interest in the IP Address Pool. This is where the IP addresses assigned to the Supervisor virtual machine network interfaces on this segment are retrieved. One other thing to note the subnet 10.244.0.1/28 associated with the segment. This is part of the Namespace Network CIDR (10.244.0.0./20) that was provided with the Workload Network configuration at Supervisor Cluster creation time.

Figure 145: NSX-T Segment - Detailed

The ports can be examined in greater detail. This view appears if the port count number highlighted in the previous figure is clicked in the NSX Manager UI.

Figure 146: NSX-T Segment Ports

IP Address Pool information is also available. This view can be found under **Networking > IP Management > IP Address Pools**. There are 3 IP Address Pools created in total when the Supervisor Cluster is enabled.

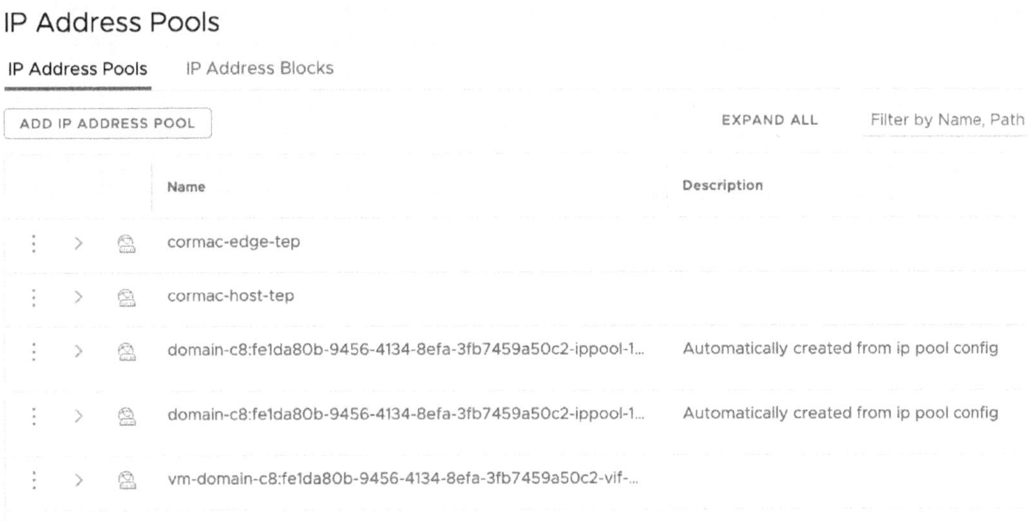

IP Address Pools

IP Address Pools   IP Address Blocks

| ADD IP ADDRESS POOL | | EXPAND ALL | Filter by Name, Path |

		Name	Description
⋮ >	🔒	cormac-edge-tep	
⋮ >	🔒	cormac-host-tep	
⋮ >	🔒	domain-c8:fe1da80b-9456-4134-8efa-3fb7459a50c2-ippool-1...	Automatically created from ip pool config
⋮ >	🔒	domain-c8:fe1da80b-9456-4134-8efa-3fb7459a50c2-ippool-1...	Automatically created from ip pool config
⋮ >	🔒	vm-domain-c8:fe1da80b-9456-4134-8efa-3fb7459a50c2-vif-...	

Figure 147: NSX-T IP Address Pools

One IP Address Pool is for the Namespace Network which we saw populated in the Workload Management UI. The other two are IP Address Pools for the **Ingress** and **Egress** ranges which were also provided with the Workload Network configuration at Supervisor Cluster creation time. As the name suggests, the Ingress is used for 'Load Balancer' or 'Ingress' type services on the Supervisor Cluster. The Egress is used when there is a SNAT (Source Network Address Translation) requirement for traffic exiting the Supervisor Cluster Namespace to access external services. The Ingress and Egress enable communication between objects running inside of the vSphere Namespace to the outside world, and vice-versa.

That completes the explanation on the automatically created Segment and IP Address Pools. The next step is to examine the Network Services associated with the Tier-1 Gateway which is also automatically created, and to which the segment examined above is attached. Earlier, when examining the Tier-1 Gateway in the Network Topology view, three services were observed. The three services are Gateway Firewall Rules, Load Balancer and NAT Rules. These are automatically created during deployment. Clicking on the Tier-1 Gateway allows them to be viewed in more detail.

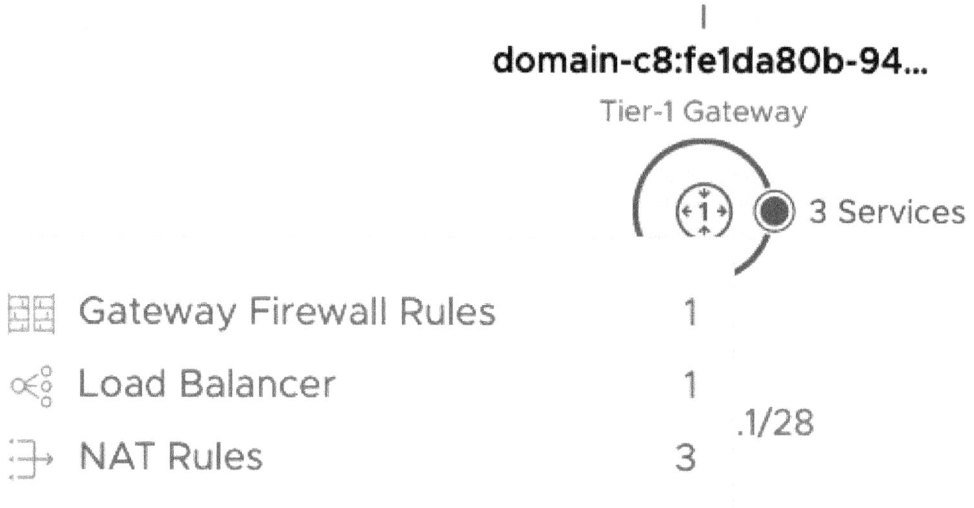

domain-c8:fe1da80b-94...

Tier-1 Gateway

(1) ⦿ 3 Services

⊞ Gateway Firewall Rules	1
⚬⚬ Load Balancer	1
⤷ NAT Rules	3

.1/28

Figure 148: NSX-T Tier-1 Services

Checking the server and distributed load balancers (**Networking** > **Network Services** > **Load Balancing** > **Load Balancers**), there are a number of virtual servers associated with each. The server load balancer has **4**, whilst the distributed load balancer can have **29** or more.

On the server load balancer **Virtual Servers** column, click on the number 4. This shows that there are two ports on each virtual server. There are two for CSI metrics and two for the Supervisor cluster API server. The first Kubernetes port is 6443. But also available is port 443 which, when you connect to it, displays the Kubernetes tools landing page for interacting with vSphere with Tanzu.

Note that the IP addresses assigned to virtual servers on the server load balancer come from the **Ingress** range provided during Supervisor Cluster setup. These provide services that can be accessed externally to the cluster (e.g. Kubernetes LoadBalancer Service type).

We can also list the virtual servers on the distributed load balancer. These are Supervisor Cluster services which do not need to reach out externally (e.g. Kubernetes ClusterIP Service type). The IP addresses come from the Services CIDR (**10.96.0.0/23**) which is also configured in the vSphere with Tanzu wizard during setup time, as seen in the workload networking configuration shown above. You can get a similar list by running a *kubectl get svc -A* on the Supervisor Cluster.

There are 3 NAT rules created as shown here; 2 are "No SNAT" rules, and one is a "SNAT" rule. The "No SNAT" rules relate to East-West (internal) traffic. The "SNAT" rule relates to North-South (external) traffic.

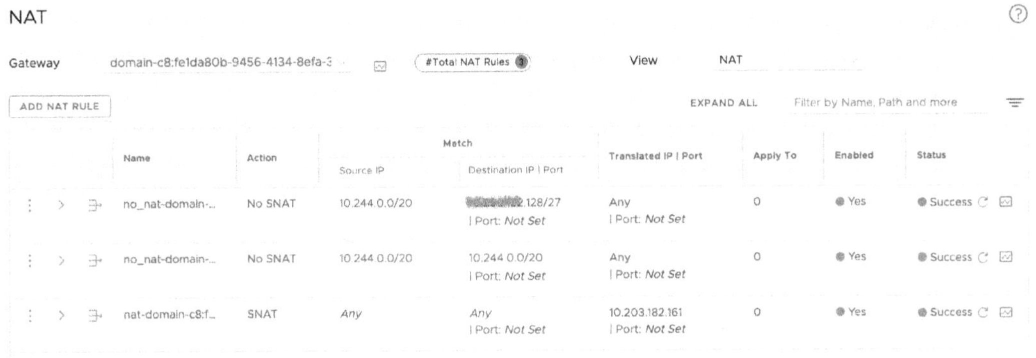

NAT

		Name	Action	Match		Translated IP | Port	Apply To	Enabled	Status
				Source IP	Destination IP | Port				
⋮ > ⋺		no_nat-domain-...	No SNAT	10.244.0.0/20	●●●●●●● 128/27 | Port: *Not Set*	Any | Port: *Not Set*	0	● Yes	● Success ↻ ☑
⋮ > ⋺		no_nat-domain-...	No SNAT	10.244.0.0/20	10.244.0.0/20 | Port: *Not Set*	Any | Port: *Not Set*	0	● Yes	● Success ↻ ☑
⋮ > ⋺		nat-domain-c8:f...	SNAT	*Any*	*Any* | Port: *Not Set*	10.203.182.161 | Port: *Not Set*	0	● Yes	● Success ↻ ☑

Gateway: domain-c8:fe1da80b-9456-4134-8efa-3   #Total NAT Rules 3   View NAT

ADD NAT RULE   EXPAND ALL   Filter by Name, Path and more

Figure 149: NSX-T Tier-1 NAT

These rules work as follows:

- The first "No SNAT" rule matches the **Ingress range**. Each vSphere Namespaces, including the system namespace used by the Supervisor Cluster, will get its own separate network setup. This includes a network segment as well as its own tier-1 gateway and Load Balancer. This first "No SNAT" rule is for traffic between vSphere namespaces through its allocated Load Balancer, and facilitates communicate to other Load Balancer services / vSphere namespaces.
- The second "No SNAT" is for traffic between standard Kubernetes namespaces in the Supervisor Clusters. This facilitates East-West communication.
- The last rule is a SNAT rule which used an **Egress** IP address, and as mentioned earlier, this is a requirement for traffic between entities within the Supervisor Cluster Namespace (Native Pods, TKG clusters, VMs) to external entities. All workloads running in the same vSphere Namespace share the same SNAT IP for North-South connectivity.

The final service on the tier-1 relates to Gateway Firewall rules. To look at these more closely, change contexts to the *Security* tab, and then select *Gateway Firewall* under Policy Management. Here you will observe a policy for the Tier-0 and another for the Tier-1. The firewall rules, by default, appear to allow all traffic between the namespaces and services in the Supervisor Cluster.

vSphere Namespace - NSX-T objects and Services

The act of creating a new vSphere namespace with default settings means that the existing Tier-0 gateway is used, NAT mode is enabled, and Load Balancer size set to small. Namespace network and Namespace subnet are left at the defaults (10.244.0.0/20). After creating the new vSphere namespace, the Network Overview reports the following new objects and services.

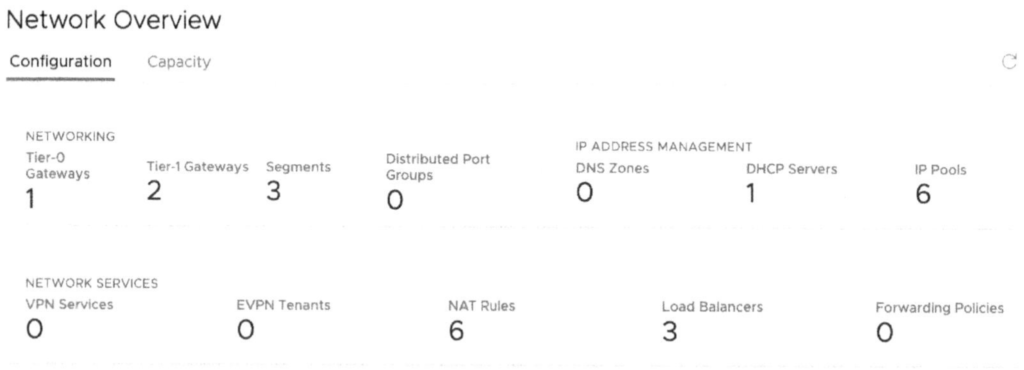

Network Overview

Configuration   Capacity

NETWORKING

Tier-0 Gateways	Tier-1 Gateways	Segments	Distributed Port Groups
1	2	3	0

IP ADDRESS MANAGEMENT

DNS Zones	DHCP Servers	IP Pools
0	1	6

NETWORK SERVICES

VPN Services	EVPN Tenants	NAT Rules	Load Balancers	Forwarding Policies
0	0	6	3	0

Figure 150: NSX-T Namespace Objects and Services

From the updated items, a new namespace resulted in the creation of the following network objects and services:

- **1 x Tier-1 Gateway** (connected to Tier-0)
- **1 x Segment** (no ports used until something is deployed in the namespace, e.g. vSphere Pod, TKG cluster)
- **1 x IP Pool** (with IP range taken from Namespace network range)
- **3 x NAT Rules** (for the new Tier-1. These are the same as seen previously but with a new SNAT IP address for this namespace)
- **1 x Load Balancer** (of type server, as seen before)

Hopefully this gives you, the vSphere administrator, a pretty good idea of the kinds of networks and services that get created when enabling vSphere with Tanzu Workload Management using NSX-T networking, and successfully deploying a Supervisor Cluster. Every new vSphere Namespace gets allocate a separate network and its own set of networking resources shared by applications inside the namespace. From the list above, you can see resource such as a tier-1 gateway, a load balancer service, and SNAT IP address. Note that there are additional controls available when creating a vSphere Namespace with NSX-T which are not available in non-NSX-T environments.

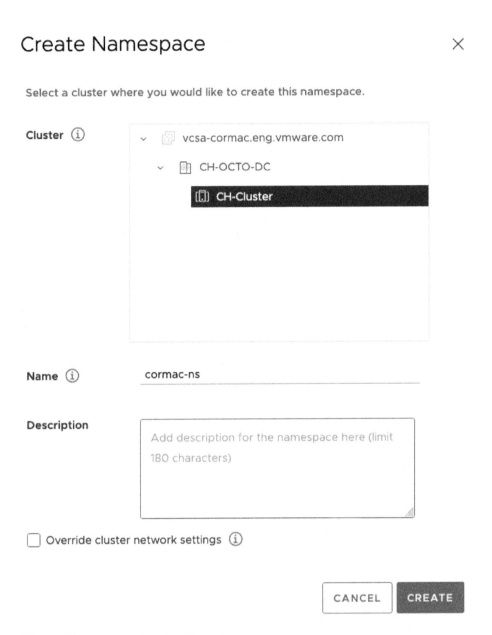

Create Namespace   ✕

Select a cluster where you would like to create this namespace.

Cluster ⓘ

    ∨ ▣ vcsa-cormac.eng.vmware.com

        ∨ ▥ CH-OCTO-DC

            ▥ **CH-Cluster**

Name ⓘ   cormac-ns

Description

Add description for the namespace here (limit 180 characters)

☐ Override cluster network settings ⓘ

CANCEL   CREATE

Figure 151: NSX-T Namespace Creation (Simple)

This looks much the name as the other vSphere Namespaces we have built in the past. However, on this occasion, there is the option to override the cluster network settings. When that option is selected, several network configuration parameters become available.

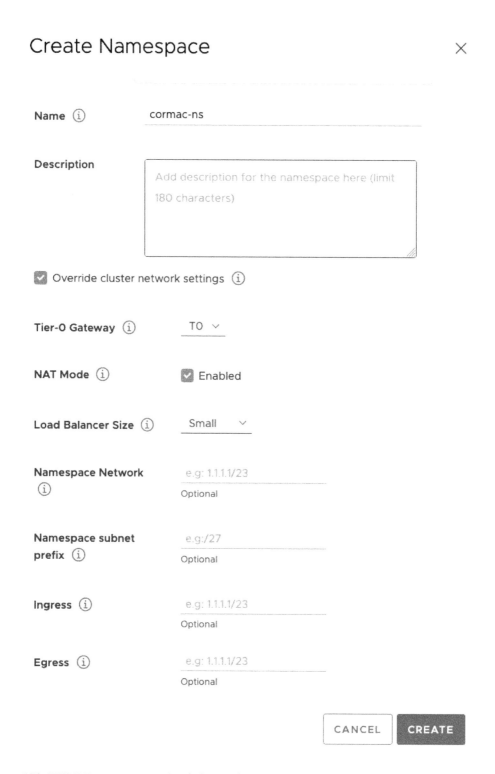

Create Namespace ✕

Name ⓘ cormac-ns

Description
> Add description for the namespace here (limit 180 characters)

☑ Override cluster network settings ⓘ

Tier-0 Gateway ⓘ T0 ⌄

NAT Mode ⓘ ☑ Enabled

Load Balancer Size ⓘ Small ⌄

Namespace Network ⓘ e.g: 1.1.1.1/23
Optional

Namespace subnet prefix ⓘ e.g:/27
Optional

Ingress ⓘ e.g: 1.1.1.1/23
Optional

Egress ⓘ e.g: 1.1.1.1/23
Optional

CANCEL   **CREATE**

Figure 152: NSX-T Namespace Creation (Advanced)

As you can see, this option provides the ability to select a different tier-0 gateway if multiple ones exist. It gives control over the size of the load balancer, as well as the ability to change the range of IP addresses for namespace, ingress and egress which were all defined when vSphere with Tanzu was first enabled. You may never need to use these options, but nevertheless it is useful to know that this is an available option.

At this point, it is also interesting to describe a vSphere namespace that has been created in vSphere with Tanzu with NSX-T. Reference to the T1, SNAT IP Address and other information related to the vSphere Namespace are all visible.

```
% kubectl describe ns demo-ns
Name:          demo-ns
Labels:        kubernetes.io/metadata.name=demo-ns
               vSphereClusterID=domain-c8
Annotations:   ls_id-0: 31b31652-e936-44cb-a8e7-571c8a4192a2
               ncp/extpoolid: domain-c8:fe1da80b-...-ippool-192-168-182-161-192-168-182-190
               ncp/router_id: t1_3410a762-a927-4857-86b6-ed4c4d1cb8de_rtr
               ncp/snat_ip: 192.168.182.165
               ncp/subnet-0: 10.244.0.16/28
               vmware-system-resource-pool: resgroup-18285
               vmware-system-vm-folder: group-v18286
Status:        Active
Resource Quotas
  Name:                                                                   demo-ns-
storagequota
  Resource                                                         Used  Hard
  --------                                                         ---   ---
  vsan-default-storage-
policy.storageclass.storage.k8s.io/requests.storage  100Gi  9223372036854775807
No LimitRange resource.
```

At this point, you should have a good idea of what the NCP (NSX Container Plugin) CNI does on the Supervisor Cluster. We've mentioned this CNI a few times throughout the book, and it is this plugin that is controlling the interaction between the Supervisor Cluster and the NSX-T networking stack, and making requests to the NSX-T API to build the components needed by vSphere Namespaces. When a new vSphere Namespace is created on the Supervisor Cluster, it is the NCP that provides the interface to NSX-T to build out the necessary networking infrastructure to accommodate it.

vSphere with Tanzu features available with NSX-T

I have mentioned several times throughout this book that there are certain features that are only available when vSphere with Tanzu is configured with NSX-T. Now that vSphere with Tanzu has been configured with NSX-T, let's look at some of those features in action.

Embedded Harbor Image Registry

vSphere with Tanzu, when configured with NSX-T, provides an embedded Harbor Image Registry. This can be extremely useful as it provides a secure location for the storing and retrieving of container images. This avoids developers pulling images from an external registry. It is also multi-tenanted so that each vSphere Namespace is provided with its unique Project within Harbor. A project in Harbor holds all the container images (repositories) for a vSphere Namespace.

To enable the Image Registry, select the vSphere Cluster in the vSphere Client inventory, and select **Configure > Supervisor Cluster > Image Registry**. Here you will find the 'Enable Harbor' button.

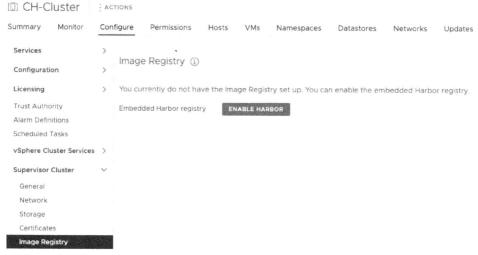

Figure 153: Harbor – Enable Embedded Registry

There is only a single configuration setting that needs to be selected, and that is to choose the storage policy for the persistent volumes (PVs) that are used to store the container images when Harbor is deployed. Harbor is deployed as a set of Native Pods. The deployment now creates a new vSphere Namespace called `vmware-system-registry`.

A total of 7 Native Pods (or PodVMs) are created for the registry. The list is shown below but includes a web server front end using nginx, an in-memory store using Redis and a backend database. The namespace view for the registry shows the vSphere Pods view, with 7 of them entering a running state soon after enablement.

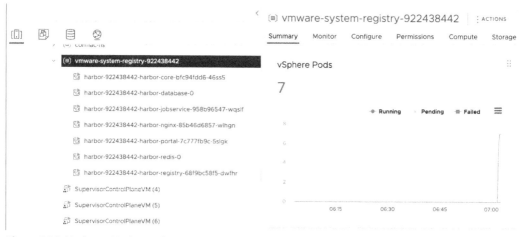

Figure 154: Harbor – Native Pods

Returning to the **Configure > Supervisor Cluster > Image Registry**, details regarding the Harbor Image Registry, and how to access it, are now shown.

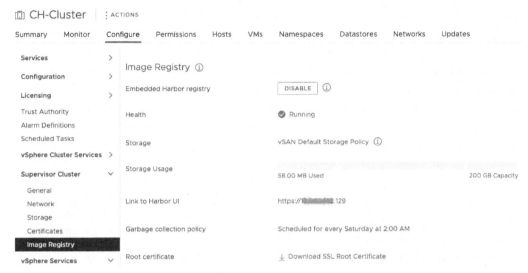

Figure 155: Harbor – Image Registry Details

Clicking on the link to Harbor UI will open a browser to the registry. It is linked to vSphere Single Sign-On so there is no need to worry about managing another set of credentials. The owner of a namespace has automatic access to Harbor. Let's now look at how the embedded Harbor Image Registry can be used for the safe storing of container images on a per vSphere Namespace basis.

Pushing and Pull images to the Image Registry

For the purposes of this exercise, I have created a new vSphere namespace called `demo-ns`. When I login to the embedded Harbor image registry UI as the SSO user who owns this namespace, I see a new project created for this namespace, but it currently has 0 images / repositories.

Figure 156: Harbor – Project automatically created

You may remember that earlier in this chapter when vSphere with Tanzu was first deployed, our first vSphere Namespace was created. On the Summary card of that vSphere Namespace, the ability to download tools to allow a Platform Operator to interact with the environment was displayed. As well as the CLI plugin, some additional tools enabled interaction with the embedded Harbor image registry. This is the vSphere Docker Credential Helper, and we are going to familiarise ourselves with this next.

vSphere Docker Credential Helper

Download the vSphere Docker Credential Helper to securely pull
and push image to the embedded Harbor registry in vSphere.

SELECT OPERATING SYSTEM ˅

DOWNLOAD FOR MAC OS ⬇

Checksum for Docker Credential Helper Mac OS ⬇

VIEW INSTALL INSTRUCTIONS ˅

Figure 157: Harbor - vSphere Docker Credential Helper

To use the vSphere Docker Credential Helper, download the zip file containing the docker credentials binary. Unzip it and move it to a location that is in your PATH. I have placed it in */usr/local/bin* on my local desktop. The next step is to try to log in to the Harbor image registry. Continue to use the SSO credentials. This should provide access to the projects to which you have permission to access the image registry.

```
% /usr/local/bin/docker-credential-vsphere login -h
The developer needs to provide the vSphere username and password, who will be granted to
login to the specified Harbor server.

Usage:
  docker-credential-vsphere login [harbor-registry] [flags]

Flags:
  -h, --help               help for login
  -s, --service string     credential store service
      --tlscacert string   location to CA certificate (default
"/etc/docker/certs.d/*.crt")
  -u, --user string        vSphere username and password
```

Next, attempt to log in. In the example below, this step failed with an x509 error.

```
% /usr/local/bin/docker-credential-vsphere login 192.168.182.129
FATA[0002] Error getting API master info: Get "https://192.168.182.129/api/systeminfo":
x509: certificate signed by unknown authority
```

The command needs a reference to the TLS certificate for the Harbor registry. This is available for download from the vSphere Client via **Configure** > **Supervisor Cluster** > **Image Registry**, as shown earlier. The link is called 'Download SSL Root Certificate'. Once downloaded, place it in a location that can be referenced via the login command. I renamed the certificate to harbor-ssl-root-crt and placed it in my home directory. Now the login succeeds.

```
% /usr/local/bin/docker-credential-vsphere login 192.168.182.129 \
--tlscacert harbor-ssl-root-crt
Username: administrator@vsphere.local
Password: INFO[0010] Fetched username and password
INFO[0012] Fetched auth token
INFO[0012] Saved auth token
%
```

OK. We appear to have logged in. Now to see if it is possible to push a container image to the registry. Way back in chapter 2, when we built an ingress example, we saw how to pull, tag and push container images to a registry. The steps are identical for the embedded Harbor image registry.

Note: The embedded Harbor registry does not allow unsecured connections with docker, so the certificate for the Harbor image registry must be added to `~/.docker/certs.d/<registry>/` on your desktop (this is correct for Mac, it may be different for other distributions). The downloaded Harbor registry cert must also be renamed to `ca.crt`. This will also allow *docker push* and *docker pull* commands to work. Otherwise, these will also generate x509 errors.

Let's see this in action. First, I will *pull* the busybox image from docker.io. Then I will *tag* it. Then I will try to *push* it to the embedded Harbor image registry after it has been tagged. Take note of the tag. It is the IP address of the registry, followed by the name of the vSphere namespace (e.g., demo-ns) followed by the name of the image (busybox) and the version (latest). As noted, the project was created automatically in the embedded registry and matches the name of the namespace.

```
% docker pull busybox:latest
latest: Pulling from library/busybox
19d511225f94: Pull complete
Digest: sha256:3614ca5eacf0a3a1bcc361c939202a974b4902b9334ff36eb29ffe9011aaad83
Status: Downloaded newer image for busybox:latest
docker.io/library/busybox:latest

% docker images
REPOSITORY              TAG             IMAGE ID        CREATED         SIZE
busybox                 latest          62aedd01bd85    13 days ago     1.24MB

% docker tag busybox:latest 192.168.182.129/demo-ns/busybox:latest

% docker push 192.168.182.129/demo-ns/busybox:latest
The push refers to repository [192.168.182.129/demo-ns/busybox]
Get "https://192.168.182.129/v2/": x509: certificate signed by unknown authority
```

This failed as expected. I need to put the image registry certificate in a location expected by docker, and name it appropriately. This is the same certificate referred to during the vSphere Docker Credential Helper login, but has been renamed to ca.crt. Now the push succeeds.

```
% ls ~/.docker/certs.d/192.168.182.129
ca.crt

% docker push 192.168.182.129/demo-ns/busybox:latest
The push refers to repository [192.168.182.129/demo-ns/busybox]
7ad00cd55506: Pushed
latest: digest: sha256:dcdf379c574e1773d703f0c0d56d67594e7a91d6b84d11ff46799f60fb081c52
size: 527
%
```

Success! The image has been uploaded. Let's now check in the Harbor UI.

Figure 158: Harbor – Image successfully Uploaded

Everything looks good. There is now a single repository for the busybox image in the demo-ns project in the registry. In the next section, we will see how to create a Native Pod using this image, which is only accessible from within the demo-ns namespace context. This image is not accessible outside of the demo-ns namespace, which is an important feature of vSphere with Tanzu multi-tenancy.

Before we leave the embedded Harbor image registry, there are a few additional docker commands that might be useful. One of these is how to untag an image so it no longer appears in the docker images output. The command *docker rmi* (remove image) can be used. Note that this does not delete the actual image until the command is run against the very last instance of the image.

```
% docker images
REPOSITORY                          TAG       IMAGE ID      CREATED       SIZE
192.168.182.129/demo-ns/busybox     latest    62aedd01bd85  13 days ago   1.24MB
busybox                             latest    62aedd01bd85  13 days ago   1.24MB

% docker rmi 192.168.182.129/demo-ns/busybox:latest
Untagged: 192.168.182.129/demo-ns/busybox:latest
Untagged: 192.168.182.129/demo-
ns/busybox@sha256:dcdf379c574e1773d703f0c0d56d67594e7a91d6b84d11ff46799f60fb081c52

% docker images
REPOSITORY                          TAG       IMAGE ID      CREATED       SIZE
busybox                             latest    62aedd01bd85  13 days ago   1.24MB
```

The previous command removed the tagged image but not the original. If you fat-fingered some tags, this is a way to clean them up. Lastly, to log out of the registry, run the following command.

```
% /usr/local/bin/docker-credential-vsphere logout 192.168.182.129
INFO[0000] Deleted auth token
```

Let's now use this image in the embedded Harbor image registry to create a Native Pod, also known as a vSphere Pod, also known as a PodVM.

Native Pods

A Native Pod can be thought of as a virtual machine, but a very lightweight, optimized, highly opinionated and fast booting virtual machine which in turn can run containers. It offers the flexibility of containers with the security and isolation of a VM. We already saw how the Harbor image registry utilizes Native Pods to provide its service. By way of a simple demonstration, a new Native Pod will be built. It will use the busybox image that was stored in the Harbor image registry in the previous exercise. Note the YAML is identical to a manifest that one would deploy to a standard TKG or upstream Kubernetes cluster. Instead, on this occasion, it is being sent to the Supervisor Cluster with a request to create it in a vSphere Namespace.

```
apiVersion: v1
kind: Pod
metadata:
  name: native-pod-busybox
  namespace: demo-ns
  labels:
    app: podvm
spec:
  containers:
  - image: 192.168.182.129/demo-ns/busybox:latest
    command:
      - sleep
      - "3600"
    imagePullPolicy: IfNotPresent
    name: busybox
  restartPolicy: Always
```

The only thing that is different here is the image. It is being pulled from the Harbor image registry. Let's now login to vSphere with Tanzu, set the context to the correct namespace, and deploy the Native Pod.

```
% kubectl vsphere login \
--vsphere-username administrator@vsphere.local \
--server=https://192.168.182.130 \
--insecure-skip-tls-verify

KUBECTL_VSPHERE_PASSWORD environment variable is not set. Please enter the password below
Password:
Logged in successfully.

You have access to the following contexts:
   192.168.182.130
   demo-ns


If the context you wish to use is not in this list, you may need to try
logging in again later, or contact your cluster administrator.

To change context, use `kubectl config use-context <workload name>`

% kubectl config use-context demo-ns
Switched to context "demo-ns".

% kubectl apply -f podvm.yaml
pod/native-pod-busybox created

% kubectl get pods
NAME                   READY   STATUS    RESTARTS   AGE
native-pod-busybox     1/1     Running   0          26s
```

Success! The Pod is running. Let's check on the UI.

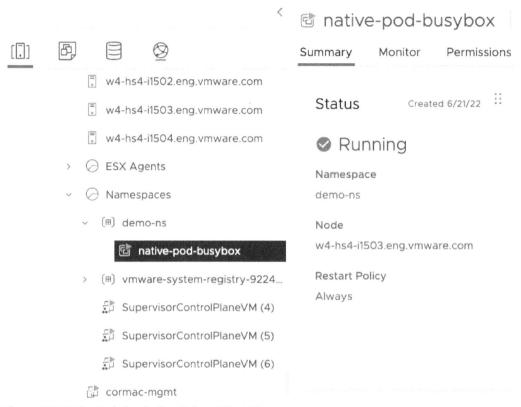

Figure 159: Native Pod view in the vSphere Client UI

As a vSphere administrator, it is useful to be able to see, at a glance, what developers are creating within a vSphere Namespace, or to be more precise, what Platform Operators are building for developers. It is possible to see TKG clusters, normal VMs or Native Pods. All this is visible from the vSphere Client.

One thing to note about Native Pods is that they behave just like Kubernetes Pods. Therefore, and stateless standalone Pod such as the one that we have just created will be deleted in the event of a failure, or a drain operation on the node on which it resides. It has no built-in protection and is not migrated using vMotion via DRS in the event of some failure as you might expect. A drain operation evacuates a Kubernetes node and could be done as part of an upgrade. The node, in this case, is of course the ESXi host, which is acting as a Kubernetes node. So even a maintenance mode operation as part of a vSphere upgrade could impact the standalone Pod, just like in normal Kubernetes. We have seen in chapter 2 how to provide the availability to applications using constructs such as deployments and stateful sets. These can also be built using the Native Pod building block if you wish to create a highly available application on native Pods. This is something for vSphere administrators to think about when dealing with Native Pods since it is a different thought process to dealing with virtual machine availability.

It is important to keep in mind that there is a caveat with ReplicaSets, Deployments and StatefulSets in the Supervisor Cluster. Native Pods that are part of such a ReplicaSet, Deployment or a StatefulSet do not necessarily get evenly spread across different ESXi nodes of the Supervisor Cluster. Instead, Native Pods are placed based on the cluster load at the time they are scheduled.

This means that Native Pods that are part of the same ReplicaSet, Deployment or StatefulSets may or may not end up on the same ESXi host.

Before leaving Native Pods, it is worth highlighting one difference between them and Kubernetes Pods which may not be obvious at first glance. It is not possible, at the time of writing, to use a NodePort service. NodePort was discussed in chapter 2, as a way of allowing a Kubernetes Service to be exposed on a specific port on all nodes in the cluster. It's a relatively simple way of exposing a cluster service externally. While NodePort service is not necessarily something you would do in production, keep in mind that it is not available with Native Pods.

vSphere Services

In the initial release of vSphere Service in vSphere 7.0U2, the only available services were those that had a dependency on the vSAN Data Persistence platform (DPp). These services were embedded within vCenter and could be enabled with the click of a button. However, in 7.0U3, vSphere Services were extended to include services that did not have a DPp dependency. Several vSphere Services are currently available as of vSphere with Tanzu with vSphere 7.0U3, which is the latest release at the time of writing. These are predominantly services that are provided through VMware partners. These services are typically deployed as a Kubernetes Operator on the Supervisor Cluster in vSphere with Tanzu. The necessary tooling is then made available through vSphere Client plugins to create instances of the service on different vSphere Namespaces for different end-users. As a vSphere administrator responsible for setting up a vSphere Service, it is important to note that these are no longer built-in services, which is how they appeared in the 7.0U2 release. Today, as a vSphere administrator, you would need to retrieve the appropriate YAML manifests for the partner product to apply it on the Supervisor cluster, essentially registering the service. After this step is complete, the vSphere Service (operator) may be installed. The final step is making an instance of the service available to developers who wish to use these services, most likely with Kubernetes workloads. In particular, there are several S3-compatible object stores available from partners such as MinIO, Cloudian and Dell Technologies. There is also a Velero Supervisor Service for backup and restore. Note that all of these services rely on Native Pods for instantiating the management components, so NSX-T is a necessity. There may also be a dependency on vSAN, VMware's Hyperconverged Infrastructure solution, as many of the S3-compatible object stores require the vSAN Data Persistence platform (DPp). This depends on the nature of the vSphere service.

The vSphere Service manifests are available in the following JFROG repository at the time of writing (June 2022): https://vmwaresaas.jfrog.io/. Simply navigate to the appropriate partner folder under **Artifactory > Artifacts > vDPP-Partner-YAML** and select a YAML file to download. The path to the Velero Supervisor Service is shown below:

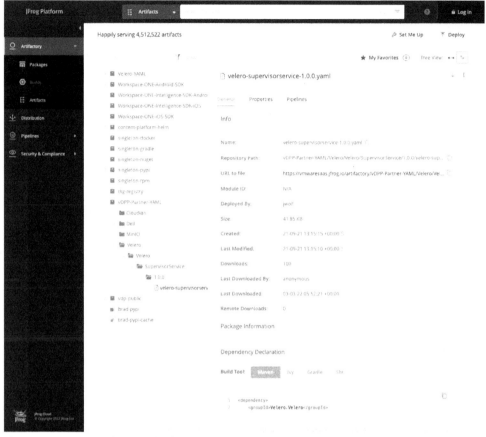

Figure 160: Data Persistence Platform Service Manifests

vSphere CSI Considerations in vSphere with Tanzu

Since we are on the topic of storage, it is probably a good point to discuss some considerations around the vSphere CSI driver in vSphere with Tanzu. Previously the discussions around the vSphere CSI driver have been related to the upstream vSphere CSI driver. This is the vSphere Container storage plug-in that runs in a native Kubernetes cluster, deployed on vSphere infrastructure. For the most part, we can also think of the multi-cloud version of Tanzu Kubernetes Grid (TKG) as an upstream Kubernetes cluster. The difference between TKG and upstream Kubernetes is that our Tanzu team selects components from the plethora of open-source products that are available for Kubernetes. The team tests this Kubernetes stack, validates and signs it, and then offers VMware support for customers who purchase it. In other words, the team chooses the CSI drivers for storage, the CNI drivers for networking, various Load Balancers, IAM components for identity management, and so on. Once deployed into production, VMware can now support this Kubernetes platform and your vSphere platform. Thus, what we have read so far about the vSphere Container Storage Plug-in/upstream vSphere CSI driver applies to TKG, once the Tanzu team has completed their tests, and released it with a TKG build/version. However, it is important to note that the Tanzu team also needs to do their qualification of the vSphere CSI driver, so the latest upstream version may not be the version that is found in TKG. There may be a lag before a new version of vSphere CSI is introduced into TKG.

But VMware offers more Kubernetes offerings than just TKG as we have just seen. Through vSphere with Tanzu, VMware offers TKG clusters via the TKG Service. This is important as vSphere with Tanzu does not use the upstream CSI driver at the time of writing. This is because vSphere with Tanzu has the concept of a Supervisor Cluster which is deployed when vSphere with Tanzu is enabled on a vSphere Cluster. And while workloads can be deployed directly onto the Supervisor Cluster using Native Pods, the Supervisor Cluster is not considered a general-purpose workload cluster. General purpose Kubernetes clusters are those provisioned using a TKG Service, through some simple YAML manifest files which describe the cluster configuration.

This brings us to the reason why the TKG clusters cannot use the upstream vSphere CSI driver. TKG clusters created by the TKG Service are placed on their own workload networks which are not designed to have access to the management network where the vCenter Server resides. This means that if the upstream vSphere CSI driver is deployed on a TKG workload cluster in vSphere with Tanzu, it would be unable to reach the vCenter Server, nor would it be able to communicate to its associated CNS component for persistent volume lifecycle management. So how are persistent volumes created in TKGS provisioned clusters you might ask?

The creation of persistent volumes is achieved through a paravirtual CSI (pvCSI) running in the workload clusters that have been provisioned by the TKG Service. This is a modified version of the upstream CSI driver. The reason it is called pvCSI is that it "proxies" requests from the TKG guest cluster to the Supervisor Cluster which in turn communicates to vCenter and CNS to create persistent volumes on the appropriate vSphere storage. The Supervisor Cluster control plane nodes are multi-homed with one network interface on the vSphere management network and the other network interface on the workload network (the one used by the TKGS workload clusters). In this way, PV operations from TKGS workload clusters are sent to the Supervisor Cluster, which in turn sends it onto CNS in vCenter.

Note that the CNS views of the persistent volumes in vSphere with Tanzu reveal this proxying of volumes. For a PV created in a TKG workload cluster, a vSphere administrator will be able to see the relationship between it and the volume that is created on the Supervisor Cluster on its behalf, as well as information about which TKG workload cluster it was created for.

There is one additional consideration with the CSI driver in vSphere with Tanzu. While it is possible to change the storage policy of a persistent volume in upstream, vanilla Kubernetes that are attached to Kubernetes nodes/virtual machines, the same is not possible for volumes that are attached to nodes in TKG clusters deployed by the TKG Service in vSphere with Tanzu. This is also true for Native Pods that are using volumes. While this may change at some point in the future, it is a limitation at the time of writing. The figure below shows a simplified relationship between the pvCSI in a TKG and the CSI-CNS component in the Supervisor Cluster which in turn communicates to vCenter for volume requests on vSphere storage.

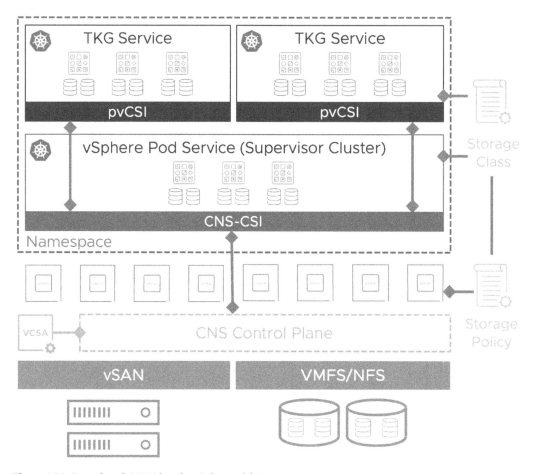

Figure 161: Paravirtual CSI Driver in vSphere with Tanzu

The reason why the pvCSI driver is called out as a consideration is that new CSI features typically get developed for the upstream CSI driver for vanilla Kubernetes distributions before filtering down to vSphere with Tanzu. Examples of this would be the support for read-write-many volumes (RWX) using vSAN File Service, which has been in upstream Kubernetes for some time, but only became available for vSphere with Tanzu TKG workload clusters in June 2022. Support for RWX is now available in Tanzu Kubernetes release (TKr) version 1.22. Similarly, CSI snapshot support was announced in the upstream CSI driver version 2.5 in March 2022, but there will be a lag before the feature appears in TKG workload clusters in vSphere with Tanzu.

Thus, it is extremely important to check whether a particular CSI driver capability is specifically available in vSphere with Tanzu, and not to rely on seeing feature support in upstream Kubernetes, then assuming that it is also available in vSphere with Tanzu.

Summary

As mentioned at the beginning of this chapter, vSphere with Tanzu is specifically built with the vSphere administrator in mind. In many larger organization, it is expected that there would be a clear delineation between the person responsible for the vSphere infrastructure (the vSphere administrator) and the person responsible for creating developer infrastructure (the platform operator). vSphere with Tanzu is a great product to allow collaboration between these two personas. It allows a vSphere administrator to control and manage vSphere resources, while the Platform Operator can use many self-service tools to carve out resources through the Namespace Service, build Kubernetes clusters through the TKG Service and create virtual machines through the VM Service. All this can be done under the watchful eye of the vSphere administrator who can view resource usage at the granularity of a namespace or project.

Other key features make this a great platform for developers, since a built in Image Registry is available along with other vSphere Services if NSX-T is used as the networking stack. NSX-T also enables the use of Native Pods, giving developers the flexibility of containers, with the isolation and security of virtual machines. Even if NSX-T is not used, and vSphere distributed networking is used instead, other Load Balancer provider options are available such as NSX ALB and the HA-Proxy.

07

Day 2 Operations

So far in this book, we have been discussing mostly Day-0 operations, which is mostly involved in standing up developer platforms such as Kubernetes. However, getting a platform deployed is only a small part of the lifecycle of the platform. Mostly time is spent in making sure the platform is available, secure and up to date. In this chapter, these day 2 operations are considered. While most of these operations can be considered as falling under the responsibilities of a Platform Operator, it is important for vSphere administrators to be aware of these function as well. Many of these operations are directly connected to responsibilities of the vSphere administrator in the underlying vSphere platform.

RoleBinding, ClusterRoleBinding & ClusterRole

At this point, the various personas involved in running Kubernetes on top of a vSphere platform should be well understood. By way of a recap, let's mention them one more time.

- **vSphere Admin** – responsible for vSphere resource management on behalf of Platform Operator. May involve creation and management of vSphere Namespace with vSphere with Tanzu, making resource available to Platform Operator
- **Platform Operator** – responsible for deploying developer platforms. This most likely involves Kubernetes cluster lifecycle/registry management and user management of developers
- **Developer** – Creates/Tests/Debugs code as containers. Consumer of Kubernetes clusters.

Let's assume that this is a vSphere with Tanzu environment. In that case, the vSphere administrator would use the vSphere Client UI extensively to create and manage vSphere Namespaces. The Platform Operator would access to the namespace via the *kubectl-vsphere* command, and from there can create virtual machines and TKG clusters for the developers. Thus, the expectation is that we would not have vSphere administrators dealing with YAML manifests, and we would not have developers requiring vSphere SSO credentials.

This definition of roles might certainly be true for the larger customers, who are running at scale. But in smaller environments, there may not be such a clear distinction between the role of vSphere administrator and Platform Operator. I have mentioned a number of times already that the role of a Platform Operator is something that a vSphere administrator could absolutely transition into, in much the same way as they transitioned into managing storage with vSAN or perhaps transitioned into managed networking with NSX-T.

No matter who is responsible, whether it is a dedicated Platform Operator, or a combined vSphere administrator/Platform Operator role, one thing is clear. There needs to be a mechanism to control access and privileges to the TKG clusters. This applies to the TKG clusters that are deployed standalone or deployed through the TKG Service in vSphere with Tanzu. You probably do not want to grant every user who accesses the cluster admin access through KUBECONFIG. What is needed is a way to create a Kubernetes context for a particular developer which has privileges to a particular namespace. Unfortunately this process is a little bit complex, so I will try to outline the steps here. Note that this references TKG clusters, but the process is the same for upstream, vanilla clusters. These steps need to be carried out with admin privileges.

1. The wish is to provide users with permissions to a single namespace on the TKG cluster. Therefore the first step for the Platform Operator is to select an existing Kubernetes namespace or to create a new Kubernetes namespace on the TKG cluster.
2. Next, they must create a certificate signing request (CSR) and a key for the developer with the developer's username. This can be done with the *openssl req* command.
3. Using the data created in step 2, the Platform Operator now creates a certificate signing request YAML manifest
4. The CSR manifest is applied to the TKG cluster to create a certificate signing request with the developer's details
5. Use the *kubectl certificate approve*, the Platform Operator can approve the new certificate signing request
6. Next, the Platform Operator uses *kubectl get csr* to retrieve the newly created user certificate
7. The TKG cluster's Certificate of Authority can be retrieved using *kubectl config view*
8. With the CA certificate from the TKG cluster, a secure KUBECONFIG can be created for the developer using *kubectl config set-cluster --embed-certs*.
9. Using the secure KUBECONFIG from the previous step, the developer's user cert retrieved in step 6, and the key created in step 2, user credentials can now be applied to this config using the *kubectl config set-credentials* command.
10. A new context for the developer can now be created with the new secure config.

There does seem to be a lot of work with certificates, doesn't there? I agree. Even the default admin access in KUBECONFIG is created with a certificate and key. Take a look at any ~/.kube/config file and you will see that every user, even the admin user, has this information associated.

However, even at this point, even though the user has been given access through KUBECONFIG, the user does not have any privileges on the cluster at this point. This is where the Platform Operator can decide what sort of privileges a user can have on the cluster, now that the user exists on the Kubernetes cluster. Two role bindings are available which decide if a user has access to just a namespace, or whether they have permissions to do tasks on the cluster as a whole. These are RoleBinding (namespace permissions) or ClusterRoleBinding (overall cluster permissions). The Platform Operator, once the boundary has been decided, can then grant a user or developer permissions through the *--clusterrole* option. The command to create a RoleBinding (bound to a namespace) with an admin clusterrole is as follows:

```
$ kubectl create rolebinding ${user}-admin \
--namespace=${namespace} \
--clusterrole=admin \
--user=${user}
```

The user/developer has now been granted full access to a namespace to build their applications but does not have access to do anything in any other namespace in the cluster. Note that the scope could be changed to the whole of the cluster using a ClusterRoleBinding rather than a RoleBinding.

There is a lot of work involved in giving users access to a Kubernetes cluster, especially when dealing with certificates. This script might be useful in such a scenario, as it automates a lot of the steps involved - https://github.com/cormachogan/Setup-K8s-User. This is the accompanying blog post - https://cormachogan.com/2020/11/06/creating-developer-users-and-namespaces-scripted-in-tkg-guest-clusters/

Admittedly, this may not be an area that a vSphere administrator gets involved in. However, the objective is to highlight that there are controls in place that prevent granting full Kubernetes cluster admin access to every user. An area where the vSphere administrator might get involved is when the developer accounts are managed via Lightweight directory access protocol (LDAP) or OpenID Connect (OIDC), as this might be the same functionality integrated with vSphere user accounts.

Identity Management with Pinniped and Dex

TKG v1.3 introduced OIDC and LDAP identity management with Pinniped and Dex. Pinniped provides a mechanism to plug external OpenID Connect (OIDC) or LDAP identity providers (IDP) into Tanzu Kubernetes clusters. This, in turn, allows you to control access to those clusters. Pinniped uses Dex as the endpoint to connect to the upstream LDAP identity provider, e.g. Microsoft Active Directory. If you are using OpenID Connect (OIDC), Dex is not required. This example show how to configure TKG v1.5.4 to control user access to Tanzu Kubernetes cluster(s) via Active Directory. This exercise won't go through a complete deployment, as this has already been shown in chapter 3. Instead, the focus will be on the LDAP integration component.

Requirements

If deploying TKG from a desktop, you will need a graphical user interface capable of opening a browser. This is because a browser tab is opened so that AD/LDAP credentials can be provided in the Dex endpoint when an AD user first tries to interact with a workload cluster. You will also need to retrieve the Base 64 root certificate of authority (CA) from your identity provider, e.g. from your Microsoft Active Directory Certificate Service. A good understanding of LDAP directory attributes, such as OU, CN, DC, etc, will also be needed as these fields will need to be populated during setup. The official TKG documentation does not go into details regarding LDAP configuration options. Lastly, determine if your LDAP service is also a global catalog server. Secure LDAP communicates over TCP port 636. If there is also a global catalog server, then communication occurs over TCP port 3269.

Management Cluster Deployment

As we saw back in chapter 3, a TKG cluster can be deployed via the UI or the tanzu CLI. If using the CLI approach, the configuration details for identify management can be added to the management cluster configuration file. Here is a snippet of the relevant details.

```
IDENTITY_MANAGEMENT_TYPE: ldap
LDAP_BIND_DN: cn=Administrator,cn=Users,dc=rainpole,dc=com
LDAP_BIND_PASSWORD: <encoded:VnhSYWlsITIz>
LDAP_GROUP_SEARCH_BASE_DN: dc=rainpole,dc=com
LDAP_GROUP_SEARCH_FILTER: (objectClass=group)
LDAP_GROUP_SEARCH_GROUP_ATTRIBUTE: ""
LDAP_GROUP_SEARCH_NAME_ATTRIBUTE: ""
LDAP_GROUP_SEARCH_USER_ATTRIBUTE: ""
LDAP_HOST: dc01.rainpole.com:636
LDAP_ROOT_CA_DATA_B64: LS0t***
LDAP_USER_SEARCH_BASE_DN: cn=Users,dc=rainpole,dc=com
LDAP_USER_SEARCH_FILTER: ""
LDAP_USER_SEARCH_NAME_ATTRIBUTE: userPrincipalName
LDAP_USER_SEARCH_USERNAME: userPrincipalName
```

However, if the UI approach is used, there is a nice validation mechanism which can be used to validate that the LDAP integration is correct.

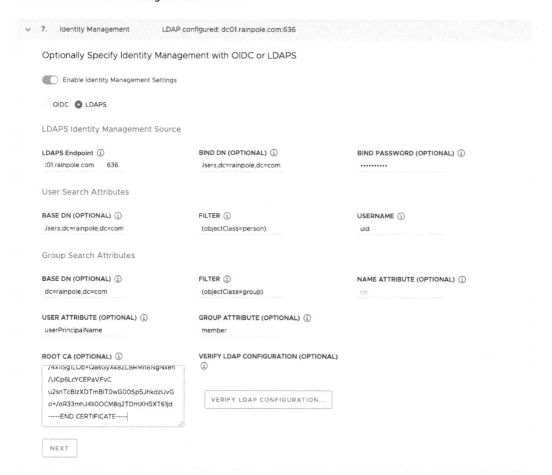

Figure 162: TKG - LDAP Identity Management

Notice that there is also a 'Verify LDAP Configuration' button. If, like me, you are not well-versed in the various LDAP attributes that needs to be populated above, this is a really nice way of making sure that what you have populate here is working correctly.

When the Verify LDAP Configuration wizard launches, you can add a name or a group and then have it run through a quick test to make sure that the credentials are valid.

Figure 163: TKG — Verify LDAP Configuration

Using the LDAP configuration, and an NSX ALB Load Balancer, we can proceed with the deployment of the new TKG v1.5.4 management cluster. Once the management cluster has been deployed, the Pods for Pinniped and DEX can be examined, and we can give privileges to use an LDAP user to access the TKG cluster.

```
% kubectl get pods -A | grep pinniped
pinniped-concierge    pinniped-concierge-9fc77d4b6-gf7q9              1/1 Running    0   9m20s
pinniped-concierge    pinniped-concierge-9fc77d4b6-rhsrl             1/1 Running    0   9m20s
pinniped-concierge    pinniped-concierge-kube-cert-agent-...-k2n4s   1/1 Running    0   9m2s
pinniped-supervisor   pinniped-post-deploy-job--1-4kr6g             0/1 Error      0   9m20s
pinniped-supervisor   pinniped-post-deploy-job--1-hd954             0/1 Error      0   8m36s
pinniped-supervisor   pinniped-post-deploy-job--1-msxw5            0/1 Completed 0   7m50s
pinniped-supervisor   pinniped-supervisor-6c8b4cccdf-c44wt          1/1 Running    0   5m21s
pinniped-supervisor   pinniped-supervisor-6c8b4cccdf-rrxxc          1/1 Running    0   5m21s

% kubectl get pods -A | grep dex
tanzu-system-auth     dex-5f59d75785-ncbtn                          1/1 Running    0   9m33s
```

You can ignore some of the pinniped-post-deploy-job errors. These are expected. Usually they error waiting for the pinniped-concierge deployment to have enough replicas spun up. Note that both Pinniped and Dex use a Load Balancer service. Since we deployed this management cluster with the NSX ALB, it should be possible to check in the NSX ALB UI that these virtual services are coming online.

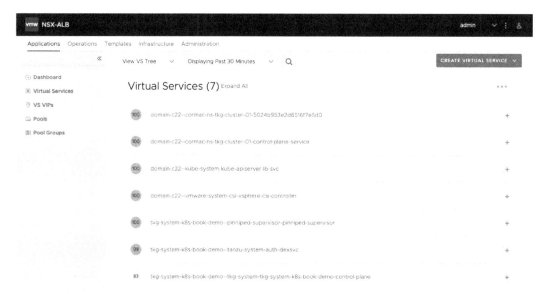

Figure 164: NSX ALB – Pinniped and Dex virtual services

Once the management cluster is deployed, the next step is to retrieve the KUBECONFIG. In previous examples, the –admin option was used with the *tanzu management-cluster kubeconfig get*. This meant that an admin KUBECONFIG was retrieved, giving full privileges to whomever used that context. This is what we are trying to avoid. If *tanzu management-cluster kubeconfig get* is used without the --admin option, we get a non-admin context. Through Pinniped and Dex integration, it is now possible to authenticate an LDAP user to have non-admin access to the cluster. However, we must still set privileges for this user, so a ClusterRoleBinding/Rolebinding with a ClusterRole must still be created before the LDAP user can do anything on the TKG cluster.

Let's see this in action. I'll begin by retrieving the non-admin context from the TKG management cluster, and then try to query some details about the cluster. Note that the non-admin context for TKG clusters uses the preface `tanzu-cli-`, but otherwise is looks very like the admin context. Note that I am not allowed to query anything on the Kubernetes cluster until I have been authorized to do so. This is apparent when I try to query the nodes in the cluster.

```
% tanzu management-cluster kubeconfig get
You can now access the cluster by running 'kubectl config use-context tanzu-cli-k8s-
book@k8s-book'

% kubectl config use-context tanzu-cli-k8s-book@k8s-book
Switched to context "tanzu-cli-k8s-book@k8s-book".
```

```
% kubectl get nodes
Log in by visiting this link:

    https://10.27.62.39/oauth2/authorize?access_type=offline&client_id=pinniped-
cli&code_challenge=A2X6hFDTw9ixDILr4LQ6ws1ZLT6huOfPuZhKKY8PGvk&code_challenge_method=S256&
nonce=00822491472ea5af8a8269c13783ad11&redirect_uri=http%3A%2F%2F127.0.0.1%3A60468%2Fcallb
ack&response_mode=form_post&response_type=code&scope=offline_access+openid+pinniped%3Arequ
est-audience&state=b3f0ad4d69e70569b919106abfe5acff

    Optionally, paste your authorization code: [...]
```

Immediately, at this point, the following popup appears in a local browser.

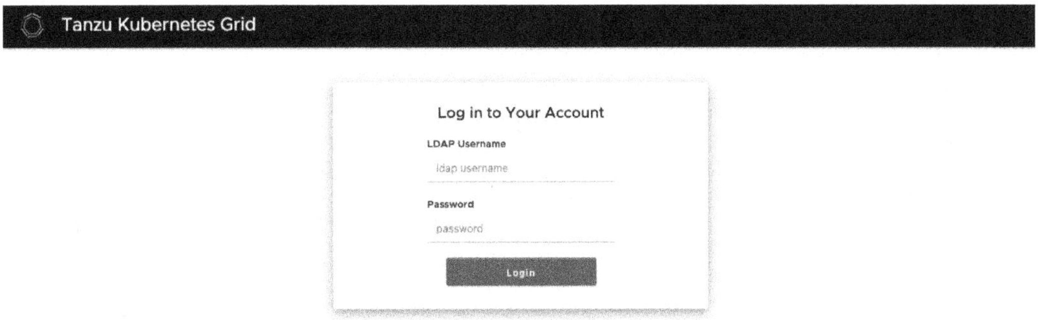

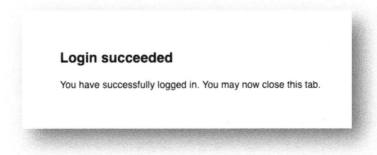

Figure 165: DEX UI

This is the Dex authentication mechanism. If you are on a remote ssh to the system where you are running the tanzu CLI commands, and it does not have a GUI, then simply copy the link displayed at the command line into your local browser to continue. This is the load balancer IP address allocated to the Dex service, so is accessible outside the cluster. The IP address shown in the output is from the load balancer virtual services created for Dex. Next, add the LDAP user credentials for the developer that you wish to have access to the TKG cluster. In my case, I will have a user called `chogan@rainpole.com`. Once added, the LDAP user is authenticated to access the cluster.

Login succeeded

You have successfully logged in. You may now close this tab.

Figure 166: DEX LDAP User Login Success

However, as mentioned, this user still does not have any privileges to the cluster – in other words, they can log in to the cluster but they can't do anything. You will see an error similar to the following appear at the command line:

```
Error from server (Forbidden): nodes is forbidden: User "chogan@rainpole.com" cannot list
resource "nodes" in API group "" at the cluster scope
```

Therefore, the ldap user/developer must now be granted the appropriate privileges by the Platform Operator through the Role Binding mechanism discussed earlier. But they will need to do this step using the admin context of the cluster. Below, the context is being switched back to admin, and a ClusterRoleBinding for user `chogan@rainpole.com` is being created with a cluster-admin ClusterRole.

```
% cat chogan-crb.yaml
kind: ClusterRoleBinding
apiVersion: rbac.authorization.k8s.io/v1
metadata:
  name: chogan
subjects:
  - kind: User
    name: chogan@rainpole.com
    apiGroup:
roleRef:
  kind: ClusterRole
  name: cluster-admin
  apiGroup: rbac.authorization.k8s.io

% kubectl config use-context k8s-book-admin@k8s-book
Switched to context "k8s-book-admin@k8s-book".

% kubectl apply -f chogan-crb.yaml
clusterrolebinding.rbac.authorization.k8s.io/chogan created

% kubectl get clusterrolebinding chogan
NAME       ROLE                          AGE
chogan     ClusterRole/cluster-admin     9s

% kubectl config use-context tanzu-cli-k8s-book@k8s-book
Switched to context "tanzu-cli-k8s-book@k8s-book".

% kubectl get nodes
NAME                              STATUS   ROLES                   AGE   VERSION
k8s-book-control-plane-995jl      Ready    control-plane,master    40m   v1.22.9+vmware.1
k8s-book-md-0-7fb4d4d855-4hpkf    Ready    <none>                  39m   v1.22.9+vmware.1
```

Success! The LDAP user can now access the cluster but without using the admin cluster context (although we have still given them admin privileges). The point is that the Platform Operator does not need to give out the admin context to all cluster users, but can control access through LDAP integration with Pinniped and Dex.

Workload Cluster Deployment

In the previous deployment, we saw how to integrate LDAP with a management cluster. How does it work for workload clusters. In fact, it is almost identical. Let's deploy a workload cluster, and see.

```
% tanzu cluster create workload --file workload.yaml
Validating configuration...
Creating workload cluster 'workload'...
Waiting for cluster to be initialized...
cluster control plane is still being initialized: WaitingForControlPlane
cluster control plane is still being initialized: ScalingUp
Waiting for cluster nodes to be available...
```

```
Waiting for addons installation...
Waiting for packages to be up and running...

Workload cluster 'workload' created
```

```
% tanzu cluster list
  NAME      NAMESPACE  STATUS   CONTROLPLANE  WORKERS  KUBERNETES       ROLES    PLAN
  workload  default    running  1/1           1/1      v1.22.9+vmware.1  <none>   dev
```

Let's get the admin context for the workload cluster and do some checks.

```
% tanzu cluster kubeconfig get workload --admin
Credentials of cluster 'workload' have been saved
You can now access the cluster by running 'kubectl config use-context workload-
admin@workload'
```

```
% kubectl config use-context workload-admin@workload
Switched to context "workload-admin@workload".
```

```
% kubectl get nodes
NAME                                STATUS  ROLES                 AGE  VERSION
workload-control-plane-mwps2        Ready   control-plane,master  10m  v1.22.9+vmware.1
workload-md-0-7dfb8598cb-p924q      Ready   <none>                10m  v1.22.9+vmware.1
```

Looks good. Let's try that for the non-admin context next.

```
% tanzu cluster kubeconfig get workload
   You can now access the cluster by running 'kubectl config use-context tanzu-cli-
workload@workload'
```

```
% kubectl config use-context tanzu-cli-workload@workload
Switched to context "tanzu-cli-workload@workload".
```

```
% kubectl get nodes
Error from server (Forbidden): nodes is forbidden: User "chogan@rainpole.com" cannot list
resource "nodes" in API group "" at the cluster scope
```

As expected, I am unable to query the cluster with the non-admin context, since the user I am
authenticated with (chogan@rainpole.com) has no privileges. As we did in the management
cluster, let's go ahead and provide those privileges. To do that, the admin context must be used as
before.

```
% kubectl config use-context workload-admin@workload
Switched to context "workload-admin@workload".
```

```
% kubectl apply -f chogan-crb.yaml
clusterrolebinding.rbac.authorization.k8s.io/chogan created
```

```
% kubectl config use-context tanzu-cli-workload@workload
Switched to context "tanzu-cli-workload@workload".
```

```
% kubectl get nodes
NAME                                STATUS  ROLES                 AGE  VERSION
workload-control-plane-mwps2        Ready   control-plane,master  17m  v1.22.9+vmware.1
workload-md-0-7dfb8598cb-p924q      Ready   <none>                16m  v1.22.9+vmware.1
```

```
% kubectl get pods -A
NAMESPACE                 NAME                                        READY
STATUS      RESTARTS      AGE
avi-system                ako-0                                       1/1
Running     0             15m
```

```
kube-system          antrea-agent-6pzq8                                         2/2
Running      0           14m
kube-system          antrea-agent-8cwjm                                         2/2
Running      0           14m
kube-system          antrea-controller-7c755d9f5-5cfhn                          1/1
Running      0           14m
kube-system          coredns-67c8559bb6-4sw5v                                   1/1
Running      0           17m
kube-system          coredns-67c8559bb6-mvqvf                                   1/1
Running      0           17m
kube-system          etcd-workload-control-plane-mwps2                          1/1
Running      0           17m
kube-system          kube-apiserver-workload-control-plane-mwps2                1/1
Running      0           17m
kube-system          kube-controller-manager-workload-control-plane-mwps2       1/1
Running      0           17m
kube-system          kube-proxy-8jcjl                                           1/1
Running      0           16m
kube-system          kube-proxy-fw7j4                                           1/1
Running      0           17m
kube-system          kube-scheduler-workload-control-plane-mwps2                1/1
Running      0           17m
kube-system          kube-vip-workload-control-plane-mwps2                      1/1
Running      0           17m
kube-system          metrics-server-77dbc8c4c7-bkxlg                            1/1
Running      0           15m
kube-system          vsphere-cloud-controller-manager-qm9ml                     1/1
Running      0           14m
kube-system          vsphere-csi-controller-86cbc5fb4-b7dzg                     6/6
Running      0           13m
kube-system          vsphere-csi-node-gjhsk                                     3/3
Running      2 (12m ago)  13m
kube-system          vsphere-csi-node-gkb4t                                     3/3
Running      1 (12m ago)  13m
pinniped-concierge   pinniped-concierge-fdc68bc55-gkv46                         1/1
Running      0           14m
pinniped-concierge   pinniped-concierge-fdc68bc55-w5nz8                         1/1
Running      0           14m
pinniped-concierge   pinniped-concierge-kube-cert-agent-58f87f544b-cjgth        1/1
Running      0           13m
pinniped-supervisor  pinniped-post-deploy-job--1-5kgd2                          0/1
Error        0           14m
pinniped-supervisor  pinniped-post-deploy-job--1-k6wfq                          0/1
Completed    0           12m
tanzu-system         secretgen-controller-58497959dd-pgf9q                      1/1
Running      0           14m
tkg-system           kapp-controller-f9fdd4d95-l822k                            1/1
Running      0           17m
tkg-system           tanzu-capabilities-controller-manager-676fbf6c8f-wb7tx     1/1
Running      0           17m
```

```
% kubectl get svc -A
NAMESPACE            NAME                     TYPE        CLUSTER-IP        EXTERNAL-IP
PORT(S)                  AGE
default              kubernetes               ClusterIP   100.64.0.1        <none>
443/TCP                  20m
kube-system          antrea                   ClusterIP   100.70.145.248    <none>
443/TCP                  17m
kube-system          kube-dns                 ClusterIP   100.64.0.10       <none>
53/UDP,53/TCP,9153/TCP   19m
kube-system          metrics-server           ClusterIP   100.64.159.165    <none>
443/TCP                  17m
kube-system          vsphere-csi-controller   ClusterIP   100.67.239.176    <none>
2112/TCP,2113/TCP        16m
```

```
pinniped-concierge    pinniped-concierge-api    ClusterIP  100.67.94.228   <none>
443/TCP               17m
pinniped-concierge    pinniped-concierge-proxy  ClusterIP  100.68.200.49   <none>
443/TCP               17m
tkg-system            packaging-api             ClusterIP  100.69.17.254   <none>
443/TCP               19m
```

And now everything is working as expected. I've included some additional outputs here to show the workload cluster configuration. There is the AKO (Avi Kubernetes Operator) controller for integration with the NSX ALB. Antrea is the CNI, and the vSphere CSI is also deployed. Note that these is no load balancer service for Pinniped or Dex in the workload cluster; this is managed via the management cluster. The final entity to point out is the kapp-controller, which is used for add-on package management. These packages are looked at next.

Tanzu Packages

Tanzu has a range of additional package that can be added to a TKG cluster post deployment. These range from Prometheus and Grafana for monitoring, through to Fluent Bit for log shipping. To access the packages, the TKG cluster needs to be told about the repository where they reside. In this example, I am have used the name tkgv154repo to identify the package repository on projects.registry.vmware.com. To add the Tanzu repository to a TKG cluster, run the following commands.

```
% tanzu package repository list
- Retrieving repositories...

  NAME  REPOSITORY  TAG  STATUS  DETAILS

% tanzu package repository add tkg154repo \
--url projects.registry.vmware.com/tkg/packages/standard/repo:v1.5.4
/ Adding package repository 'tkg14repo'

 Adding package repository 'tkg154repo'

 Validating provided settings for the package repository

 Creating package repository resource

 Waiting for 'PackageRepository' reconciliation for 'tkg154repo'

 'PackageRepository' resource install status: Reconciling

 'PackageRepository' resource install status: ReconcileSucceeded

Added package repository 'tkg154repo' in namespace 'default'

% tanzu package repository list
- Retrieving repositories...

  NAME        REPOSITORY                                              TAG     STATUS
DETAILS
  tkg154repo  projects.registry.vmware.com/tkg/packages/standard/repo  v1.5.4  Reconcile
succeeded
```

The available packages can now be displayed, either via tanzu CLI or kubectl. Unfortunately, due to the lengthy descriptions, the formatting is a little difficult to read due to text wrapping.

```
% tanzu package available list
| Retrieving available packages...

  NAME                            DISPLAY-NAME   SHORT-DESCRIPTION
LATEST-VERSION
  cert-manager.tanzu.vmware.com   cert-manager   Certificate
management
1.5.3+vmware.2-tkg.1
  contour.tanzu.vmware.com        contour        An ingress controller
1.18.2+vmware.1-tkg.1
  external-dns.tanzu.vmware.com   external-dns   This package provides DNS synchronization
functionality.                                                 0.10.0+vmware.1-tkg.1
  fluent-bit.tanzu.vmware.com     fluent-bit     Fluent Bit is a fast Log Processor and
Forwarder                                                      1.7.5+vmware.2-tkg.1
  grafana.tanzu.vmware.com        grafana        Visualization and analytics software
7.5.7+vmware.2-tkg.1
  harbor.tanzu.vmware.com         harbor         OCI Registry
2.3.3+vmware.1-tkg.1
  multus-cni.tanzu.vmware.com     multus-cni     This package provides the ability for
enabling attaching multiple network interfaces to pods in Kubernetes  3.7.1+vmware.2-tkg.2
  prometheus.tanzu.vmware.com     prometheus     A time series database for your metrics
2.27.0+vmware.2-tkg.1

% kubectl get packages
NAME                                                      PACKAGEMETADATA NAME
VERSION                  AGE
cert-manager.tanzu.vmware.com.1.1.0+vmware.1-tkg.2        cert-manager.tanzu.vmware.com
1.1.0+vmware.1-tkg.2     5m53s
cert-manager.tanzu.vmware.com.1.1.0+vmware.2-tkg.1        cert-manager.tanzu.vmware.com
1.1.0+vmware.2-tkg.1     5m53s
cert-manager.tanzu.vmware.com.1.5.3+vmware.2-tkg.1        cert-manager.tanzu.vmware.com
1.5.3+vmware.2-tkg.1     5m53s
contour.tanzu.vmware.com.1.17.1+vmware.1-tkg.1           contour.tanzu.vmware.com
1.17.1+vmware.1-tkg.1    5m53s
contour.tanzu.vmware.com.1.17.2+vmware.1-tkg.2           contour.tanzu.vmware.com
1.17.2+vmware.1-tkg.2    5m53s
contour.tanzu.vmware.com.1.17.2+vmware.1-tkg.3           contour.tanzu.vmware.com
1.17.2+vmware.1-tkg.3    5m53s
contour.tanzu.vmware.com.1.18.2+vmware.1-tkg.1           contour.tanzu.vmware.com
1.18.2+vmware.1-tkg.1    5m53s
external-dns.tanzu.vmware.com.0.10.0+vmware.1-tkg.1      external-dns.tanzu.vmware.com
0.10.0+vmware.1-tkg.1    5m53s
external-dns.tanzu.vmware.com.0.8.0+vmware.1-tkg.1       external-dns.tanzu.vmware.com
0.8.0+vmware.1-tkg.1     5m53s
fluent-bit.tanzu.vmware.com.1.7.5+vmware.1-tkg.1         fluent-bit.tanzu.vmware.com
1.7.5+vmware.1-tkg.1     5m53s
fluent-bit.tanzu.vmware.com.1.7.5+vmware.2-tkg.1         fluent-bit.tanzu.vmware.com
1.7.5+vmware.2-tkg.1     5m53s
grafana.tanzu.vmware.com.7.5.7+vmware.1-tkg.1            grafana.tanzu.vmware.com
7.5.7+vmware.1-tkg.1     5m53s
grafana.tanzu.vmware.com.7.5.7+vmware.2-tkg.1            grafana.tanzu.vmware.com
7.5.7+vmware.2-tkg.1     5m53s
harbor.tanzu.vmware.com.2.2.3+vmware.1-tkg.1             harbor.tanzu.vmware.com
2.2.3+vmware.1-tkg.1     5m53s
harbor.tanzu.vmware.com.2.2.3+vmware.1-tkg.2             harbor.tanzu.vmware.com
2.2.3+vmware.1-tkg.2     5m53s
harbor.tanzu.vmware.com.2.3.3+vmware.1-tkg.1             harbor.tanzu.vmware.com
2.3.3+vmware.1-tkg.1     5m53s
multus-cni.tanzu.vmware.com.3.7.1+vmware.1-tkg.1         multus-cni.tanzu.vmware.com
3.7.1+vmware.1-tkg.1     5m53s
multus-cni.tanzu.vmware.com.3.7.1+vmware.2-tkg.1         multus-cni.tanzu.vmware.com
3.7.1+vmware.2-tkg.1     5m53s
multus-cni.tanzu.vmware.com.3.7.1+vmware.2-tkg.2         multus-cni.tanzu.vmware.com
3.7.1+vmware.2-tkg.2     5m53s
```

```
prometheus.tanzu.vmware.com.2.27.0+vmware.1-tkg.1        prometheus.tanzu.vmware.com
2.27.0+vmware.1-tkg.1   5m53s
prometheus.tanzu.vmware.com.2.27.0+vmware.2-tkg.1        prometheus.tanzu.vmware.com
2.27.0+vmware.2-tkg.1   5m53s
```

Deploying packages to TKGS deployed clusters

It is also possible to use the tanzu CLI to install packages to TKG clusters deployed by the TKG Service in vSphere with Tanzu, as well as to standalone TKG clusters. There are several additional steps that will need to be followed to make this happen. These steps are already taken care of in standalone TKG (TKGm) clusters but are needed for TKGS. The first is to create a default StorageClass. In the example below, I am using the vSAN Default Storage Policy and making it the default StorageClass.

```
% kubectl get sc
NAME                        PROVISIONER             RECLAIM  VOLBINDMODE ALLOWVOLEXP AGE
vsan-default-storage-policy csi.vsphere.vmware.com  Delete   Immediate   true        5d

% kubectl patch storageclass vsan-default-storage-policy -p \
'{"metadata": {"annotations":{"storageclass.kubernetes.io/is-default-class":"true"}}}'
storageclass.storage.k8s.io/vsan-default-storage-policy patched

% kubectl get sc
NAME                                  PROVISIONER             RECLAIM  VOLBMODE   AVE  AGE
vsan-default-storage-policy (default) csi.vsphere.vmware.com  Delete   Immediate  true 5d
```

The next step is to create a `ClusterRole` and a `ClusterRoleBinding` for Service Accounts. The reason for this was discussed back when we created the first TKG cluster via the TKG Service in vSphere with Tanzu. Since the majority of the packages will have their own service accounts, we need to ensure that these service accounts have the appropriate privileges to carry out tasks, such as the ability to create Pods in the workload cluster. While it is possible to create a new PodSecurityPolicy, it is also possible to use one of the predefined ones such as *vmware-system-privileged.* Include it as a resource to a new ClusterRole, and then bind this new ClusterRole to the service accounts through a new ClusterRoleBinding. How to do this was shown back in chapter 6.

Now the `kapp-controller` manifest must be deployed. The kapp-controller is an integral part of Carvel package management. This is what makes it possible to install and manage packages on vSphere with Tanzu TKG workload clusters. There are two parts to this step. The first part is to create a Pod Security Policy for the kapp-controller service account, not to be confused with the PSP made earlier for the various package service accounts. The second step is to deploy the kapp-controller manifest. As we have seen in chapter 6, there are two PSPs already on TKG clusters. This step creates a third.

```
% cat tanzu-system-kapp-ctrl-restricted.yaml
apiVersion: policy/v1beta1
kind: PodSecurityPolicy
metadata:
  name: tanzu-system-kapp-ctrl-restricted
spec:
  privileged: false
  allowPrivilegeEscalation: false
  requiredDropCapabilities:
    - ALL
  volumes:
    - configMap
```

```
      - emptyDir
      - projected
      - secret
      - downwardAPI
      - persistentVolumeClaim
    hostNetwork: false
    hostIPC: false
    hostPID: false
    runAsUser:
      rule: MustRunAsNonRoot
    seLinux:
      rule: RunAsAny
    supplementalGroups:
      rule: MustRunAs
      ranges:
        - min: 1
          max: 65535
    fsGroup:
      rule: MustRunAs
      ranges:
        - min: 1
          max: 65535
    readOnlyRootFilesystem: false
```

Once this new Pod Security Policy is created, there should now be a third PSPs on this TKG cluster.

```
% kubectl apply -f tanzu-system-kapp-ctrl-restricted.yaml
podsecuritypolicy.policy/tanzu-system-kapp-ctrl-restricted created
```

```
% kubectl get psp
NAME                            PRIV    CAPS   SELINUX     RUNASUSER        FSGROUP
SUPGROUP     READONLYROOTFS  VOLUMES
tanzu-system-kapp-ctrl-
restricted    false           RunAsAny MustRunAsNonRoot MustRunAs  MustRunAs    false
      configMap,emptyDir,projected,secret,downwardAPI,persistentVolumeClaim
vmware-system-
privileged              true    *      RunAsAny RunAsAny          RunAsAny  RunAsAny   f
alse          *
vmware-system-
restricted              false          RunAsAny MustRunAsNonRoot MustRunAs  MustRunAs  f
alse          configMap,emptyDir,projected,secret,downwardAPI,persistentVolumeClaim
```

There is no need to manually create any ClusterRole or ClusterRoleBinding for this PSP. These are already included in the kapp-controller YAML manifest. The kapp-controller YAML manifest is available here - https://docs.vmware.com/en/VMware-Tanzu-Kubernetes-Grid/1.4/vmware-tanzu-kubernetes-grid-14/GUID-packages-prep-tkgs-kapp.html#kapp-controller-manifest-file-3. This is required to deploy the kapp-controller, so I am not going to reproduce it in the book since it is quite large. Once copied into a local file, apply it to the workload cluster. As you can see below, there are a significant number of Custom Resource Definitions (CRDs) added to the clusters, many of which we can query using kubectl, which we will see shortly.

```
% nano kapp-controller.yaml     ### paste the manifest contents here and save it
```

```
% kubectl apply -f kapp-controller.yaml
namespace/tkg-system created
namespace/tanzu-package-repo-global created
apiservice.apiregistration.k8s.io/v1alpha1.data.packaging.carvel.dev created
service/packaging-api created
customresourcedefinition.apiextensions.k8s.io/internalpackagemetadatas.internal.packaging.
carvel.dev created
```

```
customresourcedefinition.apiextensions.k8s.io/internalpackages.internal.packaging.carvel.d
ev created
customresourcedefinition.apiextensions.k8s.io/apps.kappctrl.k14s.io created
customresourcedefinition.apiextensions.k8s.io/packageinstalls.packaging.carvel.dev created
customresourcedefinition.apiextensions.k8s.io/packagerepositories.packaging.carvel.dev
created
configmap/kapp-controller-config created
deployment.apps/kapp-controller created
serviceaccount/kapp-controller-sa created
clusterrole.rbac.authorization.k8s.io/kapp-controller-cluster-role created
clusterrolebinding.rbac.authorization.k8s.io/kapp-controller-cluster-role-binding created
clusterrolebinding.rbac.authorization.k8s.io/pkg-apiserver:system:auth-delegator created
rolebinding.rbac.authorization.k8s.io/pkgserver-auth-reader created

% kubectl get pods -n tkg-system -w | grep kapp-controller
kapp-controller-5d8f7d9477-9z7n2    0/1    ContainerCreating    0    19s
kapp-controller-5d8f7d9477-9z7n2    1/1    Running              0    93s

% kubectl get all -n tkg-system
NAME                                         READY    STATUS     RESTARTS    AGE
pod/kapp-controller-5d8f7d9477-9z7n2         1/1      Running    0           7m48s

NAME                      TYPE         CLUSTER-IP       EXTERNAL-IP    PORT(S)     AGE
service/packaging-api     ClusterIP    100.70.177.69    <none>         443/TCP     7m50s

NAME                                 READY    UP-TO-DATE    AVAILABLE    AGE
deployment.apps/kapp-controller      1/1      1             1            7m49s

NAME                                           DESIRED    CURRENT    READY    AGE
replicaset.apps/kapp-controller-5d8f7d9477     1          1          1        7m49s

% kubectl get crd | grep -v antrea
NAME                                                  CREATED AT
apps.kappctrl.k14s.io                                 2022-02-14T11:16:36Z
internalpackagemetadatas.internal.packaging.carvel.dev    2022-02-14T11:16:36Z
internalpackages.internal.packaging.carvel.dev        2022-02-14T11:16:36Z
packageinstalls.packaging.carvel.dev                  2022-02-14T11:16:37Z
packagerepositories.packaging.carvel.dev              2022-02-14T11:16:37Z
```

The setup is now complete. You can now add the TKG package repository to the cluster, and deploy packages from it.

Deploy a monitoring stack with Prometheus & Grafana

Now that the packages are available, the next step is to deploy some of them. In this example, a monitoring stack will be installed. This stack uses Prometheus to gather metrics from a TKG cluster and then deploy Grafana. Grafana has some pre-canned dashboards for displaying the metrics. This stack will install the following packages which are available from VMware. Some packages will install without the need to provide any configuration information. Others will require some additional information to be provided to complete the setup and integrate with other components in the stack. The following table shows the packages that will be installed to create a monitoring stack for the TKG cluster.

Package Name	Configuration Required
Cert Manager	None
Contour	Set service type to Load Balancer and use the Cert Manager
External-DNS	Set DNS integration type
Prometheus	Enable ingress and set the FQDN
Grafana	Enable ingress, reference the Prometheus data source URL, and set the FQDN

Table 4: Monitoring stack configuration steps

Let's now look at how to install these packages, one at a time, to build the monitoring stack on a TKG cluster. Begin by ensuring that the context is correctly set to the TKG cluster, and not the Supervisor cluster.

Deploy Cert Manager Package

Cert Manager is deployed with no changes to its default configuration. The only required step is to retrieve the version of the package, and then deploy that version.

```
$ tanzu package available get cert-manager.tanzu.vmware.com
- Retrieving package details for cert-manager.tanzu.vmware.com...
NAME:                 cert-manager.tanzu.vmware.com
DISPLAY-NAME:         cert-manager
SHORT-DESCRIPTION:    Certificate management
PACKAGE-PROVIDER:     VMware
LONG-DESCRIPTION:     Provides certificate management provisioning within the cluster
MAINTAINERS:          [{Nicholas Seemiller}]
SUPPORT:              Support provided by VMware for deployment on TKG 1.4+ clusters. Best-
effort support for deployment on any conformant Kubernetes cluster. Contact support by
opening a support request via VMware Cloud Services or my.vmware.com.
CATEGORY:             [certificate management]

$ tanzu package available list cert-manager.tanzu.vmware.com
- Retrieving package versions for cert-manager.tanzu.vmware.com...
  NAME                           VERSION               RELEASED-AT
  cert-manager.tanzu.vmware.com  1.1.0+vmware.1-tkg.2  2020-11-24T18:00:00Z

$ tanzu package install cert-manager \
--package-name  cert-manager.tanzu.vmware.com \
--version 1.1.0+vmware.1-tkg.2
/ Installing package 'cert-manager.tanzu.vmware.com'
| Getting namespace 'default'
| Getting package metadata for 'cert-manager.tanzu.vmware.com'
| Creating service account 'cert-manager-default-sa'
| Creating cluster admin role 'cert-manager-default-cluster-role'
| Creating cluster role binding 'cert-manager-default-cluster-rolebinding'
- Creating package resource
| Package install status: Reconciling

Added installed package 'cert-manager' in namespace 'default'

$ tanzu package installed list
/ Retrieving installed packages...
  NAME          PACKAGE-NAME                   PACKAGE-VERSION       STATUS
  cert-manager  cert-manager.tanzu.vmware.com  1.1.0+vmware.1-tkg.2  Reconcile succeeded
```

Cert Manager is now installed on the TKG cluster.

Deploy Contour Package

We have already seen a Contour Ingress deployment in chapter 2. The reason for installing Contour here is because Prometheus has a requirement on an Ingress. Contour provides this functionality via an Envoy Ingress controller. Contour is an open-source Kubernetes Ingress controller that acts as a control plane for Envoy. Since this deployment is using an NSX ALB, we can provide a bespoke Contour data values file to set the Envoy service type to Load Balancer, as well as set the number of Contour replicas.

In order to be able to ascertain the available configuration values, the package version is required. To get the Contour package version, run this command:

```
$ tanzu package available list contour.tanzu.vmware.com
- Retrieving package versions for contour.tanzu.vmware.com...
  NAME                        VERSION                RELEASED-AT
  contour.tanzu.vmware.com    1.17.1+vmware.1-tkg.1  2021-07-23T18:00:00Z
```

Once the package version has been retrieved, the default Contour package configuration values can also be retrieved. The same methodology is used to retrieve the values file from every other package. Therefore, the detailed procedure is shown here for the Contour package, but will not be repeated for every other packages that is installed.

```
% image_url=$(kubectl get packages contour.tanzu.vmware.com.1.17.1+vmware.1-tkg.1 \
-o jsonpath='{.spec.template.spec.fetch[0].imgpkgBundle.image}')

% echo $image_url
projects.registry.vmware.com/tkg/packages/standard/contour@sha256:73dc13131e6c1cfa8d3b56ae
acd97734447acdf1ab8c0862e936623ca744e7c4

% mkdir ./contour

% imgpkg pull -b $image_url -o ./contour
Pulling bundle
'projects.registry.vmware.com/tkg/packages/standard/contour@sha256:73dc13131e6c1cfa8d3b56a
eacd97734447acdf1ab8c0862e936623ca744e7c4'
  Extracting layer
'sha256:93c1f3e88f0e0181e11a38a4e04ac16c21c5949622917b6c72682cc497ab3e44' (1/1)

Locating image lock file images...
One or more images not found in bundle repo; skipping lock file update

Succeeded
```

The values file is now available in `./contour/config/values.yaml`. These are the default values with which the package is deployed, but can be modified to meet various requirements.

```
infrastructure_provider: vsphere
namespace: tanzu-system-ingress
contour:
  configFileContents: {}
  useProxyProtocol: false
  replicas: 2
  pspNames: "vmware-system-restricted"
  logLevel: info
envoy:
```

```
  service:
    type: null
    annotations: {}
    nodePorts:
      http: null
      https: null
    externalTrafficPolicy: Cluster
    aws:
      LBType: classic
    disableWait: false
  hostPorts:
    enable: true
    http: 80
    https: 443
  hostNetwork: false
  terminationGracePeriodSeconds: 300
  logLevel: info
  pspNames: null
certificates:
  duration: 8760h
  renewBefore: 360h
```

The recommendation is to make a copy of the values file before making any changes. Note that not every field needs to be added to your own bespoke values file. For the purposes of deploying this package on a TKG cluster, a service type of LoadBalancer is set for Envoy, and there is a requirement to leverage Cert Manager to allow for secure communication. Thus, a simple Contour configuration manifest is created as shown below.

```
$ cat contour-simple.yaml
envoy:
  service:
    type: LoadBalancer
certificates:
  useCertManager: true
```

The manifest is provided as an argument to the command line option `--values-file`.

```
$ tanzu package install contour -p contour.tanzu.vmware.com \
--version 1.17.1+vmware.1-tkg.1 \
--values-file contour-simple.yaml
/ Installing package 'contour.tanzu.vmware.com'
| Getting namespace 'default'
| Getting package metadata for 'contour.tanzu.vmware.com'
| Creating service account 'contour-default-sa'
| Creating cluster admin role 'contour-default-cluster-role'
| Creating cluster role binding 'contour-default-cluster-rolebinding'
| Creating secret 'contour-default-values'
- Creating package resource
| Package install status: Reconciling

Added installed package 'contour' in namespace 'default'
```

To check the Contour deployment, ensure that the envoy service of type load balancer as allocated an IP address from the load balancer range defined in the provider, in this case the NSX ALB. Then check that the Pods are up and running.

```
$ tanzu package installed list
- Retrieving installed packages...
  NAME          PACKAGE-NAME                  PACKAGE-VERSION        STATUS
```

```
      cert-manager   cert-manager.tanzu.vmware.com   1.1.0+vmware.1-tkg.2   Reconcile succeeded
      contour        contour.tanzu.vmware.com        1.17.1+vmware.1-tkg.1  Reconcile succeeded

$ kubectl get pods -A | grep 'contour\|envoy'
tanzu-system-ingress   contour-648456fdbf-bpbl6                1/1    Running  0              114s
tanzu-system-ingress   contour-648456fdbf-z7q8d                1/1    Running  0              114s
tanzu-system-ingress   envoy-fvddk                             2/2    Running  0              115s

$ kubectl get svc -A | grep envoy
tanzu-system   ingress   envoy   LoadBalancer   100.68.160.66   192.168.62.197
80:30836/TCP,443:31826/TCP 2m4s

$ tanzu package installed list
- Retrieving installed packages...
  NAME            PACKAGE-NAME                    PACKAGE-VERSION        STATUS
  cert-manager    cert-manager.tanzu.vmware.com   1.1.0+vmware.1-tkg.2   Reconcile succeeded
  contour         contour.tanzu.vmware.com        1.17.1+vmware.1-tkg.1  Reconcile succeeded

$ kubectl get pods -A | grep contour
tanzu-system-ingress   contour-648456fdbfbpbl6                 1/1    Running  0              4m47s
tanzu-system-ingress   contour-648456fdbf-z7q8d                1/1    Running  0              4m47s

$ kubectl get pods -A | grep 'contour\|envoy'
tanzu-system-ingress   contour-648456fdbf-bpbl6                1/1    Running  0              5m8s
tanzu-system-ingress   contour-648456fdbf-z7q8d                1/1    Running  0              5m8s
tanzu-system-ingress   envoy-fvddk                             2/2    Running  0              5m9s

$ kubectl get svc envoy -n tanzu-system-ingress
NAME    TYPE           CLUSTER-IP      EXTERNAL-IP      PORT(S)                       AGE
envoy   LoadBalancer   100.68.160.66   192.168.62.197   80:30836/TCP,443:31826/TCP    5m21s
```

Everything looks good, and the Envoy service has a Load Balancer IP Address. We can even test if Envoy is working correctly by attempting to reach the Envoy admin page.

```
$ ENVOY_POD=$(kubectl -n tanzu-system-ingress get pod -l app=envoy -o name | head -1)
$ echo $ENVOY_POD
pod/envoy-fvddk


$ kubectl -n tanzu-system-ingress port-forward $ENVOY_POD 9001
Forwarding from 0.0.0.0:9001 -> 9001
Handling connection for 9001
```

Now if a browser is pointed at `localhost:9001`, or if the command *curl localhost:9001* is used, the Envoy Admin page is displayed. One verified, control-c the port-forward command.

Deploy External-DNS Package

External-DNS is an optional package. It allows the FQDNs associated with Kubernetes services to be automatically added to your external DNS. This is useful for Grafana dashboards, as an FQDN can be used to access them rather than the IP address. In this example, insecure connections to Microsoft DNS are being used, as per these instructions - https://github.com/kubernetes-sigs/external-dns/blob/master/docs/tutorials/rfc2136.md#microsoft-dns-insecure-updates. At the time of writing, only insecure connections to Microsoft DNS could be made. There are 2 steps to be carried out on the Microsoft DNS configuration for the domain that you plan to integrate with: (1) Allow both secure and non-secure dynamic updates, and (2) allow zone transfers to any server. I am using the **RFC2136** provider. This allows any RFC2136-compatible DNS server to be used as a provider for External-DNS, such as Microsoft DNS. This integration is to the `rainpole.com` domain. Included is a copy of the External-DNS values file. Note the inclusion of the rfc2136-insecure argument (support insecure dynamic updates) and the rfc2136-tsig-axfr (support zone transfers). Zone transfers are needed for the deletion of records. Notice also that the source has been set to **contour-httpproxy**, implying that services created using it will be added to the DNS, e.g. Prometheus and Grafana.

```
$ cat external-dns.yaml
namespace: tanzu-system-service-discovery
deployment:
  args:
    - --registry=txt
    - --txt-prefix=external-dns-
    - --txt-owner-id=tanzu
    - --provider=rfc2136
    - --rfc2136-host=192.168.51.252
    - --rfc2136-port=53
    - --rfc2136-zone=rainpole.com
    - --rfc2136-insecure
    - --rfc2136-tsig-axfr
    - --source=service
    - --source=contour-httpproxy
    - --source=ingress
    - --domain-filter=rainpole.com
```

Let's now deploy this package with the above values.

```
% tanzu package available list external-dns.tanzu.vmware.com
- Retrieving package versions for external-dns.tanzu.vmware.com...
  NAME                            VERSION                 RELEASED-AT
  external-dns.tanzu.vmware.com   0.8.0+vmware.1-tkg.1    2021-06-11 19:00:00 +0100 IST

% tanzu package install external-dns -p external-dns.tanzu.vmware.com \
-v 0.8.0+vmware.1-tkg.1 \
--values-file external-dns.yaml
| Installing package 'external-dns.tanzu.vmware.com'
/ Getting namespace 'default'
- Getting package metadata for 'external-dns.tanzu.vmware.com'
| Creating service account 'external-dns-default-sa'
| Creating cluster admin role 'external-dns-default-cluster-role'
| Creating cluster role binding 'external-dns-default-cluster-rolebinding'
| Creating secret 'external-dns-default-values'
\ Creating package resource
/ Package install status: Reconciling

 Added installed package 'external-dns' in namespace 'default'

%
```

External-DNS deploys package resources into the `tanzu-system-service-discovery`. If we examine the logs of the `external-dns` Pod, we should see a message stating the RFC2136 has been configured.

```
% kubectl -n tanzu-system-service-discovery logs external-dns-777f74bd6c-zs7bn
.
time="2022-02-15T15:08:09Z" level=info msg="Instantiating new Kubernetes client"
time="2022-02-15T15:08:09Z" level=info msg="Using inCluster-config based on
serviceaccount-token"
```

```
time="2022-02-15T15:08:09Z" level=info msg="Created Kubernetes client
https://100.64.0.1:443"
time="2022-02-15T15:08:10Z" level=info msg="Created Dynamic Kubernetes client
https://100.64.0.1:443"
time="2022-02-15T15:08:12Z" level=info msg="Configured RFC2136 with zone 'rainpole.com.'
and nameserver '192.168.51.252:53'"
```

If the above is observed in the logs, everything is working as expected. The next step is to deploy Prometheus.

Deploy Prometheus Package

Prometheus is another open-source application which records real-time metrics and provides alerting capabilities. It has a requirement for an Ingress (or HTTPProxy) and that requirement is met by Contour, which has been previously installed. Prometheus has quite a number of configuration options, most of which are not displayed here. This is showing a minimal configuration. In this example, Prometheus is configured to use an **Ingress**, and uses an FDQN that is part of the external DNS domain – `prometheus-tkgs-cork.rainpole.com` (you may need to change this to something that fits with your own DNS). It also has some StorageClasses defined for Persistent Volumes, which need to already exist before they can be used. The Prometheus server requires persistent storage for the metrics. Therefore a 150GB volume is requested. Also, alert manager also requires persistent storage, in this case a 2GB volume. Here is the configuration/values file for Prometheus.

```
% cat prometheus.yaml
ingress:
  enabled: true
  virtual_host_fqdn: "prometheus-tkgs-cork.rainpole.com"
  prometheus_prefix: "/"
  alertmanager_prefix: "/alertmanager/"
  prometheusServicePort: 80
  alertmanagerServicePort: 80
prometheus:
  pvc:
    storageClassName: vsan-default-storage-policy
alertmanager:
  pvc:
    storageClassName: vsan-default-storage-policy
```

Prometheus is deployed with the above values.

```
% tanzu package available list prometheus.tanzu.vmware.com
- Retrieving package versions for prometheus.tanzu.vmware.com...
  NAME                          VERSION                  RELEASED-AT
  prometheus.tanzu.vmware.com  2.27.0+vmware.1-tkg.1  2021-05-12 19:00:00 +0100 IST

% tanzu package install prometheus \
--package-name prometheus.tanzu.vmware.com \
--version 2.27.0+vmware.1-tkg.1 \
--values-file prometheus.yaml
- Installing package 'prometheus.tanzu.vmware.com'
| Getting namespace 'default'
/ Getting package metadata for 'prometheus.tanzu.vmware.com'
| Creating service account 'prometheus-default-sa'
| Creating cluster admin role 'prometheus-default-cluster-role'
| Creating cluster role binding 'prometheus-default-cluster-rolebinding'
| Creating secret 'prometheus-default-values'
\ Creating package resource
```

```
| Package install status: Reconciling

 Added installed package 'prometheus' in namespace 'default'
```

This creates a significant number of package resources for Prometheus in the namespace `tanzu-monitoring-system`. There should also be a new `httpproxy` object created for Prometheus.

```
% kubectl get deploy,rs,pods -n tanzu-system-monitoring
NAME                                            READY   UP-TO-DATE   AVAILABLE   AGE
deployment.apps/alertmanager                    1/1     1            1           5m11s
deployment.apps/prometheus-kube-state-metrics   1/1     1            1           5m13s
deployment.apps/prometheus-pushgateway          1/1     1            1           5m12s
deployment.apps/prometheus-server               1/1     1            1           5m13s

NAME                                                      DESIRED   CURRENT   READY   AGE
replicaset.apps/alertmanager-669c4f497d                  1         1         1       5m11s
replicaset.apps/prometheus-kube-state-metrics-6ccbc7bfc  1         1         1       5m13s
replicaset.apps/prometheus-pushgateway-6d7bc967f9        1         1         1       5m12s
replicaset.apps/prometheus-server-7cc7df4dd6             1         1         1       5m13s

NAME                                                  READY   STATUS    RESTARTS   AGE
pod/alertmanager-669c4f497d-wsx2s                     1/1     Running   0          5m11s
pod/prometheus-cadvisor-fxhw8                         1/1     Running   0          5m13s
pod/prometheus-cadvisor-m758x                         1/1     Running   0          5m13s
pod/prometheus-cadvisor-mzzm7                         1/1     Running   0          5m13s
pod/prometheus-kube-state-metrics-6ccbc7bfc-fsggg     1/1     Running   0          5m13s
pod/prometheus-node-exporter-24rc7                    1/1     Running   0          5m13s
pod/prometheus-node-exporter-9b9nh                    1/1     Running   0          5m13s
pod/prometheus-node-exporter-g6vtp                    1/1     Running   0          5m13s
pod/prometheus-node-exporter-p8tkk                    1/1     Running   0          5m13s
pod/prometheus-pushgateway-6d7bc967f9-stctt           1/1     Running   0          5m12s
pod/prometheus-server-7cc7df4dd6-ncbhz                2/2     Running   0          5m13s

% kubectl get httpproxy -n tanzu-system-monitoring
NAME                 FQDN                                TLS SECRET        STATUS   STATUS
DESCRIPTION
prometheus-httpproxy prometheus-tkgs-cork.rainpole.com   prometheus-tls    valid    Valid
HTTPProxy

% kubectl get pvc,pv -n tanzu-system-monitoring
NAME                                          STATUS   VOLUME
   CAPACITY   ACCESS MODES   STORAGECLASS                 AGE
persistentvolumeclaim/alertmanager            Bound    pvc-912dacdd-6533-45a4-948a-
34b9fd383d37   2Gi          RWO                vsan-default-storage-policy   5m29s
persistentvolumeclaim/prometheus-server       Bound    pvc-08e145e4-a267-4e1e-89d2-
513cff467512   150Gi        RWO                vsan-default-storage-policy   5m29s

NAME                                                          CAPACITY   ACCESS
MODES    RECLAIM
POLICY   STATUS   CLAIM                                 STORAGECLASS
   REASON    AGE
persistentvolume/pvc-08e145e4-a267-4e1e-89d2-
513cff467512   150Gi        RWO                Delete        Bound       tanzu-system-
monitoring/prometheus-server   vsan-default-storage-policy            3m20s
persistentvolume/pvc-912dacdd-6533-45a4-948a-
34b9fd383d37   2Gi          RWO                Delete        Bound       tanzu-system-
monitoring/alertmanager        vsan-default-storage-policy            5m27s
```

```
% kubectl get svc -n tanzu-system-monitoring
NAME                       TYPE        CLUSTER-IP       EXT-IP   PORT(S)        AGE
alertmanager               ClusterIP   100.71.143.203   <none>   80/TCP         6m15s
prometheus-kube-state-
metrics                    ClusterIP   None             <none>   80/TCP,81/TCP  6m17s
prometheus-node-
exporter                   ClusterIP   100.67.91.192    <none>   9100/TCP       6m17s
prometheus-pushgateway     ClusterIP   100.70.217.119   <none>   9091/TCP       6m17s
prometheus-server          ClusterIP   100.67.174.220   <none>   80/TCP         6m17s
```

When the httpproxy has been successfully created, and external DNS is working, it should now be possible to connect to the FQDN of the Prometheus service via a browser. If you did not integrate with DNS, then you optionally can add the Prometheus FQDN and the Envoy Load Balancer IP address to the local /etc/hosts file. This should also work. It should then display something similar to the following:

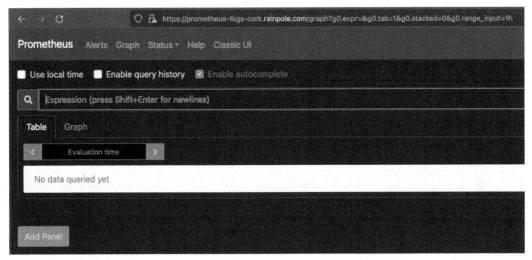

Figure 167: Prometheus UI

With Prometheus successfully installed, the next step is deploying the Grafana package. This will provide dashboards for the metrics captured by Prometheus.

Deploy Grafana Package

As seen in the Contour section already, the Grafana configuration values can be retrieved using the same method. There are quite a number of values, but as before, this deployment is trying to keep the values file quite simple. Through the values file, we can provide a data source (to Prometheus). The Prometheus URL provided is the internal Kubernetes URL, made up of the Pod Name and Namespace of the Prometheus Server. Since Grafana is also running in the same cluster, Prometheus and Grafana can communicate using internal Kubernetes networking. This is the sample Grafana values file. Grafana is requesting an ingress as well, and its FQDN is provided. Again, this may need to be changed to suit your own DNS. There is also a requirement for a 2GB persistent volume, so the StorageClass is included in the configuration. Just like with Prometheus, this StorageClass must be already available.

```
% cat grafana.yaml
namespace: tanzu-system-dashboard
ingress:
  virtual_host_fqdn: "graf-tkgs-cork.rainpole.com"
grafana:
  config:
    datasource_yaml: |-
      apiVersion: 1
      datasources:
        - name: Prometheus
          type: prometheus
          url: prometheus-server.tanzu-system-monitoring.svc.cluster.local
          access: proxy
          isDefault: true
  pvc:
    storageClassName: vsan-default-storage-policy
```

Next deploy the Grafana application, and verify that the Grafana UI can be reach via the FQDN, which if integrated with External-DNS, should be automatically added.

```
% tanzu package available list grafana.tanzu.vmware.com
\ Retrieving package versions for grafana.tanzu.vmware.com...
  NAME                       VERSION              RELEASED-AT
  grafana.tanzu.vmware.com   7.5.7+vmware.1-tkg.1  2021-05-19 19:00:00 +0100 IST


% tanzu package install grafana \
-p grafana.tanzu.vmware.com \
-v 7.5.7+vmware.1-tkg.1 \
--values-file grafana.yaml
- Installing package 'grafana.tanzu.vmware.com'
| Getting namespace 'default'
/ Getting package metadata for 'grafana.tanzu.vmware.com'
| Creating service account 'grafana-default-sa'
- Creating cluster admin role 'grafana-default-cluster-role'
| Creating cluster role binding 'grafana-default-cluster-rolebinding'
| Creating secret 'grafana-default-values'
\ Creating package resource
| Package install status: Reconciling

 Added installed package 'grafana' in namespace 'default'
```

Once again, a number of different Grafana package resources are created in the `tanzu-system-dashboard` namespace. Note that Grafana gets a Load Balancer IP and its own **httpproxy**. The Grafana FQDN should also be automatically added to your external DNS, if configured.

```
% kubectl -n tanzu-system-dashboard get pods
NAME                     READY   STATUS    RESTARTS   AGE
grafana-7fc98dd5b8-bq2mw  2/2    Running   0          2m25s

% kubectl -n tanzu-system-dashboard get svc
NAME      TYPE          CLUSTER-IP      EXTERNAL-IP    PORT(S)       AGE
grafana   LoadBalancer  100.67.139.55   192.168.62.21  80:31126/TCP  2m33s

% kubectl -n tanzu-system-dashboard get httpproxy
NAME                FQDN                         TLS SECRET    STATUS   STATUS
DESCRIPTION
grafana-httpproxy   graf-tkgs-cork.rainpole.com  grafana-tls   valid    Valid HTTPProxy
```

```
% kubectl -n tanzu-system-dashboard get pvc
NAME          STATUS   VOLUME                                CAPACITY   ACCESS
MODES    STORAGECLASS               AGE
grafana-pvc   Bound    pvc-72e06aa7-9944-439a-80e0-
40fecd61915b   2Gi           RWO            vsan-default-storage-policy   2m54s
```

Assuming everything is working correctly, it should now be possible to connect to the Grafana FQDN to see the dashboards. Again, if you haven't integrated with DNS, just add the Grafana FQDN and Grafana Load Balancer IP Address shown above to the local /etc/hosts file. The default login for Grafana is `admin/admin`, and you are then prompted to set a new admin password. Then navigate to **Dashboards > Manage** on the left hand side and select one of the two existing dashboards to see some metrics. This is the TKG Kubernetes cluster monitoring dashboard. Of course, you can then proceed to build your own bespoke dashboards if you wish.

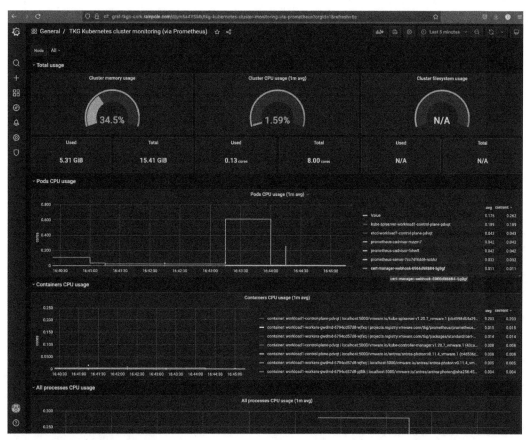

Figure 168: Grafana Dashboards

The TKG cluster is now being monitored. As you can hopefully appreciate, VMware has made it very easy it is to stand up a Prometheus and Grafana monitoring stack on a TKG cluster. Here are the full list of packages that have now been installed on the cluster, which can be queried in two ways.

```
% tanzu package installed list
- Retrieving installed packages...
  NAME            PACKAGE-NAME                   PACKAGE-VERSION        STATUS
  cert-manager    cert-manager.tanzu.vmware.com  1.1.0+vmware.1-tkg.2   Reconcile succeeded
  contour         contour.tanzu.vmware.com       1.17.1+vmware.1-tkg.1  Reconcile succeeded
  external-dns    external-dns.tanzu.vmware.com  0.8.0+vmware.1-tkg.1   Reconcile succeeded
  grafana         grafana.tanzu.vmware.com       7.5.7+vmware.1-tkg.1   Reconcile succeeded
  prometheus      prometheus.tanzu.vmware.com    2.27.0+vmware.1-tkg.1  Reconcile succeeded

% kubectl get apps
NAME            DESCRIPTION          SINCE-DEPLOY   AGE
cert-manager    Reconcile succeeded  58s            172m
contour         Reconcile succeeded  29s            35m
external-dns    Reconcile succeeded  39s            25m
grafana         Reconcile succeeded  2m20s          2m24s
prometheus      Reconcile succeeded  22s            17m
```

Log shipping with Fluent Bit

VMware provides another package which facilitates the shipping of container logs to a monitoring system. This destination could range from VMware Log Insight to what is commonly referred to as an ELK stack, made up of products called Elastic and Kibana. While the setup of the ELK stack is outside the scope of this book, the steps to install and configure Fluent Bit on a TKG cluster will be shown. The Fluent Bit package will be configured to ship logs to Elasticsearch since fluent-bit has an Elasticsearch plugin. Finally an index pattern will be built in Kibana to allow us to visualize and search on our Kubernetes cluster logs, and use the Dashboard view to see the logging activity.

Let's begin by getting the values file for the Fluent Bit package.

```
% kubectl get packages fluent-bit.tanzu.vmware.com.1.7.5+vmware.2-tkg.1 \
-o jsonpath='{.spec.template.spec.fetch[0].imgpkgBundle.image}'
projects.registry.vmware.com/tkg/packages/standard/repo@sha256:264bfbefb2430c422cb69163700
4ed5dbf4a4d0aac0b0cb06ee19a3c81b1779e%

% image_url=$(kubectl get packages fluent-bit.tanzu.vmware.com.1.7.5+vmware.2-tkg.1 \
-o jsonpath='{.spec.template.spec.fetch[0].imgpkgBundle.image}')

% echo $image_url
projects.registry.vmware.com/tkg/packages/standard/repo@sha256:264bfbefb2430c422cb69163700
4ed5dbf4a4d0aac0b0cb06ee19a3c81b1779e

% mkdir fluent-bit

% imgpkg pull -b $image_url -o ./fluent-bit
Pulling bundle
'projects.registry.vmware.com/tkg/packages/standard/repo@sha256:264bfbefb2430c422cb6916370
04ed5dbf4a4d0aac0b0cb06ee19a3c81b1779e'
  Extracting layer
'sha256:9117de69d77240fa52e38e1a434bcda69b9185f5fafd2a85eedbd06c06beb57c' (1/1)

Locating image lock file images...
The bundle repo (projects.registry.vmware.com/tkg/packages/standard/repo) is hosting every
image specified in the bundle's Images Lock file (.imgpkg/images.yml)

Succeeded
```

```
% ls -R ./fluent-bit
config

./fluent-bit/config:
_ytt_libfluent-bit.yaml values.yaml

./fluent-bit/config/_ytt_lib:
bundle

./fluent-bit/config/_ytt_lib/bundle:
config

./fluent-bit/config/_ytt_lib/bundle/config:
overlaysupstreamvalues.yaml

./fluent-bit/config/_ytt_lib/bundle/config/overlays:
overlay-configmap.yaml   overlay-daemonset.yaml   overlay-namespace.yaml

./fluent-bit/config/_ytt_lib/bundle/config/upstream:
fluentbit

./fluent-bit/config/_ytt_lib/bundle/config/upstream/fluentbit:
configmap.yaml   daemonset.yaml   namespace.yaml   rbac.yml
```

```
% cat ./fluent-bit/config/_ytt_lib/bundle/config/values.yaml
#@data/values
#@overlay/match-child-defaults missing_ok=True
---
namespace: "fluent-bit"
#! Required params for supported output plugins
fluent_bit:
  config:
    #! https://docs.fluentbit.io/manual/administration/configuring-fluent-bit/variables
    service: |
      [Service]
        Flush          1
        Log_Level      info
        Daemon         off
        Parsers_File   parsers.conf
        HTTP_Server    On
        HTTP_Listen    0.0.0.0
        HTTP_Port      2020
    outputs: |
      [OUTPUT]
        Name              stdout
        Match             *
    inputs: |
      [INPUT]
        Name tail
        Path /var/log/containers/*.log
        Parser docker
        Tag kube.*
        Mem_Buf_Limit 5MB
        Skip_Long_Lines On

      [INPUT]
        Name systemd
        Tag host.*
        Systemd_Filter _SYSTEMD_UNIT=kubelet.service
        Read_From_Tail On
    filters: |
      [FILTER]
        Name              kubernetes
        Match             kube.*
```

```
        Kube_URL                https://kubernetes.default.svc:443
        Kube_CA_File            /var/run/secrets/kubernetes.io/serviceaccount/ca.crt
        Kube_Token_File         /var/run/secrets/kubernetes.io/serviceaccount/token
        Kube_Tag_Prefix         kube.var.log.containers.
        Merge_Log               On
        Merge_Log_Key           log_processed
        K8S-Logging.Parser      On
        K8S-Logging.Exclude On

    [FILTER]
        Name                    modify
        Match                   *
        Rename message text
  parsers: |
    [PARSER]
        Name    json
        Format json
        Time_Key time
        Time_Format %d/%b/%Y:%H:%M:%S %z
  streams: ""
  plugins: ""
#! optional configuration for the daemonset
daemonset:
  resources: { }
  #! limits:
  #!   cpu: 100m
  #!   memory: 128Mi
  #! requests:
  #!   cpu: 100m
  #!   memory: 128Mi
  podAnnotations: { }
  podLabels: { }
```

There is a considerable amount of documentation available for configuring fluent bit with Elastic - https://docs.fluentbit.io/manual/pipeline/outputs/elasticsearch. A simple configuration file might look similar to the following, where the output is set to "es" (elastic search) with an index called cjh_index, and the plugin also called "es" for Elasticsearch. The Host IP address is the Elasticsearch master service ClusterIP, and 9200 is the port that it is using. All of the inputs remain the same, which is to tail the container logs and well as the kubelet service. Since they are the same, they are not included in this configuration. A much simpler values file is shown here.

```
$ cat ./fluent-bit-values.yaml
fluent_bit:
  service: |
    [Service]
      Flush         5

  outputs: |
    [OUTPUT]
      Name          es
      Match         *
      Host          100.66.166.36
      Port          9200
      Index         cjh_index
      Type          doc

  plugins: "es"
```

With the values file in place, we can deploy the Fluent Bit package.

```
% tanzu package install fluent-bit \
-p fluent-bit.tanzu.vmware.com \
-v 1.7.5+vmware.2-tkg.1 \
--values-file ./fluent-bit-values.yaml
- Installing package 'fluent-bit.tanzu.vmware.com'
 Installing package 'fluent-bit.tanzu.vmware.com'
 Getting package metadata for 'fluent-bit.tanzu.vmware.com'
 Creating service account 'fluent-bit-default-sa'
 Creating cluster admin role 'fluent-bit-default-cluster-role'
 Creating cluster role binding 'fluent-bit-default-cluster-rolebinding'
 Creating secret 'fluent-bit-default-values'
 Creating package resource
 Waiting for 'PackageInstall' reconciliation for 'fluent-bit'
 'PackageInstall' resource install status: Reconciling
 'PackageInstall' resource install status: ReconcileSucceeded
 'PackageInstall' resource successfully reconciled

 Added installed package 'fluent-bit'
```

At this point, the index should be visible in the Elasticsearch catalog, and in the Kibana interface, it should be possible to select Manage Index Lifecycles. Kibana should detect that there is now data in Elasticsearch and prompt you to create a new Index Pattern for the Elasticsearch source (cjh_index). Once completed, it should now be possible to use Kibana to display some logs. Returning to the Kibana Main Menu (top left), select **Analytics** > **Discover** and it should be possible to see logging information from your TKG cluster now displayed.

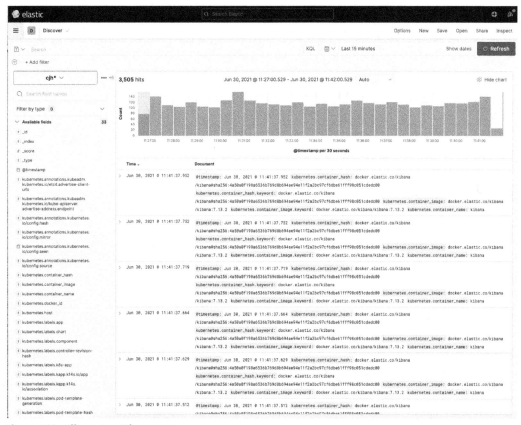

Figure 169: Kibana Log Discovery

Backup & Restore with Velero

Way back in 2018, VMware announced its intent to purchase a company called Heptio. As part of the acquisition, VMware acquired a backup product called Velero to provide backup and restore capabilities to Kubernetes applications. In this section, we will take a look at Velero, and how to use it.

Note: For vSphere administrators who are running vSphere with Tanzu, vCenter Server backups are also an essential component. The vCenter backups will also capture the state of the Supervisor Cluster. On restore, vCenter will recreate all three Supervisor Cluster control plane VMs. This should be used in combination with Velero to provide cluster workload backups. Also note that if you are using NSX-T as the networking stack, additional steps should be carried out to ensure a successful backup and restore of the NSX-T database. This captures the state of the load balancer and ingress services. NSX-T backups can be configured via the NSX-T manager.

Velero Deployment

At the time of writing, Velero v1.8.1 was the most recent release. Velero does require an S3-compatible bucket as a backup storage location. To get you started, the Velero quick start guides provides details on how to create a MinIO instance on your Kubernetes cluster. Thus, 3 components are needed to run Velero, the client binary installed to your local laptop / desktop, the server component installed in the Kubernetes cluster and an S3 bucket as a backup destination.

Velero can be downloaded from `https://github.com/vmware-tanzu/velero`. Once the gzip bundle is download, it must be extracted as follows, and moved to your PATH.

```
% tar zxvf velero-v1.8.1-darwin-amd64.tar.gz
x velero-v1.8.1-darwin-amd64/LICENSE
x velero-v1.8.1-darwin-amd64/examples/README.md
x velero-v1.8.1-darwin-amd64/examples/minio
x velero-v1.8.1-darwin-amd64/examples/minio/00-minio-deployment.yaml
x velero-v1.8.1-darwin-amd64/examples/nginx-app
x velero-v1.8.1-darwin-amd64/examples/nginx-app/README.md
x velero-v1.8.1-darwin-amd64/examples/nginx-app/base.yaml
x velero-v1.8.1-darwin-amd64/examples/nginx-app/with-pv.yaml
x velero-v1.8.1-darwin-amd64/velero

% mv velero-v1.8.1-darwin-amd64/velero /usr/local/bin/velero

% chmod +x /usr/local/bin/velero

% which velero
/usr/local/bin/velero

% velero version
Client:
        Version: v1.8.1
        Git commit: 18ee078dffd9345df610e0ca9f61b31124e93f50
I0620 11:50:58.371185   57020 request.go:665] Waited for 1.175735556s due to client-side
throttling, not priority and fairness, request:
GET:https://192.168.51.178:6443/apis/identity.concierge.pinniped.dev/v1alpha1?timeout=32s
<error getting server version: no matches for kind "ServerStatusRequest" in version
"velero.io/v1">
```

The server part of the version output failed as expected. Velero server still needs to be installed in the TKG cluster. The next step however is to set up an S3-compatible object store. For evaluation purposes, Velero ships with a minimal MinIO (https://min.io) configuration to create an object store and bucket backup destination. This is found in the download examples folder.

```
% cd velero-v1.8.1-darwin-amd64

% ls
LICENSE          examples
```

A credentials file called `credentials-velero` must be created with a key id and an access key, as shown below.

```
% cat credentials-velero
[default]
aws_access_key_id = minio
aws_secret_access_key = minio123
```

Next, apply the MinIO deployment manifest so that the S3-compatible object store is created.

```
% kubectl apply -f examples/minio/00-minio-deployment.yaml
namespace/velero created
deployment.apps/minio created
service/minio created
job.batch/minio-setup created
```

Velero server can now be installed. This deployment is going to use restic to do backups and restores. Restic leverages file copy technology rather than snapshots. The snapshot mechanisms available for Kubernetes deployments on vSphere shall be discussed later on. However, this restic mechanism also works for Kubernetes deployments on vSphere.

The S3-compatible object store is referenced via the provider, bucket name and secret file in the install command.

```
% velero install  \
--provider aws \
--bucket velero \
--secret-file ./credentials-velero \
--use-volume-snapshots=false \
--plugins velero/velero-plugin-for-aws:v1.0.0 \
--use-restic \
--backup-location-config \
region=minio,s3ForcePathStyle="true",s3Url=http://minio.velero.svc:9000
CustomResourceDefinition/backups.velero.io: attempting to create resource
CustomResourceDefinition/backups.velero.io: attempting to create resource client
CustomResourceDefinition/backups.velero.io: created
CustomResourceDefinition/backupstoragelocations.velero.io: attempting to create resource
CustomResourceDefinition/backupstoragelocations.velero.io: attempting to create resource
client
CustomResourceDefinition/backupstoragelocations.velero.io: created
CustomResourceDefinition/deletebackuprequests.velero.io: attempting to create resource
CustomResourceDefinition/deletebackuprequests.velero.io: attempting to create resource
client
CustomResourceDefinition/deletebackuprequests.velero.io: created
CustomResourceDefinition/downloadrequests.velero.io: attempting to create resource
CustomResourceDefinition/downloadrequests.velero.io: attempting to create resource client
CustomResourceDefinition/downloadrequests.velero.io: created
CustomResourceDefinition/podvolumebackups.velero.io: attempting to create resource
CustomResourceDefinition/podvolumebackups.velero.io: attempting to create resource client
CustomResourceDefinition/podvolumebackups.velero.io: created
```

```
CustomResourceDefinition/podvolumerestores.velero.io: attempting to create resource
CustomResourceDefinition/podvolumerestores.velero.io: attempting to create resource client
CustomResourceDefinition/podvolumerestores.velero.io: created
CustomResourceDefinition/resticrepositories.velero.io: attempting to create resource
CustomResourceDefinition/resticrepositories.velero.io: attempting to create resource
client
CustomResourceDefinition/resticrepositories.velero.io: created
CustomResourceDefinition/restores.velero.io: attempting to create resource
CustomResourceDefinition/restores.velero.io: attempting to create resource client
CustomResourceDefinition/restores.velero.io: created
CustomResourceDefinition/schedules.velero.io: attempting to create resource
CustomResourceDefinition/schedules.velero.io: attempting to create resource client
CustomResourceDefinition/schedules.velero.io: created
CustomResourceDefinition/serverstatusrequests.velero.io: attempting to create resource
CustomResourceDefinition/serverstatusrequests.velero.io: attempting to create resource
client
CustomResourceDefinition/serverstatusrequests.velero.io: created
CustomResourceDefinition/volumesnapshotlocations.velero.io: attempting to create resource
CustomResourceDefinition/volumesnapshotlocations.velero.io: attempting to create resource
client
CustomResourceDefinition/volumesnapshotlocations.velero.io: created
Waiting for resources to be ready in cluster...
Namespace/velero: attempting to create resource
Namespace/velero: attempting to create resource client
Namespace/velero: already exists, proceeding
Namespace/velero: created
ClusterRoleBinding/velero: attempting to create resource
ClusterRoleBinding/velero: attempting to create resource client
ClusterRoleBinding/velero: created
ServiceAccount/velero: attempting to create resource
ServiceAccount/velero: attempting to create resource client
ServiceAccount/velero: created
Secret/cloud-credentials: attempting to create resource
Secret/cloud-credentials: attempting to create resource client
Secret/cloud-credentials: created
BackupStorageLocation/default: attempting to create resource
BackupStorageLocation/default: attempting to create resource client
BackupStorageLocation/default: created
Deployment/velero: attempting to create resource
Deployment/velero: attempting to create resource client
Deployment/velero: created
DaemonSet/restic: attempting to create resource
DaemonSet/restic: attempting to create resource client
DaemonSet/restic: created
Velero is installed! ⛏ Use 'kubectl logs deployment/velero -n velero' to view the status.
```

As reported in the output, the logs of the velero deployment, in the namespace velero, can be checked to make sure there are no errors. The output is too long to reproduce here, but it should be possible to observe the backup location being validated and marked as available:

```
time="2022-06-20T10:54:27Z" level=info msg="Validating backup storage location" backup-
storage-location=default controller=backup-storage-location
logSource="pkg/controller/backup_storage_location_controller.go:114"
time="2022-06-20T10:54:27Z" level=info msg="Backup storage location valid, marking as
available" backup-storage-location=default controller=backup-storage-location
logSource="pkg/controller/backup_storage_location_controller.go:121"
```

It should also be possible to see the list of entities created in the velero namespace.

```
% kubectl get all -n velero
NAME                        READY   STATUS    RESTARTS   AGE
pod/minio-5b84955bdd-76dd8  1/1     Running   0          3m37s
```

```
pod/minio-setup--1-pxb6p      0/1     Completed   1     3m36s
pod/restic-798lb              1/1     Running     0     2m13s
pod/restic-bjfzf              1/1     Running     0     2m13s
pod/restic-gjx5r              1/1     Running     0     2m13s
pod/velero-5c8fc4f8c7-94l7k   1/1     Running     0     2m13s

NAME             TYPE        CLUSTER-IP       EXTERNAL-IP   PORT(S)     AGE
service/minio    ClusterIP   100.66.12.13     <none>        9000/TCP    3m36s

NAME                    DESIRED  CURRENT  READY  UP-TO-DATE  AVAILABLE  NODE SELECTOR  AGE
daemonset.apps/restic   3        3        3      3           3          <none>         2m14s

NAME                      READY  UP-TO-DATE  AVAILABLE  AGE
deployment.apps/minio     1/1    1           1          3m38s
deployment.apps/velero    1/1    1           1          2m14s

NAME                                 DESIRED  CURRENT  READY  AGE
replicaset.apps/minio-5b84955bdd     1        1        1      3m38s
replicaset.apps/velero-5c8fc4f8c7    1        1        1      2m14s

NAME                    COMPLETIONS  DURATION  AGE
job.batch/minio-setup   1/1          19s       3m38s
```

Finally, you can check the version of the velero client and the velero server.

```
% velero version
Client:
        Version: v1.8.1
        Git commit: 18ee078dffd9345df610e0ca9f61b31124e93f50
Server:
        Version: v1.8.1
```

Everything is now ready to take the first backup and restore.

Velero Backup and Restore

For a sample application, I will leverage our familiar nginx web server application. This will result in deployment and service entities getting created on the TKG workload cluster in the namespace nginx. It also creates a virtual service on the NSX ALB, to which the TKG cluster is integrated.

```
apiVersion: v1
kind: Service
metadata:
  labels:
    app: nginx
  name: nginx-svc
  namespace: nginx
spec:
  type: LoadBalancer
  ports:
    - name: http
      port: 80
  selector:
    app: nginx
---
apiVersion: apps/v1
kind: Deployment
metadata:
  name: nginx-deployment
  namespace: nginx
```

```
spec:
  selector:
    matchLabels:
      app: nginx
  replicas: 2
  template:
    metadata:
      labels:
        app: nginx
    spec:
      containers:
      - name: nginx
        image: nginx:latest
        ports:
        - containerPort: 80
```

```
% kubectl apply -f nginx-deployment-lb.yaml
service/nginx-svc created
deployment.apps/nginx-deployment created
```

After the nginx deployment, the following are the objects created in the Kubernetes cluster.

```
% kubectl get all -n nginx
```

NAME	READY	STATUS	RESTARTS	AGE
pod/nginx-deployment-585449566-4n995	1/1	Running	0	3m2s
pod/nginx-deployment-585449566-f22b2	1/1	Running	0	3m2s

NAME	TYPE	CLUSTER-IP	EXTERNAL-IP	PORT(S)	AGE
service/nginx-svc	LoadBalancer	100.68.119.197	192.168.62.41	80:30462/TCP	3m2s

NAME	READY	UP-TO-DATE	AVAILABLE	AGE
deployment.apps/nginx-deployment	2/2	2	2	3m2s

NAME	DESIRED	CURRENT	READY	AGE
replicaset.apps/nginx-deployment-585449566	2	2	2	3m3s

Velero will now be used to back it up. The resulting backup is stored in the Minio S3-compatible object store bucket. In this example, Velero is instructed to back up the nginx namespace only.

```
% velero backup create nginx --include-namespaces nginx
Backup request "nginx" submitted successfully.
Run `velero backup describe nginx` or `velero backup logs nginx` for more details.
```

The command `velero backup describe <backup-name>` can be used to retrieve the status of the backup.

```
% velero backup describe nginx
Name:          nginx
Namespace:     velero
Labels:        velero.io/storage-location=default
Annotations:   velero.io/source-cluster-k8s-gitversion=v1.22.9+vmware.1
               velero.io/source-cluster-k8s-major-version=1
               velero.io/source-cluster-k8s-minor-version=22

Phase:  Completed

Errors:    0
Warnings:  0

Namespaces:
```

```
     Included:  nginx
     Excluded:  <none>

 Resources:
   Included:       *
   Excluded:       <none>
   Cluster-scoped: auto

 Label selector:  <none>

 Storage Location:  default

 Velero-Native Snapshot PVs:  auto

 TTL:  720h0m0s

 Hooks:  <none>

 Backup Format Version:  1.1.0

 Started:    2022-06-20 12:42:57 +0100 IST
 Completed:  2022-06-20 12:43:10 +0100 IST

 Expiration:  2022-07-20 12:42:57 +0100 IST

 Total items to be backed up:  53
 Items backed up:              53

 Velero-Native Snapshots: <none included>
```

The `velero backup logs <backup-name>` can only be used if the MinIO service is exposed externally to the Cluster. The logs are stored in the S3-compatible bucket along with the backup information, so unless the client can reach it through a NodePort type service, the command will fail. The official Velero documentation has details on how to do this.

Checking the backup can also be done with the following command:

```
% velero backup get
NAME    STATUS     ERRORS  WARNINGS  CREATED                        EXPIRES  STORAGE
nginx   Completed  0       0         2022-06-20 12:42:57 +0100 IST  29d      default
```

Let's now delete the application namespace and all of its objects. Afterwards, let's restore the backup via Velero and see if the application is recovered.

```
% kubectl delete ns nginx
namespace "nginx" deleted

% velero restore create nginx-restore --from-backup nginx
Restore request "nginx-restore" submitted successfully.
Run `velero restore describe nginx-restore` or `velero restore logs nginx-restore` for
more details.

% velero restore describe nginx-restore
Name:         nginx-restore
Namespace:    velero
Labels:       <none>
Annotations:  <none>

Phase:                        Completed
Total items to be restored:   40
Items restored:               40
```

```
Started:    2022-06-20 12:58:59 +0100 IST
Completed:  2022-06-20 12:59:00 +0100 IST

Backup:  nginx

Namespaces:
  Included:  all namespaces found in the backup
  Excluded:  <none>

Resources:
  Included:         *
  Excluded:         nodes, events, events.events.k8s.io, backups.velero.io,
restores.velero.io, resticrepositories.velero.io
  Cluster-scoped:  auto

Namespace mappings:  <none>

Label selector:  <none>

Restore PVs:  auto

Preserve Service NodePorts:  auto
```

The restore appears to have been completed successfully. Let's check if everything was restored.

```
% kubectl get all -n nginx
NAME                                    READY   STATUS    RESTARTS   AGE
pod/nginx-deployment-585449566-db7zh    1/1     Running   0          73s
pod/nginx-deployment-585449566-tdmnx    1/1     Running   0          73s

NAME                  TYPE           CLUSTER-IP       EXTERNAL-IP     PORT(S)        AGE
service/nginx-svc     LoadBalancer   100.70.210.249   192.168.62.41   80:30511/TCP   73s

NAME                                READY   UP-TO-DATE   AVAILABLE   AGE
deployment.apps/nginx-deployment    2/2     2            2           74s

NAME                                          DESIRED   CURRENT   READY   AGE
replicaset.apps/nginx-deployment-585449566    2         2         2       74s
```

Success! Velero has taken a backup of the application and successfully restores it. A few observations on the previous test should be mentioned. The first is that this was a stateless application, so there was no consideration given to persistent data. If you wish to use the restic plugin to backup and restore Pod volumes, the Pods will need to be annotated using the `backup.velero.io/backup-volumes` annotation. Otherwise, Velero will not backup the Pods. Refer to the official Velero + Restic documentation for further details.

An alternative to using restic with annotations is to use the `EnableCSI` feature when installing the Velero server. This will allow for the CSI snapshotting of PVCs rather than restic file copies. CSI Snapshots are available in the vSphere CSI driver since version 2.5.

vSphere Service – Velero Plugin for vSphere

Note that, at the time of writing, CSI snapshots were not available in TKGS or the Supervisor Cluster of vSphere with Tanzu. Instead, a backup/restore product called the **Velero Plugin for vSphere** is available that provides a mechanism to take vSphere snapshots of Pod volumes. This mechanism installs as a vSphere Service on vSphere with Tanzu and then provides a central point for backing up and restoring TKG workloads. The installation leverages PodVMs or Native Pods on the Supervisor Cluster, thus this solution can only be used when vSphere with Tanzu is deployed with NSX-T. An S3-Compatible Object Store is also required as a backup destination. The solution also required a Data Manager VM to be deployed. This appliance is involved in the movement of snapshot data from the volumes to the S3 object store, and vice-versa. It is also recommended that a dedicated network be created for backup and restore traffic. The network should be configured to support a dedicated network block device (NBD) transport. This is done by setting the tag `vSphereBackupNFC` on each NIC connected to the network. This service is available in vSphere 7.0U3. A subtlety different version called the Velero vSphere Operator was available in vSphere 7.0U2, but on upgrade to 7.0U3, this is automatically converted to a vSphere Service.

Deployment and configuration of the Velero Plugin for vSphere is rather lengthy, so beyond the scope of this book. Readers who are interested in such a solution are urged to refer to the official vSphere with Tanzu documentation for instructions on how to deploy the Velero Plugin for vSphere.

Management through Tanzu Mission Control

For Platform Operators who are responsible for managing Kubernetes clusters across many different platforms, either multiple on-prem vSphere platforms and different Cloud platforms, Tanzu Mission Control (TMC) can make management a lot easier. TMC is a management service offered via SaaS (Software as a Service) from VMware. This section is not going to cover all the features of Tanzu Mission Control but will highlight some of the interesting management features that it offers.

Adding Kubernetes Cluster to Tanzu Mission Control

TMC provides manifests that allow a Platform Operator to quickly integrate TKG management clusters and vSphere with Tanzu Supervisor Clusters. Under **Administration > Management** clusters, a button to register a management cluster is available. This provides the ability to select TKG, vSphere with Tanzu or even TCE clusters, the latter being Tanzu Community Edition. In this example, we will look at vSphere with Tanzu registration. After assigning a name, and a few other necessary settings, TMC provides the Platform Operator with a URL as shown below.

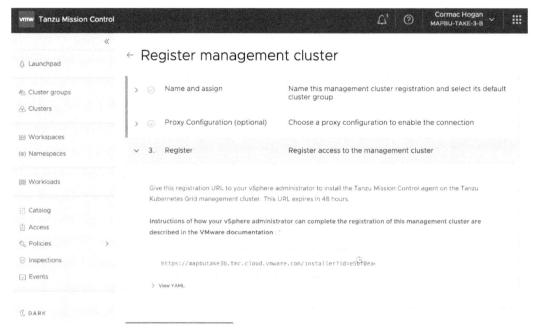

Figure 170: Tanzu Mission Control – Registration URL

Back on the vSphere Client UI where vSphere with Tanzu is running, navigate to **Cluster** > **Configure** > **TKG Service** > **Tanzu Mission Control** and add the URL from TMC.

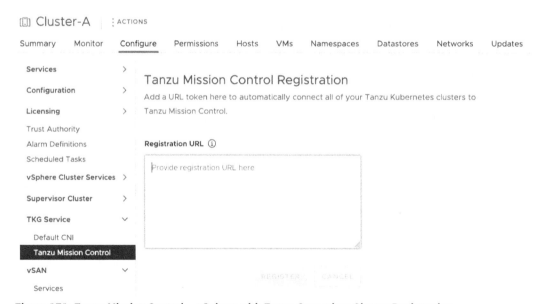

Figure 171: Tanzu Mission Control – vSphere with Tanzu Supervisor Cluster Registration

This will pull down and install the necessary TMC components onto the Supervisor Cluster. It will also discover any existing TKG workload clusters that have already been deployed, and these will automatically appear in TMC. TMC also provides a UI driver mechanism to deploy new TKG workload clusters to the vSphere with Tanzu environment, rather than using the YAML manifest.

The following sections talk about some of the other useful operations that TMC makes available in a centralized portal to a Platform Operator.

Tanzu Mission Control Inspection with Sonobuoy

TMC through Sonobuoy can offer a centralized location to check the security compliance (CIS benchmark) and conformance of the different Kubernetes clusters that have been deployed and are under your control. In TMC, these are called inspections. This conformance inspection will ensure that your Kubernetes cluster (whether is an upstream version or a third-party packaged version) supports all of the necessary Kubernetes APIs. The CIS benchmark checks whether Kubernetes is deployed according to security best practices as defined in the CIS Kubernetes Benchmark. Both can be run against a cluster directly from TMC.

Tanzu Mission Control Data Protection with Velero

TMC enables the selection of an S3-compatible Object Store that can then be used as the "backup target" for TMC Data Protection. TMC Data Protection uses the Velero product from VMware. Once configured, it can be used to initiate backup and restore operations. Tanzu Mission Control allows restoration of a selected namespace from a cluster backup, as well as allowing the ability to restore without overwriting an existing namespace.

3 steps need to be completed to set up Tanzu Mission Control with Data Protection. These can be summarized as follows:

1. Create the backup credentials for the S3 Object Store
2. Add the S3 Object Store bucket as a backup target location
3. Enable Data Protection on the cluster(s)

Once data protection is enabled, there should be 2 additional Pods created in the velero namespace on the target cluster that is being backed up. Backup and restore jobs can now be created and managed via TMC rather than the command line, which makes for a much more elegant user experience. TMC also caters for scheduled backups which can be run regularly.

Tanzu Mission Control Network Policies with Antrea

Another interesting feature of TMC is its ability to create network policies for the Antrea CNI. Antrea was discussed way back in chapter 4, but network policies were not. Suffice to say that network policies can control communication between different cluster entities in a Kubernetes cluster. A network policy could be created to prevent communication between Pods based on either Pod selectors or labels. For example, perhaps a namespace contains a web server deployment and a standalone Pod. The Pod can access the web server when no network policies are in place. With a network policy, it is possible to control which Pods are allowed to communicate with each other based on whether or not the Pod selector/label matches the rule defined in the policy. These policies can also be configured via Tanzu Mission Control.

A network policy in Tanzu Mission Control (TMC) is created at the workspace level. A workspace is an organizational tool that helps you monitor and manage your Kubernetes namespaces within and across clusters. Once the workspace is created, the namespaces that you wish to manage, i.e.

control with network policies, are added to it. Network policies created at the workspace level are then applied to any namespaces attached to that workspace. This way you can apply a network policy across very many namespaces at the same time. A very useful way to manage multiple environments simultaneously, rather than manually setting network policies at a per namespace or per cluster basis.

Upgrades & Lifecycle Management

When managing vSphere with Tanzu, upgrades need to be considered across several components, namely, vCenter, the Supervisor Cluster and the TKG workload clusters provisioned by TKGS.

Note: There are only ever three releases of Kubernetes supported in the Supervisor Cluster. When support for a new release of Kubernetes is introduced, support for an earlier version is removed. This is a significant consideration for vSphere administrators who may have upgraded their vCenter Server very infrequently in the past. Since upstream Kubernetes releases on a cadence of three releases a year, vSphere administrators may need to consider more frequent vCenter Server updates to provide the Kubernetes distributions required by the Platform Operators in their organization.

vCenter Server Update

Let's run through the scenario with the following example. vCenter Server is reporting that there is a new update available. It is also a critical update, so a reboot of the vCenter Server is required. This means that the client will be unavailable for some time, so be sure to plan your maintenance accordingly. This environment already has vSphere with Tanzu configured. From Workload **Management > Supervisor Clusters**, I can see that the version is `v1.21.0+vmware.wcp.2-vsc0.0.13-19411006`. At this point, I am not yet sure if a new Supervisor Cluster update comes with the vCenter Server update.

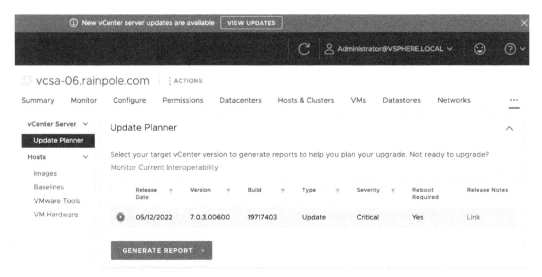

Figure 172: vCenter Server updates are available

From the Generate Report, both interoperability and pre-update checks are possible. If the pre-update checks pass, you will be prompted to open the appliance management of the vCenter Server. From here, the vCenter upgrade can be initiated.

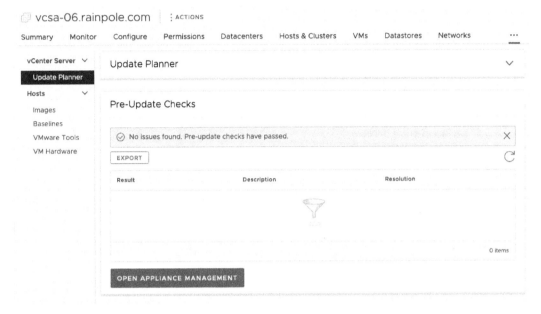

Figure 173: Pre-Update Checks - Open Appliance Management

Navigate to the Update section in the vCenter Server Appliance Management. The same update as seen in the vSphere Client should be visible in the appliance view.

Figure 174: Available Updates view

Once the update is selected, there are 2 options. The first is to stage the upgrade items but not yet install them. The second option is to do the stage and install it in a single step. Once the stage and install step is chosen, you will be prompted to take a backup of your vCenter Server before proceeding with the upgrade. You must confirm that a backup has been taken before proceeding.

Figure 175: Backup vCenter Server

The upgrade will now proceed. After installing the patches, rebooting vCenter and converting data as part of the post-install, it is now possible to check to see if there are any Supervisor updates. If there are any new components to upgrade on the Supervisor Cluster, these will also be reflected in the vSphere Client.

Figure 176: vCenter Server Upgrade Complete

Caution: the vCenter Server may go through multiple reboots. Don't start any activity on the Supervisor Cluster until you have confirmed via the vCenter appliance portal that the vCenter upgrade has been completed successfully.

Supervisor Cluster Update

To check if there is a new update for the Supervisor Cluster, open Workload Management, select Updates and any available updates should be visible. In this scenario, it would appear that there is a new version of the Supervisor available – a v1.22.6.

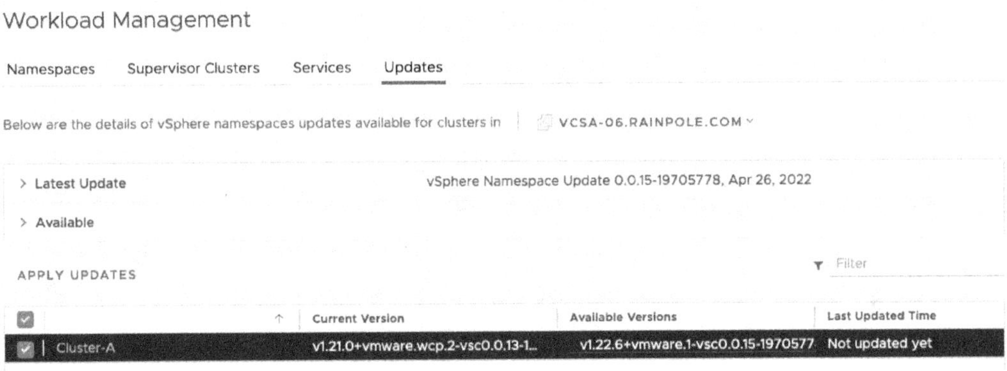

Workload Management
Namespaces
Supervisor Clusters
Services
Updates
Below are the details of vSphere namespaces updates available for clusters in
VCSA-06.RAINPOLE.COM
Latest Update
vSphere Namespace Update 0.0.15-19705778, Apr 26, 2022
Available
APPLY UPDATES
Filter
Current Version
Available Versions
Last Updated Time
Cluster-A
v1.21.0+vmware.wcp.2-vsc0.0.13-1...
v1.22.6+vmware.1-vsc0.0.15-1970577
Not updated yet

Figure 177: Supervisor Cluster Updates Available

To upgrade the Supervisor Cluster, click on the "Apply Updates". This will deploy a new version of the Supervisor Cluster. You may recall way back when the first Supervisor Cluster was installed, five IP addresses were set aside. Three were for the nodes, one was for the API server/etcd, and there was one additional one set aside. Well, the purpose of that fifth IP address should now be clear. It is used to roll out an additional, upgraded Supervisor control plane node. This mechanism maintains quorum in the cluster whilst the upgrade of the other nodes takes place.

Namespaces
cormac-ns
SupervisorControlPlaneVM (1)
SupervisorControlPlaneVM (2)
SupervisorControlPlaneVM (3)
SupervisorControlPlaneVM (4)

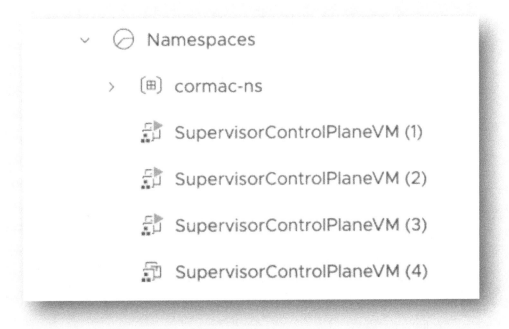

Figure 178: Supervisor Control Plane VM Updates

Once the new SV Control Plane VM is powered on and configured onto the management network and the workload network, the rolling upgrade will proceed with the older version nodes removed and new version nodes added to the Supervisor Cluster. On a Supervisor Cluster that has been through several updates, the Supervisor Control Plane numbering sequence could be very high. This process can take as long as the initial deployment of workload management since all of the Supervisor control plane nodes have to be redeployed and reconfigured. Note however that this has no impact on the TKG workload clusters that have been deployed with TKG Service. These clusters are not impacted by the Supervisor Cluster update.

Automatic Upgrades of Supervisor Cluster

If vCenter Server is upgraded to a release which no longer supports the current version of Kubernetes used on the Supervisor Cluster, the Supervisor Cluster will undergo an automatic upgrade to the supported release. No vSphere administrator intervention is required at this point. It would be a very good idea to check the vCenter Server Release Notes for any new update, and check to see if the Supervisor Cluster is still on a supported release, or whether an automatic update will occur when the vCenter Server is updated. This will avoid being caught unaware of such an activity, resulting in a longer maintenance window than originally planned.

TKG Workload Cluster Update

vSphere with Tanzu also supports three versions of upstream Kubernetes in the TKG Service. Be aware that if TKG workload clusters are running a Kubernetes version that is no longer supported, the TKG cluster will be automatically updated to keep it supported. Therefore, after the Supervisor Cluster has been updated, the TKG workload clusters may also automatically start to update as well. Like the Supervisor Cluster, workload cluster nodes should begin to deploy and replace the existing cluster nodes in a rolling fashion. This may also happen if there is a critical patch that needs to be applied to the OS image used by the cluster nodes.

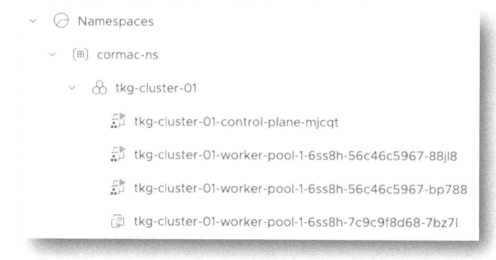

Figure 179: TKG Cluster Updates

If the current version of a TKG cluster is still supported even after an update to a new Supervisor version, it is possible that the updates introduced new versions of Kubernetes. Thus, the Platform Operator might like to update the version of your TKG workload clusters and leverage some of the new enhancements found in the later releases. There is no UI-driven mechanism to do an upgrade of a TKG cluster in vSphere with Tanzu. Instead, the cluster must be edited using *kubectl edit* and the version number changed. This will automatically instigate an upgrade of the TKG cluster to the desired version.

The following procedure describes how to upgrade a TKG cluster. First, login to the vSphere Namespace context, and query for any Tanzu Kubernetes Grid clusters.

```
% kubectl vsphere login \
--vsphere-username administrator@vsphere.local \
--server=https://supervisor \
--insecure-skip-tls-verify \
--tanzu-kubernetes-cluster-namespace cormac-ns \
--tanzu-kubernetes-cluster-name tkg-cluster-01

KUBECTL_VSPHERE_PASSWORD environment variable is not set. Please enter the password below
Password:
Logged in successfully.

You have access to the following contexts:
   supervisor
   cormac-ns

If the context you wish to use is not in this list, you may need to try
logging in again later, or contact your cluster administrator.

To change context, use `kubectl config use-context <workload name>`

% kubectl get tkc
NAME            CP  WK  TKR NAME                             AGE  READY  TKR COMPATIBLE
UPDATES AVAILABLE
tkg-cluster-01  1   2   v1.20.7---vmware.1-tkg.1.7fb9067    4d   True   True
[1.21.6+vmware.1-tkg.1.b3d708a 1.20.12+vmware.1-tkg.1.b9a42f3]
```

The above command displays all Tanzu Kubernetes clusters (tkc). In the output, it is showing one cluster. However, the output also shows that there are two Tanzu Kubernetes releases (TKr) available for updating this Tanzu Kubernetes Cluster (TKC).

Note: There are currently two versions of TKC object types supported. The TKC upgrade method is dependent on the version of the API of the cluster object. The two supported versions of TKC are v1alpha1 and v1alpha2.

For v1alpha2, the `spec.topology.controlPlane.tkr.refernece.name` for the control plane and `spec.topology.nodePools[*].tkr.reference.name` for the workers both need to be modified by live editing the cluster yaml. Here is an edited cluster, with these fields populated with the new version (v1.21.6) of the image for the cluster. The image name can be displayed via the *kubectl get vmimage* command.

```
spec:
  distribution:
    fullVersion: v1.20.7+vmware.1-tkg.1.7fb9067
    version: ""
  settings:
    network:
      cni:
        name: antrea
      pods:
        cidrBlocks:
        - 192.168.0.0/16
      serviceDomain: cluster.local
      services:
        cidrBlocks:
        - 10.96.0.0/12
```

```
topology:
  controlPlane:
    replicas: 1
    storageClass: vsan-default-storage-policy
    tkr:
      reference:
        name: v1.21.6---vmware.1-tkg.1.b3d708a
    vmClass: guaranteed-small
  nodePools:
  - name: worker-pool-1
    replicas: 2
    storageClass: vsan-default-storage-policy
    tkr:
      reference:
        name: v1.21.6---vmware.1-tkg.1.b3d708a
    vmClass: guaranteed-small
```

After editing and saving the v1alpha2 TKC spec, the cluster should set READY to False after a moment or so.

```
% kubectl edit tkc/tkg-cluster-01
tanzukubernetescluster.run.tanzu.vmware.com/tkg-cluster-01 edited
```

```
% kubectl get tkc
NAME           CP WK  TKR NAME                          AGE   READY  TKR COMPATIBLE
tkg-cluster-01 1  2   v1.21.6---vmware.1-tkg.1.b3d708a  4d1h  False  True
```

In the vSphere UI, new node deployments should be visible, replacing the current nodes in the cluster with the newer images in a rolling upgrade fashion. Note that v1.21.6 is currently the latest version at the time of writing, and that there are no other updates available. After a number of minutes, the TKG cluster should be back online and ready.

```
% kubectl get tkc
NAME           CP WK  TKR NAME                          AGE   READY  TKR COMPATIBLE
tkg-cluster-01 1  2   v1.21.6---vmware.1-tkg.1.b3d708a  4d1h  True   True
```

That completes the upgrade overviews for vSphere with Tanzu.

Troubleshooting vSphere with Tanzu

So far, all the demonstrations that we have shown have worked seamlessly. But what if something goes wrong. In this section, we look at what you can do if things are not behaving as expected?

Restarting the WCP Service on vCenter

One step you might consider taking is restarting the WCP service which is essential for workload management, or the workload control plane. This could be useful if the WCP service on vCenter is not responding, or some tasks appear to be in a "stuck" state. For example, after a licensing expiry issue, I deleted the embedded image registry and then re-enabled it when the licensing issue was resolved. However, I noticed it would not create projects on re-enabling. After a restart of the service, it worked as expected, creating projects for new vSphere namespaces.

```
# vmon-cli -r wcp
Completed Restart service request.
```

It would also be useful to monitor the wcpsvc.log file shown later when the service is restarted.

Workload Management Logs on vCenter

Troubleshooting should normally begin with the vCenter Server. You may have observed something in the vSphere Client UI or in the outputs from one of the kubectl commands. Indeed, if the issue is with the deployment of Workload Management and the Supervisor Cluster has not been deployed, vCenter Server logs are the only place to look.

wcpsvc.log

This is a very verbose log and will show details about the creation of the Supervisor nodes. This log file is probably most useful in determining why a Supervisor Cluster did not get created. Once the Supervisor nodes are created, you will see attempts to reach the Supervisor Control Plane VIP over port 6443. If there is an issue with the VIP, and it never gets assigned to the control plane, or it is assigned but not reachable for some reason, then this will retry indefinitely to reach it. This is because, once again, Kubernetes is a desired state system.

```
# cd /var/log/vmware/wcp
# tail -f wcpsvc.log
```

vpxd.log

The standard vCenter operations logs. It could be useful to examine the state of the Supervisor control plane VMs from this log as well, using the virtual machine id reported in the wpcsvc.log. Usually good to review this log if there are problems with the Supervisor Cluster nodes getting created or initialized successfully.

```
# cd /var/log/vmware/vpxd
# tail -f vpxd.log
```

eam.log

This is the ESX Agent Manager log file. It is used by several vSphere features today, such as vSAN File Service, vSphere Cluster Services (vCLS) virtual machines for vSphere DRS and vSphere HA, as well as by the Supervisor Cluster. When there is a request to create virtual machines to make up the Supervisor Cluster, EAM received the request from the WCP service on vCenter Server and sends it onto VPXD to carry out the task of creating the VMs. It also monitors the progress of the rollout. If there are issues with the deployment of Supervisor nodes, this is also a useful place to check.

```
# cd /var/log/vmware/eam
# tail -f eam.log
```

Workload Management Logs on ESXi

When vSphere with Tanzu is configured with NSX-T, the spherelet component is added to the ESXi hosts. This could be useful when determining why ESXi hosts are not getting successfully added to the Supervisor cluster, or why Native Pods are not being successfully deployed. SSH to the ESXi host and monitor the spherelet.log file as follows.

```
[root@w4-hs4-i1501:~] cd /var/log
[root@w4-hs4-i1501:/var/log] tail -f spherelet.log
```

Supervisor Cluster Control Plane Node Access

Getting onto a Supervisor node can also be a very useful step in troubleshooting. You can use it to examine whether the Supervisor node started up and got configured successfully, or to determine if Kubernetes is running successfully. You might even need to drop in here to figure out why a particular service is not running the way it should be.

Warning: No changes to the cluster should be made directly from the Supervisor control plane nodes. This may cause the vCenter server to become confused about the actual state of the Supervisor cluster. Access to the control plane nodes should only be used to examine the state of the cluster and assist with troubleshooting. It should not be used to change anything.

The first step is to gain access. This is done from the vCenter Server once again. Run the following command to get the root password of the nodes. Then open an *ssh* session from vCenter to the Supervisor node and provide the password.

```
# cd /usr/lib/vmware-wcp/
# ./decryptK8Pwd.py
Read key from file

Connected to PSQL

Cluster: domain-c22:4df0badc-1655-40de-9181-3422d6c36a3e
IP: 192.168.51.151
PWD: S/*******WWI=
---------------------------------------------------------

# ssh root@192.168.51.151
FIPS mode initialized
The authenticity of host '192.168.51.151 (192.168.51.151)' can't be established.
ECDSA key fingerprint is SHA256:ZUkZUBD0C+tRHJEu3RDEPitgZ9qaceXZXPu9xmDgLcU.
Are you sure you want to continue connecting (yes/no)? yes
Warning: Permanently added '192.168.51.151' (ECDSA) to the list of known hosts.
Password: ********
 13:44:55 up 20:21,  0 users,  load average: 0.44, 0.54, 0.55

21 Security notice(s)
Run 'tdnf updateinfo info' to see the details.
```

Once logged in, kubectl commands may be issued.

```
root@422450f331929273e040fdfa576b1621 [ ~ ]# kubectl get nodes
NAME                                  STATUS ROLES                   AGE  VERSION
4224010ae4399578af7d5df4e7e80f1f      Ready  control-plane,master    20h  v1.21.0+vmware.wcp.2
42243f72ad9460bd8636d41ebcbc6abb      Ready  control-plane,master    20h  v1.21.0+vmware.wcp.2
422450f331929273e040fdfa576b1621      Ready  control-plane,master    20h  v1.21.0+vmware.wcp.2
```

Workload Management Logs on SV Control Plane Nodes

Now that we have access to the Supervisor Control Plane nodes, let's examine some of the supervisor control plane node logs next.

cloud-init.log

Once logged in, there are many troubleshooting steps a vSphere administrator can take. One useful thing to check on the Supervisor nodes is their initial configuration and start-up, and whether everything went ok. The `cloud-init.log` is in `/var/log`. It may look something like this. Again, there are a lot of content in this file, so I snipped a bunch of it. However, this log file should be somewhere to look if the Supervisor VMs are not coming online successfully.

```
# cat /var/log/cloud-init.log
2022-06-14 17:24:04,427 - util.py[DEBUG]: Cloud-init v. 21.3 running 'init' at Tue, 14 Jun
2022 17:24:04 +0000. Up 10.62 seconds.
2022-06-14 17:24:04,428 - main.py[DEBUG]: No kernel command line url found.
2022-06-14 17:24:04,428 - main.py[DEBUG]: Closing stdin.
2022-06-14 17:24:04,431 - util.py[DEBUG]: Writing to /var/log/cloud-init.log - ab: [644] 0
bytes
2022-06-14 17:24:04,432 - util.py[DEBUG]: Changing the ownership of /var/log/cloud-
init.log to 0:16
2022-06-14 17:24:04,432 - util.py[DEBUG]: Writing to /var/lib/cloud/data/python-version -
wb: [644] 3 bytes
2022-06-14 17:24:04,433 - subp.py[DEBUG]: Running command ['ip', 'addr', 'show'] with
allowed return codes [0] (shell=False, capture=True)
2022-06-14 17:24:04,449 - subp.py[DEBUG]: Running command ['ip', '-o', 'route', 'list']
with allowed return codes [0] (shell=False, capture=True)
2022-06-14 17:24:04,451 - subp.py[DEBUG]: Running command ['ip', '--oneline', '-6',
'route', 'list', 'table', 'all'] with allowed return codes [0, 1] (shell=False,
capture=True)
.
.
.--snip--
.
.
2022-06-14 17:24:05,953 - subp.py[DEBUG]: Running command ['ssh-keygen', '-t', 'ecdsa', '-
N', '', '-f', '/etc/ssh/ssh_host_ecdsa_key'] with allowed return codes [0] (shell=False,
capture=True)
2022-06-14 17:24:05,968 - subp.py[DEBUG]: Running command ['ssh-keygen', '-t', 'ed25519',
'-N', '', '-f', '/etc/ssh/ssh_host_ed25519_key'] with allowed return codes [0]
(shell=False, capture=True)
2022-06-14 17:24:05,982 - util.py[DEBUG]: Reading from /etc/ssh/ssh_host_rsa_key.pub
(quiet=False)
2022-06-14 17:24:05,982 - util.py[DEBUG]: Read 391 bytes from
/etc/ssh/ssh_host_rsa_key.pub
2022-06-14 17:24:05,982 - util.py[DEBUG]: Reading from /etc/ssh/ssh_host_ed25519_key.pub
(quiet=False)
2022-06-14 17:24:05,982 - util.py[DEBUG]: Read 91 bytes from
/etc/ssh/ssh_host_ed25519_key.pub
2022-06-14 17:24:05,982 - util.py[DEBUG]: Reading from /etc/ssh/ssh_host_ecdsa_key.pub
(quiet=False)
2022-06-14 17:24:05,982 - util.py[DEBUG]: Read 171 bytes from
/etc/ssh/ssh_host_ecdsa_key.pub
2022-06-14 17:24:05,983 - util.py[DEBUG]: Reading from /etc/ssh/sshd_config (quiet=False)
2022-06-14 17:24:05,983 - util.py[DEBUG]: Read 3294 bytes from /etc/ssh/sshd_config
2022-06-14 17:24:05,984 - util.py[DEBUG]: Reading from /root/.ssh/authorized_keys
(quiet=False)
2022-06-14 17:24:05,985 - util.py[DEBUG]: Read 15 bytes from /root/.ssh/authorized_keys
2022-06-14 17:24:05,985 - util.py[DEBUG]: Writing to /root/.ssh/authorized_keys - wb:
[600] 15 bytes
2022-06-14 17:24:05,986 - handlers.py[DEBUG]: finish: init-network/config-ssh: SUCCESS:
config-ssh ran successfully
2022-06-14 17:24:05,986 - main.py[DEBUG]: Ran 15 modules with 0 failures
2022-06-14 17:24:05,987 - atomic_helper.py[DEBUG]: Atomically writing to file
/var/lib/cloud/data/status.json (via temporary file /var/lib/cloud/data/tmpzzlxctr6) - w:
[644] 487 bytes/chars
```

```
2022-06-14 17:24:05,987 - util.py[DEBUG]: Reading from /proc/uptime (quiet=False)
2022-06-14 17:24:05,987 - util.py[DEBUG]: Read 12 bytes from /proc/uptime
2022-06-14 17:24:05,987 - util.py[DEBUG]: cloud-init mode 'init' took 1.593 seconds (1.59)
2022-06-14 17:24:05,987 - handlers.py[DEBUG]: finish: init-network: SUCCESS: searching for
network datasources
```

As well as the `cloud-init.log`, there is a `cloud-init-output.log` file which has the outputs from the various command that were run during the initialization of the VM. This can be a useful place to check that everything went ok with the creation of the Supervisor VMs in the Supervisor Cluster, or narrow down if something failed during initialization of the nodes/VMs.

configure-wcp.log

On occasion, you might find that only one supervisor control plane node is powered on. A good place to check why the rest of the cluster failed to come up successfully might be found in the following logs. These detail the configure steps that were/are taking place on the node to configure it for Workload Management.

- `/var/log/vmware-imc/configure-wcp.log`
- `/var/log/vmware-imc/configure-wcp.stderr`

kubelet

One other thing to check on the Supervisor Cluster nodes is the status of the `kubelet`, the Kubernetes node agent. Each Supervisor node will have (or should have) one running. This can be examined as follows:

```
# systemctl status kubelet
● kubelet.service - kubelet: The Kubernetes Node Agent
   Loaded: loaded (/etc/systemd/system/kubelet.service; enabled; vendor preset: enabled)
  Drop-In: /etc/systemd/system/kubelet.service.d
           └─10-kubeadm.conf
   Active: active (running) since Tue 2022-06-14 17:31:05 UTC; 21h ago
     Docs: http://kubernetes.io/docs/
 Main PID: 47770 (kubelet)
    Tasks: 23 (limit: 19179)
   Memory: 91.2M
   CGroup: /system.slice/kubelet.service
           ├─29561 /usr/bin/sleep 180s
           ├─47770 /usr/bin/kubelet --bootstrap-kubeconfig=/etc/kubernetes/bootstrap-
kubelet.conf --kubeconfig=/etc/kubernetes/kubelet.conf --config=/var/lib/kubele>
           └─47778 /bin/bash /usr/lib/vmware-wcp/kubelet-watchdog/kubelet --bootstrap-
kubeconfig=/etc/kubernetes/bootstrap-kubelet.conf --kubeconfig=/etc/kubernetes>
```

It should be in an active (running) if all is well. If something is not right, check the logs using the following command.

```
# journalctl -u kubelet
-- Logs begin at Tue 2022-06-14 17:23:55 UTC, end at Wed 2022-06-15 14:51:04 UTC. --
Jun 14 17:23:57 changeme systemd[1]: Started kubelet: The Kubernetes Node Agent.
Jun 14 17:23:57 changeme kubelet[766]: kubelet-watchdog: Running /usr/lib/vmware-
wcp/kubelet-watchdog/kubelet as pid=766 on changeme
Jun 14 17:23:57 changeme kubelet[766]: /usr/lib/vmware-wcp/kubelet-watchdog/kubelet: line
251: /usr/bin/kubelet: No such file or directory
Jun 14 17:23:57 changeme systemd[1]: kubelet.service: Main process exited, code=exited,
status=127/n/a
Jun 14 17:23:57 changeme systemd[1]: kubelet.service: Failed with result 'exit-code'.
```

```
Jun 14 17:24:07 None systemd[1]: kubelet.service: Service RestartSec=10s expired,
scheduling restart.
Jun 14 17:24:07 None systemd[1]: kubelet.service: Scheduled restart job, restart counter
is at 1.
Jun 14 17:24:07 None systemd[1]: Stopped kubelet: The Kubernetes Node Agent.
Jun 14 17:24:07 None systemd[1]: Started kubelet: The Kubernetes Node Agent.
Jun 14 17:24:07 None kubelet[3020]: kubelet-watchdog: Running /usr/lib/vmware-wcp/kubelet-
watchdog/kubelet as pid=3020 on None
Jun 14 17:24:07 None kubelet[3020]: /usr/lib/vmware-wcp/kubelet-watchdog/kubelet: line
251: /usr/bin/kubelet: No such file or directory
Jun 14 17:24:07 None kubelet[3020]: kubelet-watchdog: Monitoring kubelet process 3020
```

Again, be careful not to get distracted by errors that are commonplace, and may have no bearing on the issue you are trying to solve. Familiarise yourself with these outputs when the system is healthy so you know what to expect.

etcdctl

The command *etcdctl* enables the status of the etcd configuration to be checked. All 3 Supervisor control plane node should be available to maintain the highly available etcd key-value store. This can be checked by running the command *etcdctl member list* on the Supervisor control plane node.

```
# etcdctl member list
6e7efece3a39d5f5, started, 4224410461c3458fe2cd4e70a657e3c5, https://192.168.51.153:2380,
https://192.168.51.153:2379, false
8c3f83234691f037, started, 4224504ccbbf33eb915c46b9480d3004, https://192.168.51.152:2380,
https://192.168.51.152:2379, false
ac43f7d64142d5d7, started, 4224b3558391211cc3cfb0a4f284a608, https://192.168.51.155:2380,
https://192.168.51.155:2379, false
```

crictl

The Supervisor control plane nodes ship with a tool called *crictl*. This is a CLI tool for CRI-compatible container runtimes. This is because docker is not the container runtime on the supervisor control plane nodes, so the docker CLI cannot be used to examine containers. If there are issues with the Supervisor control plane starting successfully, *crictl* could prove very useful as it allows container status to be examined, as well as logs displayed, as per the following example which first list containers, and then displays the logs from one of the containers.

```
# crictl ps
CONTAINER       IMAGE          CREATED      STATE     NAME              ATT  POD ID
f9c759fe62bd6   8b68d15d90431  6 days ago   Running   hostvalidator     2    af0cea2c89fc9
df35080468fd7   a7f39213cb509  6 days ago   Running   manager           2    fddda35126c4f
f1300c70b1f7e   e31e0a18bb701  6 days ago   Running   kube-rbac-proxy   1    3f95d060e655e
f735aae47dc7e   8b68d15d90431  6 days ago   Running   manager           1    3f95d060e655e
5dd3f67af4ebd   3d6ad8e999c7f  6 days ago   Running   manager           1    2b8fcf185a5de
5344922810d29   e31e0a18bb701  6 days ago   Running   kube-rbac-proxy   1    814a695437ac8
7abb83d1ea158   c769c2adfff0e  6 days ago   Running   manager           1    59b7553fd6b43
.
.
419e4799f9340   67756bacecc6f  6 days ago   Running   kube-contlr-mgr   3    e5b7faf175203
```

```
# crictl logs 419e4799f9340
Flag --address has been deprecated, This flag has no effect now and will be removed in
v1.24.
Flag --port has been deprecated, This flag has no effect now and will be removed in v1.24.
I0623 15:50:19.894526      1 serving.go:375] Generated self-signed cert in-memory
```

```
I0623 15:50:20.483339      1 controllermanager.go:186] Version: v1.22.6+vmware.wcp.2
W0623 15:50:20.485410      1 secure_serving.go:69] Use of insecure cipher
'TLS_ECDHE_ECDSA_WITH_AES_128_CBC_SHA256' detected.
W0623 15:50:20.485426      1 secure_serving.go:69] Use of insecure cipher
'TLS_RSA_WITH_AES_128_CBC_SHA256' detected.
W0623 15:50:20.485431      1 secure_serving.go:69] Use of insecure cipher
'TLS_ECDHE_RSA_WITH_AES_128_CBC_SHA256' detected.
I0623 15:50:20.486775      1 dynamic_cafile_content.go:155] "Starting controller"
name="client-ca-bundle::/etc/vmware/wcp/tls/vmca.pem"
I0623 15:50:20.486977      1 dynamic_cafile_content.go:155] "Starting controller"
name="request-header::/etc/kubernetes/pki/front-proxy-ca.crt"
I0623 15:50:20.487316      1 secure_serving.go:216] Serving securely on 127.0.0.1:10257
I0623 15:50:20.487399      1 tlsconfig.go:345] "Starting
DynamicServingCertificateController"
I0623 15:50:20.489969      1 leaderelection.go:248] attempting to acquire leader lease
kube-system/kube-controller-manager...
```

Supervisor Cluster Pod logs

There are significant number of Pods on the Supervisor Cluster. Some of them you might be able to recognise at this point. For example, core Kubernetes Pods are in the `kube-system` namespace. All the Pods that are in the `vmware-system-capw` namespace are related to ClusterAPI and are responsible for the lifecycle management of TKG clusters via the TKG service. The vsphere-csi-controller Pod for storage is found in `vmware-system-csi` namespace. Depending on the load balancer, different namespaces exist for the different solutions. For NSX-T and the NCP, the namespace is `vmware-system-nsx`. For NSX ALB, the namespace is called `vmware-system-ako`, and for the HA-Proxy, the namespace is called `vmware-system-lbapi`. The `vmware-system-tkg` namespace has Pods related to the TKG service, and `vmware-system-vmop` is the namespace where the VM Service functionality is found.

The recommendation is to use commands such as *kubectl get ns -A* and *kubectl get pods -A* to get a good idea about the running Pods on your Supervisor Cluster, and which namespace they reside in.

Troubleshooting Load Balancer Controller Pods

When discussing the NSX ALB, it was mentioned that the Kubernetes cluster has an AKO (Avi Kubernetes Operator) installed, and this communicates with the NSX ALB to create virtual services such as load balancers on behalf of Kubernetes objects. Now that we know how to access the Supervisor Cluster, we can examine the logs of this Pod that does that communication. This can be useful when the NSX ALB is not behaving as expected when the Supervisor Cluster has been deployed as part of Workload Management. Note that the namespace below will be the same on your system, but the AKO Pod name should be different.

```
# kubectl get pods -A | grep ako
vmware-system-ako                              vmware-system-ako-ako-controller-manager-
548f76584f-gvbm7         1/1     Running    0       20h

# kubectl logs vmware-system-ako-ako-controller-manager-54..4f-gvbm7 -n vmware-system-ako
2022-06-14T17:34:52.029Z INFO    api/api.go:52    Setting route for GET /api/status
2022-06-14T17:34:52.029Z INFO    ako-main/main.go:65    AKO is running with version: ob-
18719385-ee6e861-5a23951
2022-06-14T17:34:52.029Z INFO    api/api.go:110   Starting API server at :9999
2022-06-14T17:34:52.029Z INFO    ako-main/main.go:71    We are running inside kubernetes
cluster. Won't use kubeconfig files.
2022-06-14T17:34:52.126Z INFO    ako-main/main.go:122    Kubernetes cluster apiserver
version 1.21
```

```
2022-06-14T17:34:52.128Z INFO     utils/ingress.go:36       networking.k8s.io/v1/IngressClass
not found/enabled on cluster: ingressclasses.networking.k8s.io is forbidden: User
"system:serviceaccount:vmware-system-ako:default" cannot list resource "ingressclasses" in
API group "networking.k8s.io" at the cluster scope
2022-06-14T17:34:52.128Z INFO     utils/utils.go:167       Initializing configmap informer
in vmware-system-ako
2022-06-14T17:34:52.128Z INFO     lib/cni.go:96    Skipped initializing dynamic informers
2022-06-14T17:34:52.371Z INFO     utils/avi_rest_utils.go:126      Setting the client
version to the current controller version 21.1.4
2022-06-14T17:34:52.863Z INFO     cache/avi_ctrl_clients.go:74      Setting the client
version to 21.1.4
2022-06-14T17:34:54.012Z INFO     cache/controller_obj_cache.go:2299      Avi cluster state
is CLUSTER_UP_NO_HA
2022-06-14T17:34:54.092Z INFO     cache/controller_obj_cache.go:2827      Setting cloud
vType: CLOUD_VCENTER
2022-06-14T17:34:54.180Z INFO     cache/controller_obj_cache.go:2972      No Marker
configured usable networks found.
2022-06-14T17:34:54.180Z INFO     lib/lib.go:162   Setting AKOUser: ako-domain-c22 for Avi
Objects
2022-06-14T17:34:54.230Z INFO     cache/controller_obj_cache.go:2666      No Marker
configured Service Engine Group found.
2022-06-14T17:34:54.230Z INFO     cache/controller_obj_cache.go:2559      Setting Default-
Group for VS placement.
2022-06-14T17:34:54.231Z INFO     cache/controller_obj_cache.go:2566      Skipping the
check for SE group labels
2022-06-14T17:34:54.231Z INFO     cache/controller_obj_cache.go:2482      All values
verified for advanced L4, proceeding with bootup
```

A similar approach can be taken when using NSX-T. The NCP Pod (NSX Container Plugin) is called `nsx-ncp` and is in the `vmware-system-nsx` namespace on the Supervisor Cluster. If NSX-T is not responding correctly to requests to build networking infrastructure from vSphere with Tanzu operations, then this is a good place to start looking for a root cause.

Caution: Keep in mind that Kubernetes is a desired state / eventually consistent system. This means that there may be errors in the logs which eventually get resolved as the deployment proceeds over time. It might be a good idea to spend some time looking at these logs on a healthy system to familiarise yourself with what sorts of warnings and errors are expected, and which ones are unexpected.

Troubleshooting the TKG Service

A very common mistake is to attempt to create a TKG cluster (TKC) with a VM class which is not available in the vSphere Namespace. This was not so easy to troubleshoot in earlier versions of vSphere with Tanzu.

In the latest releases, if you try to build a cluster with a missing VM class or missing image, you get notified immediately, as per the following examples:

Missing or incorrect VM Class

The following error is reported when the VM class is not available in the namespace. This could be because the correct VM Class has not been associated with the namespace.

```
% kubectl apply -f tanzucluster-v1alpha2-v1.21.6.yaml
Error from server (could not find spec.topology.controlPlane.class "guaranteed-small",
could not find VMClass "guaranteed-small" for nodepool worker-pool-1): error when creating
```

```
"tanzucluster-v1alpha2-v1.20.7.yaml": admission webhook
"default.validating.tanzukubernetescluster.run.tanzu.vmware.com" denied the request: could
not find spec.topology.controlPlane.class "guaranteed-small", could not find VMClass
"guaranteed-small" for nodepool worker-pool-1
```

Missing or incorrect VM image

The following error is reported when the VM image is not available in the namespace. This could be because the correct content library has not been associated with the namespace.

```
% kubectl apply -f tanzucluster-v1alpha2-v1.21.6.yaml
Error from server (unable to get Kubernetes distribution by ref
'&ObjectReference{Kind:,Namespace:,Name:v1.21.7---vmware.1-
tkg.1.b3d708a,UID:,APIVersion:,ResourceVersion:,FieldPath:,}':
tanzukubernetesreleases.run.tanzu.vmware.com "v1.21.7---vmware.1-tkg.1.b3d708a" not
found): error when creating "tanzucluster-v1alpha2-v1.20.7.yaml": admission webhook
"version.mutating.tanzukubernetescluster.run.tanzu.vmware.com" denied the request: unable
to get Kubernetes distribution by ref '&ObjectReference{Kind:,Namespace:,Name:v1.21.7---
vmware.1-tkg.1.b3d708a,UID:,APIVersion:,ResourceVersion:,FieldPath:,}':
tanzukubernetesreleases.run.tanzu.vmware.com "v1.21.7---vmware.1-tkg.1.b3d708a" not found
```

Missing or incorrect StorageClass

The following error is reported when the storage class is not available in the namespace. This could be because the correct storage policy has not been associated with the namespace.

```
% kubectl apply -f tanzucluster-v1alpha2-v1.21.6.yaml
Error from server (storage class is not valid for control plane VM: StorageClass 'vsan-
dfault-storage-policy' is not assigned for namespace 'demo-ns', storage class is not valid
for nodepool worker-pool-1: StorageClass 'vsan-dfault-storage-policy' is not assigned for
namespace 'demo-ns'): error when creating "tanzucluster-v1alpha2-v1.21.6.yaml": admission
webhook "default.validating.tanzukubernetescluster.run.tanzu.vmware.com" denied the
request: storage class is not valid for control plane VM: StorageClass 'vsan-dfault-
storage-policy' is not assigned for namespace 'demo-ns', storage class is not valid for
nodepool worker-pool-1: StorageClass 'vsan-dfault-storage-policy' is not assigned for
namespace 'demo-ns'
```

kubectl get / describe

A *kubectl get* and *kubectl describe* on the Tanzu Kubernetes Cluster (TKC) can also be useful during a deployment. Once again, be cognizant of the fact that it is a desired state / eventually consistent system so errors will be shown during a normal healthy deployment as well. Look at the Status section in the describe outputs below. Note the errors from the various addon components while the cluster is on its way up, which eventually resolve. I have included a snippet from various *kubectl describe tkc* commands below, taken from different times during a TKC deployment.

```
% kubectl get tkc
NAME                CONTROL  WORKER   TKR NAME                             AGE   READY   TKR
tkg-cluster-01      1                 v1.21.6---vmware.1-tkg.1.b3d708a     7s            True
```

At this point, the nodes have not yet come online. The addons are still waiting for the nodes to be ready.

```
% kubectl describe tkc tkg-cluster-01
Name:          tkg-cluster-01
Namespace:     demo-ns
Labels:        run.tanzu.vmware.com/tkr=v1.21.6---vmware.1-tkg.1.b3d708a
Annotations:   <none>
```

```
API Version:   run.tanzu.vmware.com/v1alpha2
Kind:          TanzuKubernetesCluster
    .
    .
    .
Status:
  API Endpoints:
    Host:  10.203.182.132
    Port:  6443
  Conditions:
    Last Transition Time:  2022-06-21T08:50:23Z
    Message:               Waiting for control planes to be ready
    Reason:                WaitingForControlPlane
    Severity:              Info
    Status:                False
    Type:                  Ready
    Last Transition Time:  2022-06-21T08:50:23Z
    Message:               Waiting for control planes to be ready
    Reason:                WaitingForControlPlane
    Severity:              Info
    Status:                False
    Type:                  ControlPlaneReady
    Last Transition Time:  2022-06-21T08:50:20Z
    Message:               node pools [] are unknown, [] are failed, [worker-pool-1] are
updating
    Reason:                NodePoolsUpdating
    Severity:              Info
    Status:                False
    Type:                  NodePoolsReady
    Last Transition Time:  2022-06-21T08:50:20Z
    Message:               0/1 Control Plane Node(s) healthy. 0/2 Worker Node(s) healthy
    Reason:                WaitingForNodesHealthy
    Severity:              Info
    Status:                False
    Type:                  NodesHealthy
    Last Transition Time:  2022-05-13T07:57:05Z
    Status:                True
    Type:                  TanzuKubernetesReleaseCompatible
    Last Transition Time:  2022-05-13T07:57:07Z
    Reason:                NoUpdates
    Status:                False
    Type:                  UpdatesAvailable
  Phase:                   creating
  Total Worker Replicas:   2
Events:                    <none>
```

A short time later, the TKC control plane node(s) are now online but the controllers and other objects for the addons are not yet available, so there are a lot of 'not found' message with 'ProvisioningFailed' as the reason. As stated, this is expected to resolve as more components come online.

```
% kubectl describe tkc tkg-cluster-01
    .
    .
Status:
  Addons:
    Conditions:
      Last Transition Time:  2022-06-21T08:51:57Z
      Status:                True
      Type:                  Provisioned
    Name:                    defaultpsp
    Type:                    PSP
    Version:                 v1.21.6+vmware.1-tkg.1.b3d708a
```

```
    Conditions:
       Last Transition Time:  2022-06-21T08:51:58Z
       Message:                unable to retrieve system:coredns clusterrole from the guest
cluster: clusterroles.rbac.authorization.k8s.io "system:coredns" not found
       Reason:                 ProvisioningFailed
       Severity:               Warning
       Status:                 False
       Type:                   Provisioned
    Name:
    Type:                      DNS
    Conditions:
       Last Transition Time:  2022-06-21T08:51:58Z
       Message:                unable to retrieve kube-proxy daemonset from the guest
cluster: daemonsets.apps "kube-proxy" not found
       Reason:                 ProvisioningFailed
       Severity:               Warning
       Status:                 False
       Type:                   Provisioned
    Name:
    Type:                      Proxy
    Conditions:
       Last Transition Time:  2022-06-21T08:51:58Z
       Message:                failed to update owner reference for antrea secret in
supervisor cluster: secrets "tkg-cluster-01-antrea" not found
       Reason:                 ProvisioningFailed
       Severity:               Warning
       Status:                 False
       Type:                   Provisioned
    .

    .
    Name:                      pvcsi
    Type:                      CSI
    Version:                   v2.3.0-d154d1c
    Name:
    Type:                      AuthService
    Name:
    Type:                      MetricsServer
  API Endpoints:
    Host:   10.203.182.132
    Port:   6443
  Conditions:
    Last Transition Time:  2022-06-21T08:52:00Z
    Message:                5 errors occurred:
                           * failed to configure DNS for /, Kind= demo-ns/tkg-cluster-01:
unable to retrieve system:coredns clusterrole from the guest cluster:
clusterroles.rbac.authorization.k8s.io "system:coredns" not found
                           * failed to configure kube-proxy for /, Kind= demo-ns/tkg-
cluster-01: unable to retrieve kube-proxy daemonset from the guest cluster:
daemonsets.apps "kube-proxy" not found
                           * failed to configure CNI for /, Kind= demo-ns/tkg-cluster-01:
failed to update owner reference for antrea secret in supervisor cluster: secrets "tkg-
cluster-01-antrea" not found
                           * failed to configure AuthService for /, Kind= demo-ns/tkg-
cluster-01: secrets "tkg-cluster-01-auth-svc-cert" not found
                           * failed to configure Metrics Server for /, Kind= demo-ns/tkg-
cluster-01: secrets "tkg-cluster-01-metrics-server-cert" not found

    Reason:                 AddonsReconciliationFailed
    Severity:               Warning
    Status:                 False
    Type:                   Ready
    Last Transition Time:  2022-06-21T08:52:00Z
    Message:                5 errors occurred:
```

```
                                * failed to configure DNS for /, Kind= demo-ns/tkg-cluster-01:
unable to retrieve system:coredns clusterrole from the guest cluster:
clusterroles.rbac.authorization.k8s.io "system:coredns" not found
                                * failed to configure kube-proxy for /, Kind= demo-ns/tkg-
cluster-01: unable to retrieve kube-proxy daemonset from the guest cluster:
daemonsets.apps "kube-proxy" not found
                                * failed to configure CNI for /, Kind= demo-ns/tkg-cluster-01:
failed to update owner reference for antrea secret in supervisor cluster: secrets "tkg-
cluster-01-antrea" not found
                                * failed to configure AuthService for /, Kind= demo-ns/tkg-
cluster-01: secrets "tkg-cluster-01-auth-svc-cert" not found
                                * failed to configure Metrics Server for /, Kind= demo-ns/tkg-
cluster-01: secrets "tkg-cluster-01-metrics-server-cert" not found


  .
  .
  Phase:                     creating
  Total Worker Replicas:     2
Events:                      <none>
```

A little later, the worker nodes get configured and addons get applied. Some addon installations do not need the worker nodes to come online, whereas others do. You can see messages relating to the NodePool status.

```
% kubectl describe tkc tkg-cluster-01
  .
  .
Status:
  Addons:
    Conditions:
      Last Transition Time:  2022-06-21T08:51:57Z
      Status:                True
      Type:                  Provisioned
    Name:                    defaultpsp
    Type:                    PSP
    Version:                 v1.21.6+vmware.1-tkg.1.b3d708a
    Conditions:
      Last Transition Time:  2022-06-21T08:52:01Z
      Status:                True
      Type:                  Provisioned
    Name:                    CoreDNS
    Type:                    DNS
    Version:                 v1.8.0_vmware.9
    Conditions:
      Last Transition Time:  2022-06-21T08:52:01Z
      Status:                True
      Type:                  Provisioned
  .
  .
    Name:                    metrics-server
    Type:                    MetricsServer
    Version:                 v0.4.0+vmware.1
  API Endpoints:
    Host:  10.203.182.132
    Port:  6443
  Conditions:
    Last Transition Time:    2022-06-21T08:52:17Z
    Message:                 node pools [] are unknown, [] are failed, [worker-pool-1] are
updating
    Reason:                  NodePoolsUpdating
    Severity:                Info
    Status:                  False
    Type:                    Ready
```

```
          Last Transition Time:  2022-06-21T08:52:08Z
          Status:                True
          Type:                  AddonsReady
          Last Transition Time:  2022-06-21T08:52:17Z
          Status:                True
          Type:                  ControlPlaneReady
          Last Transition Time:  2022-06-21T08:50:20Z
          Message:               node pools [] are unknown, [] are failed, [worker-pool-1] are
updating
          Reason:                NodePoolsUpdating
          Severity:              Info
          Status:                False
          Type:                  NodePoolsReady
          Last Transition Time:  2022-06-21T08:52:41Z
          Message:               1/1 Control Plane Node(s) healthy. 0/2 Worker Node(s) healthy
          Reason:                WaitingForNodesHealthy
          Severity:              Info
          Status:                False
          Type:                  NodesHealthy
          Last Transition Time:  2022-06-21T08:51:57Z
          Status:                True
          Type:                  ProviderServiceAccountsReady
          Last Transition Time:  2022-06-21T08:51:57Z
          Status:                True
          Type:                  RoleBindingSynced
          Last Transition Time:  2022-06-21T08:51:58Z
          Status:                True
          Type:                  ServiceDiscoveryReady
          Last Transition Time:  2022-06-21T08:51:57Z
          Status:                True
          Type:                  StorageClassSynced
          Last Transition Time:  2022-05-13T07:57:05Z
          Status:                True
          Type:                  TanzuKubernetesReleaseCompatible
          Last Transition Time:  2022-05-13T07:57:07Z
          Reason:                NoUpdates
          Status:                False
          Type:                  UpdatesAvailable
  Phase:                         creating
  Total Worker Replicas:         2
Events:                          <none>
```

Eventually, the TKC cluster comes ready, and the events reports a message to say that the TKC has entered running phase.

```
% kubectl describe tkc tkg-cluster-01
.
.
Phase:                      running
  Total Worker Replicas:    2
Events:
  Type      Reason          Age    From
Message
  ----      ------          ----   ----
-------
  Normal    PhaseChanged    78s    vmware-system-tkg/vmware-system-tkg-controller-
manager/tanzukubernetescluster-status-controller   cluster changes from creating phase to
running phase


% kubectl get tkc
NAME              CONTROL WORKER   TKR NAME                            AGE     READY   TKR
tkg-cluster-01    1       2        v1.21.6---vmware.1-tkg.1.b3d708a    6m2s    True    True
```

Troubleshooting the VM Service

Let's look at another service now, the VM Service. We saw how to deploy virtual machines with the VM Service back in chapter 6. Like we saw with the TKG, obvious items such as VM image, VM Class and so on are checked, and report on.

Missing or incorrect VM image

The following error is reported when the VM image is not available in the namespace. This could be because the correct content library has not been associated with the namespace.

```
% kubectl apply -f ubuntu-vm.yaml
configmap/ubuntu-vm-configmap-broken created
Error from server (spec.imageName: Invalid value: "ubuntu-20-1633387172196":
VirtualMachineImage.vmoperator.vmware.com "ubuntu-20-1633387172196" not found): error when
creating "ubuntu-vm.yaml": admission webhook
"default.validating.virtualmachine.vmoperator.vmware.com" denied the request:
spec.imageName: Invalid value: "ubuntu-20-1633387172196":
VirtualMachineImage.vmoperator.vmware.com "ubuntu-20-1633387172196" not found
```

Missing ConfigMap

In this example, a deployment of a VM through the VM Service was attempted, but there was an a mistake with the name of the ConfigMap. The VM was deployed referencing a non-existing ConfigMap for customization. Let's then see if we can determine what the problem is.

```
% kubectl apply -f ubuntu-vm.yaml
virtualmachine.vmoperator.vmware.com/my-ubuntu-vm created
configmap/ubuntu-vm-configmap-broken created
```

It appears to have deployed ok. Let's try to have a closer look. Note that when I query virtual machines this command also returns the TKC nodes. I can simply specify the name of the VM to get details about it on its own.

```
% kubectl get vm
NAME                                                  POWERSTATE   AGE
my-ubuntu-vm                                                       8s
tkg-cluster-01-control-plane-ls79h                    poweredOn    17h
tkg-cluster-01-worker-pool-1-6ss8h-c7db67f69-9dx78    poweredOn    16h
tkg-cluster-01-worker-pool-1-6ss8h-c7db67f69-lq42q    poweredOn    16h

% kubectl get vm my-ubuntu-vm
NAME            POWERSTATE   AGE
my-ubuntu-vm                 15s

% kubectl describe vm my-ubuntu-vm
Name:        my-ubuntu-vm
Namespace:   cormac-ns
  .
  .
Spec:
  Class Name:  best-effort-small
  Image Name:  ubuntu-20-1633387172196
  Network Interfaces:
    Network Name:  vm-32-dvs-a
    Network Type:  vsphere-distributed
  Power State:     poweredOn
  Storage Class:   vsan-default-storage-policy
```

```
Vm Metadata:
  Config Map Name:   ubuntu-vm-configmap
  Transport:         OvfEnv
Events:              <none>
```

So nothing about a missing ConfigMap here. However, there is no task about deploying the VM that appears in the vSphere UI either. Something is wrong. Where do I look now? We need to take a look at the VMOP controllers, the Pods that take care of VM Operations. Here they are:

```
% kubectl get pods -n vmware-system-vmop
NAME                                                      READY   STATUS    RESTARTS   AGE
vmware-system-vmop-controller-manager-7b9544dcdb-2dqm2    2/2     Running   0          17h
vmware-system-vmop-controller-manager-7b9544dcdb-76gwz    2/2     Running   0          17h
vmware-system-vmop-controller-manager-7b9544dcdb-bqjbr    2/2     Running   0          17h
vmware-system-vmop-hostvalidator-5ff465c7d-h67mp          1/1     Running   0          17h
```

So we need to see which one of these picked up our request to create a VM. Rather than displaying all the logs from when the controller started, let's look at just the last 30 minutes. Also notice that there are 2 containers in each Pod, so we could display the logs from all containers using `--all-containers`, or just specify the container we want to view. Note that if you try to look at the logs without specifying a container, the error will return the names of the container in the Pod, and tells you to choose one.

```
% kubectl logs vmware-system-vmop-controller-manager-7b9544dcdb-bqjbr \
-n vmware-system-vmop
error: a container name must be specified for pod vmware-system-vmop-controller-manager-
7b9544dcdb-bqjbr, choose one of: [manager kube-rbac-proxy]
```

With this information, we can ask to look at the manager container logs for the last 30 minutes.

```
% kubectl logs vmware-system-vmop-controller-manager-7b9544dcdb-bqjbr \
-n vmware-system-vmop manager \
--since=30m
I0621 09:21:26.802288       1 response.go:42] vmware-system-vmop-controller-manager-
7b9544dcdb-bqjbr/default-validate-vmoperator-vmware-com-v1alpha1-virtualmachine/cormac-
ns/my-ubuntu-vm "msg"="validation denied"  "code"=422 "reason"="spec.imageName: Invalid
value: \"ubuntu-20-1633387172196\": VirtualMachineImage.vmoperator.vmware.com \"ubuntu-20-
1633387172196\" not found"
```

Ah! This isn't the controller we want as it is reporting our previous error, the missing or incorrect image. Let's try another controller.

```
% kubectl logs vmware-system-vmop-controller-manager-7b9544dcdb-76gwz \
-n vmware-system-vmop manager \
--since=10m
.
.
I0621 09:25:55.707352       1 virtualmachine_controller.go:352] VirtualMachine
"msg"="Reconciling VirtualMachine" "name"="cormac-ns/tkg-cluster-01-worker-pool-1-6ss8h-
c7db67f69-9dx78"
E0621 09:25:55.710380       1 virtualmachine_controller.go:376] VirtualMachine
"msg"="Failed to reconcile VirtualMachine" "error"="configmaps \"ubuntu-vm-configmap\" not
found" "name"="cormac-ns/my-ubuntu-vm"
I0621 09:25:55.710402       1 virtualmachine_controller.go:365] VirtualMachine
"msg"="Finished Reconciling VirtualMachine" "name"="cormac-ns/my-ubuntu-vm"
E0621 09:25:55.710416       1 virtualmachine_controller.go:263] VirtualMachine
"msg"="Failed to reconcile VirtualMachine" "error"="configmaps \"ubuntu-vm-configmap\" not
found" "name"="cormac-ns/my-ubuntu-vm"
```

```
E0621 09:25:55.710691        1 controller.go:302] controller-
runtime/manager/controller/virtualmachine "msg"="Reconciler error" "error"="configmaps
\"ubuntu-vm-configmap\" not found" "name"="my-ubuntu-vm" "namespace"="cormac-ns"
"reconciler group"="vmoperator.vmware.com" "reconciler kind"="VirtualMachine"
.
.
```

Success! This has found the problem. The logs on this controller are reporting that it cannot find the ConfigMap called `ubuntu-vm-configmap`. That's our problem. If we delete the current VM, fix up the ConfigMap reference, and deploy it again, we should be good to go. There are lots of other options for tail'ing (–tail) and following (-f) Pod logs which are well worth familiarizing yourself with.

Troubleshooting storage issues on vSphere with Tanzu

I am going to finish with a discussion on troubleshooting storage issues on vSphere with Tanzu. The reason for this is because of the pvCSI used in TKG clusters, which was discussed in chapter 6. When there is a request to create a Persistent Volume in a TKG cluster, that request is forwarded to the Supervisor Cluster, who in turn forwards it to vCenter to create the volume on the correct vSphere datastore. Therefore, the logs will need to be examined on both the CSI Pods on the TKC and on the CSI Pods on the Supervisor to discover where the problem might reside.

Let's do a simple example and see this in action. To do this, I'll create a simple PVC manifest which will create a volume on a vSAN datastore. The vSAN default storage policy will already be added to the vSphere Namespace. Remember that you do not manually create StorageClasses in vSphere Namespaces – you assign storage policies to the Namespace and these appear as StorageClasses . Let's see the request pass from the TKC to the Supervisor Cluster and over to vCenter.

CSI controller on TKC

In the current TKC, the CSI controller Pod has 6 containers. You can get the list of containers by once more requesting the logs from the Pod. In this example, the vsphere-csi-controller is being monitored, but you may have to look at the logs on other containers when troubleshooting actual issues. Note that on this occasion, I will use the -f to follow any new logs.

```
% kubectl logs vsphere-csi-controller-55bb79b978-rj56f -n vmware-system-csi
error: a container name must be specified for pod vsphere-csi-controller-55bb79b978-rj56f,
choose one of: [csi-attacher vsphere-csi-controller vsphere-syncer liveness-probe csi-
provisioner csi-resizer]

% kubectl logs vsphere-csi-controller-55bb79b978-rj56f \
-n vmware-system-csi \
vsphere-csi-controller -f
{"level":"info","time":"2022-06-
20T16:28:20.573610883Z","caller":"logger/logger.go:41","msg":"Setting default log level to
:\"PRODUCTION\""}
{"level":"info","time":"2022-06-20T16:28:20.574491625Z","caller":"vsphere-
csi/main.go:55","msg":"Version : ","TraceId":"3e4a80b3-fef2-4d4d-aa22-a844e97546c1"}
{"level":"info","time":"2022-06-
20T16:28:20.576375617Z","caller":"logger/logger.go:41","msg":"Setting default log level to
:\"PRODUCTION\""}.
.
```

```
{"level":"info","time":"2022-06-
20T16:28:21.41656724Z","caller":"wcpguest/controller.go:157","msg":"Adding watch on path:
\"/etc/cloud/pvcsi-config\"","TraceId":"afb49bf5-c6f0-49db-afd7-58304dbd5522"}
{"level":"info","time":"2022-06-
20T16:28:21.416611448Z","caller":"wcpguest/controller.go:163","msg":"Adding watch on path:
\"/etc/cloud/pvcsi-provider\"","TraceId":"afb49bf5-c6f0-49db-afd7-58304dbd5522"}
{"level":"info","time":"2022-06-
20T16:28:21.416632437Z","caller":"service/driver.go:107","msg":"Configured:
\"csi.vsphere.vmware.com\" with clusterFlavor: \"GUEST_CLUSTER\" and mode:
\"controller\"","TraceId":"9d9092ae-eace-4aed-b334-59c68a695823"}
time="2022-06-20T16:28:21Z" level=info msg="identity service registered"
time="2022-06-20T16:28:21Z" level=info msg="controller service registered"
time="2022-06-20T16:28:21Z" level=info msg=serving endpoint="unix:///csi/csi.sock"
```

CSI controller on Supervisor Cluster

This can be done from the same laptop/desktop where the TKC was examined, but sometimes it is easier to do it from the Supervisor node. It means that you do not have to keep switching contexts to look at updated logs. We have seen the steps to get onto the Supervisor Cluster nodes earlier. To do this, we need to access the Supervisor node as follows:

```
[ /usr/lib/vmware-wcp ]# ./decryptK8Pwd.py
Read key from file

Connected to PSQL

Cluster: domain-c22:4df0badc-1655-40de-9181-3422d6c36a3e
IP: 192.168.51.151
PWD: mJGM*****=
-----------------------------------------------------------

[ /usr/lib/vmware-wcp ]# ssh root@192.168.51.151
FIPS mode initialized
The authenticity of host '192.168.51.151 (192.168.51.151)' can't be established.
ECDSA key fingerprint is SHA256:ZrrORHPUxV+UqUA6vwA1APlr5W8qCBBLJ3tSUTwwNqg.
Are you sure you want to continue connecting (yes/no)? yes
Warning: Permanently added '192.168.51.151' (ECDSA) to the list of known hosts.
Password:
 10:05:06 up 19:18,  0 users,  load average: 0.26, 0.45, 0.57

14 Security notice(s)
Run 'tdnf updateinfo info' to see the details.

[ ~ ]# kubectl get pods -n vmware-system-csi
NAME                                         READY   STATUS    RESTARTS        AGE
vsphere-csi-controller-794dfb6998-bwhn6      6/6     Running   12 (7h35m ago)  18h
```

Again, there are 6 containers in the controller Pod. Let's follow the controller container again using -f.

```
[ ~ ]# kubectl logs vsphere-csi-controller-794dfb6998-bwhn6 -n vmware-system-csi
error: a container name must be specified for pod vsphere-csi-controller-794dfb6998-bwhn6,
choose one of: [csi-provisioner csi-attacher csi-resizer vsphere-csi-controller liveness-
probe vsphere-syncer]

[ ~ ]# kubectl logs vsphere-csi-controller-794dfb6998-bwhn6 \
-n vmware-system-csi \
vsphere-csi-controller -f
{"level":"info","time":"2022-06-
21T02:32:11.424117592Z","caller":"logger/logger.go:41","msg":"Setting default log level to
:\"PRODUCTION\""}
```

```
{"level":"info","time":"2022-06-21T02:32:11.424353769Z","caller":"vsphere-
csi/main.go:56","msg":"Version : ","TraceId":"e894dee6-28b7-45fc-be1a-9dcbb96fd96c"}
{"level":"info","time":"2022-06-
21T02:32:11.424382435Z","caller":"commonco/utils.go:40","msg":"Defaulting feature states
configmap name to \"csi-feature-states\"","TraceId":"e894dee6-28b7-45fc-be1a-
9dcbb96fd96c"}
{"level":"info","time":"2022-06-
21T02:32:11.424392092Z","caller":"commonco/utils.go:44","msg":"Defaulting feature states
configmap namespace to \"vmware-system-csi\"","TraceId":"e894dee6-28b7-45fc-be1a-
9dcbb96fd96c"}
{"level":"info","time":"2022-06-
21T02:32:11.424773718Z","caller":"logger/logger.go:41","msg":"Setting default log level to
:\"PRODUCTION\""}
.
.
{"level":"info","time":"2022-06-
21T02:32:11.502183209Z","caller":"service/driver.go:109","msg":"Configured:
\"csi.vsphere.vmware.com\" with clusterFlavor: \"WORKLOAD\" and mode:
\"controller\"","TraceId":"eb9bed6f-8305-4f87-abc5-c0c316b8713f"}
time="2022-06-21T02:32:11Z" level=info msg="identity service registered"
time="2022-06-21T02:32:11Z" level=info msg="controller service registered"
time="2022-06-21T02:32:11Z" level=info msg=serving endpoint="unix:///csi/csi.sock"
```

Now let's try to create the simple volume and see what happens.

```
apiVersion: v1
kind: PersistentVolumeClaim
metadata:
  name: demo-pvc
  namespace: default
spec:
  storageClassName: vsan-default-storage-policy
  accessModes:
    - ReadWriteOnce
  resources:
    requests:
      storage: 1Gi
```

```
% kubectl apply -f simple-pvc.yaml
persistentvolumeclaim/demo-pvc created
```

```
% kubectl get pvc
NAME       STATUS  VOLUME            CAP  ACC  STORAGECLASS                  AGE
demo-pvc   Bound   pvc-34c81088-22c2-.. 1Gi  RWO  vsan-default-storage-policy   2m4s
```

```
% kubectl get pv
NAME                 CAP ACC RECLAIM STATUS CLAIM            STORAGECLASS
pvc-34c81088-22c2-.. 1Gi RWO Delete  Bound  default/demo-pvc vsan-default-storage-policy
```

It looks like the volume was successfully created. Let see what appeared in the logs.

CSI Controller Logs on TKC

In this pvCSI controller log snippet on the Tanzu Kubernetes cluster, we can see the
CreateVolume call.

```
{"level":"info","time":"2022-06-
21T11:08:35.047396092Z","caller":"wcpguest/controller.go:235","msg":"CreateVolume: called
with args {Name:pvc-34c81088-22c2-4aa6-8e2e-d225ab30079b
CapacityRange:required_bytes:1073741824  VolumeCapabilities:[mount:<fs_type:\"ext4\" >
access_mode:<mode:SINGLE_NODE_WRITER > ] Parameters:map[svStorageClass:vsan-default-
```

storage-policy] Secrets:map[] VolumeContentSource:<nil> AccessibilityRequirements:<nil>
XXX_NoUnkeyedLiteral:{} XXX_unrecognized:[] XXX_sizecache:0}","TraceId":"94b59ed1-193b-
4436-aaec-a5a8ab574abe"}
{"level":"info","time":"2022-06-
21T11:08:35.050187539Z","caller":"k8sorchestrator/k8sorchestrator.go:750","msg":"file-
volume feature state set to false in internal-feature-states.csi.vsphere.vmware.com
ConfigMap","TraceId":"94b59ed1-193b-4436-aaec-a5a8ab574abe"}
{"level":"info","time":"2022-06-
21T11:08:35.136721161Z","caller":"wcpguest/controller_helper.go:239","msg":"provisionTimeo
ut is set to 4 minutes","TraceId":"94b59ed1-193b-4436-aaec-a5a8ab574abe"}
{"level":"info","time":"2022-06-
21T11:08:35.136756124Z","caller":"wcpguest/controller_helper.go:197","msg":"Waiting up to
240 seconds for PersistentVolumeClaim 6cda75f9-e27e-418c-b2fc-cf94f621af78-34c81088-22c2-
4aa6-8e2e-d225ab30079b in namespace cormac-ns to have phase Bound","TraceId":"94b59ed1-
193b-4436-aaec-a5a8ab574abe"}
{"level":"info","time":"2022-06-
21T11:08:36.659286702Z","caller":"wcpguest/controller_helper.go:219","msg":"PersistentVolu
meClaim 6cda75f9-e27e-418c-b2fc-cf94f621af78-34c81088-22c2-4aa6-8e2e-d225ab30079b in
namespace cormac-ns is in state Bound","TraceId":"94b59ed1-193b-4436-aaec-a5a8ab574abe"}
{"level":"info","time":"2022-06-
21T11:08:36.659556054Z","caller":"k8sorchestrator/k8sorchestrator.go:750","msg":"file-
volume feature state set to false in internal-feature-states.csi.vsphere.vmware.com
ConfigMap","TraceId":"94b59ed1-193b-4436-aaec-a5a8ab574abe"}

CSI Controller Logs on Supervisor node

Similarly, in the CSI controller log snippet on the Supervisor, the `CreateVolume` call is visible. The call is reported as successful less than a minute later.

{"level":"info","time":"2022-06-
21T11:08:35.198611114Z","caller":"wcp/controller.go:523","msg":"CreateVolume: called with
args {Name:pvc-6c306232-53bb-4224-9c79-a5c75f82d4c6
CapacityRange:required_bytes:1073741824 VolumeCapabilities:[mount:<fs_type:\"ext4\" >
access_mode:<mode:SINGLE_NODE_WRITER >] Parameters:map[storagePolicyID:aa6d5a82-1c88-
45da-85d3-3d74b91a5bad] Secrets:map[] VolumeContentSource:<nil>
AccessibilityRequirements:<nil> XXX_NoUnkeyedLiteral:{} XXX_unrecognized:[]
XXX_sizecache:0}","TraceId":"1427fc7a-bbd6-4dbb-a5a9-e9ac9320e6e4"}
{"level":"info","time":"2022-06-
21T11:08:36.571536364Z","caller":"volume/manager.go:504","msg":"CreateVolume: VolumeName:
\"pvc-6c306232-53bb-4224-9c79-a5c75f82d4c6\", opId: \"07015864\"","TraceId":"1427fc7a-
bbd6-4dbb-a5a9-e9ac9320e6e4"}
{"level":"info","time":"2022-06-
21T11:08:36.573743392Z","caller":"volume/util.go:322","msg":"Volume created successfully.
VolumeName: \"pvc-6c306232-53bb-4224-9c79-a5c75f82d4c6\", volumeID: \"c0f826af-7dd1-43d8-
9425-f07ba1fa48c3\"","TraceId":"1427fc7a-bbd6-4dbb-a5a9-e9ac9320e6e4"}

wcpsvc.log

At the same time as the `CreateVolume` request is passed through the TKC to the SV, the WCP service log on the vCenter Server also logs the request. We can see that there are some quota checks done on the vSphere namespace `cormac-ns`, which is where the TKC cluster resides. At the end of the snippet, we can see a request for 1Gi of storage using the vsan-default-storage-policy storage class.

2022-06-21T11:08:35.12Z debug wcp [kubestats/kubernetes_remote.go:436] Full resourceQuota
object &ResourceQuota{ObjectMeta:{cormac-ns-storagequota cormac-ns
/api/v1/namespaces/cormac-ns/resourcequotas/cormac-ns-storagequota db914539-3dc1-4390-
83a5-84c36c73678d 3130098 0 2022-06-16 14:45:56 +0000 UTC <nil> <nil> map[] map[] [] []
[{kube-controller-manager Update v1 2022-06-16 14:45:56 +0000 UTC FieldsV1
{"f:status":{"f:hard":{".":{},"f:vsan-default-storage-
policy.storageclass.storage.k8s.io/requests.storage":{}},"f:used":{}}} } {wcpsvc Update v1

2022-06-16 14:45:56 +0000 UTC FieldsV1 {"f:spec":{"f:hard":{".":{},"f:vsan-default-storage-policy.storageclass.storage.k8s.io/requests.storage":{}}}} } {kube-apiserver Update v1 2022-06-21 11:08:35 +0000 UTC FieldsV1 {"f:status":{"f:used":{"f:vsan-default-storage-policy.storageclass.storage.k8s.io/requests.storage":{}}}} status}]},Spec:ResourceQuotaSpec{Hard:ResourceList{vsan-default-storage-policy.storageclass.storage.k8s.io/requests.storage: {{0 0} {0xc0014f55c0} DecimalSI},},Scopes:[],ScopeSelector:nil,},Status:ResourceQuotaStatus{Hard:ResourceList{vsan-default-storage-policy.storageclass.storage.k8s.io/requests.storage: {{0 0} {0xc0014f5620} DecimalSI},},Used:ResourceList{vsan-default-storage-policy.storageclass.storage.k8s.io/requests.storage: {{1073741824 0} {<nil>} 1Gi BinarySI},},},}

While this is a very simple example, hopefully, it helps to tie together the various components that are at work to service a storage request from a TKC cluster. If we looked at the logs on the other containers, more activity would be visible. Hopefully, this is enough of a guide to get you started.

Summary

This chapter focused on day 2 operations, and the kind of tasks a Platform Operator might need to handle when running Kubernetes on vSphere. It is also an area that a vSphere administrator should become familiar with since much of the developer infrastructure is sitting on vSphere infrastructure. Activities at the vSphere level must now take into account any potential impact on the developer platforms that are running on vSphere, and what impact an upgrade or a maintenance mode can have.

The developer platforms and the vSphere platforms may share systems for management, monitoring and backup/restore. Some of the tools that are commonly used for managing and monitoring Kubernetes were described, with details on how easy it is to deploy them via Tanzu packages. In particular, Prometheus and Grafana are used heavily to capture metrics and display dashboards. For backup and restore, VMware's Velero has a lot of users in the Kubernetes community, as is quite a popular solution.

The ability to examine log files, and knowing which Pods are responsible for which task, is a skill that you build up over time. Most containers will have some sort of log output, and it is certainly advisable to set up log shipping using something like Fluent Bit, or similar. It is also useful to have someplace to ship logs to so that you can look back over log history, as well as raise alerts if certain events or patterns are observed. We saw how Fluent Bit could ship logs to an ELK stack, but it could also be set up to ship to Splunk or vRealize Log Insight too. Familiarizing yourself with log outputs, both in good times and in bad times, will help you to troubleshoot Kubernetes, and void getting stuck on errors and events that resolve themselves over time in an eventually consistent system.

08

What's next?

The hope is that by the time you get to this chapter, you will have some idea about the considerations that a vSphere administrator will need to keep in mind when Kubernetes is being deployed on top of vSphere. At this point, it should have become obvious that we are dealing with the complexity of running platforms upon platforms. Actions taken and objects created on the Kubernetes platform communicate to the vSphere platform for resources. Building Kubernetes nodes as VMs is the obvious relationship between the platforms, but we have also come across examples of a Kubernetes Persistent Volume calling the vSphere CSI driver to create a virtual disk on a vSphere datastore, and request for a Load Balancer type Service calling either the AKO (Avi Kubernetes Operator) to make a call to the NSX ALB to create a virtual service, or NCP (NSX Container Plugin) doing something similar with NSX-T. These are all areas that the vSphere administrator may need monitor, lifecycle manage, and indeed troubleshoot if something goes wrong.

Now let's assume that you're starting to become comfortable with the idea of managing vSphere infrastructure which is hosting Kubernetes clusters. You might even start to enjoy it. If so, you may be thinking what's next? Are you considering stepping into the role of a Platform Operator, and managing the Kubernetes platforms running on vSphere? At this point, I hope the book has provided a certain amount of guidance around the role of a Platform Operator. As I said at the outset, I think this is a role that vSphere administrators could aspire to. While we touched on many parts of the Platform Operator role, it is very much tied to providing developer infrastructure. At the end of the day, most developers don't care too much about infrastructure, be it vSphere or Kubernetes. They simply want to commit some new code on GitHub, have it automatically tested and validated, easily troubleshoot it if it goes wrong with some decent pointers as to why it failed, and if there are no issues, have it moved into production. This whole process is orchestrated by what is known as a 'pipeline', or to use the industry standard terms, continuous integration (CI) and continuous deployment. In essence, a CI/CD pipeline is a way to do software delivery, automating a series of steps that take new code from the developer and puts it into production. In this final chapter, I will introduce you to some tooling that we at VMware are using to provide orchestration or choreography for software development. This is simply to show you, the vSphere administrator, what a Platform Operator might be expected to manage and monitor on top of Kubernetes clusters.

Note that the assumption here is that the Kubernetes cluster is static. However, this is not always the case. In fact, often, it is not just applications made up of Pods, Services, and PVs that are deployed in a repeated fashion. Sometimes it is infrastructure that is deployed and destroyed in an automated fashion, repeatedly, in a pipeline, as Platform Operators figure out the optimal size of a Kubernetes cluster to put into production.

In this final chapter, I wanted to share some further thoughts with you, whilst also introducing you to the Tanzu Application Platform (TAP). This chapter will not automatically make you a Platform Operator, but after reading this short chapter, you will hopefully have an even better understanding on what else you can achieve with your new container and Kubernetes skills, and what other paths are available for you to follow.

CI/CD Pipelines

Let's talk about some of things that might happens in a Continuous Integration / Continuous Deployment pipeline (commonly referred to as a CI/CD pipeline) to ship code into production. Many of the tasks have already been discussed in this book, albeit these tasks have been carried out in a manual way. In chapter 1, the task of packaging code into a container was discussed. A number of docker tools, such as docker build and docker compose, were used to achieve this. Another task that is more than likely a part of a pipeline is the storing of container images in an image registry. In chapter 1, we saw how to pull, tag and push container images to the external docker hub image registry. We saw this again when building the Ingress demo in chapter 2. We also came across it in chapter 6 when we went through an exercise with the embedded Harbor Image Registry in vSphere with Tanzu. Finally, in the same exercises, we saw how these container images could be used to build applications in Kubernetes using Pods, Deployments, etc, and more importantly, run then on a Kubernetes cluster. These are very much tasks that could be automated in a pipeline, but there needs to be some orchestration or choreography implemented. For example, there needs to be a trigger mechanism which detects changes, as well as a way to define the series of steps for the pipeline to follow. When one step completes, something needs to monitor for it and then initiate the next step. This involves, in many cases, retrieving the output of the previous step (e.g. new code), and passing it as input to the next step (e.g. build an image). This is what is typically known as a supply chain. A supply chain is subtlety different to a CI/CD in that you can add additional steps required for an application to reach production. This is where a product called Tanzu Application Platform (TAP) comes in. What follows is a brief introduction to TAP by way of demonstrating a supply chain for software delivery.

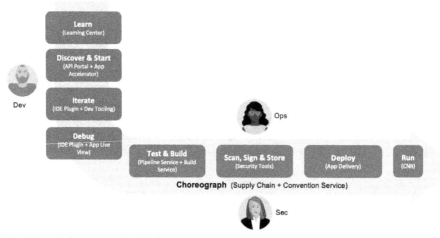

Figure 180: TAP - Software Supply Chain

Tanzu Application Platform (TAP)

Tanzu Application Platform is a relatively new product, with the first version becoming generally available to purchase on 11th January 2022. The whole idea is to provide choreography of supply chains so that when a developer commits some new code on somewhere like GitHub, the code is passed through a supply chain or pipeline, and when it comes out the other end, it is as a secure, containerized application that can be deployed and run on a Kubernetes cluster. This section introduces a few of the building blocks associated with TAP, just so you can appreciate what is going on. Many of these building blocks in the supply change are pluggable, where other products can be used in place of the ones described here. Note that this is not a deep-dive. This is purely written so that you, as a vSphere administrator, can appreciate some of the additional functions associated with a Platform Operator role. In many cases, it is not limited to just getting Kubernetes up and running.

What do developers want?

Let's begin by discussing what a developer wants, but keeping it as a very high level and simplifying it as much as possible. In a lot of cases, as already mentioned, they don't really care about infrastructure. Sure, some of them took a particular interest in containers and Kubernetes in the early days to help them get more productive. But today, Kubernetes is just another platform and containers are just a way to wrap up code and make it portable to any flavour of Kubernetes. What developers really want is a way to have their code tested automatically and quickly, once it is committed to a repository, say on a platform like GitHub. After committing their code, they want to quickly ascertain if it was built without any problems, and whether it works. If it was successfully built, they want to make it easily run. Then, they want to able to easily access it and verify that it is functioning as expected. Lastly, if there were any problems, they want to be able to examine the application to see where in the code they should debug and fix things.

A choreographed pipeline/supply chain example

We can see that there are a few things here to deal with. The first is how to trigger a pipeline when there is a new code commit by the developer on GitHub, testing the code and perhaps scanning it for vulnerabilities. The second part is the build itself — what tooling is available to take code and convert it to a container. This can be considered the Continuous Integration part of the CI/CD pipeline. The next thing is storing the image in an image registry, somewhere that is secure. This could be an internal registry such as Harbor or an external registry such as Docker Hub. In today's world, there is most likely a desire to ensure that the image is secure. This is twice we've mentioned security in the pipeline. This is becoming so important that the DevOps role is transitioning to a DevSecOps role. With security becoming more and more critical, there should be something in the pipeline that will scan and check the container image for vulnerabilities. Lastly, the application needs to be run. Since this is a Kubernetes book, we will assume that there is a desire to deploy this application on Kubernetes. If fact, Kubernetes can make this very easy. Therefore, this test setup using Kubernetes could be a deployment type object if the application is stateless, or a StatefulSet if it is stateful. It will also need some sort of service associated with it. This is the Continuous Deployment part of the CI/CD pipeline, where the application is continuously updated with new images based on new commits from the developer. Let's talk about some of the components of TAP that can meet these requirements. Again, this is just a simple overview to show you what a supply chain can do, especially when deployed on Kubernetes. It should also help to explain why Kubernetes has become a popular development platform for new, containerized, twelve-factor applications.

FluxCD

Flux - https://fluxcd.io/ - provide a set of tools to enable continuous application deployment (CD). It has the ability to sync with a configuration source (in this case, a GitHub repository) and carry out tasks and trigger notifications when there is new code to deploy. Flux can be pointed at a particular branch on a Git repository which it will then poll. TAP can leverage FluxCD to watch for new commits of code by a developer.

Tekton

The developer has committed some new code. Now it is time to run the code, test it out and create a container image. In TAP, this role of running and testing the code is carried out by Tekton – https://tekton.dev. Developers leverage various tools to run and test their code. The most common ones would be Apache Maven - https://maven.apache.org/, used primarily for Java projects. Another tool is Gradle - https://gradle.org/. All are geared towards accelerating developer productivity through automated testing and building of code. Tekton runs the test suite, and then calls next step in the pipeline to create the image. You may or may not have come across these in your role as a vSphere administrator depending on whether or not you have application developers in your organization, and how closely you work with them. If not, I shouldn't worry. At the moment, it is enough to just be aware that this is another part of a software development supply chain.

kpack

kpack - https://github.com/pivotal/kpack/blob/main/README.md - builds Open Container Initiative (OCI) images. In our supply chain example, the source code would be located on a Git repository and branch. The building of images needs to be controlled so that only approved artefacts, such as base OS images, should be used to build application images. kpack does this through the concept of buildpacks. TAP can leverage kpack to create images from code, after receiving a trigger that new code has been committed by FluxCD, and that running and testing of the code has been passed by Tekton.

Grype

Grype - https://github.com/anchore/grype - is a vulnerability scanner for container images and file systems. It enables the DevSecOps management in the supply chain. It checks for vulnerabilities in major operating system packages as well as language specific packages. It supports both OCI image formats, as well as docker image formats. Therefore, once kpack has containerized the application, Grype can scan it and report on any vulnerabilities found.

Once the image is scanned and signed off as compliant, it also needs to be stored somewhere. We've seen numerous options around container image registries already in the book. Part of the pipeline would most likely include pushing the new image to the container image registry.

Cartographer

Let's assume that both FluxCD, Tekton, kpack and Grype have all done their work. There is now a new image available for the deployment. The goal is to deploy it in a Kubernetes cluster. A next manual step might be a *kubectl edit* to update the new image in a deployment YAML manifest. Again, a Platform Operator doesn't want to be involved in manually editing the YAML manifests and running *kubectl* commands every time there is new code to test. The desire is to have the supply chain do this for us when the application is ready to be run.

The whole supply chain should be automated. Ideally, this whole process should be choregraphed together as a series of supply chain steps, with a supply chain which is completely parameterised so that new code triggers the building of code, testing it out, and then creating a new application image that in turn is simply passed as a variable value that is plugged into the supply chain. Again, this can be considered Continuous Deployment (CD). In TAP, one way to do this is through Cartographer - https://cartographer.sh/ - a Supply Chain choreographer for Kubernetes. This is the part which allows a Platform Operator to define all of the steps that an application must go through to create an image and Kubernetes configuration. This is achieved through a series of template definitions:

- Source Template
- Image Template
- Config Template
- Generic Template

As you can probably imagine, the source template would have a definition for FluxCD, monitoring source code changes on the Git repository and branch. This would create an source code bundle that could then be consumed by the next step in the supply chain, Tekton. When Tekton has finished running the test suite, it passes the code to kpack. The image template would contain the kpack steps. It would know how to retrieve the source code bundle from Tekton, and create the OCI compatible image. The config template would define how to make a new or updated Kubernetes configuration with most recent new image. The generic template can be used to instantiate Kubernetes objects that have no supply chain dependencies.

What Cartographer allows Platform Operators to do is to tightly couple the various tools in the CI/CD toolchain, rather than have a series of loosely coupled tools. And since TAP is modular and all the products used are templated definitions, different tools in the supply chain could be used, rather than the ones which I have highlighted above. For example, your developers might prefer to use Jenkins instead of Tekton, so it should be a simple matter of changing out Tekton for Jenkins via the Template mechanism. This is the intention of TAP.

And the important point from all of this is that the developer is simply committing code. They are not worrying about the underlying infrastructure or how the code is getting turned into a Kubernetes application. The one nice thing is that since the application is deployed on Kubernetes, developers could be granted access to the cluster. This means that they can use standard Kubernetes commands to check the deployment status, check logs, view events, etc. if they so wish. However, they can also get these events and logs directly sent to their integrated development environment (IDE). Integrated developer environments such as Visual Studio Code and IntelliJ integrate with TAP features such as Live Debug and Live Update. This means that developers never need to interact with *kubectl*, nor do they never need to leave their development environment.

For the Platform Operator, they can continue to use standard Kubernetes tools to monitor the supply chain, and also if and when something breaks. All of supply chain tools mentioned previously are deployed on a Kubernetes cluster, so if there is a problem with any of the components in the supply chain, whether it is FluxCD or kpack, they can use the same *kubectl get*, *kubectl describe*, *kubectl logs* commands to see where the issue lies. Of course, for production you might have something like Fluent Bit shipping logs to a central location, like we saw in chapter 7, so they can be viewed, searched and help with triaging.

Summary

Hopefully, that has given you some idea of where the role of a Platform Operator might take you once you begin to get to grips with containers and Kubernetes. Note that this is only a very high-level overview of a CI/CD pipeline or a supply chain to be more specific. And this is also only one simple example of a supply chain. This is not meant to give you a complete overview of all the nuances of supply chains, nor does it give you any meaningful depth into the capabilities of the Tanzu Application Platform. But as you begin to delve into the world of Kubernetes more and more, perhaps starting with managing and monitoring vSphere resources used by Kubernetes, and progress to managing Kubernetes clusters as a Platform Operator, you can see where this skillset might take you going forward.

The End

You have made it to the end of the book. Congratulations! Hopefully, you now have a good idea of how Kubernetes works and some of the integration points with vSphere infrastructure. It should have also given you, the vSphere administrator, a reasonable appreciation of what it takes to manage the vSphere infrastructure onto which Kubernetes clusters are deployed. Throughout this book, I have tried to simplify some of the concepts to make them easier to understand. However, I acknowledge that some concepts can still be difficult to grasp. Kubernetes is a lot of work. I would urge all readers to get as much hands-on with Kubernetes as possible.

Many of you are on different parts of this journey with Kubernetes. Maybe you are just getting started, and the very first Kubernetes clusters are only just being deployed onto the vSphere infrastructure that you manage. This book should at least have raised some awareness around the impact this will have as you manage the vSphere infrastructure where Kubernetes is deployed – the platform on platform paradigm. I hope that reading this book will provide you with enough confidence to take your first steps with Kubernetes.

Some of you might be further along on this journey. Perhaps you are already considering your next steps, which might be to take on the role of the Platform Operator and become responsible for managing and maintaining Kubernetes clusters running on vSphere. Maybe after reading chapter 8, you are thinking about getting more into the DevOps space, managing CI/CD pipelines and developer infrastructure. For those of you considering a career path as a Platform Operator or even becoming more immersed in the DevOps world, I wish you the very best and hope that this book helps in some way.

If there are any questions, please reach out via Twitter, Reddit or LinkedIn. I will do my best to answer your questions. As mentioned in the introduction, all examples used in this book are available on the following Git repository – https://github.com/cormachogan/vsphere-book-examples.

Thanks for reading,

Cormac

www.ingramcontent.com/pod-product-compliance
Lightning Source LLC
LaVergne TN
LVHW081331050326
832903LV00024B/1111